Apostles of Rock

Apostles of Rock

The Splintered World of Contemporary Christian Music

Jay R. Howard and
John M. Streck

THE UNIVERSITY PRESS OF KENTUCKY

Publication of this volume was made possible in part
by a grant from the National Endowment for the Humanities.

Scholarly publisher for the Commonwealth,
serving Bellarmine College, Berea College, Centre
College of Kentucky, Eastern Kentucky University,
The Filson Club Historical Society, Georgetown College,
Kentucky Historical Society, Kentucky State University,
Morehead State University, Murray State University,
Northern Kentucky University, Transylvania University,
University of Kentucky, University of Louisville,
and Western Kentucky University.

Editorial and Sales Offices: The University Press of Kentucky
663 South Limestone Street, Lexington, Kentucky 40508–4008

03 02 01 00 99   5 4 3 2 1

Frontispiece: Wendi Kaiser of Resurrection Band, performing at the 1992
Cornerstone Festival. Photograph courtesy of Rose Capanna.

Library of Congress Cataloging-in-Publication Data

Howard, Jay. R., 1959–
    Apostles of Rock : the splintered world of Contemporary Christian music /
Jay R. Howard and John M. Streck.
    p.   cm.
    Includes bibliographic references and index.
    ISBN 0-8131-2105-1 (cloth : alk. paper)
    1. Christian rock music—History and criticism.   I. Streck, John M.
II. Title.
ML3187.5.H68   1999
781.66—dc21   98-44113

Contents

Illustrations

Acknowledgments

It is perhaps only appropriate that a book drawing so heavily on Howard Becker's concept of an art world and premised on the notion that works of art emerge from complex social systems rather than from the efforts of single individuals should begin with the recognition that the pages it comprises could not have been produced without the assistance and contributions of many, many people. The title page mentions only Jay R. Howard and John M. Streck, but there are myriad others who must be recognized for their assistance in our pursuit of this project.

We are indebted to the many friends, acquaintances, and strangers who provided otherwise unobtainable source materials, information, and perspectives on contemporary Christian music. These include Brian Blair, Rose Capanna, Fred Clark, Rob Davis, Rodney Ho, Rick Jackson, Tudor Lance, Larry Lein, Diana Morris, Burt Matteson, Tom Niemoeller, Dwight Ozard, Matt Roddin (a/k/a Chris MacIntosh), Bill Romanowski, Dave Severance, Dave Stephens, John Travis, Phill Walton, John Warren, Charles Wolff, and the innumerable contributors to the Usenet newsgroup rec.music.christian who, through their debates and diatribes, offered important insights into the fans' opinions of what contemporary Christian music is and ought to be. Photographer Joe Harpring's assistance in reproducing many of the album covers included in the book is also greatly appreciated.

We would further like to acknowledge the blessed few in the Christian music industry who were courteous enough to return our phone calls or respond to email. We are particularly grateful to those who, in addition, sent us photographs and/or gave the permission necessary under copyright law for reproducing the images that appear in the book.

We must also acknowledge the efforts of the reviewers who provided comments on an earlier draft of the work. Identifying the strengths and weaknesses of the submitted manuscript and offering suggestions for its improvement, these readers undoubtedly enhanced the final work through their critiques. The responsibility for the shortcomings that remain is, of course, wholly our own.

Finally, on a more personal note, thanks from John go to the members of my family for their unceasing support and encouragement; the faculty and grad students (1992–94) of the School of Communications at the University of Washington for helping me to transform undisciplined thinking on Christian music into something resembling rigorous analysis; the faculty of the Department of Communication Studies at the University of Iowa for looking the other way while I devoted precious time to this manuscript when I should have been focusing on my dissertation; Elaine Ackerman for the impromptu web searches; Greg Becker for riding along and thinking big thoughts; and Leann Ruff, wherever she may be, who couldn't possibly have known back in 1984 that the merciful act of lending me a Walkman and a bag of cassettes when I was trapped on a tour bus with my mother, sister and forty-odd middle-aged women would lead to this.

And from Jay: Acknowledgments to my wife, Brenda, and my children, Amalia and Dylan, for their love and support; all those folks at the Cornerstone Festival who have engaged in discussion and debate regarding CCM around campfires, in seminar tents, and while waiting for concerts to begin; the early 1980s Cedar Road Missionary Church Youth Group that forced me to begin thinking critically about Christian music as we listened to and discussed CCM in its infancy; Tony Campolo, Ron Sider, and Don Kraybill, whose work demonstrated that one can both think critically and Christian-ly; Terry Taylor for twenty plus years of music that appealed to a thinking person; Jo Davis at the IUPUC library, who cheerfully sought and obtained one obscure book after another through interlibrary loan; WHME and WFRN radio for setting me on an alternative career path; the faculty of the sociology departments at Indiana University South Bend and the University of Notre Dame who helped me to acquire and refine sociological skills; and my colleagues and students at IUPUI and IUPUC for their support, interest, and encouragement.

✝ Prelude: Ichthus '93

It is April in Kentucky; the air cool, the sun shining. Some fourteen thousand teenagers (drawn largely from Methodist youth groups in the region) have, along with their adult sponsors, packed themselves on the rural hillside like an occupying army. At the foot of the hill stands a covered wooden stage, currently the home of Hoi Polloi, a band that, despite the energetic melodies and distorted guitars, has yet to attract the attention of the crowd. There are perhaps two hundred people crowded against the security fence in front of the stage, but beyond this crush the audience seems unimpressed. Most are milling about visiting with friends or standing in line at one of the many food vendors (including Subway and Taco Bell) that surround the viewing area. Hundreds have spread out blankets and lie about chatting amongst themselves or perusing magazines—copies of *Campus Life, Seventeen, Vogue,* and *Prom* are seen scattered around one group's blanket—they've brought along to help pass the time as they wait for the bands they want to hear from to take the stage. For most, Hoi Polloi doesn't make the cut. But, although to this point indifferent to what the band has had to say, the crowd suddenly takes interest when the blonde lead singer steps forward with her fashion-model looks to assure the audience that "God is thinking about you!" A raucous cheer erupts from the hillside as people stand and begin swaying to music that only moments before seemed to effect little but boredom. For this audience, however, it's not the music that matters but the message, and Hoi Polloi's effort to connect with the audience through the vehicle of song is no match for their singer's sloganeering. Having finally attracted the crowd's attention, the band plays one last song before departing the stage with an invitation for fans to join them in the press tent.

An hour or so later, The Choir takes the stage. Known for personal and poetic lyrics set to the music of heavily processed and effects-laden guitars, the band is a longtime critic's favorite and a pioneer of alternative Christian rock. Critical favor and longevity, however, have yet to

The Ichthus music festival. (Photograph by Randy Patrick, *Jessamine Journal*. Used with permission.

coalesce into significant sales, and at Ichthus the band does no better than Hoi Polloi at attracting the crowd's attention. The only ones who seem to hear the music are the hundred or so young males who have formed a mosh pit directly in front of the stage. As the sweaty dancers swirl, bounce, and crash their way through "(Something Wonderful) About Love," two preteen boys stand at the rear of the pit grinning from ear to ear. They're close enough to feel the energy, close enough to tell their friends back home they "moshed" at Ichthus, but not so close that they get jostled about. They watch, fascinated, as a body is lifted and surfs its away across the top of the crowd. The music continues, and the energy increases. A few of the younger moshers weave their way out of the crowd as the dancing gets rougher. Still the majority seem to effectively use their hands to bounce off each other and avoid the most painful of collisions. Nonetheless, one mosher staggers out with a bloody nose and stands near me pinching his nostrils shut. With a nod of his head, he accepts the tissues I pull from a pocket and offer to him. As another person offers him a "wet wipe," he realizes that he has lost his wallet. Just then a hand goes up at the edge of the pit holding a brown wallet aloft. The dancer, whose nose has stopped bleeding, walks over and taps the shoulder of the mosher with the wallet, and it is returned to its owner. This is an usually friendly mosh pit. As the music fades, the frenzy grinds to a halt and drummer Steve Hindalong apologetically warns the crowd, "We're gonna do a few love songs. We hope that's okay with you." The crowd in the pit cheers, but the people on the hillside offer no response, apparently more interested in developing their tans than in love songs from The Choir.

Following The Choir, Jacob's Trouble takes the stage for a much more successful effort at engaging the crowd in the waning afternoon sunshine. The alternative rock continues, though this is the second generation of alternative CCM. The Choir's post-punk derivatives, rooted in the influence of bands such as U2 and The Police, gives way to jangly pop more directly linked to groups such as The Byrds and The Beatles, but, most tellingly, flowing through early Christian rock acts such as Daniel Amos as well. Indeed, in a rare effort at maintaining a sense of history within Christian music, the band begins playing "Walls of Doubt," a song first written and recorded by Daniel Amos in 1981. Unapologetically a "Christian band," Jacob's Trouble further distinguishes itself from Hoi Polloi and The Choir by recognizing that at Ichthus the music doesn't speak for itself. So, as the band moves into the bridge of "Walls of Doubt," lead singer Jerry Davison shouts a question to the crowd. "What are we here for?" he asks, and then answers the question himself by singing a few lines from the hymn, "Brethren We Have Met to Worship." The crowd responds with wild cheers and Davison begins to lead them through hyperkinetic versions of the Sunday School choruses, "Jesus Loves Me" and "The B-I-B-L-E." Continuing this rock and roll revival, Davison exhorts the enthusiastic crowd: "No President Clinton, Vice President Gore. No Hillary Rodham Clinton gonna do nothin' for you! No Republican. No Democrat. No MTV. No rock star. Don't put your trust in anything but *Jesus*!" At the mention of the name, the crowd goes wild. Suddenly, the band stops, allowing Davison to sing the chorus from "Amazing Grace." Then, just as suddenly, the band resumes its frantic playing. The crowd is on its feet. Many have their hands raised in a gesture of praise and sway with the music. Jacob's Trouble has finally delivered what fourteen thousand people came to receive: a clear affirmation of their most fundamental beliefs wrapped in a package of rock and roll music and fun, fun, fun.

Introduction: What, Pray Tell, is Contemporary Christian Music?

Pilgrim makes his progress in today's world not on foot with staff but in a batmobile.

Marshall Fishwick

In his cultural manifesto *The Closing of the American Mind*, Allan Bloom argues that "nothing is more singular about this generation than its addiction to music. . . . Today, a very large proportion of young people between the ages of ten and twenty live for music. It is their passion; nothing else excites them as it does; they cannot take seriously anything alien to music."[1] Music, in this case, refers of course to rock and roll. Its appeal is explained by Evan Eisenberg, who argues that "rock music is at once eagerly social and deeply solipsistic—a condition of adolescence—and the rock musician mediates not as musician, but as alter ego."[2] Indeed, despite critics on the right who disdain what they find to be banality and hedonism and critics on the left who lament the music's commercialization by the co-optive forces of corporate capitalism, for much of America's youth rock and roll would seem to remain a source of faith, hope, and refuge, and it is the first and best medium for carrying creative and powerful stories about the things that count most in their daily lives.[3] And as one young listener so succinctly puts it, "Kids don't want to be left out just because they're Christian."[4]

It is an understandable sentiment. From its earliest days, rock and roll has offered powerful resources to its adolescent listeners. At times the moves may seem illusory and gestural, but, by offering a rejection of dominant cultural values (or at least a particular subset of those values), rock and roll provides its audiences with the opportunity to create identities through difference.[5] And while the lines of division may be ambiguous, the positions untenable (as Robert M. Pirsig notes, "Degeneracy can be fun but it's hard to keep up as a serious lifetime occupation"), and "resistance" little more than a particular consumer choice (through what Dick Hebdige describes as "a struggle within signification"), rock music nevertheless allows individual listeners to coalesce into subcultures that see themselves as somehow separate from and/or in opposition to mainstream social values.[6] Listening may be an act of consumption, but it is also an act of identity-building; as anyone who has visited a high-school campus can confirm, musical taste and style are clear components of cultural awareness.[7] At the same time, however, while rock and roll can usefully serve the ends of identity formation and the creation of community, access to the tools that rock music provides is limited for audience members who hold values they believe to be contradicted by the messages they hear in the music. And, as has been repeatedly documented, for much of the last half century, rock and roll has been perceived to pose a clear threat to middle-class America's cultural values. This is even more true for fundamentalist and evangelical Christians. From Elvis Presley's swinging pelvis to Marilyn Manson's celebration of satanism (with points in between too numerous to mention), there has been much about rock music for Christians to abhor. The dilemma for Christian adolescents then is clear. On the one hand, rock and roll music plays a critical role in establishing identity and defining their social groups, but, at the same time, it appears to contradict many of the values they hold as Christians. Since 1969, contemporary Christian music (CCM) has attempted to offer the resolution to this quandary.

Standing in the gap between evangelical Christianity on the one side and youth culture on the other, contemporary Christian music offers evangelical Christians who cannot identify with what they see on MTV their own set of alter egos. With its angelic waifs, strutting arena rockers, choreographed girl groups, guitar-strumming folkies, flannel-encased grunge acts, posturing rappers, and wordy singer-songwriters, contemporary Christian music provides the evangelical audience with the same ethereal voices, the same driving guitars, and the same chunky rhythms that can be found anywhere on the radio dial—but with one important difference: rather than challenging predominant evangelical values, this music affirms them. Consequently, if names like The Altar Boys, Susan Ashton, Audio Adrenaline, Barren Cross, Margaret Becker, Black Eyed Sceva, Caedmon's Call,

Christafari, Clash of Symbols, Dance House Children, DC Talk, Dimestore Prophets, Gospel Gangstas, Amy Grant, Holy Soldier, Jars of Clay, Mad at the World, Sarah Masen, MxPx, Newsboys, Larry Norman, Charlie Peacock, Point of Grace, Poor Old Lu, Sometimes Sunday, Rebecca St. James, Starflyer 59, The Waiting, and Whiteheart remain meaningless to most, these (along with hundreds more like them) are the artists who for tens of millions of fans provide the soundtrack to the contemporary Christian life.

Of course it should be remembered that contemporary Christian music is only one element in the cultural identity of America's evangelical Christian community. Rooted in a broad range of evangelical and mainline Protestant churches and supported by parachurch organizations such as Young Life, Youth for Christ, and Campus Crusade for Christ as well as religious book publishers, filmmakers, television producers, and magazine publishers, American evangelicalism is a highly productive and vital subculture. Contemporary Christian music, however, remains its most vibrant expression. Through this music we intend to explore the ways in which participants in this subculture define themselves both in relation to mainstream society and in relation to one another. What sense of identity does CCM provide for those who listen to it? Does/can CCM provide a basis for critique of church and/or society, or is it merely self-congratulatory consumerism that makes no significant challenges to the dominant economic, political, and religious institutions? Recognizing that music is not only important in youth culture but also vitally important within evangelicalism more generally, we explore the nature of evangelicalism as it is expressed through contemporary Christian music.[8] Among evangelicals music is believed to facilitate a more authentic and active religious experience. Thus, debates over the nature of Christian music and its appropriate manifestations—traditional hymns versus contemporary praise choruses, positive pop versus angst-ridden rock, for example—are to a large degree debates about the nature of Christianity and the Christian experience. Contemporary Christian music has also been hailed as a tool for reaching the non-Christian with the Gospel message. Through CCM, then, one can find the essential characteristics of that message as it is currently being formulated. Contemporary Christian music represents a microcosm of the contemporary American evangelical religious experience and, as such, offers important inroads to an understanding of the American cultural landscape.

Face the Music

"When the shaking comes, if it's real it will stand; if it's solid it will stand. If it's not, through the mercy of God, this shaking—things that aren't real are going to fall away."[9] So stated recording artist Russ Taff in the opening salvo of what was to emerge as a two-hour apologetic for himself, his colleagues, Myrrh Records, and the genre of popular music known as contemporary Christian music. The occasion was *Shake: Christian Artists Face the Music,* a prerecorded radio program that aired on religious radio stations across America on February 6, 1988. Produced by Jon Rivers for Myrrh Records (a key subsidiary of the largest of the Christian music corporations, Word, Inc.), *Shake* was a collection of interviews with twenty-one of the artists signed to Myrrh.[10] Introduced with the claim that the program would give listeners direct access to the "hearts and minds" of the Myrrh artists and that "more than ever," it was "a time for honesty, integrity, vulnerability," the intent of the program was obvious: this was an opportunity for the Christian music industry, in the person of the Myrrh artist, to respond to and distance itself from the widely publicized scandals then plaguing the evangelical church.[11] As a result of Jim Bakker's extramarital affair, Jimmy Swaggart's solicitation, and Oral Roberts's spiritual extortion, the American evangelical church was, to use Taff's language, shaking. As Rivers prompted the Myrrh artists for comments on issues such as sin, temptation, accountability, cleansing, commitment, and the power of music, it became quite clear that the function of *Shake* was to buttress the foundations beneath Myrrh Records and, more generally, the foundations beneath the contemporary Christian music genre to which the label's (and artists') fortunes were inextricably tied.

A decade later the televangelism scandals have been largely forgotten, as, to be honest, have many of the artists heard from in that February 1988 broadcast. The program, however, remains a significant moment in the history of contemporary Christian music. Whatever the crisis to which it was a response and whatever its immediate goals, *Shake* was fundamentally an opportunity for a group of Christian recording artists, a Christian record label, and, in many ways, contemporary Christian music itself to explicitly and publicly grapple with their identities. "The music was created by God," claimed Jimmy Lee of The Imperials, an idea perhaps in part contradicted by producer Brown Bannister's suggestion that the artists "know it's a business" and Phil Keaggy's claim that in his case making music was simply a vocation. But then Bannister further argued that despite the necessary evils of doing business, "the bottom line is that they want to touch people—they want to touch kids." On this point Bannister himself was contradicted by Steve Hindalong and Derri Daugherty of The Choir, who claimed, "We don't view music as a tool. We didn't say, 'Let's change the world for Christ and music is the way we should do it.'"[12] Consequently, while the "Statement of Faith" printed on the album jacket that was sent to broadcasters implied a unified front, the reality of the broadcast suggested something far different.[13] Presumably united in vocation, faith, and contractual commitments to Myrrh Records, the twenty-one artists heard on the broadcast nevertheless presented vastly different interpretations of what contemporary Christian music was all about. While *Shake* shaped itself into an effort to (re)define Christian music, the definition that emerged was far from clear.

What, then, is contemporary Christian music? According to Deena Weinstein, a musical genre must, at minimum, have a particular set of fundamental sounds by which it is distinguished from other genres.[14] So, while the outer boundaries of a genre are generally blurred, at core there must be a "code of sonic requirements" to which a piece must adhere if it is to be included under the generic label. In the case of contemporary Christian music, however, Weinstein's argument is unworkable, for there is no *sound*—no sonic code—that defines CCM.[15] As characterized by former teen idol Pat Boone (an initial investor in a number of early Christian record labels), contemporary Christian music's raison d'être has been the rhetorical question, "Why not talk to young people about Jesus in their own language, and with the sound of their own music?"[16] Consequently, as the sound of young people's music changes, so too does CCM. While contemporary Christian music began in the late sixties and early seventies with a relatively homogeneous folk-pop sound (think James Taylor), today one can find the adjective "Christian" applied to most styles of contemporary popular music. Christian heavy metal ("heavenly metal" as some have dubbed it), Christian industrial, Christian punk, Christian blues, Christian folk, Christian rap, Christian new age, Christian Celtic, Christian alternative rock, Christian electronica—all of these and still others not listed can be found on the shelves of the Christian bookstores where the music is generally sold. All are identified as CCM. And if the last thirty years have shown anything, it is that no form of popular music exists that cannot be translated or transformed into a contemporary Christian strain. But if contemporary Christian music cannot be defined by its sound, then how can it be considered a musical genre? What is it that unifies this heterogeneous collection of musical styles?

Historically, three distinct entities have routinely been offered and accepted as the unifying elements of the CCM genre: artist, lyric, and organization. Ultimately problematic, the three arguments are nonetheless relatively straightforward. For many, the single defining characteristic of contemporary Christian music is the faith of the artists who produce it. Most frequently adopted by fans (as evidenced by letters to the editor and discussion groups on the Internet), the artist-based conception for contemporary Christian music requires a connection between the beliefs of the artist and his or her creative output. The end result, then, is a genre defined not by the texts (songs and albums) that constitute it, but by the individuals responsible for producing those texts. As a result, defining Christian music becomes an effort in defining Christianity—or, more accurately, in identifying the signifiers of the faith. This, then, leads to debates over the difference between so-called "artists who are Christians" and "Christian artists" and a morass of competing doctrines, religious views, and religious prejudices. At one extreme are those who attempt to include mainstream artists such as Bruce Cockburn, U2, The Indigo Girls, Sheryl Crow, and others under the CCM umbrella on the basis of those artists' acknowledged or, more frequently, inferred acceptance of the Christian faith. At the opposite end of the continuum are those who work to exclude (Christian) artists such as Sandi Patty and Michael English from the fold on the basis of these artists' break with accepted conventions of Christian behavior. The end result, then, is a genre with as many definitions as there are interested observers. Not surprisingly, most find the approach inadequate.

Hearing little musical difference between mainstream pop and CCM—but at the same time hoping to avoid the task of judging someone else's faith—some have argued that the distinguishing characteristic of contemporary Christian music is the words that are sung. It is the "message" in the music that defines CCM. Don Cusic, for example, contends that for the Christian there are two types of music: music with lyrics about Jesus Christ and the Christian life ("gospel music"), and music with lyrics about everything else ("secular music"). Christian music, therefore, is music that includes lyrics that explicitly address religious (Christian) themes. When artists do not directly address such themes, their music is not Christian.[17] Similarly, in his monthly column in *Contemporary Christian Music* (CCM's premiere trade publication), pioneer Christian music artist John Fischer has argued that Christian songs "tell people who God is, what He did on the Cross, what was wrong with us in the first place, how desperate we are without Him, what it means to follow Him every day, and where we're all going to end up after this is all over."[18] Or, as yet another musician puts it, Christian music must "instruct" in "the ways of the Lord."[19]

While defining contemporary Christian music as music that necessarily addresses religious themes seems reasonable on its face, in practice this approach has proven to be extremely problematic. Because contemporary Christian music is largely a product of evangelical Christianity, the factions, viewpoints, and variants on theology that characterize contemporary evangelicalism have come to be reflected in the realm of CCM. Consequently, to define contemporary Christian music as necessarily addressing religious themes (if not doctrine) is to open a Pandora's box of follow-up questions concerning who God is, what it means to follow Him, and what qualifies as biblical and/or Christian. Tensions are commonplace. Music critic and pastor Brian Quincy Newcomb, for example, has repeatedly dismissed the work of the rock duo DeGarmo & Key as "bumper sticker theology," while they in turn have accused him of being unbiblical.[20] Similarly, when Carman titled his 1993 album *Addicted to Jesus* (Sparrow)—the title presumably intended to illustrate the strength and vitality of his Christian faith as well as to offer a counterpoint to Robert Palmer's "Addicted to Love"—many criticized the move for equating Christianity with codependency.[21] The list of examples goes on. More generally, however, even when specific doctrinal tenets are not at stake the range of topics that can be addressed under the heading of "what it means to follow Him" remains ambiguous. Would, for example, music that addresses human conflicts within a Christian worldview be accepted as Christian music? Some would say yes, and some no. In either case, to define contemporary Christian music as music with religious content is to beg the question of what qualifies as religious.

Working from a set of assumptions that raise as many questions as they answer (as well as conflicting with the de facto generic boundaries adopted by the Christian music press and Christian music retailers), most who favor a lyric-based definition of contemporary Christian music have been forced to complicate their views. Inspirational pop artist Michael

Card, for example, resolves the dilemmas presented in ambiguously religious lyrics as well as instrumental forms of "Christian" music—How can a genre distinction based on lyrics include, as does CCM, instrumental musics such as jazz or ambient?— by creating a new conceptual category and suggesting that there are "Christian musicians" and there is "Christian music." And while Christian music will necessarily be the product of a Christian musician, a Christian musician will not necessarily produce Christian music.[22] Card's new conceptual category, however, does little to eliminate the problems associated with the thematic approach. John Fischer, on the other hand, makes a more persuasive move to issues of infrastructure. If contradicting his earlier position, Fischer nevertheless suggests (again in an article in *Contemporary Christian Music*) that it is helpful to think of Christian music in organizational terms. Christian music, he argues here, is music that is promoted, distributed, broadcast, and sold primarily by and to Christians. At this point, then, CCM is no longer defined by the thematic content of its lyrics but by corporate relations and market characteristics. Admittedly, Fischer does attempt to take back some of his original ground by arguing, on the assumption that anything else would be a waste of resources, that such music should deal primarily with "Christian themes" (however those may be defined).[23] Still, Fischer's unwillingness to give up the thematic approach entirely does not negate the fact that what he offers here is a fundamentally different approach to defining CCM. Christian content is no longer difinitive but normative. Contracts, not content, define CCM. Even here, however, problems arise.

As exemplified by their frequent use of the term "Christian ghetto," those who articulate a definition of Christian music based on the institutional structures of record labels, retail outlets, and radio stations see a relatively deep chasm separating the likes of Warner Brothers and Word, Tower Records and Christian Family Bookstores, and Top 40 and Christian radio. And for the most part, the analysis is accurate. Despite the growth of CCM, it is still difficult to find much in the way of contemporary Christian music on mainstream record store shelves, and more elusive yet has been access to the airwaves of mainstream radio. By the same token, however, if one can identify separate institutions demarcating an isolable contemporary Christian music industry, there are nevertheless points of intersection between this industry and the music industry at large. The most obvious of these are found in the patterns of ownership and financing. Word, for example, was bought by ABC (later Capital Cities/ABC) in 1974 and was held as an independent subsidiary until 1992, when it was sold to the religious book publisher Thomas Nelson Publications. (Retaining possession of Word's book publishing interests, Thomas Nelson sold the label to the Gaylord Entertainment Company at the end of 1996.) Moreover, Word isn't the only label in the Christian music industry with ties to the major record companies. In terms of ownership, then, from Christian record labels that receive "silent corporate backing from a major music publisher" to mainstream record companies that either buy up their Christian counterparts (Word) or start their own gospel/CCM labels (Warner Alliance), institutional distinctions can be problematic at best.[24] Further muddying the institutional waters, moreover, have been the frequent, if not always successful, joint distribution agreements between Christian record companies and major (and not so major) mainstream labels. From Myrrh's deals with A&M and Epic to Sparrow's with MCA, efforts to link Christian music to the distribution channels controlled by the mainstream record industry have been far from rare.[25] Here again, we find the boundaries of contemporary Christian music less than clear.

In the absence of clear parameters for defining the generic conventions of contemporary Christian music, some have moved to negate the very concept of Christian music. "All of creation is God's handiwork," the argument runs, and thus music is simply music. There is no "Christian," no "secular."[26] However reasonable theologically, such arguments miss the fundamental point that there is both practical and analytical utility in the generic identifier CCM. So, while one might argue that music is music and there is no meaningful distinction between what is called CCM and what is not, the argument doesn't change the fact that if an individual hopes to purchase, hear, or read about the latest album from Havalina Rail Company, Marty McCall, Burlap to Cashmere, Jaci Velasquez, Third Day, This Train, or any of the other two hundred plus artists and groups that constitute CCM, they had better head to the local Christian bookstore, tune in to the local Christian radio station, or pick up a copy of *Contemporary Christian Music* or *True Tunes News* because they won't likely find what they're seeking on the shelves at Sam Goody or in the pages of *Rolling Stone*.[27] That is to say, they must recognize, intuitively if not explicitly, that what they seek is "Christian music." Similar lessons must be learned by those who hope to understand the activities and motivations of these artists and the corporations and organizations that support them. As numerous artists, critics, and executives have learned, music is *not* simply music, and the practices surrounding the production of contemporary Christian music are something unique. God's creation notwithstanding, CCM is, and will remain, a viable generic category.

One appropriate way to combat the complexities surrounding contemporary Christian music is by approaching the genre within a framework appropriated from Howard Becker: the art world.[28] According to Becker, the art world is defined as the network of people whose cooperative activity produces that art world's particular type of artistic product: the artists who are immediately responsible for the creation of the artistic work; the producers who provide the funds and support necessary for its production; the distributors who bring the work to the audience; the audiences who appreciate, purchase, and collect it; and the critics, aestheticians, and philosophers who create and maintain the rationales according to which all these other activities make sense and have value.[29] Contemporary Christian music can be seen not only as an art world, but as a "splintered" art world characterized by distinct and occasionally competing rationales for the forms that are created. Borrowing further, this time from the work of film theorist Rick Altman, these competing rationales can be used to make sense of the distinctions discussed in the preceding pages.

In an effort to resurrect and redefine the concepts surrounding genre theory, Altman argues that genres "are not permanent products of a singular origin, but temporary expressions of a dynamic and ongoing process."[30] Standard genre theory, he claims, has been an effort to seek the common features among a set of texts; it has been a sorting process. So the effort to define CCM becomes a search among the artists, songs, and record labels for some common trait. In Altman's reconfiguration, however, the application of a generic label becomes not an after-the-fact categorization but rather a constitutive process of modeling patterns and possibilities. From this perspective, "every critical statement about genre— and thus any generic classification—must be understood as having a discursive as well as descriptive existence."[31] So, suggests Altman, genres are constantly undergoing a process of negotiation; producers, critics, and audiences contribute to the definition of what a particular genre "is." Ultimately, this is a process of community building. To accept the premises of a genre is to participate in a community—an art world—and to negotiate those premises is to negotiate the boundaries that define it.

These ideas can be usefully applied to the case of CCM. Contemporary Christian music cannot be defined on the basis of what is perceived to
be the shared religious faith of a particular set of musicians. Nor can it be
defined in terms of some thematic unity found among a particular set of
songs or the resources provided by a particular organizational grouping.
Contemporary Christian music can be defined, however, in terms of community. Contemporary Christian music is an artistic product that emerges
from a nexus of continually negotiated relationships binding certain artists, certain corporations, certain audiences, and certain ideas to one another. It is the art produced by an art world that surrounds a heterogeneous
grouping of sometimes competing, sometimes complementary, and sometimes unrelated discourses concerning moral values, artistic values, commercial values, social values, and religious values. Produced through the
interaction of label executives, record producers, artists, critics, audiences,
and others, it is the nature of these discourses which we intend to explore
in the pages which follow.

A Few Words on the Assumptions, Method, and Model

Approaching contemporary Christian music as a "splintered art world,"
this project rests heavily on Becker's assertion that art worlds, or at least
their boundaries, can be best understood by examining what the members
of the art world itself have to say on the subject.[32] What follows, then, is an
effort in social cartography—a mapping of the contemporary Christian
music art world based on what those who make it, criticize it, study it, and
listen to it have to say about the music. It is a study of public discourse,
one rooted in the belief that what the art world says to itself in the light of
day is, in the final analysis, far more significant than what any given individual will state or admit to in response to the questions of an outsider.
Thus, while in some cases the analysis relies upon evidence drawn from
personal interviews, the majority is taken from the public record. And for
those interested in contemporary Christian music, there is no shortage of
sources. Myriad trade publications and fanzines such as *Contemporary
Christian Music, CCM Update, CounterCulture, Cross Rhythms, (Harvest
Rock) Syndicate, Heaven's Metal, Inside Music, Kamikaze, Notebored, Release, 7Ball, The Rock, True Tunes News,* and *Visions of Gray* are (or, may
they rest in peace, were) devoted to the topic. Evangelicalism's general
interest publications, moreover, often devote time and space to CCM.

Articles on Christian music appear frequently if sporadically in magazines such as *Christianity Today, Soujourner's, The (Wittenburg) Door,* and *Prism,* while others such as *Cornerstone* and *Campus Life* regularly include album reviews, artist interviews, and features on CCM. Additionally, the growing public interest in the Internet and World Wide Web has resulted in still more sources on CCM. These include discussion-oriented Usenet newsgroups and listservs, fan-authored home pages and electronic publications, as well as the official home pages of the artists and record labels. Official or unofficial, print or electronic, this public discourse makes up the raw materials for this project.

It must be recognized, of course, that argument that depends on what people say in public for its essential premises risks validity without soundness. And in a case such as that of contemporary Christian music, there is reason to question the truth of what is claimed. Generally rooted in Christianity's more fundamentalist strains, contemporary Christian music has more than its fair share of both taboo subjects and sacred cows. Artists who are unaware of these and/or unwilling to tailor their comments to fit the mold risk abbreviating their careers. The temptation for some, then, may be to dismiss those comments as calculated, tainted, or untruthful. What such an approach fails to recognize, however, is that the conventions of the genre, not its underlying "reality," are of greater import here. The fact that an artist may be performing solely for financial remuneration is far less interesting—and far less significant—than the fact that the very same artist feels compelled to justify his or her work by claiming some alternative religious motivation; that a record label, as a publicly held corporation, may be legally required to serve the interests of its shareholders above all else is far less interesting than that same corporation's urge to present God's interests as its own; that a listener may prefer John Cougar Mellencamp to Amy Grant is far less interesting than that listener's compulsion to justify that preference in terms of religious, rather than aesthetic, differences. Ultimately, then, it is our contention that, while the material realities underlying contemporary Christian music are no doubt important, the publicly negotiated social realities are more so. What a group is trying to be or claims to be is as important as what it "really is."

With *Apostles of Rock,* then, we have attempted to make sense of the diverse public discourses that surround and define contemporary Christian music. Our brief history of the genre focuses on the conflicts that have characterized its thirty-year history. Exploring the moral and aesthetic objections against Christian music as well as the responding legitimations of the genre, we ultimately draw on the work of H. Richard Neibuhr to suggest that these conflicts can best be understood as manifestations of the age-old attempt to resolve the Christian dilemma of being called to live in the world while not becoming a part of that world.[33] Specifically, we believe that contemporary Christian music is characterized by three distinct formats, each corresponding to one of Neibuhr's resolutions to the Christ and culture paradox, which we have labeled Separational CCM, Integrational CCM, and Transformational CCM. In our view, each of these provides unique rationales for the production of Christian music and thus adheres to a unique aesthetic.

Rooted in the "Christ against culture" perspective described by Neibuhr, Separational CCM, with its rationales of evangelism, exhortation, and worship, attempts to maintain a stark distinction between Christian and secular culture while at the same time remaining committed to reaching non-Christians and making converts. The two approaches have proven difficult to reconcile because the commitment to evangelism—and the cultural relevance it requires—has routinely demanded that concessions be made to secular culture. But as the lines between mainstream music and Christian music and between mainstream artists and Christian artists grow increasingly indistinct, it becomes necessary to reaffirm the separation between the two. More often than not, this leads to an exclusive and unyielding focus on the gospel message. But even though this message produces the occasional convert, it more frequently works to isolate the music within the Christian subculture. For all its efforts at evangelism, Separational CCM emerges as music created by and almost exclusively for evangelicals.

Integrational CCM, epitomized by the music of Amy Grant but with historical precedence in the likes of The Oak Ridge Boys and B.J. Thomas, works from what Neibuhr identifies as the "Christ of culture" perspective. Opposed to the idea of withdrawing into an isolated Christian subculture, integrational artists developed new rationales for their music that would allow them to integrate themselves, as well as their Christian beliefs, into mainstream culture. Here, then, contemporary Christian music was conceived to be a wholesome alternative to mainstream rock, an alternative that served to articulate the Christian worldview to those who might not otherwise be exposed to it. As a corollary to this, evangelism—still believed to be a key element of Christian life—became a function not of the music but of the personal contacts the artist could make through his or her participation in the production of mainstream culture. Thus conceived, contemporary Christian music from the integrational perspective emerged as what would come to be known as "positive pop."

Finally, Transformational CCM, rooted in an amalgam of the mediating positions between the separational and integrational extremes and drawing on a particular set of theological and aesthetic assumptions concerning the nature of God and the purposelessness of art, has as its goal not to enter or to withdraw from mainstream culture but to enable its transformation. The end result is a music stripped of its utilitarian purposes and rendered valuable only through its ability to manifest both truth and quality. Art no longer serves religion but is drawn inextricably into it.

All that said, it is important to recognize that there are a number of key assumptions concerning the nature of music and the musical experience underlying this project. Primarily, we hold that meanings are not inherent to various forms of music but are socially derived in the course of interactions between and among an art world's participants and the social environment in which it exists and operates. As human beings, we have the capability to attach meanings to symbols through a complex process of social interaction. By their nature, then, these meanings are not fixed for all time but evolve and develop through continued interaction. For many involved with CCM, this may be a new idea.

Required to defend the concept of "Christian rock music" against those who suggest that rock music possesses and presents inherent moral dilemmas, many members of the Christian music art world have claimed that "music is neutral." Thus musician Dana Key argues, "Music is like automobiles. It's a vehicle that can be used to bring good things or bad. It can lead you closer to God, or it can lead you further away. It's a tool that can be used for many purposes."[34] Others, in contrast, claim that music does indeed possess inherent meanings. Leonard Payton, for example, argues that "contemporary Christian music is a subset of the larger pop music world, and, as such, is also driven primarily by style appetite, not verbal content . . . a catastrophe for a faith predicated on, 'In the beginning was the Word.'"[35] Payton claims that contemporary Christian music is, like pop music more generally, plagued by "thoughtless musical and poetic forms" that have the aural impact of a tidal wave. It is a cultural artifact that "demands no thought," while at the same time it creates a state in which "our aural nerves are delivering a steady torrent of overwhelming stimuli to our brains."[36] Consequently, when listening to pop music "we are truly unable to think about what we are hearing rationally; we can only experience it."[37] This, however, is precisely the point of rock and roll. Rock music is meant to be experienced. It is, however, a *social* experience. Contrary to Key's claims, rock and roll is not neutral; it does carry "inherent" meanings. But this is not to imply, as Payton suggests, that those meanings can be seen and measured with an oscilloscope. The meaning of rock is not to be found in the sonic wave-forms, nor is it to be found in lyrics transcribed and analyzed. Rock and roll is a form of music that must be understood in situ and furthermore is one that comes with a significant measure of cultural baggage. So, while it may be true that there are no inherent meanings in a syncopated beat or a I-IV-V chord progression, to strap on a Stratocaster and climb on stage is necessarily to evoke the presence of Elvis Presley, The Beatles, Jimi Hendrix, The Rolling Stones, most of those who followed, and all the meanings that have come to be attached to them. And while those meanings may be negotiated—even cleaned up and Christianized—they cannot be ignored.[38]

Flowing out of this is our belief that music, culture, and society are integrally related. The meanings associated with a particular form or piece of music can only be understood in the context of the widest range of human activities. Politics, economics, religion, education—all inform and can be informed by the meanings associated with music.[39] As a result of these social influences, groups with different forms and measures of cultural capital, different expectations, and different experiences will produce different forms of music and endow them with different meanings.[40] Because the meanings associated with the music are socially situated, if one approaches the musical art world without understanding the social context in which it originated, exists, and continues to evolve, one can assume meanings that are not shared by the art world's participants. This is the case with Flake's commentary on Christian rock in her treatise on evangelicals, *Redemptorama: Culture, Politics, and the New Evangelicalism*. Flake calls Christian rock and roll an "oxymoron," a "most peculiar hybrid," "a strange hybrid beast," and a musical product wherein there is "no organic connection between the message and the style."[41] In assuming that there is an innate, rather than socially produced, relationship between a musical style and the meanings it carries within an art world, Flake's analysis amounts to an external authority's misguided interpretation and judgment of an art world that she fails to understand. Her conclusion that Christian rock is "not so much Christianized culture as enculturated Christianity" may or may not be accurate, but she has failed to see and understand the product as do the members of the Christian rock art world.[42]

To avoid making the same error, we must follow Sara Cohen's dictum and determine not only what meanings are created through participation in the CCM art world but also for and by whom those meanings are created.[43] This challenge proves particularly difficult in CCM. Contemporary Christian music attempts to be all things to all people musically and, to a lesser extent, lyrically. The evangelical subculture out of which the CCM art world has arisen and in which it continues to exist is not a monolithic structure. "Evangelical," by one definition, is a comprehensive term that refers to that group of Christians who accept the absolute authority of the Bible, have been converted to Christ (are "born again"), and who share their faith with others; another definition argues evangelicalism to be "an umbrella term to refer broadly to conservative Protestants—including fundamentalists, evangelicals, Pentecostals, and Charismatics—who insist on some sort of spiritual rebirth as a criterion for entering the kingdom of heaven, who often impose exacting behavioral standards on the faithful."[44] Given such broad definitions, it is not surprising that evangelicals are a diverse lot, and the CCM art world both reflects and reinforces these divisions within the loosely bound evangelical subculture. Hence, not only is there is substantial debate on what does and does not and what should and should not be included within the rubric of "Christian" and/or "evangelical," there is a corresponding debate on what does and does not and should and should not be included within the rubric of contemporary Christian music.

Finally, it must be remembered that some thirty years after its inception, the jury remains out on contemporary Christian music. For some, contemporary Christian music is "the greatest revolution in the modern church," "a fresh moving of the Holy Spirit" through the landscape of American culture.[45] For others, it represents a "commercial imitation" of mainstream music "with redundant religious themes" or, in the terms of evangelicalism, "a blatant compromise with the world."[46] But if evangelicals and atheists, artists and audiences, critics and corporate sponsors are still trying to make sense of CCM, one thing remains clear: contemporary Christian music is here to stay. Despite religious leaders who continue to find Christianized pop music to be anathema to the Christian life and critics who argue the meaning of the music to be commercial consumption rather than Jesus Christ, contemporary Christian music has become, and will remain, a vital element in the contemporary evangelical experience.

What this means, of course, is up for debate, although, from the apologists who find in the music a new wrapping for a timeless message to the critics who see the growth of CCM as little more than the music industry's latest effort to capitalize on a previously untapped market, there are clearly established schools of thought. To those schools we bring an approach that, for better or worse, takes the contemporary Christian music industry at face value. We have attempted to set aside the cynicism that searches only for ulterior motives, the optimism that dismisses the existence of such motives, and the egotism that privileges an external perspective in favor of understanding contemporary Christian music on its own terms as examined by the light of established theory. From this process has emerged an understanding of contemporary Christian music not as a monolithic cultural form but as a splintered art world, characterized by difference as much as by similarity. It must be noted, however, that the splintered art world described in the pages that follow is, in the final analysis, merely a model. No artist of contemporary Christian music, at least none that we know of, would describe his or her music as "Separational," "Integrational," or "Transformational." Many still balk at the label "Christian." Consequently, one must be wary of pushing the application of our ideas too far. Change is essential to the human condition, and this is as true of Christian musicians as it is of anybody. So this week's integrational entertainer may become next week's zealous separational evangelist, and the artist who today works squarely within the separational domain, arguing that "we're trying to reach a bunch of kids with the Gospel, that's all," will by tomorrow have moved into the realm of Transformational CCM, claiming, "I've experienced a whole new realm of human problems, and that has taken precedence over Christian Cheerleading."[47] Push too hard at the categories, demand too strongly that the artists be pigeonholed, and the system will undoubtedly come crashing down.

At the same time, it is our belief that the model we have described serves to bring some order to what is currently a chaos of competing views and ideas about what contemporary Christian music is or should be. The contrasts and contradictions are there, and they are rooted as much in the culture as they are in the music. The members of Jars of Clay fawn over the mainstream celebrities that their success has allowed them to meet.

Rebecca St. James claims to be uninterested in such individuals, happily isolated in a world occupied exclusively by Christians.[48] The two manifest not only distinct approaches to making Christian music but also distinct approaches to living the Christian life. So, whatever the value of contemporary Christian music in and of itself—and whatever the value of our model for the social world responsible for CCM—it is what contemporary Christian music has to say about contemporary Christianity that makes it of greatest interest.

Interlude:
Larry Norman

The Adam's Apple in Fort Wayne, Indiana, is 662 miles from CBGB's in New York City and 2,175 miles from the Whisky a Go-Go in Hollywood. In 1979, the miles can frequently seem like light-years. Tonight, however, such is not the case. For the patrons of The Adam's Apple, northern Indiana tonight holds as much interest and excitement as New York or Southern California, and The Adam's Apple itself—the converted basement and sanctuary to the Calvary Temple Church which now makes up one of the most visible and viable of the coffeehouses that constitute the Jesus Rock "circuit"—easily stands in for its more famous coastal kin. The Whisky may have been the launching pad for bands like The Doors and Van Halen, and CBGB's the home of musical pioneers like The Ramones, Talking Heads and Blondie, but it was at The Adam's Apple that Petra and Honeytree both got their starts, and The Adam's Apple where Phil Keaggy routinely comes to play. More important still, it is The Adam's Apple where Larry Norman, regarded by most in attendance as the man responsible for the burgeoning genre of Jesus Rock, has tonight come to perform.

His shoulder-length blond hair contrasting sharply with his black shirt and jeans, Larry Norman slowly strolls from stage left to the microphone, acoustic guitar in hand. As he comes into view, the crowd of several hundred—not quite a full house—rises to its feet in spirited applause. Stone-faced, Norman shows little reaction to the crowd. Stepping to the microphone, his immediate attention is directed at the sound engineer and a monitor that's set too low. "Is this on?" he asks. After strumming several chords, each interrupted with a request to the engineer to turn up the volume, Norman begins. He hums the opening notes to "U.F.O.," and almost immediately the crowd again applauds and cheers. Norman stops, waiting until all is silent before beginning again. "He's an unidentified flying object," Norman sings, "you will see Him in the air / He's an unidentified flying object / You will drop your hands and stare."[1] The song sets the theme for the night's performance, as it is the first of many times that Norman will sing (and speak) of Christ's Second Coming. As the song ends, Norman once again humming, applause breaks forth. Norman waits for the noise to fade, his face passive and unsmiling, before beginning another song.

As Norman plays, the apocalyptic theme continues through songs like "I Wish We'd All Been Ready" ("There's no time to change your mind / The Son has come and you've been left behind") and "Six Sixty Six" ("In the midst of war he offered us peace / He came like a lover from out of the east / With the face of an angel and the heart of a beast / His intentions were six sixty six").[2] The music and its message clearly resonate with those in attendance; many know the words by heart and sing along softly. Norman's message, however, is not confined to his songs, and between and within numbers he entertains the crowd with long periods of humorous dialogue and sarcastic commentary on topics ranging from the oil crisis ("Maybe they just forgot where they put it. We should all go over and help them look through the garage") and the space program ("They brought back a big bag of rocks / Only cost $13 billion / Must be nice rocks") to Jesus Rock ("The world stole rock 'n' roll from the church. I'm just stealin' it back"), Christian jargon ("Brother, have you been washed in the blood? Gee, uh, not lately"), and the treatment he's received from the Christian media ("Spreading rumors and gossip is a real bad game / The only name to spread is Jesus' name").[3] Each time, as the audience reacts with laughter and applause, Norman waits expressionless until the crowd is silent once again. Finally, after more than two hours of music and banter about Jesus Christ, the Second Coming and current events, the solitary figure with the long blond hair and a wardrobe inspired by Johnny Cash strolls off the stage and back into the shadows.

1 Origins and Oppositions: The Founding of CCM

It is not my view that the Gospel should cause all the arts to be struck down and disappear; on the contrary, I should like to see all the arts, and especially music, used in the service of Him who gave and created them.

Martin Luther

In his history of popular music and the emergence of rock and roll, Philip Ennis opens with a metaphor drawn from the schoolyard. Describing the game Rock-Paper-Scissors, Ennis argues that in the realm of popular music "the relations among art, commerce, and politics are something like that game; each has some strong power over one other, but, at the same time, is vulnerable to a third."[1] But while power in the children's game is absolute and unidirectional—paper covers rock, rock smashes scissors, scissors cut paper—power in the music world, as in real life, varies in both magnitude and direction. Thus, while asserting the general case that "in American society, art validates money, money regulates politics, and politics defines art," Ennis suggests that there are exceptions to these rules and ways in which contradictory relationships can also be argued.[2] Ultimately, then, the history of rock and roll Ennis proposes is the tale of a "stormy relationship" between art, commerce and politics. "Rocknroll," Ennis argues, ". . . provoked trouble right from the start in all three of these areas, and it still does."[3]

Art, commerce, politics. There can be little doubt that the three are necessary for an understanding of the history and development of rock and roll. However, unless one assigns the broadest of meanings to these concepts, one can question their sufficiency. In particular, as we move from the grand narrative of rock and roll's broad history—its emergence from earlier music forms, the development of new recording technologies, the battle between ASCAP and BMI over performance rights, the payola hearings, etc.—to a more focused examination of the particular moments and forms that constitute both major and minor aspects of that history, it becomes obvious that other considerations must be brought to bear on our understanding of rock and roll as a musical form. Our case in point is contemporary Christian music, a musical genre that merges rock and roll with evangelical Protestantism. With CCM, therefore, one must add to the already convoluted mix of art, commerce, and politics the equally problematic tensions that characterize twentieth-century Christianity. Stormy relationships, indeed.

The Origins of CCM

In attempting to understand the history and development of contemporary Christian music (or any music for that matter), one must first ask a basic question: Revolution or evolution? Are we to understand the historical development of the music as a series of revolutions, with the meaningful distinctions emerging from the innovations of particularly creative individuals, or are we to understand musical history as a slow evolution from style to style? Was rock and roll born "when Elvis recorded rhythm and blues songs as a white country boy with the voice of a black gospel singer" or was rock and roll the outcome of the slow merging of various established genres of music—"pop, black pop, country pop, jazz, folk, and gospel," and/or "rhythm and blues, . . . gospel, country and urban blues, pop crooning, Anglo-American balladry and Nashville country music"?[4] Given a particular style of music, does it make any sense to ask who invented it?

Popular discourse would suggest that it certainly does make sense. There is no shortage of people who would assert that rock and roll was indeed invented by Elvis Presley, and, as we will see here, there are those who actively argue this or that artist to be the "father" (rarely "mother") of contemporary Christian music. That said, however, there are reasons to move away from this revolutionary approach. Simply put, music, like any cultural form, cannot exist in a vacuum, and, if it is to communicate at all, music must draw from an established set of symbols and signs. Thus, while the popular discourse of music suggests each new genre to be the result of the lone artist creating something completely new, this discourse masks the communal nature of artistic production. As Jane Gaines writes in her discussion of entertainment law, "the very concept of authorship overrides the generic and conventional indebtedness that would mark . . . works as the product not so much of individuals as of societies."[5] This is as true of the genre as it is of the particular work. Music is evolution.

Turning, then, to the specific evolutionary history of contemporary Christian music, one faces the complication of three sometimes distinct histories—one in the music itself and two more in the musics from which it developed. To employ a frequently used metaphor, contemporary Christian music can be seen as the merging of two distinct musical streams: the safe, acceptable church musics of the evangelical church on the one hand and rock and roll on the other. This bucolic imagery, however, is somewhat misleading. For one thing, it implies a distinction between church music and rock and roll that is more imagined than real. As discussed above, music evolves; included in the ancestors of rock and roll were the very church musics that would later recombine with their secular progeny to produce CCM. This, then, points to a second issue. While the development of CCM is frequently discussed as a simple, linear progression—first there was church music, then there was rock, and then church music and rock combined to form CCM—the fact of the matter is that these "streams" twist, turn, merge, separate, dive underground, change names, and merge yet again. Metaphorically speaking, then, the history of CCM is not a history of merging streams but of woven threads. When CCM was born, church music and rock and roll did not cease to exist but rather continued on their own evolutionary paths. These paths continue to intersect with contemporary Christian music, with innovations in rock and roll being absorbed directly into CCM and innovations in CCM altering the landscape of church music. To write the history of CCM is, at least to some extent, to write the histories of rock and roll and of church music as well.

The religious roots of rock and roll are by now well documented. Ennis argues that Elvis Presley was "religiously soaked," and Curtis suggests that both his vocal style and his stage presence were modeled after the southern gospel groups that Presley heard as a young man growing up in a Pentecostal church. Curtis claims that the Blackwood Brothers, a pioneering southern gospel group, were a particularly strong influence on Presley and a "harbinger for musical trends."[6] And Elvis Presley was not the only early rocker connected to religious traditions. Jerry Lee Lewis and Little Richard both came from Pentecostal backgrounds similar to Presley's, and both brought the energy of the Pentecostal church service to the performances of rock music.[7] Similarly, Chuck Berry (the son of a

Baptist preacher), Buddy Holly ("a devout Baptist to the end of his life"), Ray Charles, Sam Cooke, and Aretha Franklin had all started out as church or gospel singers.[8] Clearly, more than a few of rock's pioneers had ties to the Christian church.

The ties between early rock and roll and American religion, however, went well beyond the personal faith of particular musicians. In some cases, gospel songs became hits on the pop charts, either in their original form— "Oh Happy Day" (said to have originally been played as a joke) or "Amazing Grace"[9]—or with a few judicial changes that would translate "lyrics that sang of the mystical love of God into lyrics that celebrated the earthly love of woman."[10] Ray Charles made use of this latter approach in his songs "This Little Girl of Mine" and "Talking about You," which as gospel songs had been "This Little Light of Mine" and "Talking about Jesus." More generally, it is claimed that gospel "showed rock how to sing," with groups like The Beatles, who "echoed one another's phrases, dragged out words across several beats, shouted 'yeah' and went into falsetto cries," mimicking classic gospel style.[11] Indeed, the quintessential vocals of a rock band—a male quartet, one singing lead and the remaining three backup— is said to be "a gospel form by origin."[12] According to Anderson, "Black gospel provided white rock with the style, songs, and artists to imitate." Taking this to its logical conclusion, Richard Stanislaw, music columnist for *Eternity* magazine and professor of music at Taylor University (a prominent Evangelical liberal arts college), argued, "Rock was first Christian music, then appropriated by the popular secular culture."[13] Religious roots, however, do not necessarily make for a religious medium, and, though there were numerous ways in which the various forms of gospel music had influenced rock and roll, religious leaders nevertheless found an abundance of reasons to condemn this new musical form.

Despite its gospel roots, rock and roll was quickly distanced from religion, with each side antagonistic toward the other. For their part, the teenagers who constituted the music's intended audience began to react "against everything they perceived as aligned with the stuffy, restrictive adult world," including the church.[14] Rock and roll provided the soundtrack to this rebellion. In reaction, church leaders quickly attacked the new music. But with Southern fundamentalists leading the way, these early attacks on rock music focused on racial as much as religious concerns.[15] So, for example, it was claimed that the interracial nature of early rock and roll presented a "new outbreak of cultural miscegenation" that "could only spell trouble for white America."[16] With the coming of the sixties, however, the opposition between rock and religion moved past the issue of race to that of lifestyle—specifically, the "permissive attitude toward sex, drugs and revolution" critics found embodied in rock and roll music.[17] "'Rock and roll,'" evangelist Bob Larson would later claim, "actually means 'promiscuous sexual relationship music.'"[18] So, while the hippies who now defined rock and roll were able to justify their cultural ménage à trois of sex, drugs, and rock and roll "as some sort of epic journey," to the adult world it was little more than degeneracy and hedonism.[19] Degeneracy has never been a church-approved lifestyle.

While the antagonism between rock and roll and the church that developed concomitant with the music made it difficult to imagine Christian forms of the genre, the evolution of gospel music itself paved the way for this connection. As far back as the late nineteenth century, the Fisk Jubilee Singers were credited with providing a "refined and wholesome entertainment" suitable for Christians.[20] Cusic credits evangelist Billy Sunday's singer, Homer Rodeheaver, with revolutionizing the musical portion of revival meetings with his mixture of ministry and entertainment. Rodeheaver was, according to Cusic, gospel music's first sex symbol.[21] In the more recent past (and with no small measure of irony), televangelist Jimmy Swaggart, who continues to condemn both rock and roll and contemporary Christian music, also established openings for a merging of rock and religion with his own "honky-tonk style" of gospel playing and singing. Indeed, Swaggart himself commented, "There seemed to be more rhythm in" his music "than the four walls of the church could stand."[22] While artists like Elvis Presley combined rhythm and blues, country music, and southern gospel to make rock and roll, Swaggart combined these same elements with Pentecostalism, pushing gospel music out of its hymn-oriented style toward more contemporary forms.[23]

Throughout the sixties and seventies, vocal groups such as the Bill Gaither Trio and The Imperials, choral composers such as Ralph Carmichael, and black gospel artists including André Crouch and the Disciples gradually began to incorporate more pop- and rock-oriented styles into their music. And even though they were not the most daring of artists, this gentle pushing at the borders of what the evangelical church considered acceptable would have significant impact on the music of the church. In fact, the hymnals and projector slides of most evangelical churches today include numerous songs written by Gaither ("There's Something about That Name" and "He Touched Me") and Carmichael ("He's Everything to Me") as well as an abundance of "praise and worship" choruses from the early history of CCM. Although unwilling to adopt "secular" rock music whole-sale, the evangelical church in the late 1960s and early 1970s was willing to gradually incorporate rock-like innovations into gospel music, provided they were saturated in religious rhetoric. Consequently, the success of Carmichael, Gaither, and the like arguably had as much to do with their willingness to imbue these new musical forms (or "watered down" ver-sions of them) with overtly religious lyrics as it did with their talents as songwriters; whatever their musical abilities, a key talent for these artists was the command of the religious cliché. As long as the lyrics showed the artists to be unequivocally "gospel" in their approach, a limited amount of musical innovation could be tolerated and occasionally embraced.

By the late 1960s, rock and roll and the evangelical church were be-ginning to come back into contact. As the sixties ended and the church moved into the 1970s and the so-called Jesus Movement, the tentative incorporation of new sounds into the gospel canon would give way to the formulation of a new genre of music: Jesus Rock, or, as it would later be called, contemporary Christian music.[24] The groundwork for this genre had been slowly laid throughout the 1960s. At the same time that gospel musicians working in the sixties had begun to incorporate contemporary musical forms into the music of the church, rock and roll musicians had begun to connect their own music with a quasi-religious spirituality, if not organized religion. As suggested by music critics Robert Hilburn and Chris Willman, The Beatles' 1966 pilgrimage to the Maharishi in India had been only the beginning: "Guitarist John McLaughlin amended his name to Mahavishnu John McLaughlin after meeting up with Sri Chinmoy; Carlos Santana billed himself as Devadip Santana for a number of years. Pete Townsend and Ronnie Lane became devotees of Meher Baba; Seals and Crofts advocated the Bahai faith; Richard Thompson became a strict Sufi; and Rastafarianism . . . became a household word with most American rockers thanks to the emergence of reggae music." Soon, the writers note, "albums with blatant Eastern mystical overtones became commonplace."[25] Off the beaten path of America's traditional religions, this spiritualization of rock and roll nevertheless created opportunities for Judeo-Christian beliefs to influence rock. Though hardly expressions of Christian doc-trine, many songs following this trend (Norman Greenbaum's "Spirit in the Sky," James Taylor's "Fire and Rain") drew freely from Christian culture, if not Christian belief. Indeed, this same period saw the production of *Jesus Christ Superstar* and *Godspell,* two extraordinarily successful "rock operas" that blended popular music, rock and roll included, with Christian myths and ideas. Given this environment, Christian rock and roll—Jesus Rock—began to seem less and less a contradiction in terms.

It should be emphasized here, however, that the importance of songs such as "Spirit in the Sky" as well as the *Godspell* and *Jesus Christ Superstar* rock operas lies more in what they suggest about mainstream culture at the time than their impact on evangelicals. While such material revealed an openness on the part of mainstream culture to religious and, more specifically, Christian material, such material was generally viewed with suspicion, if not open hostility, in the evangelical community because of its perceived irreverence and the lack of emphasis on the resurrection and atonement of Christ. As James Huffman explains, "Works like *Jesus Christ Superstar,* which 'ask the right questions' but allow each individual to provide his own answers, will be appropriated by nearly all—the atheist, the agnostic, the believer."[26] So, while some evangelicals saw promise in the fact that the questions were being raised, most were disappointed in the answers that were being provided. Jesus Rock emerged as a means not only to present "the right questions" but also to offer the more strident answers evangelicalism demanded.

It is at this point, then, that one must turn to Larry Norman. Rock music has Elvis Presley, Sun Studios, and "Blue Moon of Kentucky"; contemporary Christian music has Larry Norman, Capitol Records, and "I Love You." The story is by now firmly embedded in CCM history: In April 1968 the song "I Love You (But the Words Won't Come)" by the Bay Area band People reached number fourteen on the pop charts. The band was fronted by Larry Norman, a born-again Christian who, in pursuit of his desire "to alert people to the Truth in unorthodox ways," decided to title the band's first album, on which "I Love You" was to appear, *We Need a Whole Lot More of Jesus and a Lot Less Rock and Roll.* The cover art would feature an image of Jesus Christ. Unimpressed with the idea, Capitol Records "put the proverbial foot down" and released the album as *I Love You* (Capitol, 1968) with a photo of the band—not the Christian Savior—on the cover. The day the album was released, Norman left the band. The following year Capitol Records released Norman's first solo project *Upon This Rock* (Capitol, 1969), the album generally recognized as the first bona fide Christian rock album.[27]

In the years to follow, Norman would simultaneously be hailed as the "Father of Christian Rock" and marginalized in both the realm of rock music, where he was considered too religious, and in the burgeoning Christian music industry, where his music was believed to be too aggressive. But beyond Norman, a slow but increasing trickle of rock artists who experienced religious conversions to Christianity also began to produce music consistent with their newfound faith. In a few cases, these musical expressions of faith could be contained within the artist's established contractual relationships. Bob Dylan's much-publicized (and somewhat later) conversion, for example, was played out on the stages and studios he had always used. More frequently, however, the artists found themselves signing with one of the fledgling Christian labels that were quickly springing up to establish an organizational foundation for the emerging musical form. Barry McGuire (who in his pre-conversion days had a number-one hit with "Eve of Destruction"), Love Song (featuring Chuck Girard, formerly with the Castells and the Hondells), John Michael Talbot and Terry Talbot (formerly of Mason Proffit), Noel Paul Stookey (of Peter, Paul, and Mary), and Phil Keaggy (of Glass Harp) were among the many artists who began to find a small but enthusiastic audience for their new "Christian" music. Indeed, in an effort to legitimate the developing genre and sell records, converts with previous careers in mainstream rock and roll were warmly embraced by the Christian music community and quickly— sometimes too quickly—thrust upon the stage. Even a relatively obscure connection to mainstream stardom (drumming for Paul McCartney's post-Beatles band Wings, for example, as in the case of Joe English) would be enough to make an artist a prize catch in Christian music. B.J. Thomas, Dan Peek (of America), Richie Furay (of Buffalo Springfield and Poco) were each in turn quickly marketed as Christian celebrity conversions. And as CCM sought to legitimate the quality of the music both to the world of rock and roll and to the potential audience among Christians, the search for celebrity converts would continue.

Oppositions

Throughout its history, CCM, both in general and in the person of the Christian artist, has faced significant opposition—opposition from the church; opposition from the retailers, radio stations, and record labels of the mainstream music industry; even, at times, opposition from fans. Establishment opposition to new forms of music, however, is nothing new. As McClary notes, even Plato condemned new musical forms as a potential subversion of authority and a possible seduction by means of the body.[28] Plato was by no means the last to hold such views. From the Reverend John Bentzien, who in 1907 claimed the waltz was a "dance of death" that caused the dancers to "swing off the edge of a decent life into eternal ruin" to the Parents' Music Resource Center (PMRC), which in the mid-1980s suggested that rock and roll promoted rebellion, substance abuse, sexual promiscuity/perversion, violence/nihilism, and the occult, issues of both authority and the body have been the basis for much of the criticism of new musical forms.[29] Contemporary Christian music was no exception. And while Kamin suggests that by 1958 the general controversy surrounding rock music diminished to the point that the music was viewed as a "harmless, if irritating, fixture of the teen scene," opposition in the religious community didn't peak until the late 1960s and early 1970s when the rock musicians' experiments with both Eastern religions and drugs created a tempest that still rages in certain right-wing religious circles.[30] Indeed, religious opposition to rock and roll may have peaked in the 1970s, but it has yet to die away completely.

Two of the first, most vocal, and most prolific religious critics of rock and roll are the authors and ministers David A. Noebel and Bob Larson. Manifesting the frequent conflation of religion and politics, Noebel has blamed communism for rock and roll, arguing that in 1947 communists established a number of record companies in the United States with the twin goals of "not only proletariatizing [sic] our culture, but also seeking to make a generation of our youth mentally ill."[31] According to Noebel, communists were using rock music to produce a generation of neurotic and emotionally unstable youth.[32] Less politically minded, Larson concluded in 1969 that rock and roll would be "an increasingly important tool in Satan's hand to destroy the morals of this generation."[33] Larson also claimed that the steady pounding of the rock rhythm can lead to hypnotic trances and that dancing to rock music can lead to demonic possession.[34] Noebel and Larson, however, were not the only ones to voice such fears, and in works such as *Dancing with Demons* (1988), *Backward Masking Unmasked: Backward Satanic Messages of Rock and Roll Exposed* (1983), and *The God of Rock: A Christian Perspective of Rock Music* (1982), religious critics of rock and roll have continued to expound on the evils identified by Noebel and Larson.[35] If the attention they receive ebbs and flows, evangelical critics, ready to place the blame for America's ills squarely on the shoulders of rock music nonetheless seem always to be available.[36]

Despite the religious lyrics and Christian worldview of the artists who produce it, from its inception contemporary Christian music has faced many of the same critiques leveled at secular rock and roll. Christian lyrics have not saved CCM from the wrath of televangelists such as Jimmy Swaggart and Bob Larson who focused on the underlying beats and melodies. At the same time, the opposition to CCM goes well beyond its roots in rock and roll. While Swaggart, Larson, and others condemned the music *despite* the Christian lyrics, many theologians and academic authorities on religious music have condemned CCM *because of* those lyrics, arguing that the messages put forth are somehow contradictory to the teachings of the church.[37] Finally, while critics from the religious community have been the most vocal with regard to CCM, the more significant criticism has come from the mainstream record companies and radio stations that found the lyrics too "religious," thus preventing the Christian music industry from gaining access to the distribution channels and promotional rescources necessary for success. In many ways, however, the rapid growth of CCM—by 1995, estimates of Christian music industry revenues had reached as high as $750 million per year[38]—can be credited to these critics. One result of unending assault can be the creation of a united subculture whose members are able to define themselves through their opposition to the norms and values of the surrounding cultural milieu.[39] A common sense of persecution can be, and in the case of CCM has been, the catalyst that both creates a sense of community and provides the determination to continue the struggle.

The Moralist Objections: It's the Devil's Music

With critics in the church, the music industry, and even the fan base, contemporary Christian music faced opposition in distinct forms coming from multiple fronts. The most frequent and fundamental was the moralist objection that came from within the church. Perhaps best illustrated by David Wilkerson's melodramatic take on the situation—"Where is the alarm in Zion, where is the shame, where are the prophets who should be crying aloud, 'Enough! No more music of the devils in the house of God'?"[40]— the moralist objection to contemporary Christian music argued that rock music with Christian lyrics was an abomination. Rock and roll was the devil's music and thus could not in good conscience be enjoyed, much less played, by Christians. Rock music drove listeners to a sexual frenzy. Rock music was used to summon demons. Rock music killed houseplants. Working on such assumptions and ignoring the similarities between Christian rock and his own honky-tonk Pentecostal playing, Jimmy Swaggart argued that "the new so-called contemporary 'Christian' music is incompatible with true biblical Christianity. . . . I emphatically state that it's impossible to touch anyone's heart with contemporary music. . . . The sounds are weird, strange, and odd; correspondent to the minds of the individuals who relate to this type of music."[41] After decades of hearing anti-rock sermons, many Christians had a hard time accepting the possibility that rock and roll could be redeemed for Christian use.

Eventually, this opposition came to be epitomized in a key story within evangelical folklore—CCM's vanishing hitchhiker, if you will: "Many Christians know the story about an American missionary who took his family to Africa. One day, as the man's children blasted their rock records they brought with them, terrified native tribesmen rushed up to the preacher, their faces full of fear. They asked him why he allowed his children to play music that was used to call up demons during voodoo rituals."[42] In Steve Miller's version of the tale, the rock music being played was CCM. According to Miller, the story was investigated by Al Menconi (an evangelical media watchdog), who found that the record "was an early seventies production including such songs as 'When the Roll Is Called Up Yonder' and 'He's Everything to Me.'"[43] Said Menconi of the latter title, "if this song is demonic, nearly every Christian choir in America must be in danger. The song has been popular in Bible-believing fundamental Christian churches for nearly three decades. Either the native misinterpreted what he heard or millions of born-again Christians are being ministered to by demon-possessed music—which is not possible."[44] Whether or not missionary children playing "When the Roll Is Called Up Yonder" were accused by natives of playing the music of voodoo ritual is of course beside the point. Rather, what is significant about this story is, first, its frequent employment as "proof" that rock and roll music is inherently and organically satanic in nature and therefore an unsuitable vessel for carrying the gospel message; and, second, its utility as a strawman for those who defend the genre.

At the same time, if the story of the missionary's children illustrates the moralist objection to contemporary Christian music, it also identifies one of this position's darker foundations. In charging that rock was "'demonic,' 'pagan,' and inspired by 'voodoo'" or that it had a "savage beat," critics of contemporary Christian music revealed racist assumptions similar to those that had fed the early opposition to rock and roll.[45] And while the music's critics and defenders could find themselves locked in stalemate over the veracity of the missionary story, the racism, once identified, quickly became a point of embarrassment and put CCM's critics on the defensive. Not surprisingly, many of the anti-rock crusaders quickly abandoned this particular point of critique. In some cases, the critics seemed to simply forget that they had ever made such statements, while in others, they claimed they had been misunderstood and dutifully condemned such arguments for their implicit racism.[46] By far the most interesting response came from Bob Larson who, while explicitly denying the charges of racist assumptions in his arguments, nevertheless went on to suggest that "the black has to be honest about his African culture. His African culture was to a very large extent, a pagan, demonized culture."[47] The same, he claimed, is true of Indonesian and East Indian Hindu cultures. More explicitly, Larson further argued that "it is the nonchristian spiritual environment of Africa and Asia that has historically produced the most primitive musical forms."[48] Presumably supporting this claim is yet another take on the fable of the missionary: "A missionary in an uncivilized region of Africa told me of an experiment he conducted with music. One of his tapes was a recording of semi-classical music. When he played this tape, the tribesmen smiled and indicated in their language that the sound was pleasing to their ears. They asked to hear more. Then my friend played a tape of rock and roll music. In response, the natives grabbed their spears as if intending to fight. They picked up stones to smash the recording and destroy the music."[49]

The racism here is difficult to deny, though there is an irony worth noting. At the same time African culture is dismissed as "pagan," "demonized," "primitive," and "uncivilized," by virtue of their (assumed) familiarity with pagan/demonic rituals, the people of these cultures become authorities on the evils of rock music. Larson's argument seems to be: If even "pagans" recognize the inherent evil in this form of music, then how can civilized Westerners deny it? The better question might be: When a critic labels rock music a "heathen jungle boogie," how can the racist assumptions possibly be denied?[50]

Not surprisingly, the critics of CCM, facing charges of racism, by and large abandoned the "savage beat" arguments. Turning from the evil inherent in rock, the critics focused on the evil that it promoted; and, as touched on above, critics catalogued a wide range of negative effects of rock music. It was claimed that the psychological reaction to rock music was "highly unnatural" and could potentially lead to health risks.[51] Based on an apparently undocumented experiment conducted by Dorothy Retallack at Temple Buell College in Denver, rock and roll was claimed to kill houseplants.[52] Furthermore, the syncopated rhythms of rock and roll were said to evoke a sensuous response in the listener, an "animal lust."[53] In the case of CCM, then, while the lyrics might potentially be promoting a gospel message, the music would assuredly be promoting promiscuous sex.[54] So, even without reference to a savage beat, critics could agree that Christian rock, as rock, was inherently opposed to the gospel message.[55] Ultimately, they argued that to try to pair the gospel with rock music was, in Noebel's words, "spiritual cannibalism" in which Christians "eat alive their own values."[56] The inherently evil nature of rock made any attempt to sanitize it for Christian purposes at best misguided and at worst deliberately subversive.

The Aesthetic Objections: It's Inferior

The ethical objections of the church were not the only complaints leveled at contemporary Christian music. Aesthetics, too, has been a basis for critique; and defenders of the aesthetic tradition, both inside and outside the church, have condemned Christian rock as an inferior form of music. These criticisms center around three themes. First, it is argued that CCM should be rejected because it is too commercial and hence inappropriate for religious use; second, that Christian rock inevitably presents a shallow and distorted version of the gospel; and finally, that Christian rock, by the standards of rock music more generally, is mediocre at best; it is a pale imitation of the real thing.

Although not speaking exclusively of CCM but rather the increasing use of popular forms of music in churches, Erik Routley, a respected authority on church music, concludes that pop music—as a result of its commercial nature, artist worship, and extravagant noise—has "no possible place" in Christian worship.[57] Working from his high church perspective, Routley argues that popular music is not a musical form at all, but mere gesture; it is the striking of poses.[58] In Routley's view, the artificial nature of pop music defeats the goal of "rational" worship and, rather than producing a spirit of worship, produces a trance-like state.[59] The argument is undoubtedly similar to the moralist position taken by Larson and others who condemn Christian rock as inherently commercial—a form of entertainment—and thus inappropriate for facilitating worship.[60] At the same time, however, there are differences. While both are concerned with the form of the music and its effect, the basis for this concern is different. For the moralists, it is the underlying evil that is the problem; for the aestheticists, it is the underlying banality. In the words of another aestheticist, Leonard Payton, "The forms of pop music are automatic and predictable. No thought is given to them because they demand no thought. Tupperware from the factory could not be spewed forth more regularly. And while this is just fine for refrigerator containers, it is not for art."[61] Nor, he might add, is it fine for worship.

Payton extends his critique by arguing that pop music forms are largely designed not to be listened to but to be felt. Contemporary Christian music, then, as just another subset of a more general category of popular music, suffers from "vacuity of musical and poetic form together with dense spectrum and amplitude."[62] The end result, then, is a form of music that, while "delivering a steady torrent of overwhelming stimuli to our brains," demands no thought.[63]

Of course, Routley and Payton are working from a different set of theological assumptions than those of the churches out of which the contemporary Christian music genre emerged. Routley's assumptions concerning the rational nature of worship, for example, would undoubtedly be challenged by the more emotional, experience-oriented Charismatic and Pentecostal evangelicals who fostered much of early Christian rock. Most evangelicals would be more than willing to grant that CCM is of little use if one wants to promote rational, detached worship, but they would also argue against the emptiness of such worship. On the whole, the evangelical church has attempted to replace the detached, rational religious experience with a subjective and emotional one. Different theologies lead to different aesthetics.

The second major aesthetic critique of contemporary Christian music focuses not on the music's use within the worship service but rather on its use as a tool for evangelism. Specifically, critics argue that CCM promotes a shallow, distorted gospel. Contemporary evangelical theologian J.I. Packer, for example, is troubled by contemporary Christian music. In some ways echoing Payton and Routley, Packer argues that with contemporary

Christian music "there is no kind of nurturing of the mind the way there was with the older songs. With today's music, you simply sit back and wait to be tickled."[64] In addition to his moralist complaints, critic Jeff Godwin argues that CCM records preach: (a) no Jesus at all, (b) a cardboard cut-out of Christ, and/or (c) an inoffensive love gospel designed to make you feel good.[65] In Bob Larson's words, Christian rock distorts the gospel by "trying to show *how groovy it is to be a Christian.*"[66] By focusing on the ambiguous ideals of love, peace, and philosophical humanism, it neglects to emphasize the sinfulness of humanity and the need for salvation.[67] Speaking of the evangelical church's use of the arts in general, Francis Schaeffer levels the charge that "all we have produced is a very romantic Sunday School art."[68]

Significantly, one does not have to look very hard to find many within the Christian music industry itself who agree with these charges. CCM pioneer and author John Fischer charges that the concept of sin is missing from most CCM.[69] After conducting a study of Christian hymns, Fischer concludes that, in modern Christian music, acknowledging one's inadequacy before God has disappeared in favor of a nearly exclusive emphasis on praising Him. In 1972, Enroth, Ericson, and Breckinridge warned that, because of the almost overwhelming emphasis on individual experience, the Jesus Movement would wind up empty: "Without maturity, without education, without grounding in Christian thought, the Jesus People cannot avoid a commercialized end—what Larry Norman terms 'pop Christianity.'"[70] Even today, CCM artists such as Michael Card and Glenn Kaiser (an ordained minister and member of Jesus People USA's Resurrection Band) have frequently turned a critical eye to the music of their colleagues and echoed these concerns. Thus, while some critics of CCM's incorporation into worship services can largely be dismissed by virtue of their distinct liturgical traditions, the issue of a "watered down" gospel nevertheless remains a serious one within evangelical Christianity. Given that the conversion of unbelievers is a (if not the) fundamental tenet of evangelicalism, for many an act that leads people astray with faulty gospel would be sin.

While the previous concerns focused on the use of contemporary Christian music for religious purposes, the final critique has nothing to do with religion. The charge is simply that Christian music is bad music; in the words of one tongue-in-cheek critic, CCM comprises "bad songs about God written by white people" (in contrast to gospel music: "good songs about God sung by black people").[71] More substantively, a *New York Times*

Magazine writer concludes that while there are some talented performers, "most C.C.M. is mediocre stuff, diluted by hesitation and dogmatic formula, inferior to the mainstream popular music it emulates"; and a VH-1 "4 on the Floor" roundtable once suggested CCM is "the music industry's multi-million dollar cross to bear."[72] This is hardly the response the Christian music industry had hoped to elicit from the very people it sought to impress with its music and/or persuade with its message. Similar criticism has emerged from within the castle walls as well. From disgruntled artists no longer recording for Christian labels to industry favorites, more than a few Christian artists are willing to acknowledge that there is an aesthetic inferiority permeating much of contemporary Christian music.[73]

The Need to Legitimize CCM

In the face of such overwhelming criticism, why did early Christian rock musicians bother? Why keep up the struggle when Christians and non-Christians alike are against you? The answer is not that there is a tremendous amount of money to be made in CCM or that CCM is an easy road to fame. Though some Christian artists have managed to extract fortune and fame from the genre, such artists are rare. For most, a contract with a Christian record label leads to little more than hard work, poverty, and obscurity. Most Christian artists spend years touring and recording in the hopes of building a large-enough following to allow them to simply make a living; most never do. And for every Amy Grant who successfully uses a career in CCM as a launching pad to wider stardom and wealth, there are a dozen artists like Mike Roe who, after more than a decade in the business, gives guitar lessons to put food on the table. For some, it is a vocation—work, they feel, that God has called them to. For others, the motivation stems from the (possibly naive) belief that CCM will save the world. Arguing that music is the language of youth, many musicians see Christian rock as a way to present the message of Christ to a world that they feel desperately needs it. Still others persevere for the sake of their craft/art. Their music is simply an expression of their own worldview, and they keep playing because they must.

Irrespective of their motivations for playing, Christian rock artists have been burdened with the responsibility of responding to the charges of moralist critics and aesthetic critics alike. In the face of such staunch opposition, this new pop-music hybrid has had to legitimate itself before the potential audience, religious authorities, secular critics, and even the artists themselves. Consequently, beyond making music, Christian artists must spend a large amount of time and effort attempting to justify what they do. Responses have occasionally come in musical form such as Larry Norman's "Why Should the Devil Have All the Good Music?" or in T-shirt and bumper-sticker slogans such as Petra's "Our Rock Is Not As Their Rock." Elsewhere justification has come in the form of radio interviews and other promotional materials (*Shake: Christian Artists Face the Music*). Still others have attempted to write books and teach seminars.[74] But regardless of the form in which criticism comes, a response is required.

As CCM grew and evolved, three key justifications for the music emerged. The earliest centered around the utility of the music in the work of evangelism—the ability of CCM to reach lost souls and convert them to (evangelical) Christianity. Gradually, a second rationale focusing on the idea that Christians need and want a sanitized, positive form of musical entertainment gained social currency among some evangelicals. Finally, a third defense emerged from those who saw the production of Christian music as artistic production. These musicians saw CCM as a creative product that reflected the Divine Image of God the Creator and, for that reason, as something valuable. Perhaps not surprisingly, as these divergent rationales came to be articulated and refined, the various artists, producers, distributors, critics, and audiences that subscribed to a particular school of thought frequently dismissed or criticized those operating in accordance with the assumptions of another rationale. Each group began to argue that they themselves were producing true contemporary Christian music and that the others were falling short of the goal. At times the debate has been civil and reasoned; at others, hostile and shrill. Regardless, the combatants have frequently failed to consciously understand their own assumptions, let alone those of their adversaries.

Perhaps the single best illustration of this situation can be found in the February 1986 issue of *Contemporary Christian Music*. Beginning, "It is with deep heartfelt concern and conviction that we write this appeal to you," sixty-six Christian artists wrote an open letter to several Christian magazines, including *Contemporary Christian Music*. They wrote to express their frustration with the practices they associated with the concept of a Christian music industry:

For years we have all realized the incredible growth of Christian music—
so much that it is often labeled "the industry." We who feel called as
ministers of the gospel of Jesus Christ feel that this label is reflecting an
unfortunate trend in Christian music brought on in part by the prolifera-
tion of airplay and sales charts and album reviews. . . .

Scripture exhorts us not to compare ourselves with one another nor
to compete with one another. We feel that polls such as these create an
unhealthy atmosphere of rivalry between ministries. Even though we
strive to be men and women of God, in our humanity we often fall prey
to the pride or envy which polls such as this create. We can hardly imagine
the apostles and prophets being categorized in such a way. . . .

The whole area of reviewing albums and ripping apart one another's
offerings unto the Lord is disgraceful. If you don't like an album we
simply ask that you not review it. It is not right or righteous that an
offering which has taken a year or more of our lives and an outpouring of
our hearts and labor should be torn down by the subjective opinion of
one Christian brother. It hurts and discourages us, and it damages the
potential ministry opportunities of our albums.[75]

Responding to these complaints, the editors of the magazine suggested
that "before any of us can make any sense of this . . . we must define
certain terms. Basically, is every Christian who writes or performs music
automatically involved in 'music ministry'?"[76] The editors concluded, "we
think not": "For some artists . . . music is their ministry and it is designated to lead the body of Christ in worship. Others, however, say that
they simultaneously minister and provide an entertainment alternative for
Christians. Still others talk of music as a vocation. As Christians, they hope
to make good art and, whenever possible, to 'salt' modern culture with
biblical truth."[77] Christian music, claimed the editors of *Contemporary
Christian Music,* had "to come to grips with the fact that not every artist
who is a Christian operates under the same artistic imperative."[78] Whether
their own product was designated a tool for evangelism, device for worship, or art, the artists that constituted CCM needed to learn that theirs
was not the only way. Given the roots of such assumptions, it was not an
easy lesson to learn.

Within each of these rationales for CCM, one finds certain assumptions about the proper relationship between the Christian and the world
in which the Christian must live. As H. Richard Niebuhr notes in his classic work, *Christ and Culture* (1951), Christians in all ages have had to

struggle with the biblical mandate to be in the world but not of the world. What does it mean to be a follower of Christ living at a particular point in human history? How is the Christian to relate to the surrounding culture, the realm of human activity, and its results? Given that culture includes both the material and the nonmaterial—including language, ideas, habits, social norms, beliefs, customs, social organization, and values as well as automobiles, houses, clothing, computers, fax machines, and *Monday Night Football*—how is the follower of Christ to respond to and deal with it all?

As Niebuhr illustrated, multiple answers have been proposed to this problem of the reconciliation of Christianity and culture. Christians have oscillated between abandoning the world for the sake of Christ on the one hand and embracing that same world to teach and practice the things they believe on the other.[79] In an admittedly precarious venture that is inevitably at least partly artificial, Niebuhr sought to construct a typology of responses through the history of the church. Niebuhr concludes that there have been five primary strategies for relating Christ to culture. The first two—"Christ against culture" and "Christ of culture"—represent the opposite poles of the continuum, and the remaining three—"Christ above culture," "Christ and culture in paradox," and "Christ the transformer of culture"—attempt to establish centrist positions that avoid the "errors" of either extreme.

The "Christ against culture" approach sees Christianity as opposed to culture, whatever the customs or achievements of the society in which the Christian is placed. It is a call for the Christian to abandon the world (all of society outside of the church) as a realm under the power of evil. The Christian must make a simple choice: serve God or serve mammon. There is no compromise position. At the opposite extreme lies the "Christ of culture" perspective. In this view, there is a fundamental agreement between Christ and culture. The life and teachings of Jesus are regarded as the highest human achievement, and, through Christ, the aspirations of humans are confirmed. Adopting the "Christ of culture" approach, the Christian does not seek Christian sanction for all aspects of the prevailing culture but believes the values and morals for which Christ stands to be identical to those advocated in the "best" of culture. Hence, through Christian moral training, a peaceful, cooperative society may be attained.

Each of the three mediating positions attempts to maintain the distinction between Christ and culture that is easily lost in the "Christ of culture" perspective, while avoiding the seemingly complete withdrawal from culture of the "Christ against culture" perspective. The "Christ above culture" approach, which Niebuhr also refers to as a "synthesis," recognizes the separateness of the two realms but argues that the Christian must struggle to maintain a distinctiveness that is expressed in daily life in the world. Niebuhr calls the second centrist position "Christ and culture in paradox," or the "dualist" view. In this approach, Christians are called to live a holy and perfect life—a life that is beyond their grasp. Life, therefore, is lived precariously and sinfully in the continual hope of God's grace. Niebuhr labels the third approach "Christ as transformer of culture," or the "conversionist" position. Recognizing the opposition between Christ and culture, the conversionist sees culture not as inherently evil and sinful but rather as fallen and in need of restoration to God's original intent. Christ, therefore, is the savior of both human beings and of culture.

Clearly, all five of these resolutions to the problem of "Christ and culture" have their virtues and limitations; there is no single "correct" solution to the Christian's dilemma of being in the world but not of the world. When Christian musicians produce their music, they are operating on the basis of assumptions, either articulated or implicit, about the proper resolution of this problem. And like Niebuhr's typology itself, any attempt to summarize and clarify the differing approaches inevitably brings a certain amount of distortion. Nonetheless, by tying Niebuhr's typology to the various approaches within the fragmented realm of contemporary Christian music, one can generate some insight and understanding. Throughout its relatively short history, CCM has been riddled with disagreements, from the overtly hostile to the subtly condescending, about what is and what isn't "true" Christian music. These debates can be understood in the context of the competing approaches of Niebuhr's typology. Ultimately, what one faces in contemporary Christian music is a "splintered art world," with each faction organized according to a different principle of reconciliation of Christianity and culture.[80] Each of these factions attempts to define contemporary Christian music its way, dismissing all others. In some ways, then, the greatest enemy to the genre is the division between the artists themselves.

Over time, many of the critiques of Christian music have been washed away by the burgeoning sales of CCM. In 1996, "gospel music" (a catch-all category that includes CCM, black gospel, and all other varieties of Christian religious recordings) accounted for 4.3 percent of all music sales tracked by the Recording Industry Association of America (RIAA), making it America's sixth-most-popular music genre behind rock (32.6 percent), country (14.7 percent), R&B (12.1 percent), pop (9.3 percent), and rap (8.9 percent). At that point, religious recordings outsold both classical and jazz. Additionally, gospel music's 1996 performance represented the largest increase in market share of any musical genre, a 1.2 percent increase from the previous year (a growth rate of 38.7 percent).[81] According to the Gospel Music Association (GMA), gospel music has averaged 22 percent growth each year since 1991, while other formats have seen average growth rates of 5 percent or less. Looking further across time, from 1985 to 1994, gospel music experienced a 290 percent increase in sales. The hard numbers, then, are these: in 1996, record sales in the Christian music industry reached $550 million, and when merchandising and ticket sales are added into the equation, the number jumps to an estimated $750 to 900 million.[82] Three-quarters of a billion dollars can go a long way toward quieting one's critics.

At the same time, the issue runs deeper than the dollars. In 1994, 64 percent of gospel music was sold in Christian bookstores, compared to 21 percent in the general marketplace and 15 percent by direct mail; Christian music accounted for 17 percent of total sales volume at the Christian Booksellers Association (CBA) in 1995. Contemporary Christian music, then, has become a crucial element in the larger infrastructure of the evangelical media. Further, one must also consider the audience responsible for these numbers. A CBA survey of more than eleven thousand randomly selected Christian bookstore customers revealed that most of the people buying contemporary Christian music are female (76 percent), in their thirties or forties (59 percent), and white (85 percent). Most have an annual household income of less than sixty thousand dollars (74 percent), with nearly half making between thirty and sixty thousand dollars. Christian music buyers are also surprisingly well educated (77 percent having completed some college course work and nearly 43 percent being college graduates). But most important, Christian music buyers are devout Christians. They are regular churchgoers and frequent attendees at organized Christian events (90 percent attending four or more events per month and 64 percent attending at least seven times per month). Representing Baptists (27 percent), nondenominationals (26 percent), Charismatics and Pentecostals (14 percent), Methodists (5 percent), Lutherans (5 percent), Presbyterians (4 percent), and a host of others, the people who buy and listen to contemporary Christian music are, for the most part, educated, middle- to upper-middle-class, white, dedicated Christians.[83] And while one might argue that neither morals nor aesthetics should be judged on the basis of public opinion, the fact remains that those who would criticize CCM face a large group of Christians both supporting and supported by the music.

Given the role of CCM in contemporary Christian life, it is perhaps not surprising that there are only a few, however vocal, who still argue that rock and roll is the devil's music. Furthermore, if secular rock and roll is still criticized for its influence on the morals of American youth, the moralist critiques of Christian music have lost most of their sting due to the consistently Christian lifestyles of most CCM artists and the myriad Christians who find CCM spiritually uplifting.[84] At the same time, the complaints of aesthetic critics—that CCM distorts the gospel, that CCM's commercial nature overwhelms its potential religious utility, and that CCM is inferior to its more popular secular counterparts—still seem to ring loud and clear. These—not dead house plants and communist influences—are the issues that the industry, in the person of the artist, audience, and/or critic, continues to struggle against.

Interlude:
Rebecca St. James

The church doors open, and the crowd of mostly white, mostly middle-class teens and twenty-somethings who have been waiting outside (many for more than an hour) stampedes into the sanctuary. Like wolves on the hunt, they search for open seats as far forward as possible. Once seated, their nervous energy seems only to worsen. Heads crane as individuals search for people they know, eye the merchandise tables, or take in the well-equipped stage. This is not a traditional worship service; and while flowers, candles, and a chalice might seem appropriate, tonight the stage holds speakers, lighting trusses, a drum kit, and a black fabric backdrop emblazoned with a single word: "GOD."

As the crowd settles in, the taped music being played over the sound system is replaced by the antics of a comedian who, after introducing the opening act, follows up on the music with a routine wrapping Bible studies and object lessons in comedy skits. Finishing his routine, the comedian leaves the stage. As he does so, the lights in the sanctuary begin to grow dim. The room goes black. The crowd goes wild. Screams and shouting bounce from the sanctuary walls. Fog pours from the stage, music begins to play, and the crowd is instantly on its feet. Suddenly, spotlights blaze and illuminate the figure of Rebecca St. James, who puts a harmonica to her mouth and begins to play the opening riff to the anthemic "Me without You." After two more songs, this mahogany-tressed, nineteen-year-old "evangelist in waiting" waits no longer.[1] She stops singing and begins to describe the message God has sent her. "I have this vision," she begins, "the vision that we are surrounded by people bowing, bowing to the gods of money or other worldly 'gods.' But while everyone else is bowing," she continues, "this is what we're doing." St. James throws her hands heavenward as the lights behind her come on to transform her into a striking silhouette. The crowd erupts in a cheer and, at the teenager's urging, assumes the same pose. Cries of

"Thank you, Jesus" and "Praise you, Father" ring throughout the room. St. James leads the crowd in prayer and then moves into her next number.

As the performance continues, the pattern remains much the same. Songs, monologues, and prayers to God are presented in almost equal proportions. St. James's breathy vocals work through an equal number of ballads (either stripped down and syrupy sweet or lush and melodramatic) and up-tempo modern rock numbers characterized by wordy, melancholy verses that give way to impassioned choruses. Whatever the character of the music, however, the message remains unambiguous. And indeed, St. James's between-song banter makes it clear that it is the message here that matters. Working from stories and descriptions of her own experiences, St. James talks to her audience about the issues of sexual purity and abstinence (she presents her promise ring for the audience's approval, stating plainly that she is a virgin and intends to remain one until marriage), family relationships, home schooling, and accountability to both God and fellow Christians. Clearly resonating with the parents and youth ministers in attendance, St. James's message appears to be received equally well by the teens whom she is most specifically addressing. At the very least, no one seems ready to challenge her during the question-and-answer session that precedes the intermission.

Leaving the stage, St. James encourages the crowd to visit the Compassion International booth operating in the lobby. But as the lights go up, more people seem interested in buying Rebecca St. James tapes, CDs, posters, and T-shirts (The "It's All About God" Tour) or the daily devotional that she has written (*40 Days with God*) than in sponsoring a child living in a developing nation.[2] They swarm the merchandise table until the houselights dim and fog once again begins pouring from the stage. Transactions temporarily abandoned, people dash back to their seats.

After the intermission, the earlier format continues, although the emphasis begins to change. Still talking, still praying, still reading from the Bible, St. James begins looking for the "seekers" in the crowd. Encouraging those who have mobbed the stage to return to their seats, St. James suggests that there may be those in the audience wondering why she is the way she is. Crediting her personality to God, she makes her plea to those who "feel a stirring deep down inside you" to come forward. And as St. James begins singing "Above All Things," people begin to filter out of the crowd to stand and sit in the aisle near the stage. When the song ends, she first leads them in a "sinner's prayer," then sends them to a side room where staff members offer tutoring in the essentials of the Christian faith. As they file out, St. James sings her melodramatic ballad celebrating the moment of conversion, "A Cold Heart Turns." Then, once again whipping the crowd into a frenzy, St. James moves into the title track of her most recent album and the anthem for the tour, "God." Finally, bringing the crowd back down with the final song, St. James quietly leaves the stage—"leaving the praise for God and God alone"—as the audience softly sings, "Jesus your word stands forever, changing me forever."[3]

2 | Separational CCM: "It's a Ministry"

So today we are confronted by two worlds, two spheres of authority, having two totally different and opposed characters. For me now it is no mere matter of a future heaven and hell; it is a question of these two worlds today, and of whether I belong to an order of things of which Christ is sovereign lord, or to an opposed order of things having Satan as its effective head.

Watchman Nee

A lone electric guitar playing a staccato riff behind her, Leslie Phillips starts to sing: "No distinction, no emotion for right or wrong/They tell me any choice will do/No color contrast in their dull morality/The shades of good and bad are through." The band joins in another verse, and Phillips moves to the chorus: "And I'm black and white in a grey world/Black and white in a grey world/Black and white in a grey world."[1]

The title track from her 1985 album, Phillips's "Black and White in a Grey World" offers a useful summary of the "Christ against culture" perspective that defines Separational CCM. As explained by Phillips's lyrics, to adopt the position of Separational CCM is to see the world in black and white, good and evil, right and wrong. By no means limited to the realm of Christian music or even Christian entertainment, a separational view of the Christian faith attempts to reconcile the paradox of "walking in two worlds" (to use another lyricist's words) by withdrawing into one world and out of the other as completely as possible.[2] In the separational view, the Christian and the secular are locked in opposition—God versus the world—and accepting the one necessarily entails rejecting the other. Accordingly, Christians, in this view, are by virtue of their faith set off and apart from the rest of the world. The emphasis is on difference and on the behaviors that mark those differences. Songs are sung that emphasize the need to be recognized ("They'll know we are Christians by our love..."); cars are adorned with decals of a fish or dove; and caps, ties, T-shirts, and other "witness wear" allow Christians to be marked by the clothing they wear. Understating the case significantly in the bridge to the aforementioned song, Phillips sings, "I don't mind being different/'Cuz I'm different for the truth." In fact, separational Christians not only don't mind being different, they insist on it.

Difference, of course, can be a problem; and in the specific case of Separational CCM, two significant issues arise. The first revolves around the causal chain. Ostensibly, the claim of the separational position is that, as a result of their faith, Christians will necessarily withdraw from the world; their faith will make them different. Difference, then, is seen to flow from faith. In many cases, however, the short distance between distinction flowing from faith and faith flowing from distinction is quickly elided, and rather than being considered consequences of faith, particular behaviors come to be seen as preconditions for it. Drinking, dancing, smoking, swearing, gambling—participating in any one of these, among numerous others, can be considered clear evidence that one could not possibly be a Christian. This turn to particular behavior sets as a means to evaluate adherence to a particular system of belief—something essentially beyond proof—became more and more prevalent in Christian music as the distinctions between Christian and "secular" music began to be actively erased. (More than one Christian music artist has complained of fans who check their post-show drinking cups, attempting to discern the contents therein.[3]) Demanding distinction from the world, separational Christians, including the artists constituting Separational CCM, became increasingly hard-pressed during the 1980s to identify the distinctions that mattered.

In attempting to find the distinctions that mark the Christian as "apart," the first and most intuitive move is to look to a difference in the product itself—to find a difference between CCM and whatever musical parallels it may have in mainstream culture. The problems associated with such an approach should be familiar; they are the same ones that complicate the attempt to identify the generic characteristics of CCM. Thus, while the individuals who define Separational CCM adhere to a theology of explicit division, the music they compose, the organizations they work within, and to some extent even the lyrics they write and sing frequently belie such clear distinctions. Indeed, by its very nature, Separational CCM often becomes the site of the closest connections between the secular and the Christian. In their fervent desire to preach the gospel and "make disciples of all nations," the separational artists, as the most evangelical of the evangelicals, are frequently the first to incorporate new cultural trends into their work in an effort to make their message "relevant."[4] Thus, while musical forms such as punk, heavy metal, and early rock were vociferously decried by the church, Christian versions of these new genres were first attempted by artists largely adherent to separational doctrine. CCM pioneer Larry Norman, for example, later explained that he wasn't trying to start a revolution with his music, he just "wanted . . . to learn how to explain God without using any of the language or ideas that had been taught in the church."[5] Similarly, the members of Undercover, perhaps the first Christian punk band, at one point reduced their music to "trying to reach a bunch of kids with the Gospel, that's all."[6] Hence, while defining themselves exclusively in terms of their Christian faith and the principal act of that faith as proselytism, the separational artists were forced into the contradictory position of, more than any other, looking and sounding like what they claimed to eschew. Separational CCM, in many ways, could frequently seem the least separate.

On one level, this paradoxical position of the separational artist was fairly easy to resolve. Specifically, the separational artists, far more than others, began to develop the argument that music was inherently and absolutely neutral. If their music sounded most like what could be found in secular culture, separational artists emphatically argued that such similarities were meaningless. Decrying the messages they found in mainstream rock and roll—the equation of love with sex (or sex and violence), the glorification of violence and suicide, the promotion of drugs and alcohol, a focus on image over substance, and a general disdain for God, among others—separational artists nevertheless maintained that the music itself had nothing to do with these messages.[7] No form of music, they claimed, inherently belonged either to God or to the world; no musical performance could determine one's relationship to God or mammon.

The music was not the only site of contact between the separational artists and the world they were attempting to withdraw from. Increasingly, as CCM continued to grow and evolve, not only were new musical styles incorporated by separational (and other) artists but also the fads and fashions that came with them. Separational artists were particularly fervent in maintaining a visibly distinctive "Christian" persona, but at the same time the visual distinctions that identified them began to blur right along with the sonic ones. Thus, while the artists attempted to adhere, publicly at least, to the Christian proscriptions against certain behaviors (extramarital sex, drug use, and alcohol consumption), previously distinguishing features such as clothing, hair styles, album covers, group names, and performance venues largely ceased to be reliable signifiers. Cashmere sweaters and leisure suits gave way to denim and leather; church basements to clubs and bars. Here again, the separational artists largely denied that these changes were meaningful. Consequently, while academics identified the punk rock uniform as the end result of a process that "begins with a crime against the natural order" and "ends in the construction of a style, in a gesture of defiance or contempt . . . an expression both of impotence and a kind of power—the power to disfigure," Christian music's first punk rockers considered the clothes they wore to be a costume or masquerade, empty and to be adopted or discarded at will.[8] "We may look like we are conforming to a subculture or a lifestyle that is reprobate or deviant," one band claimed, "but someone has to reach the kids who *are* part of that lifestyle."[9] The clear implication was that the clothes meant nothing and that any inference about the musicians based on what they wore was an erroneous one. Studded belts, fingerless gloves, torn shirts—Christian artists argued that these trappings, like the music itself, carried no essential meanings. As the industry moved into the 1980s, more and more artists began to accept that argument, and clear distinctions between the Christian and the secular became more difficult to find.

In their efforts to be relevant, to "talk to young people about Jesus in their own language and with the sound of their own music," those who believed that it was the Christian's responsibility to abandon the world were in many ways forced to embrace it.[10] Whatever else this meant for the music, it meant new definitions for difference. Still concentrating on the music itself, there was an ever-increasing focus on the lyrics. Operating within a separational perspective, musicians were expected to write lyrics that were explicitly and emphatically Christian. While songwriters outside the separational frame wrote songs addressing social issues and experimented with forms that left meanings ambiguous (love songs addressed only to an indeterminate "he"), the artists of Separational CCM focused on the gospel, explicitly using the name "Jesus" (often as frequently as possible) and the ideas and catch phrases familiar to the evangelical church (which many critics dismissed as "Christianese"). As early as 1981, one

The early 1980s was a period of visual innovation, as well as musical innovation, in contemporary Christian music. Due largely to the efforts of groups like Altar Boys, contemporary Christian music began to shed its obvious visual signatures. (Photograph courtesy of Nancy Stand Sorrells.)

finds separational gatekeepers voicing their concerns over the increasingly ambiguous Christian content of lyrics. The band Daniel Amos and their *Horrendous Disc* (Solid Rock, 1981), for example, were taken to task in an album review for song lyrics "very vague and obscure concerning Christ and His salvation . . . which do not clearly point to Jesus Christ as 'the way, the truth, and the life.'"[11] Separational CCM was not interested in vague, even if artistic, expression. As Leslie Phillips, by then recording as Sam Phillips for Virgin Records and looking back on her CCM career, told one interviewer, "They [audiences and industry personnel] wanted to be told over and over again what they believed in for fear they'd stop believing it."[12]

From the outside, the lyrics of Separational CCM can admittedly seem no better than propaganda. Generally simplistic ("God good/Devil bad") and frequently insipid ("Wowie zowie well He saved my soul/He's the rock that doesn't roll"), the lyrics of Separational CCM are largely focused on either maudlin expressions of God's love ("You Light Up My Life," "Life is Hard (God Is Good)," "You Are the Answer") or bombastic calls to spiritual warfare ("Boycott Hell," "This Means War!" "Run to the Battle").[13] Indeed, in the mid-1980s, the military motif—fatigues and berets in particular—became one of CCM's more prominent visual clichés.[14] At the same time, however, while outsiders may view this as propaganda, those operating within the separational perspective see clear biblical justification for their works. Criticized for what is perceived as a lack of artistic merit in their music, the separational artists respond that artistic merit is not their concern; their concern is with religious merit. Thus, while the religious lyrics of the Separational CCM artist do in fact serve as a mark of distinction, they also reflect the more significant distinction of artistic rationale. Simply put, separational artists view their music as a "ministry." Thus, Petra drummer Louie Weaver suggests that CCM bands who don't view themselves as ministers are not offering anything that cannot be found in secular music: "I'll tell you one thing I don't like: all these new bands that say, 'We just want to play. We don't want to minister, we don't want to talk about Jesus. Our songs talk about Jesus, get it out of that.' My response has been, 'Why don't you go do secular music?'"[15] As with Cusic's gospel musicians, separational artists see themselves primarily as ministers and only secondarily, if at all, as artists or entertainers.[16] Their lyrics reflect that stance.

"Ministry," of course, can be an ambiguous term. In the world of Separational CCM, the concept of ministry comprises three identifiably distinct but intertwined objectives: evangelism—the effort to convince

the non-Christian to affirm the fundamental tenets of the Christian faith
and to "accept Jesus Christ as his or her personal Savior" (which is to say,
proselytism); worship facilitation—the attempt to allow God to manifest
Himself in the presence of believers or to allow believers to communicate
with Him; and exhortation—the encouragement of the believer in his or
her "Christian walk." Thus, by rejecting the usually cited reasons for recording and performing popular music (providing entertainment, expressing through art one's feelings and experiences, seeking fame and fortune,
etc.) in favor of the tripartite elements of "ministry," separational artists
claim to be able to adopt the styles and trends of contemporary culture
while, by virtue of their motivations, remaining distinct from that culture.
More than anything else, then, ministry—evangelism, exhortation, and
worship—constitutes the rationale that defines and distinguishes
Separational CCM.

The First Rationale: Evangelism

Contemporary Christian music was born of the union of American popular culture with American evangelicalism; more correctly, it was the product of American evangelicalism's adoption and incorporation of the
particular cultural form of mainstream popular music at the particular cultural moment of the Jesus Movement in the late 1960s and early 1970s.
As the initial progeny of this alliance, Separational CCM embodied most
directly the characteristics of its dominant parent, evangelicalism. If
Separational CCM was popular evangelical culture, the focus was on "evangelical," not "popular."

As described by James Davison Hunter, evangelicals—and American
evangelicals in particular—can be described by two distinct character sets.
There is, on the one hand, what might be called evangelical doctrine—the
fundamental convictions that define evangelical theology. Although "evangelical" remains a somewhat fluid designator, Hunter argues that
evangelicals can nevertheless be grouped by their adherence to three basic
theological tenets: "(1) the belief that the Bible is the inerrant word of
God, (2) the belief in the divinity of Jesus Christ, and (3) the belief in the
efficacy of Christ's life, death, and physical resurrection for the salvation
of the human soul."[17] Evangelicalism, however, is defined by more than a
belief system, and Hunter further argues that there are characteristic evangelical behaviors. "Behaviorally," writes Hunter, "evangelicals are typi-

cally characterized by an individuated and experiential orientation toward spiritual salvation and religiosity in general and by *the conviction of the necessity of actively attempting to proselytize all nonbelievers to the tenets of the Evangelical belief system.*[18] Indeed, as suggested by the very label "evangelical," it is this need to proselytize—the requirement for evangelism—that most strongly characterizes contemporary evangelicalism. Based on the findings of his survey research into the belief systems of American religions, Hunter concludes that "in the Evangelical subculture, evangelism is considered the first priority, with the spiritual well-being of one's family and oneself being second."[19]

With the Jesus Movement, these tendencies were distilled and extended. Writing near the movement's peak, Drane argues that "the Jesus Movement is as fundamentalistic and revivalistic as the Great Awakening."[20] Music was key to this effort. Robert Lyons, Asbury Seminary professor and founder of the Icthus Festival (Christian music's longest-running festival), noted that the motivation for trying to create a "Christian Woodstock" had been "to use the medium of young people to reach young people"; in other words, evangelism.[21] Linking the Jesus Movement with traditional evangelicalism, Ellwood similarly emphasizes the use of music in proselytizing, arguing that "the great vehicle of the Jesus movement is music."[22] According to Ellwood, "the ability of Jesus rock and gospel melodies to generate rich, powerful feelings in a mood and emotion-oriented age has brought and held the movement together. It is largely music that has made the movement a part of pop culture."[23] There are clear reasons for this. As William Shaw notes, "The transcendent ecstasy of a rock gig translates easily into a religious experience."[24] This is especially true when the religion at hand is not one of intellect or profound theology, but of passion and personal faith. And indeed, the Jesus Movement's emphasis on conversion and the use of contemporary forms of music to help generate the moods and feelings that facilitate conversion led to a concept of Christianity that was overwhelmingly experience-oriented.[25] The necessary experience was that of the moment of conversion. Speaking to an estimated crowd of thirty-five thousand at the Jesus Northwest festival in the summer of 1978, CCM pioneer Keith Green (never known for his subtlety) stated, "As for me, I repent of ever having made a record or ever having sung a song unless it's provoked people to follow Jesus, to lay down their whole life before him, to give him everything."[26]

Much of the urgency driving this need to elicit a conversion experience in the listener was the commonly held belief that Christ's second coming would soon occur. "Jesus is coming soon!" was a trademark cry of the Jesus Movement.[27] The evangelical belief in the imminent return of Christ, evident in books like Hal Lindsey's best-selling *The Late Great Planet Earth* (1973), motivated much of early CCM.[28] Maranatha! Music, for example, was the name given to the CCM label begun by the Calvary Chapel in Costa Mesa, California, "Maranatha" meaning "the Lord cometh."[29] The emphasis on the end times could also be seen in the music produced. The second side of Daniel Amos's *Shotgun Angel* (Maranatha!, 1977) is based on the Book of Revelation, which contains the Apostle John's vision of the end of the world. The traditional evangelical focus on proselytism combined with an overwhelming sense of urgency suggested to early CCM artists that to make Christian music for any reason other than evangelism could potentially be conceived of as sin. Given this context, it is not surprising that most historians of CCM have noted that "Christian music began as an evangelistic tool."[30] Tied to the beliefs and motivations of the Jesus Movement, Christian music shared that movement's nearly exclusive focus on evangelism and a personal, subjective, emotion-based Christian experience.[31] For the so-called Jesus People (or, more stridently, Jesus Freaks), the individual, if he or she is to be saved from separation from God and eternal damnation, must experience a personal relationship with Jesus Christ—must be "born again." (A common cliché for evangelicals both then and now is that Christianity "isn't a religion, it's a relationship.") The evidence for this experience is largely based on subjective feelings and responses. The early Jesus rock musicians, then, primarily sought to testify to their own such experiences through music in the hopes of eliciting similar responses from the "lost souls" who heard their songs. As John W. Styll, one-time Christian music DJ and concert promoter and current publisher of the Christian music industry's premiere trade publication, writes, "The idea was something like this: If the world is listening to Rock music, then let's use Rock music to attract them, but we'll change the lyrics and get them to listen to the Gospel."[32] This theme is echoed in numerous voices of early CCM.

Best known for his mainstream pop hit "Eve of Destruction," folk-pop artist Barry McGuire was one of CCM's first "prize" converts.[33] "When I first became a Christian," McGuire related to an interviewer in 1988, "my whole emphasis was to reach the lost."[34] Middle-of-the-road songwriter Bill Gaither, a CCM forerunner who helped to bridge the gap

in the evangelical establishment between southern gospel and more contemporary musical forms, similarly argued that, while entertainment and
social conscience had their places in CCM, "proclaiming the gospel, John
3:16, is certainly the bottom line of what we're trying to do."[35] These
sentiments are further echoed by Bob Hartman, founder of one of CCM's
earliest rock bands, Petra, who describes the early days of CCM this way:
"We were totally evangelistic at the beginning; there wasn't a Christian
concert scene, per se. The people who would have us in to play were
usually people with a burden to reach the lost. They knew that rock music
was a new medium and that it would hold the kids so they would have us
come play."[36] Drawing on sentiments such as these, CCM historian William Romanowski concludes that early Jesus rock was a co-optation of
rock music for evangelistic purposes—a combination of rock music and
religious lyrics intended not so much as an artistic endeavor as an evangelistic one, a version of rock and roll that evangelical Christians could embrace by making it subservient to the preeminent goal of "saving the lost."[37]

The evangelistic frenzy that characterized the Jesus Movement imbued much of early Christian rock music—which is not surprising given
the connections between the movement and this new musical genre. But
while the Jesus Movement proved to be a singular moment in America's
cultural history, the dispersal of the movement did not result in the aban-
donment of the movement's ideals within the Christian music community. The Jesus Freaks might have been absorbed into mainstream American
culture—those, at least, who chose not to withdraw into their own isolated, if socially active, communities—and Christian music might have
begun its slow evolution toward commercial viability, but for many Christian artists the rationale of evangelism remained. To this day, it is a powerful trope for Christian music's separational artists. Thus, charismatic lounge-
singer-cum-rap-artist Carman has frequently testified to the priority he
places on evangelism: "I only have two or three hours in which to stand
before a group of people who I may never, ever see again in my whole life.
And I have the opportunity to present as much of the gospel of Jesus
Christ, as much of the Bible as I have been able to apply to my life as I can
within that given amount of time. . . . I don't just want to spend my time
on social commentary because there's too much of it going on and it
doesn't deliver anyone from sin."[38]

Carman is not alone in his sentiments—nor even, for that matter, in
his language. "Issues are great," stated the members of Undercover, "but

there's no transforming or cleansing power in them." Explicitly criticizing acts who played to predominantly Christian audiences, the band further argued that Christian music needed "to communicate basic truths."[39] Similarly, Robert Sweet, the drummer for the now-disbanded Christian heavy metal group Stryper, summed up that band's agenda by saying, "All we've ever wanted to do is help the world believe in Christ."[40]

A key component of the evangelistic rationale of contemporary Christian music is the tradition of music festivals that mark the summer season. With Christian bands for the most part lacking access to the tours and club circuits that support mainstream musicians, the Christian music industry was forced to develop its own resources in order to create opportunities for live performances.[41] And while churches and coffeehouses to some degree replaced the standard clubs and bars, it was the summer music festivals that became the focal point for CCM's live performances; here is where audiences and performers connect. The basis of this connection is evangelism. The first of these festivals, Explo '72, was conceived by Campus Crusade for Christ founder Bill Bright as part of his goal of "global saturation of the gospel" by 1980.[42] In the last twenty-five years, the Christian music festival has expanded across the United States and beyond to become the performance staple of the Christian music industry.[43] And while the festivals largely serve to create larger forums—and larger audiences—for the Christian music performer, as one artist explains, "The ultimate goal . . . is to bring people to Christ. We believe we have ultimate truth and so we . . . want others to join us."[44] As Andreas Tapia writes, with these summer festivals, "evangelicals stage their own Lollapaloozas to save teen souls."[45]

There is, however, a certain measure of irony to all of this. Consider the female vocal group Point of Grace. Winners of the Dove Award (the Gospel Music Association's version of the Grammy) for Best New Artist in 1994 and one of CCM's hottest acts, Point of Grace's sophomore album, *The Whole Truth* (Word, 1995), was designed to be a musical work that would "lay out the plan of salvation and God's love."[46] It was, in other words, an album designed to reach non-Christians with the explicit message of the Christian gospel; it was designed for evangelism. Five singles were released from *The Whole Truth,* and five singles went to number one on the CCM charts; not one, however, received airplay in the mainstream market.[47] In much the same vein, while some fifty thousand people will be drawn to the Christian music festivals in any one summer, only the smallest percentage of these will be something other than evangelical Christians. Thus, while the art world of Separational CCM claims, if not demands, evangelism as its raison d'être and uses the "passion for saving souls" as its litmus test for approval, the audience for the music mostly comprises evangelical Christians. Christian music can hardly be expected to offer salvation to an audience that already possesses it.

With albums recorded for Christian record labels and sold almost exclusively in Christian bookstores, and with performances taking place in churches, church-owned facilities, and music festivals presented as a "Taste of Heaven on Earth," many Christian artists realized that Christian music was preaching to the converted. For the separational artists who defined their mission in terms of evangelism, this presented a clear dilemma. In what sense, other than evangelism, could CCM be legitimized as a "ministry"? Additional rationales were needed to justify this form of Christian music.

The Second Rationale: Worship Facilitation

Following the disintegration of the Jesus Movement in the mid-1970s, evangelical Christians in America soon found themselves in a paradoxical position. On the one hand, events like the Jesus Movement and the Carter presidency had given evangelicals a vital new presence in American culture. On the other hand, while Carter had made "born again" a household term, as America moved on, evangelical Christians began to find themselves the members an increasingly isolated subculture.[48] Undergoing its own transformation from cottage industry to institution, contemporary Christian music was caught up in that shift. Largely unable to penetrate the institutional structures of the mainstream music industry, contemporary Christian music had turned to the business of religious publishing to provide the necessary resources of distribution and access to retail shelves. Thus, while intending to transform the larger environment of secular culture, Christian musicians soon found their music "consigned to a place where elderly women are watching every move you make, and your product is sitting there next to the plastic Jesus' [sic] and the crucifixes with the heads bobbing."[49] Bound to the conservative requirements of religious publishing and isolated from the general audiences they had hoped to reach with their music, many Christian musicians came to regard the art world of CCM as a ghetto.

While the growing perception of a Christian ghetto led to numerous responses from within CCM, the artists of Separational CCM, now denied any reasonable claim to evangelism, turned to the role of their music in the contemporary worship experience. "The worship of God," explains one CCM veteran, "is the supreme duty of any Christian."[50] For post–Jesus Movement evangelicals, music played an essential role in that worship. Relying on scriptural passages such as Ephesians 5:18–19—"be filled with the Spirit; speaking to one another in psalms and hymns and spiritual songs, singing and making melody with your heart to the Lord" (NAS)—CCM pioneer Dallas Holm argued that, biblically, music is to be used primarily for the "praise of God."[51] Thus, Holm and his supporting musicians became known as Dallas Holm & Praise. Of course this was not to deny the primacy of evangelism in the Christian experience, but rather to suggest, first, that music, designed for the praise and worship of God, was not the best tool for that goal; and second, that music's role in worship was something to be celebrated and extended. Holm, by providing a scriptural basis for this new use of contemporary Christian music—essential for the justification of new behaviors and motivations to the evangelical church—both paved the way for CCM's incorporation into the contemporary worship experience and, perhaps more important, offered a new rationale for the music of the Separational CCM artists.

Given their biblical roots, it is not too surprising that "praise and worship" were quickly and extensively employed as tropes in the justification and evaluation of contemporary Christian music. From the Second Chapter of Acts during the Jesus Movement to Sandi Patty and Steve Green today, many of the best-selling artists in the field have stressed songs of worship and praise over songs with an evangelistic message. Exemplary in this regard was Amy Grant's *Age to Age* (Myrrh, 1982). Consider the following paragraph from *Contemporary Christian Music*'s review of that album:

> Although all of the ten songs shine brilliantly in their own light, listening to "El Shaddai" (God Almighty), a worshipful song of praise to the powerful and yet gentle Creator, is a knee-bending experience. The song was written by Michael Card and John Thompson and contains the phrase, "Age to age, You're still the same," from which the album received its name. Maybe not so scripturally drenched, but equally worshipful is the single released off the album, "Sing Your Praise to the

Lord." The lavish introduction, complete with Hebrew-like riffs builds to
a full orchestral crescendo before the vocal begins.[52]

If illustrative in its own right, the obsession with praise and worship in this
review of *Age to Age* becomes all the more significant in light of Grant's
subsequent career. From the moment they took control over her career in
1980, the management team of Blanton and Harrell had pointed Grant
toward a career in mainstream music, not CCM.[53] This course charted,
1982's *Age to Age* was in many ways designed to serve two goals: first, to
begin repositioning Grant in ways that would increase her appeal to mainstream audiences, and second, to prove Grant's marketability through the
success of the album among evangelicals. The epitome of "lite gospel"
and "contemporary praise," the album was successful on both counts:
Age to Age was the first gospel album certified platinum, and by 1985 at
least some Christian music industry personnel were arguing that "a
window's open in this country for this kind of music [CCM], and it's
open because of Amy."[54] Hoping to ride (if not create) the market trends
of CCM, Amy Grant turned to songs of praise and worship.[55]

Amy Grant, however, was neither the first, nor the last, to turn to
worship as a rationale for CCM. Biographer Dan O'Neill describes a conversation between John Michael Talbot and Barry McGuire in the late
1970s that captures McGuire's turn toward worshipful lyrics over blatant
attempts to proselytize and Talbot's desire to follow suit: "'Barry, your
music touches people—it reaches people. I've seen it and I want that ability to really minister,' John said. Barry sat silently, stroking his beard, squint-
ing thoughtfully skyward. 'How can I reach people?' John repeated his
question. 'Well, brother, you don't reach people. You sing to God, you
worship God and talk to God while you're onstage, and let God reach the
people.'"[56] In this conversation Talbot's new musical rationale was crystallized. Talbot's orientation toward the worship of God over proselytism
would eventually culminate in his conversion to Catholicism (a singular
occurrence in the evangelical Protestant world of CCM) and his membership in The Third Order Secular of Saint Francis.[57] Talbot's most successful release would come in *The Lord's Supper* (Sparrow, 1979), a
worship-oriented album that utilized the Catholic mass, in particular the
Eucharist, as its central theme. Even Keith Green, with his heavy emphasis
on conversion and exhortation through his first three albums, eventually
"felt God was telling him to produce an album of worship songs, a record-

ing that would inspire people to worship instead of another 'hard message' album."[58] Whether a product of God's voice or Green's savvy in spotting trends, *Songs for the Shepherd* (Pretty Good Records) was released in April 1982.

The praise and worship trend did not end in the early eighties. Indeed, a decade later albums like *At the Foot of the Cross* (Glasshouse, 1992), *Corem Deo* (Sparrow, 1992), and *Alternative Worship: Prayers, Petitions, and Praise* (Alarma, 1994) brought a new wave of praise and worship music, this time with an alternative rock sensibility. At the same time, perhaps the best evidence for the acceptance of CCM's worship rationale is found in the degree to which contemporary Christian music has been incorporated into the worship services of innumerable churches across the United States. Surveying a thousand randomly selected churches in 1993 and 1996, *Your Church* magazine found an increasing reliance on contemporary forms of worship music. In fact, by 1996, worship services relying primarily on nontraditional styles of music had become more common than services rooted in traditional music and liturgies. Additionally, churches using these contemporary forms of Christian music were found to be more effective at attracting participants to their Sunday services, with an average Sunday morning attendance nearly twice as large as that of congregations using more traditional music (314 to 172). These churches are also more likely than their traditional counterparts to have experienced growth in attendance in the previous five years.[59] So, while churches presenting traditional music do remain, contemporary Christian music in its praise and worship forms is becoming essential to the Sunday morning experience of an increasing number of Christians.[60]

Today, many CCM artists have made praise and worship their focus, touring the church circuit without pretending to offer an outreach to the "lost." As the experiences of John Michael Talbot and Amy Grant suggest, there are resources available in praise and worship music as well as in the rationales that justify it. At the same time, as praise and worship came to be defined by a particular set of musical and rhetorical conventions—that is, as "Praise & Worship," with its lush arrangements and easily memorized choruses, moved toward becoming a genre in and of itself—some Separational CCM artists found themselves returning to the original principle of evangelism. Praise and worship music, in other words, was reconceived as a tool in the evangelistic repertoire. Known in part for her own mastery of the contemporary praise form that first made Amy Grant successful, Twila

Paris testified to the use of worship songs for evangelism in her experiences with the evangelistic/missionary group Youth With A Mission: "We used to go out in the street and one of the ways we'd draw a crowd was to gather around and start singing worship songs. Before you knew it, we had a big crowd of people around. God inhabits the praise of His people, and people are drawn to that, even if they don't understand why. They want to hear and know, and you have a chance to talk to them about Jesus Christ. Worship can be one of our front-line tools in evangelism."[61]

As Paris's comments suggest, the evangelical reading of the "plan of salvation" and the demand for proselytizing are nearly always kept in mind by the artists of Separational CCM, even when their words are addressed to God and/or to those whom have already been saved.

The Third Rationale: Exhortation

For evangelicals, the moment of conversion is the most significant point in any individual's life, whether that individual be self or other. Thus, while the editors of *Contemporary Christian Music,* responding to criticism from a group of Christian musicians, argued that "it is hard to imagine a chart of the 'Top 12 Apostles' in terms of souls won or miracles performed . . . souls and miracles are a far cry from records and tapes!," it is at the same time clear that, for many individuals working within the realm of contemporary Christian music, souls are, in fact, the relevant currency.[62] Extolling the virtues of Christian music, Steve Miller makes the following claim about Petra: "During their most recent tour it was not uncommon to see one or two hundred individuals making commitments and talking with counselors at the close of a show. Who can calculate the spiritual growth fostered by those listening to Petra's tapes from day to day?"[63] Miller similarly cites Mylon LeFevre's (of Mylon LeFevre and Broken Heart) claims that by 1989 the band's ministry "was communicating with 160 thousand people who had indicated decisions [converted] at Broken Heart concerts."[64] However, while there are those like Miller who see merit in a quantified approach to Christianity, there are also those who criticize this perspective. Arguing that the experience of Christianity only begins at the moment of conversion, critics of this hit-and-run approach to ministry argue that it fails to nurture new Christians in the ways of the faith. Without this assistance, they suggest, the bulk of the people who fill out "decision cards" in the aftermath of the emotion-filled multimedia spectacle of a concert will, with the return to the reality of daily life, fall back into their pre-Christian lifestyles and belief systems.[65]

Recognizing this need for nurturing—perhaps as a result of their continued experience with Christianity and the maturation of their belief—many Christian artists responded to the isolation of CCM within the evangelical book market not with songs of praise and worship but rather with songs of exhortation.[66] As they saw it, their task was to keep the Christian on the narrow path. Approached more schematically, the music of Separational CCM can be seen to be primarily directed at any one of three audiences. When the music is intended to evangelize, it is directed at non-Christians; when the music is intended to be used for praise and worship, it is directed at God; and when the music is intended for exhortation, it is directed at fellow believers. Realizing that it was this latter group that constituted CCM's primary audience (setting aside the issue of whether or not God would listen to CCM), astute artists turned to the task of exhortation.[67]

Throughout the 1980s and 1990s, numerous Christian musicians have turned to the tropes of encouragement, exhortation, and Christian accountability to explain their efforts. Randy Stonehill, one of CCM's pioneers, had concluded by 1981 that his "role in Christian music seem[ed] to be one of an encourager to living a more committed life."[68] Still holding out for the evangelistic role of "seed planter," Stonehill nevertheless saw his primary mission defined in the context of the church, writing songs intended to serve that particular audience.[69] In the years that followed, songs like "Hymn" ("In the end we are not forgotten/ And our journey is not in vain/For the Master who brought us here/ Will lead us home again"), "Don't Break Down" ("Don't break down/ When the sky grows dark/All around your heart/Don't break down"), and "Stand Like Steel" ("You've got to stand/Stand like steel/And carry your cross through the fire/That's part of the deal") would clearly be intended to encourage and support an audience that already shared Stonehill's Christian faith.[70]

Stonehill is just one example of CCM artists turning to exhortation as the rationale for their music. A more illuminative case is perhaps that of Petra. Petra was a band that, while "totally evangelistic at the beginning," became "the most popular Christian rock band in the world" in part by recognizing the nature of their audience and making spiritual encouragement, not transformation, the goal of their music.[71] "We know our music is aimed at the church," said guitarist Bob Hartman, describing the band's

In the songs of artists like Randy Stonehill, the Christian music industry saw evangelism give way to exhortation. Encouragement, rather than conversion, became the primary purpose for the music and performances. (Photograph courtesy of Myrrh Records.)

1991 album, *This Means War!* (Star Song, 1987). "Our lyrics seek to edify the body of Christ, and we're not writing songs that are mostly directed to nonbelievers or anything."[72] Continuing, Hartman described the album as "the most conceptual album that we've ever done. It deals with all three areas of our spiritual warfare. As Christians, our enemies are the world, the flesh, and the devil. The songs on *This Means War!* deal with one of those three issues and talk about spiritual warfare."[73] One writer described the music of Petra as "straight-ahead rock like you hear on FM radio combined with straightforward scriptural lessons like you'd hear at a church Bible study."[74]

Since Petra is the world's most popular Christian rock band, its turn to Christian exhortation is particularly significant in that it, more than any other, can be seen as emblematic of four larger issues at work within the system of contemporary Christian music. First, when Christian music came to be conceived in terms of a Christian audience, the trope of spiritual warfare became pervasive in the genre. Petra played a crucial role in developing this militaristic tone, but other groups developed variations on the theme. Sweet Comfort Band's *Hearts of Fire* (Light, 1981) and *Cutting*

Throughout the history of contemporary Christian music, the evangelical tendency to view the world through the framework of "spiritual warfare" has manifested itself as one of the genre's key visual motifs. Pictured here is Sweet Comfort Band's *Hearts of Fire!* (Light, 1981). (Used by permission of Platinum Entertainment, Inc.)

Edge (Light, 1982), Kemper Crabb's *The Vigil* (Starsong, 1980), and Arkangel's *Warrior* (Star Song, 1980) were early contributors through album art. All produced albums with covers featuring a spiritual warfare theme (though from a medieval/fantasy perspective invoking knights, swords, dragons, and the like rather than the contemporary militarism of later imagery). In the middle eighties, Christian heavy metal bands also picked up the theme. Stryper led the way for this genre with its albums

Yellow and Black Attack (Enigma, 1984), *Soldiers under Command* (Enigma, 1985) and *To Hell with the Devil* (Enigma, 1986). Other relevant examples include Saint's *Warriors of the Son* (Quicksilver Records, 1984), Philadelphia's *Search and Destroy* (Patmos, 1985), Bride's *Show No Mercy* (Pure Metal, 1986), Gideon's Army's *Warriors of Love* (A&R, 1987) and, in a country rock vein, Rob Cassells Band's *Kamikaze Christian* (Morada, 1984). More recently, the spiritual warfare cliché lives on in the music of Carman, with songs like "Satan Bite the Dust" and "R.I.O.T." (Righteous Invasion of Truth), and in songs of gospel-gangsta rap artists such as T-Bone, whose *Tha Hoodlum's Testimony* (Metro One, 1997) was claimed by one reviewer to promote a "hyper spiritual warfare that demands every Christian be 'a demon executor' tough guy."[75]

The militarism of the music was supported by the concept of the song as "scripture lesson." As exemplified in DeGarmo & Key's Pledge Tour of 1990 (which was sponsored by a Bible publisher and intended, at least in part, to encourage Christian youth to develop a habit of daily Bible reading), knowledge of the Bible was considered a primary weapon in the spiritual warfare that the bands were describing. By writing songs based on particular Bible passages and citing those passages in the liner notes, bands like DeGarmo & Key and Petra were able to further tie their music to the contemporary Christian experience. If their audiences were to be limited to Christians, the bands wanted as many Christians as possible to hear them; and in connecting their music to the fundamental Christian habit of Bible reading, bands such as Petra were able to make listening to CCM a regular feature of the contemporary Christian life. Consistent with this position, Zondervan released an edited collection of short devotional essays authored by various CCM artists, ranging from Dana Key to Steven Curtis Chapman to Michael Card, called *Rock the Planet*.[76] In 1997, the connection between CCM and Bible reading/devotional time continued as Petra's Bob Hartman authored a book sharing the title of the band's 1982 album *More Power To Ya* (Star Song) and featuring devotional essays based on Petra songs.[77]

Exemplary of CCM's move toward militarism and explicit biblical rooting for lyrics, Petra's discussion of *This Means War!* in the context of spiritual warfare points to two other trends in the genre. Conceiving of a Christian audience, artists working at Christian exhortation were now free to rely more heavily on the rhetoric of evangelical Christianity—

"Christianese"—without hesitation. Lyrics were soon overflowing with phrases and references all but incomprehensible outside of an evangelical framework. With lines such as "If you die before you die than when you die you won't die," Benny Hester's "If You Die Before You Die," Kenny Marks's "Soul Reviver," Dan Peek's "Doer of the Word," Mylon LeFevre and Broken Heart's "Love God, Hate Sin," the Michael Card–penned Amy Grant hit "El Shaddai," and numerous others proved to be highly appealing affirmations to evangelicals while being largely unintelligible and/or terribly trite to non-Christians.[78] Realizing that they weren't reaching non-Christian audiences anyway, many artists writing songs of exhortation turned to the language of evangelicalism, further alienating the few non-Christians who might be listening and thus further entrenching CCM in its self-made "gospel ghetto."

Finally, Petra's turn to Christian exhortation also marked the effective death of obsessions within much of CCM over the phenomenon of "crossing over."[79] In 1985, Petra's *Beat the System* had been included in the joint distribution agreement between A&M and Word that had brought Amy Grant and *Unguarded* to the attention of non-Christian audiences. However, while *Unguarded* had been a minor hit with mainstream audiences, climbing to number thirty-five on *Billboard*'s Pop Albums chart with singles in rotation on VH-1 and charting on *Billboard*'s Hot 100 and Adult Contemporary charts, *Beat the System* "was a complete flop and an embarrassment to executives of both companies."[80] While the occasional band generating crossover hype (e.g. Sixpence None the Richer) would still turn up, Petra showed that, for the industry as a whole, Amy Grant would be the exception rather than the rule. Writing songs explicitly for the evangelical audience, with success depending on the band's "appeal to youth pastors, who use the band's music to hold their youth group's [*sic*] interest in Bible studies," Petra showed CCM where its economic future lay.[81]

With lyrics such as "Armed and dangerous/God's enemies will scatter/Armed and dangerous/We'll see the darkness shatter," Petra's message to Christians can perhaps be understood as a musical reading of Joshua or Revelation, the armies of God rising up to conquer evil.[82] This, however, was only one way in which Separational CCM approached Christian exhortation. Artists such as Keith Green and Steve Camp read their mission not as one of militaristic cheerleading but rather prophetic introspection. Consider, for example, the lyrics to Green's "Asleep in the Light":

"The world is sleeping in the dark that the church just can't fight/'Cause it's asleep in the light/How can you be so dead when you've been so well fed?/Jesus rose from the grave, and you, you can't even get out of bed/ Oh, Jesus rose from the dead/Come on, get out of bed!"[83] The message was clearly directed at Christians, but it was a far cry from either the subtle encouragement of Randy Stonehill or the bombastic posturing of Petra. For many in the Christian music industry as well as many audience members, Green was a modern-day Ezekiel, a prophet emerging from the desert to warn twentieth-century Christians of the consequences of their lukewarm faith and inaction. The perception of Green as contemporary prophet was furthered with his decision, rooted in the belief that money had replaced God as the raison d'être for the Christian music industry, to bypass the by-then reified distribution channels of CCM, and, beginning with *So You Wanna Go Back to Egypt?* (Pretty Good Records, 1980), use his own Last Days Ministries as a mail-order distributor, offering albums for whatever amount a listener could afford or was willing to give.[84]

Whatever the particular merits of Keith Green's music, the "musician as prophet" role achieved a certain measure of popularity among Separational CCM artists. "Christian Artists: Today's Prophets?" wondered one writer for *Contemporary Christian Music*.[85] Comparing Christian musicians to Saul, David, and Solomon, the author identified these artists as people "God uses . . . in spite of their weaknesses . . . who express . . . their relationship with Almighty Yahweh mentally, emotionally, physically, and musically . . . touching the nerves of contemporary [Christian] culture with God's truth."[86] The music of many Christian artists—Steve Camp, John Fischer, Michael Card, and Glenn Kaiser (of Rez Band), for example—can certainly be understood in this context. At the same time it is worth noting that, even drawing solely on these examples, each of the four approaches the task much differently. At one extreme is Steve Camp, who has no qualms with naming names and pointing fingers—an approach that has at times angered the fans of those artists whom Camp criticizes.[87] At the other end of the spectrum is John Fischer, who uses his monthly column in *Contemporary Christian Music* as a public soapbox for what are in many cases private introspections. Chastising Christian musicians for trying to be "relevant," claiming that "we started out trying to save the world, and ended up trying to get a record contract," questioning the potential contradictions of a marketed ministry that nonetheless impacts people's lives, and occasionally deciding that "it's over . . . go home," Fischer's role as prophet is one with fewer answers than questions (and unafraid of the contradictions those questions often lead to).[88] In any case, whatever their personal approach to the issues, be it hard-line pulpit-pounding or dubious introspection, in holding their listeners to some level of Christian accountability, these modern-day prophets were clearly addressing their messages to the Christian audience. Their words make little sense in any other context.

Emerging from the Jesus Movement, with its focus on evangelism and the spreading of the Gospel, early contemporary Christian music was designed to speak through the medium of popular music to America's lost youth. Ironically, however, in their effort to expand its influence, the people of the CCM art world increasingly isolated the genre within the confines of the evangelical subculture. Albums were sold through the retail channels of religious book publishing (and thereby associated with the kitsch generally found there), performances were largely confined to church auditoriums or music festivals that seemed more religious revivals than rock concerts, and while contemporary Christian music thus emerged as an important complement to the contemporary Christian life, it concomitantly became irrelevant to almost everybody else. Thus, the self-identified motivation for creating the music (evangelism) soon came into conflict with the reality of its reception. Designed to reach the lost, the music was being heard by the found.

Still conceiving of their music as ministry and yet facing the realization that the audiences they were reaching were already part of the church, the artists of Separational CCM turned to new rationales to justify the music they made. Ministry, previously a term used to designate evangelism (the sine qua non of the evangelical faith), was self-consciously expanded to included activities appropriate for a churched audience. Without abandoning the goals of evangelism, the rationales for Separational CCM, still articulated under the rubric of "ministry," were expanded to include the praise and worship of God as well as exhortation and encouragement of Christian audiences in their pursuit of the faith. Under these new rationales, artists began making music finely tuned to the character and desires of their audience. Songs such as "Awesome God" and "How Majestic Is Your Name" became staples in evangelical worship services, while the number of radio stations specializing in CCM's light encouragement ex-ploded.[89] Ultimately, however, the turn to worship and exhortation was only one response to the growing realization that the audience for con-temporary Christian music was almost exclusively Christian. Some began to challenge the very assumption that contemporary Christian music was a "ministry" at all.

✝ Interlude: DC Talk

Most of the time, the Bren Events Center serves as the basketball arena for the University of California, Irvine. Tonight it is the setting for the debut performance of DC Talk's Jesus Freak Tour. At the end of the arena floor, a stage has been installed. Behind it hangs a white backdrop, a screen for the images and video that will be projected throughout the show. On stage, several risers covered in red fabric make up the whole of the relatively spartan arrangements.

Fenced in and guarded by security, the floor between the stage and the seating has been designated as a mosh pit. An announcement broadcast over the PA system informs the waiting crowd that those who are at least eighteen years old, hold tickets to seats on the floor, and are willing to sign an injury waiver may receive a wristband that will allow them entry to the moshing floor. It doesn't take long for the mosh pit to fill.

After an enthusiastic set from the tour's opening act, Toby McKeehan, Kevin Smith, and Michael Tait—DC Talk—walk on stage singing The Beatles' "Help." As the crowd goes wild, this deified, ridiculed, applauded, and dismissed trio moves from the Lennon-McCartney plea into their own take on the situation, "So Help Me God."[1] As the show continues, the crowd eagerly accepts everything the band throws at them—the band's early pop-rap hybrids; newer, Nirvana-influenced alternative rock; and a version of a Doobie Brothers' hit, reworked to fit the band's rap-rock leanings and its Christian audience, now titled "Jesus Is Still Alright." Backed by a six-piece band (and thus freed from the constraints of carrying instruments), the three men pace the stage like tigers in a cage. Occasionally pausing to address the audience—"We look at our skin color as God's artwork," the band's African American member tells the crowd—the focus nonetheless remains on the music. At least for now.

With a half-dozen songs completed, the tone of the performance shifts as stagehands bring out overstuffed chairs and other furnishings, laying out a living room in the middle of the stage. Making themselves comfortable, McKeehan, Smith, and Tait begin talking and joking with the audience. Following the lighthearted banter, the three embark on a brief "unplugged" set, the centerpiece of which is their take on the Larry Norman classic, "I Wish We'd All Been Ready." Following this piece, the band's Christian leanings are made emphatic as McKeehan draws out a Bible and begins to read from I John. Perhaps missing the point of the passage—"Now for this very reason also, applying all diligence, in your faith supply moral excellence, and in your moral excellence, knowledge; and in your knowledge, self-control, and in your self-control, perseverance, godliness; and in your godliness, brotherly kindness, and in your brotherly kindness, love" (I John 1:5–7, NAS)—a number of girls in the audience so disturb McKeehan with their screams of devotion that he raises the Bible and tells them, "Hey, even if you're not going to respect us, you have to respect this." As the audience settles down, McKeehan finishes reading, and the band winds up its acoustic set with a cover of Charlie Peacock's "In the Light."

The living room gone, the three are once again the rock stars, prowling the stage and stirring the audience. As in the first half of the show, the material draws freely from sources other than the band's own recordings. *Godspell*'s "Day by Day" becomes a grunge rock anthem. R.E.M.'s "It's the End of World as We Know It (And I Feel Fine)" becomes a rejoinder to the band's "What Have We Become." But the song that grabs the audience and pulls the people from their seats is the title track of the band's hit album *Jesus Freak* (Forefront, 1995). As the band moves through the grungy rock number likened by more than one listener to Nirvana's "Smells Like Teen Spirit," Smith and McKeehan leap out into the mosh pit, surfing across the bodies. Returning to the stage, the Nirvana connection is further emphasized as the band moves directly from "Jesus Freak" into their revamped (and, in some places, reworded) version of "All Apologies." As the frenzy winds to a halt, Smith, Tait, and the backing band leave McKeehan alone on stage. Having established their credentials as performers, McKeehan spends the closing moments of the show establishing their credentials as Christians, offering a sermon-like talk to the faithful in the audience.

3 Integrational CCM: "It's Entertainment"

The world exists, not for what it means but for what it is. The purpose of mushrooms is to be mushrooms; wine is in order to be wine: Things are precious before they are contributory. It is a false piety that walks through creation looking only for lessons which can be applied somewhere else.

Robert Farrar Capon

She wears black pants, a white shirt, and a leopard-print tuxedo jacket, the sleeves rolled to the elbow. The four poses are dynamic and nearly sequential: left shoulder drawn back, arm bent and drawn in close to her body, while the right shoulder dips, arm swung out, fingers snapping; elbows in close to the body, arms forward, fingers splayed; arms held wide, fingers snapping; hands in her pockets, head thrown back, hair swinging through the air. She has been caught—at four brief instants—in a moment of wild abandon.[1] Framing the images, the text reads: "You may not know this artist by name. But a million know her music by heart."[2] The year was 1985, the album *Unguarded* (Myrrh/A&M), the artist Amy Grant. Contemporary Christian music was going mainstream.

Amy Grant was, from the beginning of her career, groomed to go beyond the established boundaries of contemporary Christian music. While every one of her albums "generated surprising sales, radio airplay, and concert requests in the evangelical market," it wasn't the evangelical market alone for which Grant was aiming.[3] From *Age to Age* (Myrrh, 1982) forward, each new album represented a further step toward mainstream success: *Age to Age*—the first gospel album to sell platinum; *Straight Ahead* (Myrrh, 1984)—number one on *Billboard*'s inspirational chart for more than a year; *Unguarded* (Myrrh/A&M, 1985)—certified gold in two months and platinum in less than half the time it had taken *Age to Age*, the album eventually reached number thirty-five on the *Billboard* Pop Albums chart; *Lead Me On* (Myrrh/A&M, 1988)—the first gospel album to ship gold; *Heart in Motion* (Myrrh/A&M, 1991)—number ten on the *Billboard* Pop Albums chart and certified triple platinum in a slow economy; *House of Love* (Myrrh/A&M, 1994)—fifty-four weeks on the *Billboard* Pop Albums chart, peaking at number thirteen. Additionally, *Heart in Motion,* Grant's breakthrough album, produced her first single to reach number one on the *Billboard* Hot 100 ("Baby, Baby"), and the follow-up, "Every Heartbeat," rose to number two. And while the three singles from *House of Love* ("Lucky One," "House of Love," and "Big Yellow Taxi") couldn't match that performance, "Lucky One" and "House of Love" reached the top five on *Billboard*'s Hot Adult Contemporary Chart.[4] So, if critics could debate the reasons for Grant's success—although the release of *Behind the Eyes* (Myrrh/A&M) in 1997 would go a long way toward reaffirming her artistic credentials—there could be little doubt that Grant had successfully negotiated her way into the mainstream distribution and exhibition channels.[5]

Grant's move from gospel queen to mainstream pop star was not accomplished without transformations in the songs she sang. The contemporary praise and "lite gospel" of *Age to Age* slowly gave way to a form of music that would eventually be labeled "positive pop." At first, the explicit praise choruses of "Sing Your Praise to the Lord" ("Sing Your Praise to the Lord/Come on everybody, stand up and sing one more 'hallelujah'"), "I Have Decided" ("I have decided/I'm going to live like a believer/Turn my back on the deceiver/I'm gonna live what I believe"), and the like gave way to ambiguous sentiments of (Christian?) love such as *Unguarded*'s "Find a Way."[6] Combining the chorus of a generic love song ("Leave behind the doubt/Love's the only out/Love will surely find a way") with a bridge that attempted to position that love as divine ("If our God His Son not sparing/Came to rescue you/Is there any circumstance/That He can't see you through"), "Find a Way" could easily be integrated into both religious and secular contexts.[7] The ambiguity was further emphasized by Grant's shift in musical sensibilities. Thickly orchestrated ballads and a folk-based, down-home approach to rock and roll gave way to music that came straight from Top 40 radio. Setting aside the words she was singing, even Grant's music stopped signaling "CCM."

And the trend continued. While the underlying message of songs such as "Find a Way" might reasonably be assigned both religious and secular interpretations, even this ambiguity would give way to songs like "Baby, Baby" and "The Things We Do for Love" (originally recorded by 10cc) that only through the wildest stretches of the imagination could be given religious interpretations.[8] So, while some were suggesting that Grant, "realizing the tendencies of individuals to close their minds to that which is initially uncomfortable, . . . found a new wrapping for an old message" (the gospel), such interpretations became harder to support as Grant's career progressed.[9] One writer questioned, "Has Amy Grant traded in *hallelujah* for *hubba hubba?*"[10]

In her success, Amy Grant became the focal point for a series of debates concerning the nature and goals of CCM, with opinions ranging from those of *Contemporary Christian Music* editor John W. Styll, who at one point claimed that the success of "Baby, Baby" might "be the most significant single event in the history of contemporary Christian music," to those of the fan who sent Grant flowers accompanied by a note that read, "Turn back. You can still be saved if you renounce what you've done."[11] What attitudes such as the latter miss, however, is the fact that there is a substantial difference between Amy Grant and "Amy Grant." Among critics, fans, and scholars alike, there has been a tendency to equate the woman with the career. It is a dubious move. While Grant's individual talents, beauty, and persona undoubtedly played instrumental roles in her success, she did not rise to the top without significant assistance. And as with Elvis and Col. Tom Parker, much of the credit (or blame) for Grant's success must be laid at the feet of Dan Harrell and Mike Blanton, her managers, who have been called the "guiding lights" behind Amy Grant.[12] Beyond the question of management, moreover, there are the issues of production and authorship. Scanning the credits of Grant's albums reveals a veritable *Who's Who* of Nashville CCM: Gary Chapman (Grant's husband), Chris Eaton, Dann Huff, Wayne Kirkpatrick, Jerry McPherson, and Charlie Peacock, among a host of others. Additionally, the role of critics and writers such as John W. Styll, Bruce Brown, John J. Thompson, Dwight Ozard, and Brian Quincy Newcomb in justifying Grant's experiments to a hesitant evangelical audience should not be ignored.[13] By no means intended to diminish Grant's talents or accomplishments, the above comments point only to the fact that, in the context of contemporary Christian music, Amy Grant isn't a person, she's an empire—an empire that sits at the center of Integrational CCM. And while others (Michael W. Smith, Kathy Troccoli, Jars of Clay, Bob Carlisle) have had their brief flashes of mainstream success, to this point only Amy Grant has been able to command mainstream attention on a consistent basis and, while still releasing albums to the Christian marketplace, more or less shed the burdensome label of "Christian artist."

Ministers versus Entertainers

As with Separational CCM, Integrational CCM's defining moment came with the recognition that contemporary Christian music was trapped within the boundaries of an evangelical subculture defined not only by religious belief but also by commercial habits. It has been noted repeatedly that, while a large portion of the American population claims a Christian faith of one form or another, few of those people make it a habit to shop in the evangelical bookstores where Christian records are sold.[14] Consequently, in hitching its fortunes to the institutions of religious publishing and retail, Christian music isolated itself behind subcultural walls that not only segregated the Christian artists from the non-Christians they sought to convert but from the majority of Christian consumers as well. Recognizing the incongruity of this situation, artists and record companies began to seek ways of "crossing over" into the mainstream market. However, while virtually all of the Christian music artists sought, or would at least have accepted, attention from the mainstream media, such success stories, with the notable exception of Amy Grant, were few, infrequent, and short-lived.

For the artists of Christian music, breaking into the system for the distribution, exhibition, and promotion of mainstream popular music generally proved to be far more difficult than anyone anticipated. At each turn, the artists found themselves the victims of bad business, bad choices, bad albums, and/or bad timing. With a contract offer from Warner-Curb and what many perceived to be an exceptionally strong album in *Horrendous Disc* (Solid Rock, 1980), Daniel Amos emerged in the late 1970s as one of CCM's first crossover hopefuls. But when the band held out for a better offer and *Horrendous Disc* was held up by a vicious legal battle with Larry Norman and Solid Rock Records, the band's crossover hopes evaporated.[15] A beneficiary of the same joint distribution deal that eventually made Amy Grant a household name, Petra's first (and only) release to the mainstream market, 1984's *Beat the System* (Star Song), was characterized by one critic as a "synth fiesta," and fans of the guitar-based rock band found the album to sound nothing like what they had come to expect from Petra; non-fans simply ignored it.[16] Having negotiated for mainstream distribution through Island Records, The 77's released its 1987 album *The 77's* (Exit/Island) only to have the almost simultaneous release of U2's *The Joshua Tree* (Island, 1987) consume all of the label's promotional resources. After three well-received albums in the Christian market, Kim Hill left CCM for country music only to be dropped by her new label when her album failed to sell a million copies.[17] Darrell Mansfield Band, DeGarmo & Key, Holy Soldier, Tonio K., Dakoda Motor Company, The Choir, Russ Taff, The Prayer Chain—the list of unsuccessful crossovers goes on and on.

It perhaps goes without saying that potential success in mainstream popular culture requires that the music be commercially viable. This, for many Christian artists, requires a fundamental redefinition of their musical activities. Dakoda Motor Company provides one of the more colorful illustrations of this process. Originally signed to Myrrh, Dakoda Motor Company was a band known more for its members than its music. While the band's infectious surf-punk generally received good reviews, it was having a guitarist who was a professional surfer and the host of MTV's *Sandblast* and an attractive lead singer who appeared on stage wearing her high school cheerleading uniform that garnered the band most of its attention. However, after recording two successful albums for Myrrh *(Into the Son* [1993] and *Welcome Race Fans* [1994]), the band left Myrrh for a mainstream label. Guitarist Peter King explained the move this way: "It's really easy for a band to float by using the 'J-Word,' and get some gigs and go play for a couple of youth groups. . . . You say a couple of nice things about Jesus, you smile, you're happy, and everyone is fulfilled, and everyone leaves happy. . . . But really, we want to play for fans of music, not fans of Christianity." With no small measure of irony, King went on to add, "We're not the 'Jesus Cheerleading Squad.'"[18] Granted, not every band trying to attract the attention of the mainstream record industry and mainstream audiences has felt the need to deny its past. But still, history has proven at least minor alterations to be inevitable. So, in the case of Daniel Amos, as the band moved closer toward mainstream success, "each album . . . [became] more sensitive to the unbeliever." Strong evangelical messages gave way to the band members' increasing belief that "all we can do is plant a seed. Ultimately, a person has to make up their own mind about the truth they encounter."[19] More fundamentally, as Peter Wicke argues,

Launched with an independent album of sped up worship songs and a bidding war that landed them on Myrrh, Dakoda Motor Company soon learned that contemporary Christian music was worlds away from mainstream pop. Thus, while the band repeatedly emphasized its non-religious credentials, including the use of one of their songs in an ad campaign for the Chevy Camaro, nothing seemed able to separate the band's music from its members' religion. The band eventually left Myrrh for a mainstream label. (Photograph courtesy of Myrrh Records.)

everything that comes into contact with the music industry is made to serve the economic and ideological interests of capital.[20] If nothing else, then, to be successful in American popular music requires not only touching the hearts and minds of an audience, but also moving them to purchase the music. Consequently, as Darrell Mansfield discovered when he was dropped by Polydor, if contemporary Christian musicians were to achieve mainstream success, they had to stop thinking of themselves as primarily ministers or evangelists and start thinking of themselves as entertainers—albeit entertainers who also happened to be Christians.[21]

Defining themselves as singers who are Christians rather than Christian singers, the artists of Integrational CCM argue that, while the content of their live and recorded performances is intended to remain consistent with the message of the gospel, the primary purpose behind their singing and songwriting is not necessarily to proclaim God's plan for salvation through Christ, praise and worship the Lord, or encourage Christians in their faith. Frequently, this puts the integrational artists in an uncomfortable position regarding the established rationales of Separational CCM. In the late seventies and early eighties, singer B.J. Thomas found that his insistence on being an entertainer rather than a minister frequently led to conflict with Christian audiences. As Thomas explained, "a lot of my concerts are big, painful experiences for the Christian community. They can't seem to hear somebody *sing*. It's always got to be some kind of Christian cliché or bible song, or they feel it's their right before God to reject and judge and scoff."[22]

Coming to Christianity (and CCM) with an established career in pop music, Thomas attempted to integrate his faith into that career by maintaining a presence in both the pop and gospel arenas. This was, however, an effort frequently misunderstood by Christian music fans who had incorporated the rationales of the separational approach into their assumptions about CCM. Thomas, seeking to integrate a selection of gospel songs into his family-oriented pop show, fell victim to catcalls and heckling from Christian fans who preferred that he leave out the love songs and "Rain Drops Keep Falling on my Head" and instead sing songs about his faith.[23] Thomas worked to remain in the larger mainstream culture and exercise his influence there; but seeing the reconciliation of Christ and culture in a different way, many in his audience demanded that he withdraw. Thomas's frustration with the Christian audience's requirement that he "minister" eventually led to physical confrontations. In the face of audience members who would demand that he "sing about the Lord" when he performed his pre-conversion hits, Thomas was ultimately worn down to the point of storming off stage, smacking a stagehand, and swearing at a hall manager.[24]

Thomas, however, was by no means the last Christian artist to face problems with the "minister" label; most CCM artists have had to deal with its weight at one point or another. In this context, it is interesting to note the strategies developed by the artists and others to escape the requirement of ministry. *Contemporary Christian Music* editor John Styll, for example, argued in an early defense of Amy Grant that she was not a "music minister" but rather provided "sanctified entertainment"—something that "has all the diversionary value of entertainment, but . . . is infused with the power of the gospel."[25] According to Styll, this sanctified entertainment may not explicitly invoke the name of Jesus Christ or God, but neither does it appeal to "our lowest nature." The value of sanctified entertainment, in other words, was to be found not in what it could do, but rather in what it didn't do—a significant shift from the artist-as-minister approach of Separational CCM and one that those who adhere to the values of Separational CCM often regard as an obvious compromise of the Christian music industry's essential mission.

In moving to a concept of Christian music as sanctified entertainment, Integrational CCM clearly drew on assumptions at odds with, if not antithetical to, the principles driving Separational CCM. As described by Niebuhr, the "Christ of culture" position sees a fundamental agreement between Christ and culture.[26] In this view Jesus often appears as the great hero of human culture; his life and teachings are regarded as the greatest human achievement. Christ confirms what is best in the culture and guides civilization toward its proper goal. Culture, while imperfect and frequently misguided, is essentially good and in harmony with Christ, who will fulfill culture's hopes and aspirations. In this approach, the tensions between the church and the world are minimized. According to Niebuhr, in the "Christ of culture" approach, Christ does not require the faithful to leave their homes and kindred (cf., Luke 14:2–35) but rather enters into their homes and associations as the gracious presence that adds an aura of infinite meaning to temporal tasks. Kind and liberal guidance for good people who want to do "the right thing" is offered in the hope of bringing about a peaceful and cooperative society. It is important to note, however, that advocates of this position do not typically seek a Christian sanction for the whole of culture but for only those aspects of culture that they regard as representing its highest ideals and goals. This inevitably leads to a process of careful selection from the teachings of Christ and Christian doctrine. Those aspects of Christianity that seem to agree with what is best in civilization ("love your neighbor") are emphasized, while more discordant elements ("love your enemy," "woe to you who are rich") are excised. It is, of course, a risky endeavor. As numerous critics have pointed out, the attempt to synthesize Jesus Christ with contemporary culture can lead to a cultural Christianity that has less to do with the New Testament than with the maintenance of the social status quo—a point clearly articulated in the song "Church of Do What You Want To" by the band Jacob's Trouble: "Turn in your hymnals to hymn number one/It ain't 'Holy, Holy, Holy'/It's 'Fun, Fun, Fun'/Don't need a Savior 'cause we got no flaws/They ain't sins no more, they're more like spiritual faux pas."[27] This "Christianity-lite," however, is not the only risk associated with the "Christ of culture" approach, and it can be particularly problematic for evangelicals. Niebuhr argues that this approach is generally ineffective in converting the unbelieving to Christ.[28] For Integrational CCM artists, however, this latter issue is somewhat beside the point. They enter the marketplace not as ministers or evangelists but as entertainers. More important, while other Christian musicians languish in the ghetto of the evangelical subcultural, the Integrational CCM artists, some of them at least, are gaining access to the mainstream marketplace.

Crossover Controversies

According to the Recording Industry Association of America (RIAA), gospel music is gospel music, and, for the purpose of tracking sales, religious musics of all types have traditionally been lumped together into a single category. Despite the assumptions of the RIAA, however, not all religious music is the same. While both bear the label "gospel," white and black gospel can clearly be distinguished from one another through social, historical, theological, and musical differences. The two sit at the center of very distinct social worlds. Both have had importance for contemporary Christian music in terms of the controversies surrounding crossover artists. While black gospel has always been peripheral to CCM, in terms of audience reaction to their attempts at crossing over to mainstream success the musicians of CCM have largely followed the path of their black gospel predecessors.[29] According to Jim Curtis, because black Americans needed the church to be a refuge more than whites did, they tended to draw a strict dichotomy between sacred and profane music. Black music in the fifties and early sixties thus tended to be divided between "gospel" and "the blues," and attempts to blend the two, either stylistically or lyrically, were condemned. Curtis cites the negative reaction of the black gospel music community to the pop success of Ray Charles and Sam Cooke as illustrations of this separation.[30] So, while black gospel artists have more frequently crossed over to pop stardom, such efforts generally came at the cost of being unable to remain in, or return to, the artists' gospel music roots.

In contrast to black gospel, white gospel music (which was an important predecessor to what would develop into contemporary Christian music) had little difficulty dealing with the issue of its artists crossing over because, for the most part, those artists remained segregated within the boundaries of the church. Like contemporary Christian music, white (southern) gospel was largely characterized by subcultural isolation. Given the similarities between the two, the early forays of southern gospel artists into the mainstream arena are a useful point of departure into the larger issues surrounding crossing over for contemporary Christian music. The two most significant southern gospel bands with regard to the crossover phenomenon were The Oak Ridge Boys and The Imperials, both of which began to entertain the possibility of mainstream success during the mid-seventies. However, while the two bands shared significant commonalties in their southern gospel roots, each resolved the question of crossing over in a very different way. The difference between them usefully illustrates the separational "either/or" assumptions that defined white gospel music—and the Christian music industry—at the time.

Throughout the 1970s, both The Imperials and The Oak Ridge Boys had been riding a wave of commercial and critical approval. The Imperials' albums, *No Shortage* (Impact, 1975), *Sail On* (Impact, 1977), *Heed the Call* (Dayspring, 1979), and *Priority* (Dayspring, 1981), would all eventually win Grammy Awards. The Oak Ridge Boys picked up four Grammys for their gospel music from 1971 to 1977. And while The Imperials would win the Gospel Music Association's Dove Award for "Group of the Year" six times between 1976 and 1983, The Oak Ridge Boys would win eleven Dove Awards from 1969 to 1974.[31] At the same time, however, both bands were pushing the boundaries of southern gospel toward a mainstream pop sound. The Imperials had performed as backup singers for Elvis Presley between 1969 and 1971, appearing on his records from that era as well as in his movie *That's the Way It Was*. "You are three minutes away from stardom," The Oak Ridge Boys were told by their booking agent and eventual manager, Jim Halsey.[32] And as a result of these successes, the mid-seventies saw the first round of Christian music industry hype over crossing over, the hope being that one of these groups would be the first (white) gospel act to break through to mainstream success. Their eventual paths, however, could not have been more different.

If we picture The Oak Ridge Boys and The Imperials as riding the line between gospel music on the one side and mainstream pop on the other, the two can be seen to have moved in nearly opposite directions. The Oak Ridge Boys took their music to the secular market and, after several lean years between 1973 and 1976, transformed themselves into an extremely popular country music act that recorded nine gold and two platinum albums between 1978 and 1984.[33] One key element of that transformation, whether accidental or intentional, was an abandoning of the gospel lyrics that had defined their southern gospel music. Sounding distinctly like one working from integrational assumptions, baritone William Lee Golden described the man he replaced in The Oak Ridge Boys in 1965: "I thought the group lost the appeal, the charisma, the enthusiasm. I personally didn't think that Jim Hammill and his approach to singing—to him it's a ministry; to me it was clean, fun entertainment—. . . fit The Oak Ridge Boys."[34] Attitudes such as Golden's put the band in direct opposition to the southern gospel community. And while the group had already been soundly condemned by other gospel acts—in particular Howard and Vestal Goodman—for their long hair, their modern attire (including failure to wear neckties on stage), and their rock beat, the move from recording songs like "Because He Lives" (which won a Dove Award for songwriter Bill Gaither in 1974) to the 1977 single "The Y'all Come Back Saloon" resulted in burned bridges and little chance of return to the gospel music industry.

The Imperials took an opposite course, immersing themselves more fully in the gospel music industry. In 1972, believing they were called by God to perform gospel music developed through the resources of the gospel industry, The Imperials signed with the gospel label Impact. Moreover, while the group continued to blend traditional southern gospel with more contemporary forms of music, the members nevertheless decided to stop performing with secular artists and to avoid Las Vegas venues. The reactions of the gospel music industry and fans to the actions of The Oak Ridge Boys and The Imperials were equally polarized. The Oak Ridge Boys, considered to have sold their faith for fame and fortune, were largely abandoned by their evangelical fan base. Eliminating the explicit gospel content of their lyrics, The Oak Ridge Boys were perceived by the gospel music industry to have turned their backs on the industry, the gospel, and even Christ himself.[35] The Imperials, in contrast, despite musical and racial innovations, were for the most part embraced by the Christian music industry, at least in part as a result of their stubborn refusal to "compromise" the gospel as a way to attain crossover success.[36]

If The Imperials and The Oak Ridge Boys (and the Christian music industry of the time) had largely approached success in gospel or mainstream music as an either/or proposition, the contrast began to seem less stark as the industry moved into the 1980s. In part this can be viewed as the result of change in the institutional infrastructure that defined Christian music. The growing number of cross-ownership and joint distribution deals that linked Christian and mainstream music led the Christian music industry to again consider the question of maintaining "Christian" content while attempting to move its artists into the mainstream markets. Not surprisingly, the more optimistic artists, executives, and writers were about the potential penetration of the mainstream market, the more willing they were to dismiss the dichotomy that The Imperials and The Oak Ridge Boys had faced.[37]

Early Corporate Crossovers

With distinct forms of religious music—southern gospel, Jesus rock, hymnody, etc.—coalescing into the catchall genre of contemporary Christian music, the members of the Christian music art world began to wrestle in earnest with defining the boundaries between Christian and secular entertainment. However, while the evolution of groups like The Oak Ridge Boys and The Imperials worked to articulate clear distinctions between these two realms, the infrastructure that supported the growing Christian music industry increasingly belied such sharp division. And since at least 1974, the institutional interpenetration of the Christian and mainstream music industries has been impossible to deny.

The institutional touchstone of the contemporary Christian music industry has long been Word, Inc. Founded by Jarrell McCracken in 1950 with seventy dollars and a single record, "The Game of Life," Word has been the Christian music industry's premiere label from almost its moment of inception and, since 1960, has been the world's largest producer of religious sound recordings.[38] It is no small thing, therefore, that in

1974 the company was sold to the ABC Entertainment Corporation for $12.6 million in stock.[39] In fact, even though largely ignored by the (Christian) record buying public, the purchase was a watershed for the Christian music industry. This was the first time—but by no means the last—a secular corporation maintained ownership of a contemporary Christian record label. As such, the relationship between Word and ABC became a model for subsequent efforts. Unfamiliar with the machinations of the religious market, ABC, while providing capital and exacting profits, largely left the executives at Word to their own devices with regard to evangelical marketing. Thus, in its merger with ABC, Word became the first of the CCM labels to produce records existing in parallel universes. It was a pattern that would become common in the 1980s: "gospel personnel worked with the evangelical market, while those on the payroll of the associated mainstream label handled the affairs in the general market."[40] And while the strategy wasn't always successful, it was for ABC—so much so that the corporation kept control of Word (under the auspices of ABC Publications) when the rest of its record industry holdings were sold to MCA in 1979.[41] With the merger of ABC and Capital Cities Communications in March 1984, Word became a subsidiary of Cap Cities/ABC.

To state the obvious, between 1974 and 1992 when Word was sold for $72 million to the religious book publisher Thomas Nelson Publishers, the largest and most important of the Christian music recording companies was a wholly owned subsidiary of a secular corporation. Word, however, was not the only CCM label to come under secular ownership. After helping to develop Word into the dominant Christian music corporation, former church choir director Billy Ray Hearn left Word to form his own label, Sparrow Records, which would eventually become one of CCM's "big three" (Word, Sparrow, and Benson). Long rumored to have ties to the mainstream music industry, Sparrow was eventually purchased by EMI in September 1992.[42] According to Hearn, Sparrow was happy to take advantage of the distribution available through EMI ownership as long as "the music is still quality and carries a message of integrity that is consistent with Scripture."[43] In Hearn's view, contemporary Christian music was finally achieving through cross-ownership the long-sought goal of being readily available to all consumers, Christian or otherwise, in mainstream outlets.

Ownership was not the only form of corporate relationship being developed between mainstream and Christian music. Throughout the his-

tory of Christian music, there have been multiple attempts at joint distribution agreements between Christian and mainstream record companies.
In early 1981, Sparrow Records signed a distribution deal with MCA.
Light Records, a smaller but still significant CCM label, negotiated a similar deal with Elektra/Asylum in February 1982. Additionally, several mainstream companies launched their own gospel labels. In the fall of 1981,
CBS formed its own CCM label, Priority, using the label to launch Carman
toward a very successful career in CCM. And while the Priority roster
included gospel albums from artists who had earned fame in other musical
genres (Johnny Cash, Ray Stevens, and the Statler Brothers), the label
also signed numerous "pure" CCM artists such as Bob Bennett, David
and the Giants, and James Vincent. Prior to the distribution deal with
Sparrow, MCA had also tried its hand at marketing Christian music with
MCA/Songbird. Signing artists such as Dan Peek (America), B.J. Thomas, and B.W. Stevenson ("I'm Goin' Down to the Station"), MCA employed the strategy of working with Christian artists who had at least
minimally successful mainstream careers behind them in the hope that
those credentials would facilitate crossover success. Importantly, there was
little subterfuge in the reasoning behind efforts such as Songbird and Priority. Deputy president of CBS Dick Asher stated it plainly: "I'll not pre-
tend that we're here because of some new burst of religious faith. We're
here because of the potential to sell records in the gospel market."[44] The
goal was to transform contemporary Christian music from a specialty item
into a product with mass-market appeal. In the end, however, such efforts
were less than completely successful.

While Peek's "All Things Are Possible" made a ripple by hitting
Billboard's Hot 100, early efforts to generate mass interest in Christian
music generally emerged as abysmal failures. Songbird, in this case, was
typical. Just three years after the label was started, MCA announced that it
was putting a moratorium on signing new acts to the Songbird label because of a lack of sufficient sales. Arguably, the label had faced at least two
significant problems. First, as the executives of MCA and other mainstream labels quickly learned, while it may seem that recorded music is
recorded music, in reality things are not this simple. One MCA executive
said of the decision to shut down Songbird, "We have found that gospel's
a totally different record business than the record business MCA is in.
And we haven't found a successful way to make it tick."[45] As MCA learned

with Songbird and ABC learned when it attempted to distribute albums from Word's Myrrh label and "barely survived the debacle," the business of selling Christian records is something altogether different from that of selling mainstream music.[46] This, however, was only half the problem. Although the Christian music industry had largely weathered the recorded music industry's 1979 slump without serious damage, by 1982 Christian music, too, had begun to feel the pinch. The Benson Company and Light Records both laid off large numbers of employees. Sparrow and Word, while managing to avoid staff cutbacks, had to make significant budget cuts.[47] Between the languishing fortunes of the recorded music industry and the distinctions that separated the evangelical and mainstream markets, absent the hands-off approach of ABC in relation to Word, there was little chance for these experiments in co-ownership and/or joint distribution to find success. Thus, as early as December 1981, Sparrow president Billy Ray Hearn was forced to admit that his label's distribution agreement with MCA had resulted in only a minimal expansion of the label's sales.[48] And by 1983, when Light Records pulled out of its distribution deal with Elektra/Asylum and CBS pulled the plug on Priority after the label failed to turn a profit, Christian music was once again largely isolated within the evangelical subculture.[49] After a brief period of cooling off, however, the effort to bring contemporary Christian music to the mainstream market would begin again with new vigor.

Crossing Over in the Eighties and Nineties: New Efforts, New Critiques

Throughout the 1980s and 1990s, each new effort at joint distribution or secular ownership seemed to bring with it a new generation of Christian music artists being positioned to follow Amy Grant to mainstream stardom. Magazines such as *Contemporary Christian Music* and (*Harvest Rock*) *Syndicate* routinely identified the players involved in each developing deal and the artists who would benefit: Exit Records was going to be distributed by Island Records, and The 77's were about to become a household name; A&M and Word were joining to form What? Records, and Tonio K. would be the first to benefit; Reunion and Geffen were forming Rode Dog to promote The Prayer Chain to mainstream audiences.[50] Whatever the report on the business of contemporary Christian music, the articles also served as commentary on the very issue of Christian music crossovers. While the rest of the music industry takes "crossover" to be a relatively straightforward term identifying a song or artist that appears on two or more of the distinct popular music charts, as it comes to be applied to the artists of contemporary Christian music, the term is significantly complicated. For many, the various sales and airplay charts are understood as social cartography: gospel and CCM charts map the realm of God; the *Billboard* Hot 100 and the like map the realm of man. Success beyond the gospel charts, then, is read by some as evidence that an artist has moved outside the realm of God. Crossover success becomes tantamount to backsliding (i.e., rejecting God).

The difficulty, at core, is the belief that the mainstream media are anathema to the Christian faith, censoring direct references to Jesus Christ and deflecting Christian values while promoting immorality. The ties between the mainstream and Christian media are understood in terms of "us and them," with crossover success entailing a betrayal of Christian ideals. This dynamic is perhaps best illustrated by the example of DeGarmo & Key, whose 1994 album *Heat It Up* (Benson) included the song "I Use the J-Word." The song claimed, "They took us off the airwaves/Banned from MTV/For taking our religion/A bit too seriously."[51] The song was a reference to an incident in 1985 in which the band's video to the song "Six, Six, Six" was rejected by MTV. While some critics claimed religious bias and pointed out that "Six, Six, Six" meshed perfectly with the videos being created by the mainstream music industry, this was, in fact, the video's downfall.[52] Emerging at a time when MTV executives were being excoriated by angry parents and the Federal Government over the level of violence found in the videos they aired, DeGarmo & Key made the mistake of including the image of a figure in flames (intended to represent the Antichrist) in their video. As a result of this "senseless violence," the video—along with a number of other videos submitted by mainstream artists that were screened by MTV at the same time—was rejected. Eventually the video was modified, with the offending scene replaced by a shot of a nuclear explosion (somehow deemed less violent by all involved), and went into light rotation on MTV.[53] Still, however, hard feelings, as typified in "I Use the J-Word," remained; and for many, the experience of DeGarmo & Key regarding "Six, Six, Six" presents clear evidence of an anti-Christian bias in the mainstream entertainment media. Ultimately, such experiences led to the conclusion on the part of many individuals that a true Christian crossover (an artist who would find mainstream success while still singing about Christian themes) was an impossibility. For separational artists like DeGarmo & Key, to replace direct references to Jesus Christ with more allegorical lyrics or to exchange songs about Christ for songs about life as informed by a Christian worldview is to sell out and produce music that is no longer authentically Christian.

Of course the belief that Christian artists must produce explicitly Christian (as defined by the separational perspective) music is not a universally held viewpoint. In many cases, efforts at promoting Christian crossovers have been explicitly rooted in more open definitions of "Christian music." What? Records was a case in point. Originally conceived as an artist-run label, What? emerged in 1986 as a joint venture between Word and A&M.[54] The goal of the label was to make music that appealed to and had value for both the mainstream and Christian markets without forcing the artists to tailor their material to satisfy or condescend to either audience.[55] Within these parameters, Word would distribute the material to the religious markets, A&M to the mainstream, and recordings would be explicitly conceived to balance precariously between the two. In the words of label chief Tom Willett,

> This is material that is not for the most part about religious topics, but it's made by Christians—and I would hazard that that's "Christian music," if you must define it. Christians need to be writing songs about all areas of the human experience, not just sin, salvation, and the Second Coming of Christ. As Christians grow in their walk with the Lord, one thing that happens is that He starts dealing with you about all aspects of your life— your relationships and finances and involvement in key social issues and your emotions and dreams and fears—and it's only right that our artists should sing about that.[56]

Despite big dreams of crossover success, What? Records released only four albums in its three-year history: Tonio K.'s *Romeo Unchained* (1986), iDEoLA's *Tribal Opera* (1987), Dave Perkins's *The Innocence* (1987), and Tonio K.'s *Romeo* follow-up, *Notes from the Lost Civilization* (1988).[57] Critically acclaimed but slow to find an audience, the albums pushed hard at the edges of Christian music without generating the mainstream profits that would have made such sins forgivable.[58] This tension peaked with *Notes from the Lost Civilization,* the label's last album. Originally a ten-song offering, the album's eighth track was a song called "What Women

Want," which began with the lines, "I know what these women want/ They want sex."[59] Despite the fact that the song went on to suggest that while women may be interested in sex—not to mention money, champagne, jewelry, and German cars—what they really wanted was love, the opening line proved too much for Word. Consequently, two versions of the album were eventually released: the original ten-song version through A&M and an abbreviated nine-song version through Word. Whatever chances for success What? Records might have had arguably disappeared with the elusive eighth track to *Notes from the Lost Civilization.*

What? Records was by no means the first, last, or only effort to bridge the gap between the Christian and pop markets. Exit Records, R.E.X., and Tooth & Nail, among others, have each staked claim to territory in the space between the Christian and mainstream media. But for every individual like Billy Ray Hearn trying to expand the boundaries of CCM, there is someone else challenging the very pursuit of success outside the safe boundaries of the evangelical community. At the extreme end of the continuum, moralist critic Jeff Godwin, who believes that "all secular Rock Music is totally under Satan's control," singles out for especially strident criticism those artists who try to straddle the fence between Christian music and mainstream pop.[60] After noting the backward writing—evidence for Godwin of Satanic influence—on the flip side of Michael W. Smith's *The Big Picture* (Reunion, 1986) album, for example, Godwin concluded that Smith had sold out: "Michael W. Smith is a product of an INDUSTRY, the 'Christian' Rock industry. Any industry ultimately translates down to one thing, the dollar sign. Many involved in CCM may be trying to serve the Lord with their heart, mind, soul, and strength . . . [but] here's the bottom line: Michael W. Smith has the same choice as all CCMers—stay in a compromised industry, or get out. Obviously, he chose to stay in, and Satan has marked him for it."[61] And while the volume and frequency of moralist objections to CCM have declined, Christian entertainers who achieve any sort of crossover success still quickly become favorite targets.

More significant than the strident complaints of critics like Godwin has been the increasing suspicion of crossover success by those working within the Christian music industry. Frequently, as in the case of Stan Moser, the Word executive who negotiated Word's first distribution deal with A&M in 1985, concern comes from those who have previously pushed CCM toward the mainstream markets. The concern for Moser is the creeping materialism he believes to have resulted from the marriage of the sacred and the secular. In Moser's words,

> During that time [the mid-1980s], I had a deep concern for what the product was saying. . . . We as an industry weren't running away from the church . . . but I do think we walked away, hoping to bring enough of the church along so we could still make a living—so we could still, basically, get rich. Materialism, a lot of it, crept in and started affecting our values . . . . Now we've built our houses, we've built our companies, and we've sold them—at great profit.
>
> We've made money—and now we're accountable to make more money for the new owners. . : . In fact, I would probably be more inclined to call the industry "commercial Christian music."[62]

There are at least two interrelated issues driving Moser's comments. On the one hand, for those who, with profits now in hand, can afford idealism, the issue is commodification—the concern that the music has been transformed through its association with mainstream record labels, distribution channels, and markets. On the other hand, for those whose futures are now tied to expectations of the mainstream music industry, the question is profitability—the long-term potential for CCM. As Neil Joseph, president of Warner Alliance, points out, there are questions about what may happen if the CCM labels owned by mainstream corporations (such as Warner Alliance) fail to see a sufficient return on their investment.[63] Should CCM not experience the anticipated surge in popularity, and, more important, in sales, the deals cut between Christian companies and their mainstream counterparts can be as easily undone in the late 1990s as they were in the early 1980s. Thus, mainstream investment can bring considerable pressure to produce sufficient returns, and critics were quick to point out the concessions they felt were being made in pursuit of mainstream success.

Particularly for those working from the assumptions of Separational CCM, the redefinition of contemporary Christian music manifested in songs such as "Baby, Baby" or "Place in This World" (never mind "What Women Want") is difficult to deny. Consequently, as they position themselves for mainstream success, whether achieving success or not, artists such as Amy Grant, Michael W. Smith, and others risk being defined by their colleagues in the Christian music industry as guilty of the same compromises that were made by the Oak Ridge Boys in the 1970s. Evangelicals are generally aware that, in the attempt to gain the world's attention, one must become respectable by the world's standards. It is also recognized that, in the process of obtaining the desired respectability, evangelicals can easily lose their distinctiveness. Blatant gospel messages are replaced with "feel good" lyrics that neither proclaim nor contradict the gospel. And while defenders argue that such music—this "sanctified entertainment," to use Styll's term—is far better than the standard pop fare, critics charge that the music has merely adapted Christ to society rather than bringing society to Christ.

Arguably, this transformation of the gospel messages of Separational CCM into the "positive pop" of Integrational CCM largely parallels R. Serge Denisoff's analysis of "protest music."[64] According to Denisoff, as protest music becomes popular, the harsh confrontational lyrics and sparse music are gradually replaced by softer and smoother lyrics and fuller, lusher music. The process of commercialization makes protest music unrecognizable as such, and the songs are no longer distinguishable from popular music more generally. Similarly, Paul Friedlander argues that the criticism of the social status quo found in the popular music of the late 1960s disappeared in favor of an emphasis on the individual, relationships, and happiness as political activity directed at ending the war dissipated.[65] Hence, individual acts of rebellion ("Rock and Roll All Night") replaced analytical thinking and collective consciousness ("Southern Man") in popular music. In a similar fashion, critics of Integrational CCM charge that these entertainers, too, have lost the distinctions that make their music "Christian."

Fundamental to such arguments is the definition of the term "minister." Within the Separational CCM framework, the term "ministry" is applied to the distinct practices of evangelism, worship, and encouragement. The challenge for Integrational CCM is not to these definitions but to their application. Simply put, the question is, What defines a minister? For many, the only requirement for ministry is an audience. Accordingly, separational artist Steve Camp (a frequent critic of the integrational approach) argues that it is the responsibility of every Christian musician to speak the "words of God": "Too many Christian musicians would say, 'I'm not a teacher. I'm not a theologian. I'm not even a minister.' Now I may not be a preacher; but I have a pulpit that maybe has 300 lights and a whole bunch of sound on it and is in front of 2,500 people on a night and those people are listening to the sermon I'm giving them through music

. . . . These guys have a responsibility to talk to these kids as if they were speaking the very words of God themselves in their theology."[66]

There are those who disagree with such a position. Leonard Payton wonders how it is "that every Tom, Harry, and Mary is teaching now that he/she has a guitar and knows three chords."[67] For Payton, no fan of contemporary Christian music (or at least its incorporation into the church), the presumption that the presence of an audience makes one a minister is absurd. Ultimately, even those who choose to adopt such a position find it to be fraught with tension. So even in the above interview Camp starts to backpedal slightly, attempting to leave some room for "entertainers" like Amy Grant. "I don't think everyone has a ministry," Camp claims. "I don't think Amy Grant has a ministry, but I think she touches a lot of people for the Lord. I believe Amy's gift is one of comforting. She is a comforter so she writes more about the compassion and love of Jesus."[68] Thus, on the one hand we have those who minister, and on the other those who "touch people for the Lord." The difference between the two is less than obvious. Similar waffling comes from John W. Styll who first defends Amy Grant's music as "sanctified entertainment" (1986), then argues that such music should no longer be labeled Christian (1987), and then returns to the belief that the industry should again be "Enlarging the Vision of Contemporary Christian Music" (1992).[69] The point here is not to criticize thinkers like Camp and Styll for their inconsistency—in the words of Ralph Waldo Emerson, "A foolish consistency is the hobgoblin of little minds, adored by little statesmen and philosophers and divines"[70]— but rather to point out the problematic nature of determining how in fact the term "ministry" is to be applied. Given the widespread presumption that contemporary Christian music is a music ministry, then each new development within the genre, be it the success of Amy Grant or the failure of What? Records, will bring with it new definitions as to what precisely that equation entails. And in those moments when ministry is most narrowly defined, when it seems that "as today's Christian music . . . become[s] more and more sophisticated, it . . . [loses] much of its distinctiveness from secular music," artists who hold to integrational assumptions will be characterized as having compromised the higher calling of CCM.[71]

While the occasional "What Women Want" or "Baby, Baby" results in criticism that suggests that CCM is no better than mainstream pop music, Integrational CCM is far more frequently criticized as simply being too ambiguous in its presentation of Christian ideas or ideals. Specifically, listening to Debbie Boone sing "You Light Up My Life," André Crouch "I'll Be Thinking of You," or the Youth Choir "Anyone But You," one could understand the lyrics either to be about God or about a more earthly companion. Complaining about such songs, Bud Bultman wrote in a 1982 *HIS* magazine editorial: "I refuse to listen to one more Jesus-is-my-girlfriend song. You know the kind. You can substitute Mandy or Barbara Ann for Jesus and the rest of the lyrics still make perfect sense."[72] To be fair to the artists, however, it should be recognized that such ambiguity is as much a result of the evangelical subculture as it is any sort of duplicity on the part of the songwriters. First, evangelical Christianity defines God less as an omnipotent other than as a personal being with whom one interacts as with a best friend. It is this personalization of God that sits at the heart of such ambiguity and allows for both the short hop of Ray Charles from "Talking about Jesus" to "Talking about You" and the notion of Jesus-is-my-girlfriend songs. It should be noted as well that rock critics often contribute to the problem, educating listeners to blur the lines between songs directed to God and songs directed toward other human beings. Thus, Wilfrid Mellers argues that Bob Dylan's "I Believe in You" is "addressed at once to the woman and to Jesus."[73] In a similar vein, critic T.L. Faris's review of The Choir's *Circle Slide* (Myrrh, 1990) argues that "'Sentimental Song' emphasizes the commitments of familial love . . . [but] is as much a song of a Savior's love for all people as it is of one person's love for another."[74] However valid such interpretations may be, they further blur the already indistinct lines between songs about God and songs about humans. So, with critics presenting their ambiguous interpretations and songwriters employing the ambiguous "you" (as well as homonyms such as "sun" and "Son" and doubly-coded words like "rock"), one set of listeners can find evidence for explicit statements of faith and others can find expressions of disbelief in the very same lyric, the particular choice usually being determined by each listener's evaluation of the artist's "walk with God."[75] Regardless of the underlying causes, for those operating under the assumptions of Separational CCM, this ambiguous phrasing is a clear compromise of one's calling to minister. The prevalence of such songs has thus led to concern on the part of producers, distributors, critics, and audiences with what some dismissed as the "Jesus count"—how often a particular song or album made explicit reference to Jesus Christ. As one artist puts it, "If you say Jesus a lot . . . you'll definitely sell more albums."[76] Albums with the highest "Jesus count" are frequently the biggest sellers in the Christian bookstore distribution system, while those with low counts are equally often viewed with suspicion.

Another quagmire for integrational entertainers is self-promotion. How far can a Christian group go in pursuing celebrity status and/or taking advantage of that celebrity status before encountering the wrath of the evangelical subculture? Can one legitimately be both a Christian and a celebrity? The issues may seem trivial today, but in the early eighties, self-promotion was a serious matter. In 1982, Mark Hollingsworth of Benson Records (at the time the parent label of such popular CCM artists as Daniel Amos, Don Francisco, Phil Keaggy, and the Joe English Band) voiced his opinion that Christian musicians should avoid much of the commercial accoutrements that are typically sold by secular rock stars: "It concerns me when there's a Christian band that has T-shirts or belt buckles with their name on them. . . . To me, that kind of promotion is going to extremes. Christ preached moderation, and I don't see anything wrong with promoting a group. But let's not have yo-yos with their names on them and that kind of thing."[77]

If this weren't enough for the young industry to struggle with, some critics charged that full-page ads in *Contemporary Christian Music* were "hype," a misuse of resources, and evidence of growing "secularization." With astounding naïveté, such critics claimed that "if the artists are good, both musically and lyrically, Christians will buy their product and then, in turn, tell others and so on. . . . *Christians will buy Christian albums.*"[78] Clearly, integrational entertainers had to traverse a minefield of potential criticism for virtually every conceivable decision.

In the face of criticism that their focus is on celebrity, their songs too ambiguous, their music watered down, and that they compromise the mission of contemporary Christian music, Christians who wished to produce music that could cross over to the pop charts were forced to escape the rationales of Separational CCM—evangelism, praise, exhortation—and create their own justifications for the type of music they were making. Three rationales have emerged as the principal defense of Integrational CCM: first, the music is argued to be a wholesome alternative to the hedonism inherent in most popular music ("sanctified entertainment"); second, Christian artists working as mainstream entertainers are claimed to be potential witnesses to those working in the music industry, living a godly Christian life before them and witnessing through example; and finally, Integrational CCM is believed to be valuable because it provides a commentary on everyday life from a Christian perspective and thus serves to articulate a Christian worldview.

Integrational CCM's First Rationale: A Wholesome Alternative

Defending *Unguarded,* Amy Grant at one point argued that one of her goals had been "to make a record that musically would fit right between Madonna and Huey Lewis . . . [but would] say something deeper than 'Hey, pull down your pants, I'm going to show you what love really is.'"[79] So, while critics questioned the perceived lack of explicit gospel messages and pointed accusing fingers at Grant's leopard-skin jacket, Grant, along with her defenders, attempted to divert such criticism by pointing to the likes of Madonna in her bustier and generally implying that things could be a whole lot worse. Whether intended as such or not, Grant's words are essentially an ultimatum offered to record-buying Christians and especially record-buying Christian parents: You can buy into Madonna, decked out in her bra and rosaries and singing "Like a Virgin," or you can buy into Amy Grant, leopard-print jacket and all, singing "Find a Way." And even though Grant was the first to articulate it, she was not the last to benefit from such comparisons. Throughout the eighties and nineties, Christian audiences have been routinely presented with such choices: A bestubbled George Michael singing "I Want Your Sex" or a bestubbled Michael W. Smith singing "You're Alright"? Nirvana singing "Smells Like Teen Spirit" or The Prayer Chain singing "Shine"? Toad the Wet Sprocket singing "Hold Her Down" or Jars of Clay singing "Flood"? Consequently, while some might disapprove of the aesthetic and theological moves that the integrational artists were making, such critics were generally forced to admit that the resulting music was at least better than the alternatives.

As with the Jesus-is-my-girlfriend dilemma, where beliefs about the nature of God led to potentially ambiguous songs about Him, a number of conditions combined to give the argument that CCM was a wholesome alternative to mainstream pop music more than a little persuasive force among many evangelicals. The essential precondition is noted by Randall Balmer, who writes in *Mine Eyes Have Seen the Glory: A Journey into the Evangelical Subculture of America,* "I'm not sure there is any way I could document this, but I suspect that the greatest fear that haunts evangelical parents is that their children will not follow in their footsteps, that they will not sustain the same level of piety as their parents—stated baldly, that they are headed for hell rather than heaven."[80] Such fears can easily be exacerbated by the listening and purchasing habits of evangelical teens. Informal studies done by Word in the mid-1980s, for example, determined that roughly 40 percent of evangelical youth had never heard of Amy Grant, and, perhaps more important, that fans of bands like Petra "are buying five or six secular albums by people like Def Leppard, Journey, or Led Zeppelin for every Petra LP they buy."[81] In this context, "better than the alternative" often seemed good enough. The music might not sound all that different to adults, but for many parents—even those who don't find mainstream rock and roll to be necessarily satanic—the Christian label implies at least some church sanction for the music.

Of course, in many ways the arguments made by Grant and others regarding the status of CCM as a wholesome alternative to mainstream pop were nothing new. And while the move would ultimately prove to be extraordinarily limiting for the Christian artists, the argument came to be codified (if unknowingly) by the industry as whole. Reviews, for example, have throughout the history of CCM routinely positioned albums relative to what were perceived to be the secular soundalikes. Bruce Brown's 1984 review of Daniel Amos' *Vox Humana* (Refuge) describes the album to be "rife with quotations from the Beatles, Beach Boys, and Buffalo Springfield. Taylor's quirky melodic hooks are reminiscent of Lindsey Buckingham (Fleetwood Mac) and Ric Ocasek (The Cars)."[82] Reviewing 4•4•1's *Sacrifice* (Broken, 1988) four years later, Sheree Marion argues that "in *Sacrifice* 4•4•1 trek beyond the parameters of their previous record's stark, U2ish sound, and seemingly borrow from the spacious art rock of Simple Minds as well as the zesty harmonious pop of Crowded House."[83] More recently, Michael Ciani's review of Sunday Drive's self-titled debut suggests the album "could be characterized as rather Hootie and the Blowfish-esque."[84] In a similar fashion, Scott Thunder compares the ska band Supertones to The English Beat and Rancid, and Tiffany Arbuckle, lead singer for Plumb, has been described as bringing "a vocal delivery that isn't terribly different from the most prominent of today's female singers (Alanis Morissette, Jewel, Garbage's Shirley Manson)."[85] Unfortunately, if intended to illustrate the quality of contemporary Christian music by placing it in a context where it could be favorably judged against the standards of mainstream popular music and mainstream popular music criticism rather than by the standards of Christian charity, such reviews often had the reverse effect. Tiffany Arbuckle didn't hold her own against Morissette, Jewel, and Manson, but rather was a Christian alternative to them. Sunday Drive wasn't equal to Hootie and the Blowfish; the band was an overtly Christian version of them. As one writer at *Rolling Stone* attests, the "wholesome alternative" of Christian rock has come to "serve as a convenient connect-the-dots guide to the modern-rock landscape."[86]

Supported either intentionally or unwittingly by artists and reviewers, the tendency to map contemporary Christian music onto the broader landscape of mainstream popular music was eventually reified in the various "Christian equivalent" charts that first emerged in the mid-1980s. Paul Baker's 1985 update to *Why Should the Devil Have All the Good Music?* (the more mundanely titled, *Contemporary Christian Music: Where It Came From, What It Is, Where It's Going*) included as an appendix a table characterizing the current generation of CCM bands not only in terms of musical genre but also in terms of similar mainstream bands.[87] Arkangel was compared to King Crimson and Jethro Tull, Scott Wesley Brown to Barry Manilow, Steve Camp to Paul Young, Jackson Browne and Kenny Loggins, and so forth. With the book's publication came a flood of requests to the publisher for permission to reprint the chart.[88] Today, the chart, or at least an equivalent, can be found on the World Wide Web.[89] Given this training, it should not be surprising that many letters to the Christian music magazines and postings to the Usenet newsgroup rec.music.christian frequently seek help in identifying Christian bands that sound like the writer's mainstream favorites. Consequently, while originally designed to further the cause of integrational artists attempting to move outside the evangelical subculture as well as to further the cause of Christian music more generally, the argument that positioned CCM as the wholesome alternative to mainstream rock ultimately had a far more powerful effect: those artists unable to break into the mainstream and thus develop an independent identity were largely consigned to being "the Christian Talking Heads," "the Christian Van Halen," "the Christian . . . ."

Integrational CCM's Second Rationale: Articulating a Christian Worldview

In the face of continued debate concerning their "sanctified entertainment," integrational artists developed a second rationale in defense of their music that went beyond merely arguing that CCM, regardless of its

specific content, was better than the alternative.[90] Still comparing themselves to their mainstream counterparts, the artists formulated a new justification for their music by suggesting that, rather than being a "watered
down gospel," the pop music made by integrational Christians provided a
commentary on everyday life from a Christian perspective, thus articulating something of a Christian worldview. Integrational CCM was no longer
defined only in terms of absence—the absence of songs promoting sexual
immorality, drug use, and so forth—but in terms of presence: the presence of a viable Christian message.

Though not writing exclusively or even explicitly on contemporary
Christian music, two of Christianity's more frequently cited cultural critics, Franky Schaeffer (son of Francis Schaeffer) and Hans Rookmaaker,
have both argued that, in dealing with the fine arts from a Christian perspective, it is important to consider the artist's entire body of work rather
than expect a single work to convey the totality of that individual's
worldview.[91] No one album or one song should be taken as a definitive
expression of the artist's identity. They further suggest that the Christian
life extends beyond the Four Spiritual Laws.[92] Christians work, Christians
play, Christians fall in love, Christians fall out of love. Like everyone else,
Christians find life fulfilling at times and frustrating at others. Christians
face the same life experiences as all humans and should, in this view, have
the freedom to express those experiences. So John Fischer charges that
rather than creating an alternative subculture or a Christian version of
everything in the wider culture, Christian music should "infuse the world
with the light and salt of your faith in Christ" while addressing the whole
of life. "Your lens is much too small," Fischer writes. "Your music should
be more like the Bible. If the Bible touches all of life—its consistencies
and inconsistencies, its ups and downs, its joys and fears—and through
the whole of it points to the redemption of Jesus, then your music should
do the same."[93] John Styll echoes these views, though for different reasons. In a view particularly consistent with the integrational approach,
Styll claims that "to the extent that Christian artists restrict their vision to
devotional topics, their impact outside the Christian subculture will be
minimal."[94] The issue is, therefore, at least in part one of relevance. However, perhaps realizing that relevance offers a shaky foundation at best for
the views he's expressing, Styll goes on to suggest that dealing with life
more broadly is in fact a moral imperative for the Christian artist. Drawing
on the work of Rookmaaker, Frank Gaebelein, Leland Ryken, Francis

Schaeffer, and others, Styll argues that "Christian artists must address the issues of everyday life in addition to devotional subjects in order to avoid the trap of the unbiblical concept of sacred and secular."[95] Attempting to separate music into the sacred and secular is, he suggests, heresy. The problem lies not only with the artists, and Styll concludes his argument by charging that "Christian audiences should free themselves to enjoy any artistic expression which offers a biblical view of reality."[96]

Obviously, not everyone subscribes to such views, and Christian music fans have proven particularly hard to convince. Too much talk about falling in love and too little talk about the need for a personal relationship with Jesus Christ is evidence to many fans that an artist is "backsliding"— less vigorously pursuing his or her Christian faith (if still pursuing it at all). Not surprisingly, Amy Grant has been a frequent subject of such complaints. In a letter to *Contemporary Christian Music*, one fan charges that "it is the Amy supporters who leave their faith at home and their Bibles in the pews, creating a false dichotomy between faith and action."[97] Turning Styll's argument on its head, the writer continues: "I . . . am not saying that each song must be explicitly 'Christian.' I am saying that the issuance of a compact disc . . . is the espousal of some type of philosophy. That philosophy will either be Christian or anti-Christian. As someone has said, 'There is no neutrality. Jesus eliminated all neutrality at the cross.'"[98] Assuming the writer is correct and there is no neutrality, the difficulty still lay in identifying the line between the Christian and anti-Christian. And as numerous artists discovered, the issue went well beyond the question of "spiritual" lyrics. Continuing his argument, the above-noted letterwriter suggests that "there is more truth in John Cougar Mellencamp's 'Scarecrow' than is deducible from the insipid *Heart in Motion*" and further accuses Grant of "unbiblical irrationality" and "anti-intellectualism."[99] Thus, the problem here is not that Grant's songs aren't Christian; it is that they are rooted in emotions rather than logic. In another example, Gene Eugene of the band Adam Again responds to those who criticize his move toward more ambiguous lyrics by claiming, "I certainly don't fear 'God-phrases.' I have a thing about not writing the same song twice. Some fans of our band would like us to just kind of do the same thing all the time, because that's what made them happy when they first got saved."[100] Here the problem isn't the particular nature of the shift (from songs about God to songs about life) but change in general. As Eugene sees it, Christian music fans simply oppose things that differ from what they are used to.

"I am very disappointed in you," a fan once wrote to Amy Grant, "because of the video with Peter Cetera. You looked like a sleaze." Discussing the letter, Grant defended herself against the accusation, suggesting that, while the video represented a stretch, it wasn't a sinful stretch. Christians, Grant claimed, "sometimes . . . prefer that we all walk around like a Barbie and Ken. You know, with no real flesh. But I am not Barbie, and I don't want to be married to Ken."[101] It was imagery that would prove useful to the artists of Integrational CCM. Emphasizing their membership in the category of human being, these artists argued that their music spoke to the human condition. Life couldn't be divided into the sacred and secular, and to focus only on the spiritual was to miss much of the experience of contemporary Christianity. For many, the debate ultimately emerged as a line in the sand. Describing her move out of the "close-minded parameters" imposed on artists by the Christian music industry, Margaret Becker suggests that you "draw a line and those who are with you will step with you over it. . . . And those who do not, you do not in your heart of hearts need to speak to, and they do not need to hear from you."[102] Believing their songs offered a valuable commentary on life from a Christian viewpoint, more and more integrational artists drew more and more such lines. Sometimes the fans crossed over; sometimes they did not.

Integrational CCM's Third Rationale: Witnessing to Industry Insiders

When seeking the approval of the evangelical subculture, one sure way to win support is by claiming that what you do serves the cause of evangelism. In their articulation of a third rationale for their music, integrational artists, fans, and critics did just that. While mainstream popular culture pays tribute to the gods of money, sex, power, and self, integrational artists claim to offer their audience an opportunity to listen to and identify with entertainers who represent more traditional values. Amplifying this, Christian art critic Hans Rookmaaker argues that this process of taking part in the world's activity frequently amounts to what he characterizes as "pre-evangelism," or "seed planting," which may eventually lead to later conversion.[103] Clearly an effort to recast Integrational CCM within the light of evangelicalism's focus on proselytizing, Rookmaaker's move is extended, albeit in a slightly different direction, by those integrational artists who claim that the audience for their evangelistic messages is not the same as the audience for their music. Again picking up the label of "minister" (or at least "evangelist"), some working within the realm of Integrational CCM argue that their pulpit is not found on stage but in recording studios and board rooms. In other words, they sing to the masses but minister to their coworkers. In an industry where Christian influences are perceived to be negligible, defenders of Integrational CCM claim that Christian entertainers have the potential to have significant influence.

The move to present Integrational CCM artists as potential witnesses to music industry movers and shakers has been made most explicitly by Michael W. Smith. After a series of three successful praise-and-worship albums, Smith found himself positioned as the male Amy Grant with 1986's *The Big Picture* (Reunion), an album modeled on the anthem rock/radio pop hybrids of *Unguarded*. Described by some as "sound[ing] like contemporary Christian music" and by others as "a crafty, pop masterpiece that raised the technical standards of Christian music but . . . [was] ahead of its time," *The Big Picture* failed to generate much mainstream interest.[104] But where *The Big Picture* failed, Smith's 1990 follow-up *Go West Young Man* (Reunion) proved a bona fide, if unexpected, mainstream hit. Claiming "I didn't try to make songs to get on pop radio, I just made a record" with *Go West Young Man,* Smith turned from pop-rock to adult contemporary—and to mainstream stardom.[105] "Place in This World" became both Reunion Records' and Smith's first pop hit, climbing to number six on *Billboard*'s Hot 100 and number five on *Radio and Records'* CHR chart. A second single, "For You," was also a top-ten adult contemporary single on mainstream radio; and in *Billboard*'s year-end charts, Smith was listed among the Top 15 Pop Singles Artists (Male) and in the Top 25 Adult Contemporary Artists. Then came 1992's *Change Your World* (Reunion), an album that shipped gold (a rare event in the Christian music industry) and spawned three hit singles: "Picture Perfect," number one on Adult Contemporary charts; "Somebody Love Me," number eight on *Radio and Records'* Adult Contemporary chart; and "I Will Be Here for You," which rose to the top fifteen on Contemporary Hit Radio.[106] As a result of *Change Your World,* Smith was recognized as Best New Adult Contemporary Artist by the American Music Awards and as one of the "50 Most Beautiful People" by *People* magazine.[107]

In the wake of this success, Smith almost singlehandedly developed another rationale for Integrational CCM. While steadfastly maintaining that his desire is to reach out to kids and teenagers and at the same time denying any desire to be a "superstar" or have a music "career"—goals that would elicit suspicions in the eyes of Separational CCM fans—with his move into adult contemporary music, Smith arguably lost much of the youth audience such claims depended on. Consequently, although still speaking passionately about his desire to support his teen fans, Smith also began to stress the idea that people in the music industry need to hear the gospel just like everyone else.[108] According to Smith, "There's this whole other culture that you totally forget about, but that's who needs the gospel. . . . A lot of these people [at mainstream radio stations] were going, 'There's something different about you,' and then they'd want to know about my walk with Christ and I'd share it. I had earned the right to speak into their lives. . . . All you gotta do is love them and don't come on heavy handed. Just walk it out, and they will see Christ in you."[109] Describing such interactions in numerous interviews, Smith claimed that "just from 'Place in This World' being a hit, [there are] all these little opportunities I've gotten to really share my faith with people."[110]

Undoubtedly, this new rationale for Integrational CCM is surprisingly close to the separational rationale of evangelism, though with key differences. Emphasis here is on a personal witness through lifestyle and behavior as opposed to a verbal testimony conveyed through music. Still more significant, the audience for the music is no longer the audience for the message. At the same time, however, as with Separational CCM, the Christian commission to make disciples of all nations is still being used to justify the musical product. Therefore, it is not surprising that the separational rationale that demands evangelism through music is often reintroduced into the integrational rubric. If Smith, for example, is now witnessing predominantly to those in the studios who find "something different" about him, such efforts do not come at the expense of "reaching out to the kids."[111] In another example, André Crouch, one of the earliest contemporary Christian music artists (and one who faced considerable criticism when he recorded an album for Warner Brothers in the early 1980s), advises integrational artists to be witnesses through their music, if only occasionally. "If you want to sing rock 'n' roll or whatever style of music you want to do, then do it," Crouch suggests. "If Amy Grant wants to sing a love song with Peter Cetera, do it. She has that freedom. Deniece Williams does pop music. So does Marilyn McCoo. They're all going to heaven." That said, however, Crouch also adds that

Christian musicians should also "do an occasional gospel song."[112] So while artists are, in Crouch's view, free to produce whatever type of music they like, producing an occasional gospel song will make their faith in Christ evident.

Although mainstream attention and success had long been goals of contemporary Christian music, it wasn't until Amy Grant emerged on the scene that Christian music finally found its way onto the mainstream charts. Despite mainstream ownership of religious record labels, joint distribution agreements, and, in some cases, extremely strong albums, it took this attractive young woman in a leopard-print tuxedo jacket to make Christian music a significant cultural force outside the evangelical subculture.

In the wake of Grant's success, more and more Christian artists found the door to the mainstream marketplace opening. Obviously, not all of them made it through. For every album like *Unguarded* there were a dozen like *Beat the System;* for every band like Jars of Clay, a dozen like The Prayer Chain. The failure rate, however, was a secondary issue; the effort to attract mainstream attention was alone enough to demand new rationales for the music. Christian music as conceived by integrational artists couldn't be justified by the standard rationales of evangelism, worship, or exhortation. Integrational artists thus developed new claims to justify the music they made, arguing that their music provided a wholesome alternative to mainstream offerings and presented a Christian worldview to the astute listener. Furthermore, mainstream success opened doors to the people behind the scenes that would otherwise remain closed. Christian artists could influence culture by witnessing to those creating it. In many ways, however, these new rationales emerged as a concession to the ingrained separational orientation of the Christian music industry. While separational artists conceived of their music solely in terms of its utility for evangelism, worship, and Christian exhortation, integrational artists were moving as far as possible toward an aesthetic rooted in ontology. Music was valuable simply because it existed; the purpose of mushrooms is to be mushrooms, wine to be wine, and music simply to be music. Drawing on the work of writers like Franky Schaeffer, integrational artists dismissed the obsession with utility, claiming that "Christian art" no more exists than do "Christian bricks" and that attempting to justify art "by tacking on a few Christian slogans at the end to somehow redeem them" merely trivializes the work.[113] Responding to the separational critique of her positive pop, Amy Grant wondered, "At what point in time did we have to become the Lyric Police? I mean, is it because we are the makers and sellers of music that suddenly we're the police? Can't we just say, 'It moves me. It's really pretty. But it's not my life experience'?"[114] Taking these arguments a step further, the artists of Transformational CCM wondered if the music even needed to be pretty.

Interlude:
The 77's

The club sits at the south end of Seattle's Capitol Hill. It is early on a cold, clear evening, and people are lined up at the door. No one seems to know what to do.

While the denim, leather, and flamboyant hairstyles worn by those in line suggest this to be just another group of Seattle bar hoppers, their behavior reveals them to be something else altogether. And indeed, it is not one of Seattle's over-hyped grunge bands playing at Moe's tonight but rather a little-known act from Sacramento with strong ties to the Christian music audience. So, with tickets that were purchased from the local Christian bookstores that declare a 9:00 P.M. start time, this collection of evangelicals and other Christians have descended on Moe's. It is a stark contrast of cultures: on the one hand, an audience unused to the character of the Seattle nightlife; on the other, a club staff not sure what to do with an audience that a) buys tickets ahead of time, b) expects the show to start on time, c) lines up early, and d) for the most part won't buy drinks.

It is after nine o'clock when the staff offers a small concession to the increasingly restless crowd and opens the outer doors, allowing the line to move forward into the lobby of the building. Finally, the crowd is grudgingly allowed to fill the staging area. They respond to the opening of the doors by nearly trampling each other as they search for a place to stand. It's a small room—probably not more than thirty by thirty feet—but does have a balcony, which, like the floor below, is soon packed with eager 77's fans who are once again made to wait. Sometime after ten o'clock, Springchamber takes the stage for a forty-minute set. A local favorite generating a lot of interest among those who follow CCM's underground scene, the band has clearly brought friends, and the crowd responds quite favorably to the energetic lead singer bouncing across the stage in his love beads and bare feet. Still, it's clear from their reactions that most are here to see The 77's.

The 77's. (Photograph courtesy of Myrrh Records.)

After a brief equipment change (the musicians themselves handling the gear) and a few more minutes of waiting, The 77's take the stage as the crowd goes wild. Frontman Mike Roe starts in on the first number, and the crowd immediately falls in sync. Driven by Roe's guitar, the music is loud and chunky. The band may hail from Sacramento, but the music meshes perfectly with the Seattle sound currently nearing the height of its popularity. Even the ringing, keyboard-driven pop numbers from the band's earlier days are performed here with a heavy dose of distorted guitars and a bass-heavy bottom end. Nevertheless, few in the crowd seem to mind the changes, and most exuberantly add their voices to what are for them familar and favorite choruses.

Moving through both new and old material, the band eventually pauses, and Roe addresses the crowd. "People have complained," he admits, "that we don't play enough hymns." The statement is as close as Roe will come to identifying The 77's as a "Christian band." "Well," Roe continues, "tonight we're going to play some." With that, he steps back from the mike and begins to play. The crowd waits in anticipation as the vaguely familiar notes begin to emerge from the speakers. Still playing, Roe steps to the mike and begins to wail. Suddenly, the band kicks in, and the crowd goes wild. In a nearly perfect imitation of Robert Plant, Roe starts to sing, "It's nobody's fault but mine." Few of those waving their arms and dancing in place seem to find it ironic that, while The 77's have often been presented as evidence for the authenticity of rock and roll as written and performed by Christians, it is the band's performance of warmed-over Led Zeppelin that has most affected the audience at Moe's.

4 Transformational CCM: "It's Art"

When the flush of a new-born sun first fell on Eden's green and gold,
Our father Adam sat under the Tree and scratched with a stick in the mould;
And the first rude sketch that the world had seen was joy to his mighty heart,
Till the Devil whispered behind the leaves, "It's pretty, but is it Art?"
                                          Rudyard Kipling

Rooted in the assumptions of a "Christ of culture" perspective, Integrational CCM (especially in the persons of Amy Grant, Michael W. Smith, and, most recently, Jars of Clay), generated mainstream exposure for Christian music. Although still heard on the religious radio stations, the songs—or at least some of them—now also played on mainstream radio, MTV and VH-1; records were now shelved in the record and department stores; performances could be given to sold-out stadiums rather than half-empty church auditoriums. At the same time, while Integrational CCM sold mainstream audiences on Christian music, Separational CCM offered evangelical audiences religion through music. Whether a DC Talk performance at a Billy Graham Crusade, one of Carman's Vegas-like concert-cum-revivals, or Randy Stonehill backed only by his acoustic guitar and playing in a church sanctuary, the separational artists brought contemporary music to the contemporary (evangelical) religious experience. But while Integrational CCM worked to find the path to mainstream success and Separational CCM to bring back that old time religion, Transformational CCM brought something completely different to the mix. Listening to it all, the artists of Transformational CCM joined with Kipling's Devil in challenging, "But is it Art?"

Of course in many ways this question was, paradoxically enough, both completely different and nothing new. As Howard Becker notes,

The title "art" is a resource that is at once indispensable and unnecessary

to the producer of the works in question. It is indispensable because . . . if
you . . . intend to make art and want what you make recognized as art so
that you can demand the resources and advantages available to art—then
you cannot fulfill your plan if the current aesthetic system and those who
explicate and apply it deny you the title. It is unnecessary because even if
these people do tell you that what you are doing is not art, you can
usually do the same work under a different name and with the support of
a different cooperative world.[1]

The debates between the art worlds of Separational CCM and Integrational
CCM can in many ways be seen as debates over the status of art, with each
side attempting to control the resources and advantages that Becker associates with the term "art." However, at least with regard to contemporary
Christian music, there are a great many such unnecessary, indispensable,
and contestable terms—to the point that even the definition of "Christian" is itself up for debate. In fact, for the most part, the continual battle
between Separational CCM and Integrational CCM over the status of
that art called contemporary Christian music has been fought without the
term "art" ever being used. But a battle over art it has been. As described
by Becker, "Aestheticians study the premises and arguments people use to
justify classifying things and activities as 'beautiful,' 'artistic,' 'art,' 'not
art,' 'good art,' 'bad art,' and . . . construct systems with which to make
and justify both the classifications and specific instances of their application."[2] In contemporary Christian music, "Christian" is simply added to
that list. Thus, with regard to the Christian music industry as described so
far, while neither explicitly uses the term "art" in their debates with one
another, the personnel of Separational and Integrational CCM are nevertheless engaged in aesthetic classification and application. The terms may
be different—"ministry," "evangelism," "Christian," etc.—but the activity is the same. What makes Transformational CCM different, and significantly so, is that, while neither Integrational nor Separational CCM makes
an explicit and self-conscious claim for "art," Transformational CCM does
so emphatically. Separational CCM and Integrational CCM may each have
its own distinct aesthetic, but both avoid characterizing it as such. With
Transformational CCM, however, contemporary Christian music is no
longer approached as a religious tool or as entertainment; it's art.

Transformational CCM's introduction of explicit aesthetic concerns
to the realm of Christian music is perhaps most obvious in discussions of
the life and music of Mark Heard. With his premature death from a heart

attack in 1992 (at age forty-one), Heard emerged as a sort of patron saint for the artists of Transformational CCM. Where Separational CCM had Keith Green, Transformational CCM now had Heard. If the relationships are analogous, however, the discourse surrounding the two men is quite different, with Heard positioned as a modern-day Van Gogh to Green's Ezekiel. So, explaining their reasons for contributing to a tribute album for Heard (*Strong Hand of Love* [Fingerprint, 1994]), nineteen musicians variously describe Heard as "sensitive," "distinctive," "original," "honest," "irreverent," "abrasive," "obsessive," "obscure," "subtle," "brilliant," "scathing," "intense," and assign him the roles of "genius," "artist" (comparing him to Rembrandt as well as Van Gogh), and "prophet."[3] While these words alone suggest a distinct approach to understanding Christian music, there are additional aspects to Heard's mystique that identify key assumptions of Transformational CCM. For example, Heard is routinely distanced from commercial success, both as a matter of historical record— Heard's albums were never significant commercial successes, even for CCM—and personal desire and commitment. Pat Terry claims: "I remember him telling me one time that he tried to write some commercial pop songs one time. And I heard 'em and they were actually quite good. And he told me he couldn't sleep at night after he did it. . . . I think that tells you something about Mark's perspective on things. I don't think he was ever comfortable unless he was writing really honestly and stuff that he cared deeply about."[4] Through tales such as Terry's, Heard is clearly positioned as the quintessential artist: someone with the talent to be monetarily successful should he be willing to compromise his creative output to the demands of the marketplace but at the same time morally opposed to doing so. In John Fischer's words, Heard "had to write 'what came out'" regardless of the opinions of others. Heard's life and songwriting, Fischer claims, were "a simple call to integrity in light of a market inundated by other concerns—what sells, what will make a hit, what people feel comfortable with, what happens to be popular at the time."[5] According to Fischer, Terry, and numerous others, it was only his commitment to his art—his integrity—that prevented Heard from becoming a star.

Heard's opposition to the commercial marketplace exhausts neither his artistic credentials nor his importance for Transformational CCM. Returning to the comparison with Green, it is important to note that, while both have occasionally been assigned the label "prophet," the labels work quite differently in the two cases. In a separational context, the prophet

(Green) is generally perceived to be a mere channel through whom God speaks; it is God's voice that is heard in the prophet's song. Heard's role as prophet, however, is dependent less on the perception that God spoke through him than on his ability to express key elements of the human condition—for having "felt too much, cared too much and known too much."[6] So, if listeners claimed to hear the voice of God in Green's music, in Heard's music they claimed to hear their own. Heard emerged as some- one who could say all the things listeners would like to say if only they could find the words. Thus Heard is seen as a prophet because he was able to tap into what were perceived to be universal truths regarding the hu- man condition. Arguably, it is this ability to connect—this authenticity— that is at the core of Heard's mystique. Hence the cover of *High Noon* (Fingerprint/Myrrh, 1993). Released posthumously as a quasi–greatest- hits album—the album drew primarily from Heard's three final records, ignoring all his work prior to 1990 but containing three previously unreleased tracks and his contribution to the *At the Foot of the Cross* project—*High Noon* is perhaps most notable for its front and back covers: two photographs of Heard wearing a T-shirt emblazoned with the image of Hank Williams. Whatever the intent of the producers and art director, the images clearly worked to associate Heard with the country music icon. As described by Richard Leppert and George Lipsitz, Hank Williams was "an extraordinary artist, a songwriter with a gift for concise yet powerful expression, and a singer with exceptional phrasing and drama"; someone "heard as 'authentic' at a time when authenticity was a prime determinant in the success of in-person and radio performers."[7] The description could just as easily be applied to Heard. Largely ignored in life, as the attempt to associate him with Hank Williams suggests, in death Mark Heard became the focal point for efforts to position Christian music as authentic expres- sions of genuine human experience.[8] And what was said of Williams could be said of Heard: "Millions of fans could feel that he 'wrote their lives' because, even when they did not know him, they could feel that he knew the places they had been."[9]

Perhaps not surprisingly, in the same way that Heard came to be posi- tioned relative to Hank Williams, numerous Christian musicians began to position themselves relative to Heard.[10] Preparing their eight-song demo to be released as the full-fledged if self-distributed album *Kissers and Kill- ers* (ICCD, 1993), The Choir remixed one song "to protect the accor- dion part played by the late Mark Heard."[11] And although that band's longtime association with Heard made the move seem a genuine tribute,

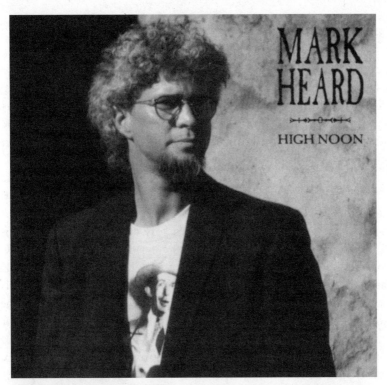

The association of Heard with Hank Williams, Sr. in the cover art of *High Noon* (Fingerprint/Myrrh, 1993) seemed intended to imbue Heard with the musical authenticity embodied by the late country music star. (Used by permission of Fingerprint Records.)

not every attempt to connect with Heard could be characterized as such. The fact that the *Strong Hand of Love* tribute album included covers from artists who "did not know Mark and [were] unfamiliar with his work and perspective" made the album seem to some less a tribute than an effort to capitalize on Heard's newfound audience—an impression reaffirmed by the fact that the album was eventually expanded into a two-disc collection and reissued as 1996's *Orphans of God* (Fingerprint).[12] Whatever the particular motives of those involved, these attempts to associate Christian music and musicians with Heard are most important in that they illustrate the significant role that Heard came to play within a particular subset of the Christian music industry, that subset here called Transformational CCM. Simply put, emerging as the quintessential Christian artist, Mark Heard became the central figure to an art world that defined itself explicitly and self-consciously in terms of art. The values that Heard was claimed to personify—the refusal to sell out to commercial concerns, the ability to tap into and express the human condition, the obsession with authenticity—were the values the musicians of the Transformational CCM art world hoped would be associated with their music. Heard was not producing religious tools or entertainment; he was creating art. The artists of Transformational CCM want the same to be said of them.

The claim that those working in the realm of Transformational CCM intend, above all else, to create art begs a significant question: How do such individuals define "art"? There is no single answer. For some, the term is clearly little more than a stylistic notation, one most frequently used to describe so-called "alternative" rock music. At risk of seeming absurdly reductive, the claim often appears to be that if it's played in a minor key, it's art. For others, "art" is a product of commercial success— or more specifically, a lack thereof. The presumption here is that if something sells, it can't be art. In another popular approach, art is defined in terms of agreement, "art" being that which the listener agrees with on some level—personally, politically, theologically, etc. Naturally, there are more rigorous and nuanced definitions of art within Transformational CCM, though for obvious reasons they are generally not articulated as frequently as the more simplistic approaches described above. For purposes here, however, the precise definition of the term is ultimately irrelevant. Far more significant is the turn to the concept of art, however it may be defined, as a justification for making music. If, as Bultman has suggested, contemporary Christian music in general is tame and innocuous, demanding nothing and requiring no response, Transformational CCM endeavors to be something altogether different.[13] However art is defined, the artists of Transformational CCM largely work to produce music that by its nature, in one way or another, challenges and confronts, making the listener face uncomfortable truths. And while the level of success in this endeavor is certainly open to debate—as much as Transformational CCM attempts to avoid the particular formulas of Integrational and Separational CCM, it often proves equally formulaic in its own right—it is the effort that is crucial. This effort is rooted in the transformational artists' distinct understanding of Christianity and their assumptions about the proper relationship between Christ and culture.

Niebuhr's "Christ As Transformer of Culture"

If Separational CCM can be connected to what Niebuhr labels the "Christ against culture" position and Integrational CCM the "Christ of culture," Transformational CCM is the product of a mediation between these two extremes. Specifically, there are three possible positions that Niebuhr claims to exist between the poles. He labels these "Christ above culture," "Christ and culture in paradox," and "Christ the transformer of culture."[14] All three can be seen at work in the rationales of Transformational CCM.

In the first mediating position, the "Christ above culture" or synthesis approach, the individual at once recognizes both the separation of Christ from human culture and his or her necessary place within that culture. Christ may be separate, but humans are not. Christian living, therefore, is rooted in an ongoing struggle to maintain distinctiveness in daily life. Furthermore, it is believed that God, who ruled in the past and will rule in the future, also rules in the present. So, while broken, corrupted and fallen, the world is neither wholly evil nor wholly good and thus should be neither completely abandoned nor uncritically embraced. This approach argues that it is crucial to recognize the danger of mistaking one's own cultural understanding of the "nature of things" as God's law, accepting fleeting realities for transcendent truths. Given these assumptions, those working from this synthetic position tend to produce theologies and cosmologies that are both tentative—with any given moment potentially leading to circumstances that would demand a reworking of assumed truths—and fragmentary, since a complete understanding of God's "truth" is not possible. Betraying his synthetic beliefs, one Christian music fan wrote in a posting to the Usenet newsgroup rec.music.christian, "I live in a world of grey. I embrace this. Does it make me a relativist? Many would say yes. I feel that many of the people who say this are trying to live in a world of black and white that they create, contrary to the world around them."[15] Musician Derri Daugherty (The Choir) echoes these sentiments with his critique of traditional (separational) contemporary Christian worship music: "For me, a lot of worship albums and Maranatha! music and those kind of things represent a lot of old baggage. It seems like a lot of the lyrics are a little too milquetoast. Everything seems to make a little too much sense. God seems too easy to understand. I tried to understand him like that, and found that I couldn't. I tend to view God now as more mysterious and awe-inspiring, as opposed to best friend and buddy-buddy, I-have-access-to-you-at-any-point."[16] Working from distinct theological assumptions, Separational and Transformational CCM create two very different Gods, one benign and one unfathomable. (Attempting to understand God, suggests one transformational band, can be best compared to a gorilla's attempt to understand an earthquake.[17]) These distinct Gods lead to distinct approaches to the Christian life. So, as the artists of Transformational CCM begin to wrestle with an unexplainable God and the difficulties associated with being in the world but not of it, they do so in terms that allow them to celebrate the mysteries, contradictions, and paradoxes rather than attempting to resolve them.

Moving on to Niebuhr's second mediating position, the "Christ and culture in paradox" or dualist view, one again finds tentative responses to the issues of living in but not of the world. Specifically, it is believed that life is to be lived precariously, and even sinfully, with an eye toward the hope of justification in the life to come. Only through divine revelation does grace come, and thus it is believed that Christians are called to do the impossible when they are called to live a holy and perfect life.[18] Consequently, the Christian will inevitably and regularly fall short, necessitating that hope be placed solely in Jesus Christ, who continuously picks up the fallen and returns them to the straight-and-narrow path. In this framework, all of culture (which includes the church) is fallen and in need of restoration.[19] Daugherty reflects this position of the Christian life being a paradox of being made perfect through grace while at the same time living sinfully in the world: "Christ says, 'It is finished,' but yet it really isn't—with me, it's not finished, because I keep screwing it up, and I still have to work to get to know God more and to experience more of his grace, and so he's not through with me yet. That's one of the things that the charis-matic movement in particular wants to make very, very simple, to see in black and white where I see them as more grey."[20] Daugherty's longtime partner Steve Hindalong adds, "The discomfort is the unresolve that I personally feel as a Christian, that I think we all feel as Christians. That's the irony, the question, if it is finished, why are we still . . . [such] unhappy people? Why isn't there peace?"[21] Called to perfection, Christians are nev-ertheless trapped through their humanity in a sinful world. And from the transformational perspective, this paradox is to be acknowledged and ex-plored rather than minimized.

Finally, there is the position Niebuhr identifies as "Christ as trans-former of culture," a conversionist position in which culture, like the hu-man beings who inhabit and create it, is believed to be redeemable. Like the synthesis and dualist views, the conversionist position sees humanity and culture as fallen and sinful but not irredeemably so. Neither humanity nor culture is ultimately evil, but both are in need of redemption from their broken state. Christ, the redeemer, can transform humans in the context of their culture and society. Thus, despite the evil, sin, and pain of this world, there is hope because Christ chose to enter the world as a human being and redeem it. It is this belief in a redeemable culture, both in the underlying conception of the world and in the concomitant sugges-tion that the dark sides of life should be explored as a way of moving through them toward redemption, that most distinguishes the transfor-mational perspective from the separational "Christ against culture" ap-proach. Consequently, transformational artists such as Mark Heard have argued that presenting the pain of life rather than focusing exclusively on its joy—which is to say, offering a tranformationalist view of the world—is enough to get you "labeled" in CCM. In attempting to present a picture of Christianity that includes the brokenness of life after the fall (if at the same time offering glimpses of hope amid the rubble), transformational artists risk being marginalized by a Christian music industry dominated by the separational view that prefers clear-cut answers over hard questions. Those unwilling to present such clear-cut answers can find themselves effectively excommunicated.[22] In response, transformational artists frequently argue that painting a rosy picture of a perfect Christian life and refusing to ask the painful questions may actually do more harm than good. According to Brian Quincy Newcomb, too many "songs repeat again and again the ideals that make us feel safe, but offer little that touches the practical issues of our lives.

We do not connect at a place of need with the concerns and fears that so demolish the lives we say we want to reach."[23] And while Newcomb sees problems in such music for the non-Christian listener, Mark Heard argues that such songs are equally problematic for Christians. "Most of the time . . . [life's] just not that crystal clear," Heard claims. "People are alone and afraid, and . . . they feel [that if] it's not crystal clear like it is in all these Christian songs, then there must be something terribly screwed-up about their lives. And that's just not true."[24] Life, these artists claim, is messy.

Despite the distinctions that separate them, Niebuhr's mediating positions of synthesis, paradox, and conversion can be linked into a single, coherent approach to reconciling Christian faith with life in secular culture through their shared approach toward contemporary culture as something fallen and broken but not inherently evil and the common belief that both humanity and society must be restored to God's original purposes and intentions. Here labeled the "transformational approach," this perspective on the relationship between Christ and culture manifests itself in contemporary Christian music as a desire to use the medium to explore rather than deny or ignore the darker sides of life. Bands named Veil of Ashes, The Blamed and Mortal; albums entitled *Prints of Darkness* (Blonde Vinyl, 1991), *A Briefing for the Ascent* (Frontline, 1987), and *Shaded Pain* (Frontline, 1987); songs called "Another Day in Limbo," "Why Are All the Children Crying" and "Walls of Doubt"—if offset by a sense of hope in the "already-but-still-to-come," with Transformational CCM the separational focus on ministry and the integrational focus on producing positive pop give way to a focus on more sober themes. Often described with words like "honest," "real," "genuine," and "authentic," considered examination suggests two essential characteristics of Transformational CCM: an overwhelming reliance on personal experience as the raw material for songwriting, and an extensive effort to use music as a means for critiquing both the church and secular society. Contemporary Christian music did not escape this critical eye.

The Transformational Critique of Competing Approaches to CCM

Reduced to its simplest components, the transformational critique of competing forms of CCM rests on the built-in assumptions each contains concerning the character of God and the character of art. According to the transformational perspective, the "ministers" of Separational CCM and the "entertainers" of Integrational CCM are guilty, like the majority of modern evangelicals, of attempting to tame God.[25] According to sociologist James Davison Hunter, the contemporary evangelical understanding of God has shifted significantly from the views held by previous generations of Christians.[26] Whatever else may be said, one of the most important transformations has been the reconception of God as something (or rather, someone) familiar. God has become a being essentially like us and, consequently, available to us; Christian faith is now a matter of "knowing God."[27] Compare, then, God as described by Bill Hybels (pastor of Willow Creek, advertised as "America's largest church") and God as described by German theologian Rudolf Otto. Separated by seventy years and the Atlantic Ocean, the perspectives couldn't be more different. Hybels writes:

> I suspect that the God I know is the God you're looking for. He's not the God of your nightmares. He's not the God of a screaming, overzealous evangelist. He's not the God who eagerly waits for you to fail so He can carry out His sentence of wrath with unbound glee.
>
> On the contrary, He's a God who wants to be in an intimate relationship with you. He's the God who has orchestrated every event of your life to give you the best chance to get to know Him, so that you can experience the full measure of His love.
>
> I bet not one person in a million fully understands how much God loves him or her. One thing I can say for sure: God cares about you more than you realize.[28]

For Otto, however, the experience of God has little to do with this kind of intimacy. According to Otto, in experiencing God

> we are dealing with something for which there is only one appropriate expression, *"mysterium tremendum."* The feeling of it may at times come sweeping like a gentle tide, pervading the mind with a tranquil mood of deepest worship. It may pass over into a more set and lasting attitude of the soul, continuing, as it were, thrillingly vibrant and resonant, until at last it dies away and the soul resumes its "profane," nonreligious mood of everyday experience. It may burst in sudden eruption from the depths of the soul with spasms and convulsions, or lead to the strangest excitements, to intoxicated frenzy, to transport, and to ecstasy. It has its wild and demonic forms and can sink to an almost grisly horror and shuddering. It has its crude, barbaric antecedents and early manifestations, and

again it may be developed into something beautiful and pure and glori-
ous. It may become the hushed, trembling, and speechless humility of the
creature in the presence of—whom or what? In the presence of that which
is a *mystery* inexpressible and above all creatures.[29]

This vision of a numinous God whose "thoughts are not our thoughts"
and "whose ways are not our ways" (see Isaiah 55:8) has all but vanished
among contemporary evangelicals; along with it has disappeared the fire,
caprice, and majesty that formerly pervaded the imagery surrounding Him.

In their ongoing struggle with modernity, Hunter argues, evangelicals,
while attempting to maintain their exclusivism, have compromised at
multiple points. Under the pressures that come with seeking to participate
in a modern society, evangelicals found themselves forced to adapt—to
become more civil, rational, tolerant, familiar, and subjective. Likewise,
the perceived character of God also became predictably rational, tolerant,
familiar, and subjective; and insofar as the image of God has come to be
defined in this way, God has become domesticated in the consciousness of
evangelical Christians.[30] Artists operating under the assumptions of the
transformational perspective conclude that this is exactly what has happened to the majority of Christian music. The God it presents is less the
divine, omnipotent, and unfathomable being than the comforting best
friend who offers support in times of trouble. Hence, Kenny Marks's "Never
Been a Stranger": "My parents always spoke of You/Great to have around/
You always were my hero/I felt so safe at night/Jesus loves me this I
know/And everything's alright [*sic*]."[31] Rebecca St. James's "Side by Side":
"Everyday [*sic*] of my life, every valley I face/ I know You'll always be
there, every step I take."[32] DeGarmo & Key's "If God Is For Us (Who
Can Be Against Us)": "If you're weary, don't lose hope in fighting the
good fight/Just remember, God is with you through the night/In the
heat of battle keep your head up high/God is marching with us, He's
always at our side."[33] The Allies' "Closer Than a Brother": "You try to go
the distance/But your heart can't take the strain/I know Someone who'll
be there/To help you start again/Someone who is closer than a brother."[34]
While both views of God, the comforting supporter and unfathomable
being, could be supported by scripture (Proverbs 18:24; Psalm 23; Romans 11:33; Isaiah 55:8), the transformational perspective, generally pre-
ferring "synthetic truth" to so-called "proof texts," nevertheless characterizes
the separational view as, to borrow Richard Lovelace's term, "biblical truth
in a glaze of corn syrup."[35]

This glaze of corn syrup is argued to be of significant consequence. When God is primarily understood as one's best friend and "ever present help in trouble" (Psalm 46:1), it is easy to lose all sense of humility and become convinced that one has God's perspective—or perhaps more accurately, that God has your perspective—on every topic. The temptation, then, is to use one's art not to enter into a dialogue as artist and audience struggle to "see through a glass darkly" (1 Corinthians 13:12), but to proclaim the final, absolute answer to any and all questions. The result is the sterilization of art through ascetic moralism and oversimplified theology.[36] The world is portrayed as being two-dimensional; everything is clearly either right or wrong without shades of gray to confuse the matter. John Fischer, reflecting on the development of contemporary Christian music, argues that this arrogance about ultimate truth can easily lead artists to overlook the truth of their own sinful and broken natures. Moreover, through their nearly exclusive focus on issues and activities that they define as uniquely "spiritual," separational artists miss seeing Christ in the mundane and "the least of these" (Matthew 25:40).[37] The point is illustrated in an oft-repeated story used by Catholic theologian Henri Nouwen to illustrate how Christians, in their fervor to experience Christ through biblical exegesis, may well miss him in daily experience:

One day a young fugitive, trying to hide himself from the enemy, entered a small village. The people were kind to him and offered him a place to stay. But when the soldiers who sought the fugitive asked where he was hiding, everyone became very fearful. The soldiers threatened to burn the village and kill every man in it unless the young man were handed over to them before dawn. The people went to the minister and asked him what to do. The minister, torn between handing over the boy to the enemy or having his people killed, withdrew to his room and read his Bible, hoping to find an answer before dawn. After many hours, in the early morning his eyes fell on these words: "It is better that one man dies than that the whole people be lost."

Then the minister closed the Bible, called the soldiers and told them where the boy was hidden. And after the soldiers led the fugitive away to be killed, there was a feast in the village because the minister had saved the lives of the people. But the minister did not celebrate. Overcome with a deep sadness, he remained in his room. That night an angel came to him, and asked, "What have you done?" He said: "I handed over the fugitive to the enemy." Then the angel said: "But don't you know that you have handed over the Messiah?" "How could I know?" the minister replied anxiously. Then the angel said: "If, instead of reading your Bible, you had visited this young man just once and looked into his eyes, you would have known."[38]

From a transformational understanding of the relationship between Christ and culture, this is exactly the shortcoming of Separational CCM. In the desire to be "biblically correct," essential tenets of the faith are missed. The brokenness of all humanity; the presence of Christ in the poor and the powerless; and the call to servanthood and self-sacrifice, compassion, humility, mercy, and grace are overlooked as the Messiah is betrayed to the enemy. As one artist complains, "Christian people are missing the chance to be Christian so much it's ridiculous. The most Christian thing you could do is . . . take care of people and be cool to people and love people, which we don't do at all. Instead, most of us waste a lot of time."[39]

Not surprisingly, this time-wasting is seen to be manifested in the songs produced by many Christian artists. In part the problem is that much of CCM, according to those working from a transformational perspective, has become reductionistic, rigid, judgmental, and arrogant. Critic Brian Quincy Newcomb, for example, complains of one band, "The bottom line with those guys is that they really believe that you can squeeze the gospel onto bumper stickers. They really believe that's the job of a Christian band, to come up with a catchy slogan that people will walk away remembering. And they believe that in four words, you can consolidate an entire theological idea. Apart from John 3:16, I personally believe that's impossible. Not only do I believe that it's impossible, I think it's wrong."[40] Based on "codes and passwords," such music, another artist argues, "doesn't give people room to be who they are at the stage they're at in life."[41] The music is, in a word, disconnected—disconnected from the Christian experience, disconnected from human experience, disconnected from the outside world. The perceived problem does not end with simplistic lyrics. Crucial to the transformational perspective is social critique, both of the church and of society. And while criticism is not exclusive to Transformational CCM—if Integrational CCM, focused on bridging the mainstream and evangelical cultures, generally avoids presenting much in the way of social critique, Separational CCM, calling Christians to distinguish themselves from a world defined by sin, at least by implication offers some critique of that world—it is argued that the social critique found in other forms of CCM often misses the point. The problems are twofold: the difference of voice and the difference of focus. While transformational artists generally write in the first person and from personal experience ("Meanwhile I dwell/On the baby that I killed/Or the drink I should have not refilled/And every heart I broke in two"), separational artists more frequently address an audience in the second person ("All those things you had to buy/Special ordered through the mail/Things you thought would change your life/Are the highlights of somebody's yard sale").[42] The separational critique is, moreover, primarily focused on issues of individual morality such as sexual behavior (see, among others: Point of Grace, "The Love He Has for You"; DeGarmo & Key, "Don't Throw Your Love Away"), abortion (see, among others: Phil Keaggy, "Little Ones"; Julie Miller, "Dangerous Place"), and selfishness (see, among others: All Star United, "Bright Red Carpet"; PFR, "Great Lengths").[43] Taking this to its logical conclusion, the early 1990s saw the appearance of a band called Lust Control. Considered by some to be little more than a novelty act, Lust Control was a punk-rock outfit whose players wore ski masks and refused to identify themselves, while at the same time performing songs about topics such as masturbation and virginity that one critic described as "ranting and fingerpointing . . . [that] reduce all women to simple chattel to be hated, dominated in marriage and slept with."[44] Singular in the extremes to which the band went to make its point, Lust Control nevertheless illustrated what was, for many, a dark side to the social critique Separational CCM had to offer. According to the transformational understanding of Christ and culture, the separational critique, even without the ranting and finger-pointing, misses larger systemic issues applicable both to society at large and to the church. Separational CCM fails to recognize the problems inherent to the social systems in which the individuals it addresses live.

If true, this shortcoming is of course far from unique to Separational CCM. Lawrence Grossberg argues in his 1994 essay on the state of rock music that "rock rarely challenges the political and economic institutions of society."[45] In a similar fashion, George Lipsitz argues that popular music and youth culture tend to offer an imminent, rather than transcendent, critique of contemporary culture and that, without some kind of political movement addressing the root causes of a given community's alienation, protest degenerates to mere posturing.[46] So while green hair, tattoos and body piercing may offend members of the "establishment," they do not fundamentally change the social situation. Generally such claims are rooted in the belief that the popular culture industry, as a part of the capitalist system, has an overwhelming ability to blunt political criticism and absorb attempts at protest. Consequently, visibility does not equal political power, and protest degenerates into a mimicking of society rather than an effort to transform it.[47] Popular music may play a role in providing group and individual identity, but, insofar as it does, that identity will largely be one of choices in consumption. As one critic, describing his moment of epiphany at a 1984 concert, puts it, "At that Cure concert I saw myself as a member of the generation that transformed rock music, once and for all, from something that could change you into something that identified you. It had become an accessory. It was an earring, a black leather jacket, a pair of shoes."[48] Expanding on these arguments, Charles Simpson makes the claim that commercially produced entertainment is able to attract a broad-based audience only to the extent that it offers a temporary escape from complex social constraints.[49] Video games offer the temporary illusion of power; soap operas offer a substitute life of exaggerated sexuality; pop music offers vicarious romantic emotion. None will create a space for critical reflection that could lead to an improved life. Thus, Simpson argues, mass entertainment forms, including music, will, in the end, tend to seek to overcome the experience of social fragmentation without being critical. Instead of critique, popular culture offers only temporary escape. The symbolic rejection of the dominant culture that is occasionally found in rock music amounts to mere posturing, to gesture. One can use popular music as an identity marker to create a real or imagined sense of community, but it is very difficult to use popular music to transform society—and more strongly, rather than being a force to change society for the better, music may merely displace the energies necessary to do so.

These arguments have important consequences for CCM. First, if such claims are correct and rock music is merely an accessory that identifies rather than an agent of substantive change, then it would follow that Christianity, through vehicles like CCM, may be reduced to such a construct. Christianity, in other words, is transformed from faith into fashion, and what sets Christians apart from non-Christians is not their belief systems but their purchasing patterns. The T-shirt may read, "They will know we are Christians by our ☐ hair ☐ ties ☒ love," but wearing the shirt, like listening to the music, belies the point.[50] Clearly, few Christians—even Christians working from a transformational perspective—would choose to take the argument this far. There may be scorn from some quarters concerning so-called "Jesus junk" ("surrounding ourselves with tacky trinkets at the expense of the poor and oppressed is a slap in Jesus' face," writes John W. Styll) and there may be some realization that the line that separates contemporary Christian music from chocolate Bibles is a blurry one, but few would go so far as to suggest that Christianity has been reduced to habits of consumption and nothing more.[51] Given the above arguments, the question is, Can Christianity as manifested in contemporary Christian music be anything more? If, as is argued, separational ministers and integrational entertainers are incapable of critique and produce little more than faith as fashion, how can transformational artists hope to do any more? How is it possible for Transformational CCM to escape these limitations of commercial culture? Can "art" accomplish anything that "entertainment" or "ministry" cannot? Transformational artists argue that it can.

A Transformational Theory of Art and Culture

Given the great diversity of evangelicals, it is perhaps not surprising to find them articulating numerous definitions for the term "art" and seriously debating its character and purpose. As described by Colin Harbinson, these evangelical debates over art can be reduced to one essential (if problematically conceptualized) conflict: the belief in art as expression versus the belief in art as communication. Harbinson writes:

> The issue is hotly debated by Christians involved in the arts. There are strong feelings on both sides. The question in point is whether the arts are for "expression" or "communication." Those who want to communicate truth through the arts are accused of using art to produce a religious tract. They are accused of prostituting art in order to moralize. On the other hand, the Christian who does not use his artistic gift in the cause of the gospel is often perceived as having little commitment to Christ and certainly no heart for the lost. Creative expression that does not contain crucifixions, make overt references to the Trinity, or portray the whole Gospel is seen as being of no value, and at worst, akin to serious backsliding.[52]

If not specifically presented in the context of contemporary Christian music, Harbinson's comments are nonetheless equally useful in understanding the production of CCM, with Transformational CCM often emerging as the sonic equivalent of abstract visual art and the same debates that motivate the conflict between abstract visual artists and those who demand iconic imagery motivating the conflict between Transformational and Separational CCM. In both cases the latter is seen by the former as guilty of the prostitution of art in order to moralize, while the former is seen by the latter as evidence of a weak Christian faith and/or backsliding. Perhaps more important, Harbinson's argument also serves as a useful introduction to two key premises of evangelical aesthetic and cultural theory. First, underlying both the "expression" and "communication" perspectives is a utilitarian, goal-oriented approach to the media of communication in which the value of any communicative form is determined solely by the ends it achieves. Whether the expression of truth or the communication of the gospel, artistic production is justified by what it effects. Additionally, even though not made explicit by Harbinson, the argument as he describes it nevertheless rests heavily on a belief in the neutrality of communicative forms—that is, in a traditional sender-message-receiver model for communication in which the medium and the message are completely separate, neither one influencing the other.

While scholars like Harold Innis, Marshall McLuhan, Walter Ong, and Eric Havelock have long been exploring the profound influence that particular media forms have on the messages they carry, the cultures that contain them, the social organizations that produce them, and the thought patterns that emerge from their use, evangelicals have largely ignored such thinking.[53] Clifford G. Christians argues that such ignorance is the product of the evangelicals' almost exclusive emphasis on the Great Commission described in Matthew 28:19–20 ("Go therefore and make disciples of all nations, baptizing them in the name of the Father and the Son and the Holy Spirit, teaching them to observe all that I commanded you" [NAS]). According to Christians, placing the need to make believers of others above all else has precluded the development of cultural theories that could powerfully animate evangelical efforts at communicating the Gospel message. Focused on what they are trying to say, evangelicals have spent little time thinking seriously about how to say it—and, perhaps more important, about the environment in which it will be said. Evangelical culture, therefore, is left largely without an intellectual basis for critiquing media institutions or evaluating the influence the media have on the messages sent.[54] Absent any theoretical understanding of culture and/or the media, evangelicals thus blindly assume the neutrality of media and use them uncritically. This conclusion is echoed by Quentin Schultze, who argues that American evangelicalism's disinterest in tradition coupled with its faith in technology has left the evangelical church without a foundation from which to work and believing in what Schultze calls the "mythos of the electronic church": "a technological optimism that uncritically links the electronic media with the providential mission of God to preach the gospel around the world before the second coming of Christ. Research clearly documents the ineffectiveness of electronic media as agents of religious conversion, yet the popular mythology holds that spiritual battles can be won technologically."[55] Successful evangelism, therefore, is seen to depend only on having access to the latest communication technologies.

Despite the evangelical belief in the mythos of the electronic church, "communication technologies," argues Schultze, "have probably secularized more than they have saved, commercialized more than they have consecrated, and propagandized more than they have proselytized."[56] This conclusion at least in part depends on Schultze's assertion that the media are far from the neutral vessels assumed by most evangelicals. Indeed, both Clifford Christians and Schultze agree that the frequent consequence of this belief on the part of evangelicals is that evangelicals involved in the mass media generally find their organizations and their messages reshaped by "the marketing ethos and stimulus-response mentality of the commercial broadcasting [or, in the case of CCM, the commercial recording] industry."[57] As Schultze puts it, "The American media were not neutral soil for planting religious messages."[58] Exacerbating this problem, suggests Christians, is the fact that evangelicals have largely failed to recognize the cultural mandate given to them in the Bible. In an argument clearly fitting with the transformational perspective described above, Christians argues that the role of the church regarding society includes, but is not limited to, the Great Commission. The church must also empower the laity to become transformers of culture for the good of humankind.[50] Evangelicals then, according to Christians, ought to use the media to articulate a moral order and stimulate the moral imagination in a manner that could help redeem popular art and fulfill a transformative purpose.[60] The media would then become sites of struggle, wherein alternative discourses and subversive texts challenge the taken-for-granted assumptions of the world. This struggle would not only focus on individual sins, but would also critique social structures so that institutional sins are also made visible.

But how can art—in this case music—challenge the dominant culture? Cone argues that black spirituals offered resistance to an oppressive system through their ability to create beauty and worth out of the ugliness of slave existence.[61] For evangelicals to offer resistance, Christians suggests, they should seek to give voice to the voiceless, to make the voices of the poor and dispossessed as clear as the voices of the establishment.[62] Christians further argues that enhancing creation's beauty and excellence, its justice and grace, has remained within the Christian mandate, despite the fall of culture and humanity, despite the Great Commission. John Fischer agrees, arguing that the purpose of contemporary Christian music is not to create an alternative world (a Christian subculture) or a Christian version of everything in the world (Christian aerobics music and Christian coffee mugs) but to infuse the world with the light and salt of faith.[63] According to Christians, accomplishing this task requires that evangelicals' media products seek to stimulate the "moral imagination." But instead of seeking to stimulate the moral imagination, evangelicals have largely focused on providing straightforward, propositional claims about God and humankind in their media products, including their music. Christians concludes, "Nothing could be less effective on the small TV screen for communicating transcendence."[64] Transformational artists would say the same principle applies to contemporary music. The straightforward, propositional claims of Separational CCM, while affirming and comforting to evangelicals themselves, fail to capture God's transcendence and the imaginations of a non-Christian audience. For separational evangelicals, the media are seen as little more than a pipeline for sending declarative statements to an unsuspecting audience; for transformational Christians, however, they are the environments in which the moral imagination of a people is engaged.

If the transformational approach can be distinguished from the separational and integrational in terms of each perspective's particular understanding of the way the media work, they can also be distinguished in terms of their particular understandings of what the media are for. This is especially true insofar as the media are equated with the production of art. As argued by Dorothy Sayers, the Christian church has never been able to make up its mind about art, alternating between puritanical denunciations of art as irreligious on the one hand and attempts to exploit art as a means of teaching religion and morals on the other.[65] According to Sayers, both approaches are misguided and degrading; art, she argues, should be seen as creation. The act of creativity is valuable in and of itself because it reflects the divine image of God-the-Creator that is found in all humans.[66] In this view, by being created in the image of God the Creator, humans are "created to create," although on a finite level using materials already available.[67] While humans and the rest of creation are in a fallen and broken state due to sin, glimpses of what God created and intended remain. Sayers therefore claims that humans are most godlike and most themselves when they are engaged in creative activity and are fully alive only to the extent that they are moved by the creativeness that proceeds from God.[68] This approach to art has been articulated by multiple spokespersons for evangelical Christianity, each of whom has made an impact on the development of multiple CCM artists, most frequently among those making what is best understood as Transformational CCM.[69]

One of the earliest apologists for Christian art to be adopted by Christian musicians was Hans Rookmaaker. According to Rookmaaker, Christian art should not be defined as art that uses biblical or other Christian themes. Indeed, in Rookmaaker's conception, there is no uniquely "Christian" art. Instead, Christian art is simply "good" art[70]—in this instance, meaning art that is "in line with the God-given structures of art, one which has a loving and free view on reality." This in contrast to "bad art," which is "false or weird in its insight into reality."[71] So for Rookmaaker, "good" art has two dimensions: it possesses aesthetic quality and it conveys a message that is true. Thus, art can succeed or fail on both aesthetic and moral dimensions. Moreover, in the process of producing "good" art, the artist's Christianity will reveal itself without turning religion into propaganda. Christians need not attempt to compose "Christian music," paint "Christian paintings," or craft "Christian sculpture"; they simply compose, paint, or sculpt while seeking both aesthetic quality and truth. In composing music as a Christian, painting as a Christian, or sculpting as a Christian, God's perspective can't help but show through, whether the topic is the fear of a boy whose parents are separating, the ecstasy of finding a lover thought to be dead, or the glimmer of a ghetto child finding that she really can succeed at something.[72] In this perspective, if an artist is a Christian, religion cannot be hidden. It will peek through the cracks and shout throughout the world the Christian perspective that is necessarily presented in the art. As John Peck writes, "Art gives us away. It always does."[73]

Despite the number of artists persuaded by Rookmaaker's theory, the ideas are largely resisted within the realm of Christian music as a whole. As Brian Quincy Newcomb notes, "the evangelical mindset is that music is merely a tool."[74] According to Rookmaaker, however, while art can be used to teach, prophesy, praise, decorate, evangelize, and exhort, it is "a perverted kind of utilitarianism" to conclude that art is only good if and when it promotes Christianity.[75] Thus, from the perspective Rookmaaker is outlining, the aesthetic judgment of art can no longer be made according to the lines of religious belief. However full of faith they might be, Christians are still quite capable of making "bad" art, while non-Christians (who as human beings also bear glimpses of the divine image of God) are equally capable of making "good" (and thus "Christian") art. In Rookmaaker's view, art is the ability to make something beautiful and pleasing (as well as useful), just as God made the world beautiful and declared, "It is good" (Genesis 1:31). Art needs no justification. Simply by being created, it is an act that reflects the divine image of God. And by reflecting the divine image, Rookmaaker concludes, art demands a response: the worship of God.[76] Furthermore, excellence in the creative activity is itself a means of praising God.[77] Thus, to try to reduce art solely into a tool for evangelism is misguided. If the supreme purpose of art is no longer to sing the praise of the Lord and be a joy to one's fellow-beings but rather to provide a tool for evangelism, then artists soon cease to ask whether art is good and beautiful, only whether it can be used effectively to convert people. In asking such questions, Christians are not far from trying to manipulate the people they want to reach.[78] In their desire to fulfill the Great Commission, evangelicals easily turn art into propaganda. But the end result is often the creation of a sectarian style and a religious subculture that is unavailable and/or uninteresting to the uninitiated.

In addition to being beautiful and a source of joy, quality art, according to Sayers, has another characteristic. Great art, she claims, allows both the audience and the artist to recognize something new about themselves. Artists experience life, express it in their art, and recognize the experience for what it is: a revelation of truth. And in the artists' expression, others can come to recognize the truth they have in common; something that was not previously understood is now made known. This new recognition of truth may be uncomfortable, startling, or even shattering, but it comes with a ring of familiarity. So, while the new truth is not something that had been consciously known, once it has been revealed by the artist, it is recognized as something that had been understood at some unconscious level.[79] Thus, John Fischer praises the music of Larry Norman because it makes you "face something you don't want to face, [namely] . . . the truth about yourselves."[80] In the view of Sayers and Fischer, quality art should make us take an honest, humbling look at our own shortcomings. The difficulty for transformational artists is that most people, Christian and non-Christian alike, neither want nor expect this type of creative and Christian art. Most audiences would rather not be upset by sudden, uncomfortable revelations about themselves or their world. They would prefer to be entertained or, in some cases, affirmed by endorsements of what they already know and believe.

Evangelicals often want their art, including their contemporary music, to contain the "truth" in clear, propositional statements that merely require intellectual assent. Yet good art is rarely so straightforward. John Fischer suggests that artists have a fundamentally different role than the pastors, teachers, and seminar leaders who otherwise characterize contemporary evangelicalism. If teachers make things clear, he argues, artists make things complex because "truth is both."[81] It is a mistake, Fischer argues, to insist that Christ be visible in clear propositional form on every page, every verse, every song, or every album. As Fischer points out, Christ is not found on every page of the Bible, although there are "shadows of Him in the Pentateuch, cries from Him in the Psalms, wisdom from Him in the Solomon writings, [and] longings for Him in the prophets."[82] Contemporary writing and music should be similarly nuanced. Echoing this sentiment, Harold Myra and Dean Merrill argue that, instead of offering pat answers, Christian artists should probe the enigmas and mysteries to show life as it really is: full of loose ends and unfinished questions. They should acknowledge that Christians don't have all the solutions to the world's problems.[83] While Christ does have those desired solutions, Christians still peer through the glass darkly and must admit that His thoughts are not our thoughts.[84] Fischer advises artists to learn a lesson from Christ's parables and "bury the truth a little," putting "it just beyond . . . [the listener's] grasp so that she has to get up out of her comfortable chair to get it." Art, Fischer claims, should "leak the truth slowly," and artists need to become "masters of compelling concealment—hiding the truth, while at the same time, inviting a search."[85] To accomplish this task, Christian artists need the freedom to create, to be misunderstood, to seek what it means to be fully human as God intended. Christians must take part in the world's activity and create art that is connected to all of life, not just prayer, worship, Bible study, and evangelism. This is the type of "art"—the type of music—that Transformational CCM attempts to create. Doing so, however, demands new rationales justifying the effort to an art world otherwise focused on ministry and/or amusement.

Working from the assumption that individuals live in a culture that is fallen from grace but able to be restored, and also from an approach to the creative arts that values the creative act in and of itself over and above any utilitarian purpose for the product of that act, transformational artists offer rationales for the production of the music that differ drastically from those of the competing CCM realms. While the activities of those producing Separational CCM are justified in terms of the music's utility for evangelism, worship, and exhortation, Transformational CCM argues that "art does not exist to tell a sermon," rejecting the focus on means and ends.[86] Similarly, the rationales that animate Integrational CCM—providing a wholesome alternative to secular rock and roll, witnessing to music-industry personnel, presenting a Christian worldview—are rejected both in their reliance on a set canon of topics and perspectives that are claimed to define a Christian worldview and in the concessions they demand with regard to artistic expression. Transformational artists conceive of their work as expression rather than communication—as (divine) revelation that exists and is valuable in and of itself, without regard to the audience or to ends. While the value of the music is not in its utility for achieving instrumental goals, it may, nonetheless, contribute to the achievement of such goals. The music, therefore, is justified on the basis of two distinct but related rationales: first, that the music, as art, is valuable in and of itself, regardless of its utility or purpose; and second, that the music reveals truth and presents possibilities in a vision of a redeemed and transformed world.

Transformational CCM's First Rationale: Art for Art's Sake

If Transformational CCM found its patron saint and sacrificed martyr in Mark Heard, in Charlie Peacock it has found its high priest and most vocal advocate. A driving force behind Exit Records in the 1980s, in the 1990s Peacock has come to be known not only for his critically acclaimed albums (*Love Life* [Sparrow, 1991], *Everything That's on My Mind* [Sparrow, 1994], *strangelanguage* [Re:think, 1996]) but also for his creation of the Art House. Peacock describes the Art House this way:

> The Art House is an independent, nonprofit foundation that exists to benefit individuals creating art within the context of historic Christianity.
> Dedicated to an artistic philosophy which places what God the Creator thinks over what man the creation thinks—the Art House Foundation is committed to art which reflects the whole of the human

Emerging from Exit Records in the 1980s and now the driving force behind The Art House, Charlie Peacock has long been an advocate of "artful living," encouraging Christians to look beyond the easy symbols and focus on the act of creation itself as a source of power. (Photograph courtesy of EMI Christian Music Group, used by permission of Sparrow Records.)

experience: not only worship, joy, and the hope of heaven, but trial, temptation, and the love between a man and a woman. . . .

Toward that goal the foundation seeks to provide education, for artists and non-artists alike, in the area of creative arts. It is not intended to be a source of inroads into the art and music industries. It seeks, rather, to inspire both the professional and the lay person to originality and creativity, to encourage them to live artfully, to develop searching minds, and to apply Biblical principles to their lives and art.

It is the further vision of the Art House Foundation that such individuals, having been well equipped, would venture into both the church and the world to create powerful and astonishing works of creativity, and that these works, created with passion and honesty, would serve the church and the culture as God in His wisdom would ordain.[87]

Designed to instruct individuals in "the fine craft of living artfully," the Art House had clear roots in Francis Schaeffer's L'Abri, an evangelical aesthetic/intellectual commune that operated in Switzerland during the fifties, sixties, and seventies. It was, in some ways, a culmination of the transformational approach to art and culture. Discussing the relationship between L'Abri and the Art House, Peacock notes that "they're probably the only model for what we're doing. . . . What they did was give people their freedom back in the arts and they modeled for people that it was all right in God's eyes to paint a flower as much as it was all right to paint Christ on the cross, and that God looks on the intents of the heart."[88] Art House, like L'Abri, was based on the premise that Christians could and should paint flowers. The problem, claims Peacock, is that too many Christian artists "play church even with art." From the crosses, doves, lambs, and lions that largely define the Christian visual arts to the clichés and buzz words of CCM, Peacock argues that "it is too easy for the artist to create 'Christian art' as symbols only, because they are trying to speak the language of a Christian culture rather than to live honestly before God."[89] According to Peacock, it is the act of creation, far more than the created product, that justifies a Christian's artistic endeavors.

Peacock's claims frequently have been echoed by those working from a transformational perspective. Unlike the separational artists who justify their music in terms of its ministry value and the integrational artists who justify their music relative to the mainstream alternatives they compete against, those working from a transformational perspective routinely justify their music not in terms of its uses or functions, but rather in terms of its essential worth. This justification can take a number of distinct forms. The most basic of these is articulated by Brian Quincy Newcomb, who, as the driving force behind *Syndicate* magazine (originally *Harvest Rock Syndicate*), emerged as one of the Christian music industry's more respected transformational critics. Newcomb writes: "I think the evangelical mindset is that music is merely a tool. And I've never in my wildest dreams thought of creativity as only valuable when it has a function. [For a]nyone who's ever been in the grand cathedrals of Europe . . . it's very clear that these paintings were not there just to provide a function, but they were there to mesmerize and amaze, to delight the eye. Certainly art does not exist to tell a sermon. Some art may, indeed, be sermonic in quality, but not all art needs to be [so] to be valuable."[90] For Newcomb and others like him, art is valuable merely because it exists. The particular form of art known as contemporary Christian music, then, becomes valuable to Newcomb only insofar as the music "rocks." The prescription, Newcomb claims, is "simple: make albums that rock, make albums that speak intelligently and relevantly to our world, make credible music . . . and say something that encourages and enlightens the road of faith that life is on." Albums are valuable when they possess "bold, artistic honesty, musical power and cultural edge," regardless of the particular message they happen to communicate.[91]

While working from these same basic assumptions, some transformational artists nevertheless take the argument a step further, arguing not only that the music is valuable in and of itself, but also that it is the joy of playing, the exercise of God-given talents, and the need for self-expression that make what they do important, with the act of creation again taking precedence over the nature of the created product. So Terry Taylor (of Daniel Amos and The Swirling Eddies, among a number of other bands) justifies his activities by claiming, "I love to play music. I love to exercise creative capacities, talents or whatever you want to call them. God has put that desire in my heart to express myself musically. I cannot cease from doing that: it's something that is just there."[92] Gene Eugene (Adam Again) argues that the members of his band "have to make music together. I feel that music and artwork is very spiritual, and that God has given us this band to express ourselves, and create something lasting and real."[93] Such statements run throughout the press given to transformational artists; however, they do not end there.

Commenting on early Christian music, Brian Quincy Newcomb notes that "many Christian artists had a tendency to say 'Jesus gave me this song' or 'Jesus told me to do . . . this or that.'" According to Newcomb, such phrases "abdicated responsibility for human action, and sometimes appeared to blame God for weak songs and stupid decisions."[94] This, however, is only one interpretation of such claims. If Newcomb's emerges as the strong reading—"Sometimes when Christians talk like that," Newcomb offers, "I'm tempted to say 'Maybe you should have given that song back. . .'"[95]—there is a weaker reading that suggests such terms are merely the parlance of CCM. As in the 1988 baseball movie, *Bull Durham*, in which Kevin Costner dictates to Tim Robbins the crucial phrases to use when talking to the media ("We just play 'em one at a time"), Christian music has its own particular catch phrases that are repeated over and over. Bands break up and band members leave over "musical differences," each new producer is committed to "allowing the artists to be themselves," every album is "the album the artist always wanted to make." As the transformational perspective has gained new ground in the Christian community, more and more Christian artists have turned to the rationales of artistic production to justify their efforts. Consider Kevin Smith, who, as part of DC Talk, has undergone a clear transformation of image from pop idol for the prepubescent set to authentic rock artist. However, while the remaining members of the band found exchanging their porkpie hats à la New

Kids on the Block for cardigan sweaters à la Kurt Cobain to be sufficient, Smith took his new role as the serious artist one step further.[96] With a solo contribution to *Strong Hand of Love* ("Lonely Moon") as different from Heard's original as it was from the pop/rap/alterno-rock that DC Talk is known for, Smith was quickly positioned as DC Talk's artist in residence; and on the heels of "Lonely Moon" came Smith's collaboration with Jimmy Abegg (a/k/a Jimmy A.), *At the Foot of Heaven*, a book comprising Smith's poetry and Abegg's paintings, which, as critics were compelled to note, had to be edited due to the "honesty" of the work involved.[97] In the wake of such efforts, Smith came to be positioned as "contemporary Christian music's John Lennon," with comparisons further extending to U2's Bono and Roxy Music's Bryan Ferry.[98] And even though the transformation was less elaborate than Smith's, the promotion of Amy Grant's 1997 release *Behind the Eyes* (Myrrh/A&M)—an album described as "deeply personal self-expression," "uncomfortably vulnerable," a "return . . . to the music that first inspired her to play guitar and write," without "question . . . the album she wanted to make, as opposed to the album that would necessarily sell a bazillion copies"[99]—was equally effective at establishing Grant as a "serious artist" despite the sugar-coated pop of the preceding albums *Heart in Motion* (Myrrh/A&M, 1991) and *House of Love* (Myrrh/A&M, 1994).

Given the image-making surrounding musicians such as Kevin Smith and Amy Grant, it is easy to dismiss the claims of all transformational artists as little more than mere mastery of the obligatory statements used by a particular set of artists to justify their activities. To some extent, such complaints must be considered. Insofar as these artists are bright people, knowledgeable in the ways of industry and audiences, there can be little doubt that in making reference to the joy and spirituality of playing, the inability to do anything else, and so forth, these artists are tapping into the tropes that resonate within their art world. To dismiss it as only that, however, misses a much larger point: the fact that such tropes do resonate within that art world. Two important considerations emerge from this fact. First, in order for such claims to have resonance, there must be some measure of truth behind them; there must be at least some belief in art for art's sake. More important, if the tropes are to have resonance, then they must, to some degree at least, be accepted as legitimate rationales for the production of contemporary Christian music. If the claims were irrelevant or ineffective, they would cease to be made. Whether they truly believe it or not, the musicians of Transformational CCM present their output as the natural consequence of their human existence and therefore valuable. In Steve Scott's words, "The fact that we *create* carries echoes of the truth that we are created beings reliant upon the grace of a creative God."[100] Transformational artists believe they are doing what God created them to do. The act of creation, however, is one thing; the output another. As Scott further notes, "*what* we create very often bears the hallmarks of our fallen nature."[101]

Transformational CCM's Second Rationale: Revealing Truth and Presenting Possibilities

While arguing that art is valuable in and of itself, as they move to justify their particular works the artists of Transformational CCM frequently claim that their creative endeavors, to use Peacock's words again, "reflect the whole of the human experience."[102] Perceiving an undue emphasis in other forms of CCM on the "pie in the sky in the great by and by," transformational artists argue that they work to reveal the unpleasant truths associated with contemporary life—the truths that many would rather not face. Generally presented in the context of "honesty," it is an approach that leads to the production of music that depicts the world, often literally, in shades of gray rather than black and white.[103] It is an approach that focuses on shortcomings and failings—the artists' own as well as those of the surrounding world—as often as it does "victory in Christ."

Catholic theologian Henri Nouwen largely captures the assumptions of the transformational approach when he calls on Christians to become "contemplative critics." Nouwen contends that Christians must recognize the sufferings of their own time in their own hearts and experiences. That recognition becomes a starting point for contemplative critique. Only one who is familiar with the pain and suffering of the world can authentically speak to it. The Christian artist is, then, one who is able to articulate his or her own experiences and offer his or her own wounded self as a source of clarification for others.[104] Mike Roe (The 77's, The Lost Dogs) offers perhaps the clearest example of this relationship. Long described by detractors as "depressing" and by fans as "real," Roe's songs routinely focus on the darker aspects of life. As Roe describes it, "Anytime that we have relationships with people that are difficult or painful, they tend to affect us much more than just about anything else. At least I know in my life that's been the case. Whether it was a parent or a friend or a sibling or a lover, it's always going to bring out the best or the worst in you."[105] Such relationships, then, "act as a deep dark well of inspiration for Roe, who writes about affairs of the heart in a sincere and honest manner."[106] The end result is that even the songs Roe writes that are focused on the outside world ("The New Physics"—"They say there's suffering here/ Suffering over there/There's suffering everywhere") are rooted in an individual experience described by one album as "drowning with land in sight."[107] When Roe claims "there's suffering here," it's because he has experienced it. As Roe explains of the decision to include "Self-Made Trap" ("a really, really upsetting song") on 1992's *The Seventy Sevens* (BAI), "I said to Dave the other day, 'how can we do this to people,' and he said, 'because we did it to ourselves.'"[108] To be a contemplative critic is to be engaged with, rather than withdrawn from, the world.

Contemplative critics, according to Nouwen, have several tasks. The contemplative critic, like Robert Parks's marginal man or Georg Simmel's stranger, exists on the borders of a group and keeps a certain distance to escape from being absorbed into the tyranny of the urgent and idolatrous values and practices of contemporary society and church.[109] At the same time, this distance, combined with the experience of the shared sufferings of the time, creates a tension that allows the contemplative critic to see those hints of the restoration that peek through the cracks of life in a broken world. Consequently, the first task of the contemplative critic is to make visible in the grit and dirt of daily reality the image of God found in all humans and the hope and promise that stem from that recognition. Exposing the divine in the dirt and exploring the tensions between life as it is lived and life as it arguably should be lived motivates much of Transformational CCM. Heard in songs like "The Pain that Plagues Creation," "Banquet at the World's End," and "Wilderness," among countless others, this approach is perhaps most clearly illustrated with the song "Window" from the album *Alternative Worship: Prayer, Petitions and Praise* (Alarma, 1994).[110] Gene Eugene sings:

> Headed down to Atlanta
> Passed a poor family that looked "in love"
> Smoke was rising from their grill
> They looked at me and smiled
>
> I see You out my window
> In the fields and the forgotten

> Moved on up to Lexington
> Saw green pastures with white fencin'
> Got off to get some gasoline
> A beggar stuck out his hand
>
> I see You out my window
> In the fields and the forgotten[111]

Believing God to be an incomprehensible mystery, transformational artists are nevertheless prepared to find Him in the widows and orphans, the strangers and forgotten. However, transformational artists frequently include themselves among this latter group. From "orphans of God" to "hollow men" to "the aboriginal [who] learns to pour the tea/In a suit they hang upon him like a cruel name," Transformational CCM is replete with images of Christians as disenfranchised creatures living in a foreign environment.[112] And if the exploration of themes of alienation are not limited to Transformational CCM (cf., DeGarmo & Key, "Aliens and Strangers"; Phil Keaggy, "Walk in Two Worlds"), the emphasis on the nature of that condition rather than the future reward it entails is.

Another task for Nouwen's critics comes by virtue of their focused examination of the world around them. Contemplative critics are able to challenge the assumptions of society and church that lead to the worship of idols such as self, wealth, or power. Unwilling to accept all of sin as a matter of individual failing, contemplative critics ask the difficult questions, looking behind the surface of the taken-for-granted practices of daily existence. They ask whether we see as clearly as we think we do. They ask if our practices are consistent with our ideals. As one of the more popular transformational artists in the 1980s, Steve Taylor spent much of his time and energy probing the underside of the church.[113] And although the herky-jerky rhythms of eighties new wave and the frequent punning sometimes detracted from Taylor's message, his early songwriting was nevertheless focused on challenging what he perceived to be the questionable practices of the church. Songs such as "I Want to Be a Clone" (which lampooned the homogenization of the Christian experience), "Colour Code" (which challenged the racial policies of Bob Jones University), and "This Disco (Used to Be a Cute Cathedral)" (which criticized the church for its self-absorption) endeared Taylor to the fans who shared his worries but left him with no shortage of critics who questioned his means and motives. The transformational critique, however, is not limited to others;

numerous artists and critics have spent a great deal of energy considering their own role in the problems they perceive. So, in the wake of CCM artists known as much for their clothing and equipment endorsements as for their music, videos that focus on the artist as clotheshorse, and other manifestations of conspicuous consumption, Kathy Pritchard wonders, "WHO ARE WE KIDDING!!??? Even if the music was on the cutting edge; even if the music was the truest fold or the purest punk, this would not be counter-cultural. Because, no matter what the words to the songs are saying, the unspoken message is clear. And it ain't the Sermon on the Mount. It's a tribute to the gods of this age. Consumerism over art. Image over substance. Red sports cars over humility. Madison Avenue over the cross."[114] Ultimately, even Taylor pondered such questions. Describing childhood visits to a Denver rescue mission, Taylor notes, "The guys in charge . . . sure had a zeal for leading people to God, even though they were not particularly sophisticated or culturally adept. . . . And probably more of us were influenced by people like that than by . . . some artsy band playing in a club and smoking clove cigarettes afterward, or something like that."[115] Ultimately led to distinct responses—Pritchard to calls for "using our artistic gifts to create the finest art ever seen or heard"; Taylor, somewhat ironically, to creating music more consistent with the goals of ministry and Separational CCM than of art and Transformational CCM—Pritchard and Taylor both reveal the willingness of those working from the transformational perspective to examine their own motives, as well as the motives of those around them.[116]

Beyond offering a critique for the way things are, Nouwen claims that the contemplative critic must also be willing to enter into the painful condition of contemporary life in order to "lead people out of the desert into the promised land."[117] As such, Christian artists should give expression to the most personal concerns. They remind us that our suffering is integral to our human condition. In the recognition that we are mortal and broken, we find a starting point for liberation and restoration. Again, this focus on individual experience characterizes much of Transformational CCM. The Choir's 1988 album *Chase the Kangaroo* (Myrrh), for example, included the song "Sad Face," a lament written in response to a miscarriage suffered by the drummer's wife. With a chorus based on Ecclesiastes 7:3 ("Sorrow is better than laughter, because a sad face is good for the heart" [NIV]), the band has noted in interviews that it is this song, more than any other, that fans mention in their letters.[118] However, while songs like "Sad Face" are embedded in specifically individual experiences, even more macro-level, global issues are individualized in Transformational CCM. In introducing the topic of world hunger on the Daniel Amos album *Alarma!* (Newpax, 1981), the songwriter presents himself as one who turns off the TV to avoid the images of starving people, only to find they still "press their faces to the window." The album ends with the "Ghost of the Heart" (a reference to the Holy Spirit) frightening the "Monster of Vanity" and the "Demon of Hatred" as the singer cries, "Oh no, who is that? Oh no, it's me!"[119] In recognizing his own hesitations to deal with or admit culpability in the problem of hunger and in his struggles with vanity and hatred, Terry Taylor gives himself and his audience a starting point for confronting the Christian's responsibility to "the least of these." Although believed to be valuable in and of itself, Transformational CCM is nevertheless routinely used to present a picture of the world that depends, first, on what is characterized to be a painful honesty applied to oneself, and second, on a humility that recognizes one's own culpability in the failures of society and church that is needed before one can begin to critique with integrity the surrounding environment of church and society.

Finally, working from assumptions that position art as valuable in and of itself but also suggest that art, when successful, will reveal truth, transformational artists find themselves in the position of using their work to present possibilities—to show how things might be if God's original intent had not been frustrated by the fall of humanity. Again, however, such possibilities are as frequently presented within the context of life on earth as they are as a future life in heaven (the approach of Separational CCM). Thus, the repeated refrain from the title track of Mark Heard's 1990 album, *Dry Bones Dance* (Fingerprint): "Every now and then I seem to dream these dreams/Where the orphans suckle and the slaves go free/Touching that miraculous circumstance/Where the blind ones see and the dry bones dance."[120] However, insofar as they offer a vision of the worlds that might be, works such as "Dry Bones Dance" also necessarily imply a critique of the world that exists. The difficulty for the transformational artists is that such critiques are not always welcomed, neither by the world nor by the church, and are frequently misunderstood by fans and critics alike. The clearest example of this occurred when The Lost Dogs—a sort of CCM equivalent to the Traveling Wilburys comprising the guitarists/vocalists from four of CCM's preeminent transformational/alternative groups[121]—included a song called "Bush League" on their album *Scenic Routes* (BAI, 1992). Written by Terry Taylor and Gene Eugene, the song was a response to the Gulf War and was addressed to President George Bush. With lines such as "Your points of light are almost gone/So here's our yellow ribbon burning song" and the repeated refrain "All I know is that you gotta go," "Bush League" was, in no uncertain terms, a vociferous critique of the Bush Administration's foreign policy.[122] Numerous fans and critics, however, read the song as a pro-choice statement in that it criticized the Republican (read: pro-life) presidential candidate. As Eugene recalls, "When that song came out, I had a lot of people come up to me with this glassy look in their eye and say that by not supporting Bush, or by supporting Clinton, that I was supporting abortion, which is ridiculous. The song has nothing to do with abortion."[123] Among transformational artists, such incidents are far from rare. It is difficult to offer an honest, truthful critique, humorous or otherwise, to an audience that is frequently uninterested in critical thinking. Consequently, transformational artists such as Taylor and Eugene come to be dismissed by many as self-indulgent, condescending, or irrelevantly "political."

The musicians of Separational CCM argue that music is designed to proselytize the nonbeliever, encourage the believer, or praise God. Integrational CCM counters that it is enough for the music to provide a wholesome alternative to the standard fare of the secular media and to give at least some voice to a Christian worldview within the larger marketplace of ideas. To this mix of reasons and rationales, Transformational CCM brings the claim that the purpose of Christian music is simply to exist; it is valuable because it is, not because it necessarily accomplishes some goal. Like the separational ministers and integrational entertainers, transformational artists occasionally (if not often) err and blunder on the road to becoming more like what God intended humans to be when He created them. Just as the evangelism of Separational CCM can seem to be little more than hollow sloganeering or tracts set to music and the wholesome alternative of Integrational CCM can emerge as warmed-over platitudes set to standard Top 40 fare, the artistry of Transformational CCM can at times emerge as the self-conscious and self-important ruminations of individuals trying too hard to claim the title "artist." The darkness and ambiguity that come from attempting to present what one feels to be an honest evaluation of the world and the human experience can at times emerge as darkness for the sake of seeming dark—as adherence to what have become the established conventions of Transformational CCM. The problem, as one musician describes it, is that Transformational CCM, as much as Separational CCM and Integrational CCM, faces the problem of selling "the most precious thing in the world . . . through this vending machine format that is pop culture."[124]

Interlude: Amy Grant

The breadth of Amy Grant's appeal is evident as the nearly sell-out crowd mills about prior to the concert at the Market Square Arena in Indianapolis with its sixteen-thousand-plus capacity. Cutting across divisions of age and ethnicity, the faces in the crowd include preschool kids holding on to Mom's or Dad's hand and gray-haired seniors; middle-aged women in their gala formals and Gen X teenagers in baggy jeans and flannel shirts; families, couples, and singles gathered in groups of various sizes; African Americans and other minorities as well as caucasians. The only obvious unifying force connecting each audience member to the next is the desire to experience Christmas music as performed by contemporary Christian music's brightest star.

The size and diversity of the crowd are not the only indications that tonight's event is something far beyond the usual CCM performance played out in small halls and church sanctuaries across America. Supporting Grant in her efforts tonight will be Michael W. Smith (himself a CCM artist with crossover success), CeCe Winans (who, in addition to her successful music career as both a solo artist and partner to her brother, hosts an acclaimed weekly talk show called "CeCe's Place" on the Odyssey channel), and the eighty-two-member Nashville Symphony. Those coming tonight to hear the pop diva sing her crossover hits like "Baby, Baby" and "Every Heartbeat" will surely be disappointed. So, too, will those hoping for long monologues explaining that "Jesus is the reason for the season" or, at the very least, renditions of Grant's early "religious" hits such as "My Father's Eyes" and "I Have Decided." This is a symphony tour (Grant will play nineteen cities besides Indianapolis) rooted in the traditions of American Christmas music, both hymns and pop standards.

Wearing a black formal pantsuit, Grant begins the night by singing "Have Yourself a Merry Little Christmas" to the cheers of the crowd. Apparently equal parts concert and fashion show, Grant's frequent costume changes throughout the evening will be used to reflect the changes in the music and the tone of the performance as the evening progresses. So, while the orchestra plays a medley of carols and other symphonic pieces, Grant heads offstage to change. When she returns, again to an eruption of applause and cheers, she wears a glamorous white ball gown with a full hoopskirt. The costume (which has the unfortunate side effect of giving Grant the appearance of a Barbie doll) sets the tone for the first half of the evening. Drawing on familiar classics such as "I'll Be Home for Christmas" and "The Most Wonderful Time of the Year," Grant's performance and costuming suggest a kind of romantic nostalgia. She is joined onstage by Michael W. Smith, and the torch songs give way to the evening's first contemporary number, "Love Has Come," co-written by Smith and Grant. Finishing this, Grant again leaves the stage, allowing Smith a pair of solo performances. Smith, in turn, gives up the stage to CeCe Winans, who performs "O Holy Night" and "Go Tell It on the Mountain." When Grant returns, she wears a sequined cape over the white dress and performs "Breath of Heaven," another contemporary Christmas song the singer co-authored. The audience is clearly enchanted. The lack of religious patter or pop hits doesn't seem to bother them.

Following the brief intermission, the orchestra plays through an eclectic series of musical selections before Grant returns for the concert's glitzier and jazzier second half. Now wearing a close-fitting red satin evening gown, Grant picks up the tempo with "Winter Wonderland" and "Jingle Bells" before CeCe Winans returns to the stage and sings "White Christmas." This is followed by a brief set of "signature songs" as Grant, Smith, and Winans each sing a song or medley from his or her solo pop repertoire. It is the only time during the evening that the audience will hear any of their contemporary Christian favorites. (Grant goes back fifteen years to her gospel breakthrough *Age to Age* for the overtly religious "El Shaddai," while Smith performs his crossover hit "Place in This World.") Following this momentary nod to their roots in pop music, the singers return to Christmas music, inviting the audience to sing along.

As the evening continues, Grant pauses to share her recollections of a grandmother who, a teetotaler throughout the year, "drank like a fish" while cooking for Christmas. Grant's admission that a sure sign of Christmas was finding Grandma a bit tipsy when they called results in roars of laughter from the crowd. The response suggests that the story is surprisingly well received by a crowd that likely includes many who believe the consumption of alcohol to be a problem for Christians. It is arguable that not every CCM artist could get away with confessing such family secrets. This, however, is not just a Christian singer. This is Amy Grant. Glamorous and talented, she is also approachable and human. And so, while others may find it necessary to explain emphatically and exhaustively their reasons for singing the songs that they do, for Grant it is enough that she merely comes to town to sing.

5 | The Materialist Critique: "It's Business"

Men make their own history, but they do not make it just as they please;
they do not make it under circumstances chosen by themselves, but
under circumstances directly encountered, given, and transmitted
from the past. The tradition of all the dead generations weighs like a
nightmare on the brain of the living.

Karl Marx

Separational CCM, Integrational CCM, Transformational CCM—it has so far been argued that these represent three distinct art worlds within the overarching generic category of contemporary Christian music. Drawing on differing assumptions concerning the necessary and proper relationship between an individual's Christian faith and his or her role in secular society, the individuals who together produce and define CCM have aligned themselves in loose social networks distinguished by philosophy, theology, and aesthetics, as well as, in many cases, geography and corporate ties. So, according to those who produce what we have labeled Separational CCM, Christian music is a religious tool. It is a tactical weapon in the spiritual warfare that they believe characterizes contemporary life. It is a way to reach nonbelievers with the gospel message, to encourage Christians in their attempt to live a Christian lifestyle, and to praise and worship God. In contrast, those working from the perspective of what we have labeled Integrational CCM do not see their music as a religious tool nor do they consider making music necessarily a religious calling. Christian music, like most popular music, is conceived as a form of entertainment. What makes it "Christian" is the fact that it is the product of a believer and presents a message that, if not an explicit expression of the gospel, is one that does not contradict it in any way. Finally, we have the music of Transformational CCM—music created in the name of artistic expression and the values of "truth" and "honesty" that are believed to be attached to it.

These constitute three distinct sets of assumptions, three distinct sets of goals, and three distinct understandings of what contemporary Christian music is or should be.

Resting on discrete resolutions to the perceived tension between adhering to the Christian faith and living within secular culture, the differences between the separational, integrational, and transformational forms of CCM have been articulated most specifically in theological and aesthetic terms—in other words, in terms of the messages communicated. Whether Separational, Integrational, or Transformational, built into the articulated self-conceptions of CCM is the presumption that contemporary Christian music is primarily an exercise in communication. If, as implied by Harbinson's discussion of "expression" versus "communication," the particular approach to communication differs, the distinct art worlds are still conceived in predominantly communicative terms.[1] From those who approach Christian music in terms of transmitting verbal messages—commenting on live performances, one critic notes, "You can tell if it's a Christian band based on the mix because . . . vocals are just so on top"[2]—to those who approach Christian music more ritualistically—"I really believe," states one musician, "that in the case of rock'n'roll, pop music, [or] any popular media, that . . . the whole atmosphere around what you're doing, the image, the style of it, the feel of it, the context in which it takes place is far more communicative as a whole than the lyric"[3]—almost everyone involved in Christian music seems to focus on the communicative elements of the music.[4] This, however, is not the only approach, and what Kevin Phillips suggested of the mainstream media twenty years ago is equally true of Christian music today: it is possible, if not necessary, to "put aside the notion of 'the media' as a moral and intellectual enterprise and think of it as a rich and powerful *industry*."[5] Less stridently, although it would be erroneous to ignore the moral, intellectual, aesthetic, and theological aspects of contemporary Christian music, any valid understanding of contemporary Christian music must, borrowing from Ennis, take into consideration the interplay between the tripartite forces of art, politics (or, here, theology), and commerce. Furthermore, despite the objections of some, with sales of contemporary Christian music generating nearly $1 billion in yearly revenues, it is hard to speak of Christian music in anything but industrial terms.[6]

Although it is not precisely clear when the term "Christian music industry" emerged, by 1986 there were those taking issue with both the label and all that it implied.[7] "Industry," it seemed, was a term more appropriate for describing steel mills and assembly lines than popular music steeped in Christian thought. Despite such misgivings, however, "Christian music industry" it was and "Christian music industry" it has remained. There is good reason for the label. The American mass media, Christian music included, are without doubt economic institutions and are economic institutions for "which analogues to research and development, production, wholesaling, and retailing can be developed."[8] And while media production and manufacturing do not, strictly speaking, run parallel and the analogies between the mass media and traditional mass production ultimately break down—as Benjamin Compaine notes, Pillsbury does not have "to introduce a new cake mix every week, pay for the research and development, promote it, get distribution on crowded supermarket shelves, and then move on to develop and promote the next cake mix, while the competition does the same thing"[9]—as a result of the increasing sums of money involved in media production, both in terms of the levels of capital necessary to participate and the concomitant potential for enormous profits, the media have increasingly come to be understood in predominantly economic/industrial terms.[10] And if in its earliest days the Christian music industry could perhaps have escaped these difficulties by virtue of its limited scope and scale, the stunning growth of Christian music sales during the 1980s led not only to increases in the scope and scale (as well as profit) of the Christian music industry itself but also to much closer ties between CCM and the larger machine of the mainstream recorded music industry.

Born in the 1960s at the nexus of numerous distinct cultural streams—the resurgent popular interest in mysticism and spiritualism, the Jesus Movement, the diversification of rock and roll, among others—and maturing through a period of rebirth in American evangelicalism, contemporary Christian music quickly came to be imbued with an industrial patina that William Romanowski and others have argued to be antithetical to the religious cause.[11] There is more behind this transformation than a mere increase in revenues. As Christian music became more popular and demand grew, those creating the music were forced to expand their vision for production and distribution; not surprisingly, they turned to the most obvious model available to them, that of the secular music industry. Seven months after Woodstock was held in Max Yasgur's pasture, Evansville, Indiana, hosted the first Faith Festival.[12] In another example of this mimicking of mainstream music, artist Randy Matthews, the first solo act signed to Word (to that point dedicated to recording religious musicals), recalls that, when his second album was rejected by the label for being "too radical," he suggested a solution based on the practices of the mainstream music industry: "I said, 'Billy, I don't know anything about the record industry, but I do know that secular labels have subsidiaries. It seems to me that if there was another name, people wouldn't know that it was a Word record.' He said, 'That's a real interesting idea.' Then about a week and a half later I got a call from him and he asked me what I thought about the name Myrrh. And I said I like[d] it."[13] Matthews's *All I Am Is What You See* (Myrrh, 1972) became the first release for Myrrh Records, which would go on to become the Christian music industry's preeminent rock label.[14] Arguably, developments such as subsidiary labels and the emerging festival circuit show that even as early as the mid-1970s the loose conglomeration of artists, churches, and coffeehouses that had to that point defined Christian music was already coalescing into an industry modeled on mainstream music. Ultimately, however, it would be the integration of Christian music and religious book publishing that would transform contemporary Christian music into a full-fledged industry.

Much as in the case of film production where "access to a film camera can make one a director, and a bit of capital can make one a producer," the barriers to entry in record production are, all things considered, quite low.[15] Still, if it takes little to record an album, it is a far more challenging prospect to distribute that album to those who would be able and willing to buy it. Unlike the process of recording, record distribution, like media distribution more generally, "is characterized by heavy capital investment costs, economies of scale, licensing, and other barriers to entry," and so, as Benjamin Compaine and his co-authors argue, the resources of the amateur filmmaker (or record producer) "yield about as much power to the individual as that enjoyed by the owner of a mimeograph machine when confronting Time Inc. or the Gannett newspaper chain."[16] In the case of contemporary Christian music, then, although distribution could at first be handled by packing Winnebagos with records, Christian recordmakers faced the challenge of finding more efficient ways to distribute their product in the wake of increasing consumer demand for the albums.[17] Recognizing the potential for profits associated with Christian music, the religious book industry—a system comprising publishers, distributors, retail chains, and independent bookstores—stepped in to meet the need. And while initial resistance to the concept of Christian music on the part of retailers (who dealt most directly with the conservative evangelical consumer base) generally shelved the albums "fifth row back, in the corner, behind the greeting cards and next to the water fountain," the success of the genre quickly gave CCM a more prominent role in the realm of Christian retail. As Romanowski puts it, "The merry ring of the cash register helped persuade stubborn Christian retailers to change their aesthetic sensibilities."[18] As early as 1984, Christian music would account for 25 percent of religious bookstore revenues.[19]

Arguably, with contemporary Christian music modeling itself on the mainstream music industry and negotiating its way into the realm of religious book publishing, there was little possibility for Christian music to escape the processes of industrialization that those associations entailed. More important, perhaps, there is little reason to believe that the personnel involved were even hoping to avoid those associations. As works such as Carol Flake's *Redemptorama,* Randall Balmer's *Mine Eyes Have Seen the Glory,* and Max Weber's *The Protestant Ethic and the Spirit of Capitalism* have repeatedly shown, industrial capitalism is far from anathema to (evangelical) Christianity.[20] The issue with regard to contemporary Christian music, then, is less industrialization and capitalism in general than it is a particular manifestation of industrial capitalism. As discussed previously, religious book publishing was not the only industry interested in the profit potential of Christian rock music; the secular music industry was interested as well. As James Lull writes, "When alternative music first develops it is resisted by industry primarily on financial grounds, then is reluctantly accommodated by them when profit potential is more clear, and finally is brought under their financial and artistic control."[21] Although not quite so smoothly as Lull's syntax suggests, this progression has certainly played itself out in regard to Christian music, with major mainstream record labels clearly attempting to either penetrate the market for Christian music and/or control the flow of Christian music to mainstream audiences. And despite the difficulties involved in merging the two in meaningful and productive ways, Christian music has clearly benefited, at least financially, from mainstream interest. According to one 1995 report, "Christian music is the fastest-growing form of popular music, driving its message home to the tune of $750 million a year."[22] As the money began to accumulate, however, and artists such as Amy Grant found themselves able to subordinate the concerns of the evangelical market to those of the mainstream, the twin fears that emerged among evangelicals were those of scale and control.[23] Simply put, there appeared to be too much money and too much ambiguity about who was in control for a supposedly religious medium. Illustrating these issues, Romanowski argues that "what was unprecedented about the contemporary Christian music (CCM) industry was that it was the most extensive attempt to merge religious music with the commercialization and industrialization of the popular entertainment industry."[24] In other words, what made CCM unusual and of particular interest to scholars and evangelicals like Romanowski was the degree (scale) to which the commercial interests of the recorded music industry had, to use Romanowski's term, co-opted religion (control). Presumably, with either fewer dollars at stake or lower levels of participation from the mainstream music industry, contemporary Christian music would be far less worrisome to contemporary evangelicals. Still, however accurate Romanowski's claim may seem at face value, there are three significant issues that should be taken into account in considering the impact of commercialism on CCM. Loosely speaking, these are: the nature of rock music (or rather, the study of rock music), the nature of evangelicalism, and the nature of co-optation.

Questioning Co-optation

While Romanowski's concern lies specifically with evangelicalism and evangelical culture, his charge that the Christian music industry has been co-opted by the commercial forces of the mainstream recorded music industry is undoubtedly a single instance of a rather widespread academic phenomenon. Reviewing the studies of popular music, one finds no shortage of scholars making similar claims concerning other forms of popular music. The issue, to borrow from the work of Simon Frith, is that of authenticity. Addressing musician and fan reactions to new technologies used in the production of music, Frith argues that "what is at stake in all these arguments is the authenticity or truth of the music."[25] And while recording technologies themselves are not directly relevant to this discussion, Frith's identification of "the slide from 'fakery' in terms of technology to 'fakery' in terms of commercial manipulation" is relevant, for embedded in this shift is the presumption that authentic music, truthful music, is noncommercial music.[26] It is this equation of the authentic with the noncommercial and the inauthentic with the commercial that drives Romanowski's analysis, but again, Romanowski is far from alone. The particular definition of "authentic" may change—here it is attached to a religious experience, there to a political movement—but the underlying concept remains the same. To choose a small sampling, R. Serge Denisoff's study of folk-rock, Holly Kruse's analysis of the alternative music scene in Champaign, Illinois, and Cynthia Lont's work with women's music and Redwood Records are similar to Romanowski's, each exploring a perceived tension between music that is perceived to comprise pure, truthful, authentic expression (folk music, alternative music, women's music, gospel) and the commercialized forms of those musics that are perceived to be inauthentic and somehow false.[27] More significant, it is an equation that sits at the heart of Marxist cultural studies more generally, characterizing studies of almost every mediated cultural form (although rock music is admittedly a favorite target).[28] The point here is not to claim that Christian music has not been affected by commercialism; indeed, such a claim would fly in the face of all available evidence. Rather, it is to suggest that claiming "co-optation" offers, if the pun can be forgiven, little more than the same old song and dance. As Lont ultimately argues with regard to Redwood Records, co-optation is simply not an adequate explanation for the relations that tie subcultures and subcultural organizations to mainstream society.[29] Ultimately, more nuanced models are required.[30]

Setting aside for the moment the assumptions that pit the commercial against the authentic, further difficulties arise with Romanowski's claim in that it seems to suggest Christian music to be a singular phenomenon in the degree to which it has blended evangelicalism with commerce. However, while contemporary Christian music has been by far the most successful of evangelical efforts to penetrate the worldwide (commercial) mass media, it is important to note that it is by no means the only such effort. Carol Flake borrows evangelist Dave Breese's reference to evangelical Christianity as "the greatest show on earth" for her 1984 treatment of the subject and extends the metaphor to suggest that American evangelicals in the 1980s "were trying to create, amid the secular wasteland of America, a new version of the city on the hill . . . an artificial paradise on earth, a kind of Christian Disneyland of model families and good clean fun."[31] According to Flake, "The attitude of the Christian counterculture was essentially censorious. If thine eye offends thee, pluck it out. If thy neighbor's eye offends thee, block his vision. But the attitude of yet another faction of conservative Christians was considerably more enterprising. If thine eye offends thee, buy Christian bifocals. If thy neighbor's eye offends thee, advise him to tune into a Christian talk show instead of those X-rated cable shows. In this approach, the Christian set out to beat the secular enemy on its own terms—by competing in the marketplace."[32] Thus, while contemporary Christian music might represent the furthest extreme of industrialized religion, the Christian music industry must nevertheless be contextualized within the larger whole of the industrialized and mediated nature of contemporary evangelicalism. Religious radio, television evangelists, evangelical book and magazine publishers, evangelical filmmaking, "Jesus junk," and, to some degree, even the practices of the modern church (especially the so-called "superchurches" such as Bob Schuller's Crystal Cathedral) all point to the fact that religion in America, at least that of the Protestant evangelical strain, is an extremely commercialized, industrialized, and institutionalized practice.[33] Can it really be the level of commercialization that makes Christian music so distinctive from the remainder of evangelical culture?

Finally, there is the issue of co-optation more generally. How are we to understand the concept? According to Cynthia Lont, "co-optation has been used to imply that the social relations of the subculture are either infiltrated or overpowered by the dominant culture," and it carries with it the notion of artists "selling-out" or being "bought off."[34] In the specific context of rock music, co-optation is understood as "the process by which rock and roll is appropriated into the contexts of the dominant organizations of affect so that it loses whatever oppositional force it may have had."[35] Within this context, Lawrence Grossberg argues that "the history of rock and roll is read as a cycle of cooptation and renaissance in which rock and roll constantly protests against its own cooptation."[36] Romanowski's description of CCM clearly falls within the parameters of this approach. According to Grossberg, however, there is another way to view co-optation within the context of rock music. "Rather than a cycle of authentic and coopted music," suggests Grossberg, "rock and roll exists as a fractured unity within which differences of authenticity and cooptation are defined in the construction of affective alliances and networks of affiliation."[37] Rock and roll, in other words, is an exercise in (temporal) community, with "authenticity" and "cooptedness" the concepts used to assign membership. And if particularly potent in its application to rock music, Grossberg's model is equally illuminating in the case of Christian music (and evangelicalism more generally). Specifically, while there can be little doubt, as Romanowski charges, that the interests of consumption, capitalism, and materialism have been incorporated into the practices of the Christian music industry as well as of the evangelical church, it is equally clear that, as with rock and roll more generally, consumption, capitalism, and materialism are *necessary components* of both Christian music and evangelicalism.[38] (That this is the case for contemporary Christian music is especially clear. This is, after all, essentially an engagement in the creation, distribution, and consumption of recorded music.) Co-optation, then, is not the final outcome of a particular set of commercial processes or decision-making that trade resistance for domination but rather the label given to a particular constellation of social forces—commercial, material, theological, artistic, etc.—as manifested in a particular social realm. The same is true of "authentic." Furthermore, which constellation(s) one believes to be co-opted and which constellation(s) one believes to be authentic are going to depend on one's personal perspective. So, while one may find Amy Grant's radio pop a corruption of the values of Christian music and evidence of religion selling out to consumption, another finds Grant's music to have remained true to the vision of CCM. Around these and other perspectives, communities develop.

It is worth remembering here as well that, as with most cultural forms (including mainstream rock and roll), the people, practices, and products that together shape and define the production of contemporary Christian music are diverse and far from homogeneous. Consequently, to argue that the process of co-optation, however one chooses to define it, sufficiently explains the whole of the Christian music industry is much like suggesting that the musics of Anthony Braxton and of Barry Manilow can both be understood in their entirety by virtue of the artists' common association with Arista Records. And while there are in fact features of both Braxton's experimental jazz and Manilow's pop treacle that can be understood in light of each one's contract with Arista—whatever their respective attitudes toward art, commerce, fame, expression, or what have you, each was inextricably involved in the business of selling records—to understand either completely demands something more.[39] The same holds for CCM.

Ultimately, then, while the myriad solo artists and bands that constitute contemporary Christian music generally provide diverse explanations for their art—"This is a business, first and foremost" (The 77's), "I think the goal is to communicate something that's important" (Petra), "We're trying to challenge people to dig deeper" (Third Day), "We're here for ministry" (Poor Old Lu), "We're here to let you know that Jesus Christ is

Lord of our lives and that you really can have fun and be a Christian too"
(Newsboys)[40]—there is little doubt that, by virtue of their participation in
a practice that routinely combines religious faith with the practices of consumption, these artists, willingly or unwillingly, consciously or unconsciously, support a system that at least to some degree equates religious
behavior with consumer behavior. At the same time, however, if these
artists share at least some common ground as a result of their involvement
with the production of commercial pop music, the relationships that tie
those artists to that capitalist system can be unique. More precisely, inas-
much as Separational CCM, Integrational CCM, and Transformational
CCM differ in terms of the assumptions held concerning the relationships
between Christian faith and secular culture, the theological rationales used
to motivate and justify the music, and the aesthetic systems that have evolved
on the basis of those theological motivations, the three can also be distinguished by virtue of their relationship to the explicitly commercial aspects
of contemporary Christian music. Thus, even if contemporary Christian
music can be described as the co-optation of religion by commercial culture, how that co-optation plays itself out—Is the potential for co-optation
acknowledged or ignored? Is it approached theologically or aesthetically?
Is it ironically embraced or flatly denied?—differs according to the particular form of CCM examined.

Transformational CCM: Artistry or Commodity?

The difficulties facing transformational artists regarding the question of
Christian music's co-optation are arguably the most straightforward, for
the nightmare (to borrow Marx's term) of Transformational CCM is the
same faced by all self-proclaimed artists as they come into contact with the
mechanisms of commercially produced culture: a capitalist system that
easily transforms art into propaganda and beauty into commodity. More
specifically, given their particular assumptions about Christ and culture
and their unique rationales for the production of their music, the artists of
Transformational CCM frequently find themselves at odds with a Christian music industry and evangelical market that, as a result of either individual belief and/or marketing savvy, for the most part adheres to
separational assumptions.[41] Simply put, transformational artists and Christian record labels often have difficulty knowing what to do with one another, and the necessary cooperative links forged between them generally

emerge as tenuous at best. The dilemma, at least for the musicians, is that of being an "artist" in a subculture that seeks "ministers" who adhere to a narrowly defined conception of Christian spirituality. Describing the experience of parsing his lyrics with a religious retailer after a customer returned an album, Steve Murray of the band Curious Fools argues that "the problem is that for some reason, some Christians don't understand or appreciate symbolism and metaphors."[42] The oft-noted desire on the part of both fans and record labels for clear, propositional statements over allegory and metaphor would seem to support this contention. It may be true, as Murray contends, that "there's no room for art and poetry" under such conditions, but while transformational artists align with Nouwen in his call for Christians to become mystics, confess their own brokenness, and engage in strenuous theological reflection, the assumption of the Christian music industry as a whole is that the majority of evangelicals want simple, even trite, affirmations of their beliefs.[43]

If it is true, as numerous artists have complained, that artistry (symbolism and metaphor) is in short supply in the Christian music industry, there are clear justifications for this state of affairs. Selling recorded music—even Christian recorded music—is an exercise in heavy investment with few guarantees of return; it is a high-stakes game with high levels of risk and uncertainty.[44] From the perspective of the Christian record labels, then, the effort to sell mystical Christianity to audiences rooted in an extremely literal evangelical version of the faith represents an increase in the risk and uncertainty that they are trying to minimize. Expressing the mystery of God may make sense from an artistic standpoint, but it makes little sense from a business standpoint.[45] Indeed, a key strategy for dealing with the inconsistency between the transformational artists' approach and the audience's assumptions is to attempt to recast transformational "artists" as separational "ministers" via the strict application of a Christian pop music formula. Bands at the start of their careers are particularly vulnerable to this endeavor. Hoi Polloi is a case in point. After what became a much-talked-about Encore Stage performance at the 1990 Cornerstone Festival (the band's first American appearance), the New Zealand group found itself with contract offers from numerous Christian record labels. After signing with Reunion, the band was paired with producer Reed Arvin, known for his success with mainstream and inspirational CCM acts, and its "gnarlier" songs were rejected by the record company. Through its actions, Reunion effectively transformed Hoi Polloi from an alternative

rock band into a pop act, with the band's first CD most closely reflecting
this latter incarnation. Ultimately, it would take a third album, a third
producer, and a second record label for Hoi Polloi to produce an album
that the band members felt captured their true sound.[46]

The members of Hoi Polloi are far from the only ones to have fallen
victim to the transformative power of a contract with a Christian record
label. Julie Miller describes her experience recording for Myrrh this way:
"I'm not for everyone; I'm sort of funky and messy. I think Myrrh wanted
to make me a poppier pop artist than I already was. So, it was just a mis-
match of artist and company."[47] Miller, however, is likely being optimistic.
The Choir, The 77's, Jacob's Trouble, Leslie Phillips, Patty Cabrera, Cindy
Morgan, Kim Hill, Michael James Murphy, Bryan Duncan—the list of
artists (transformational, integrational, and separational) whose music has
been transformed through their association with the Christian music industry goes on and on.[48] If the desires of the audience are ultimately un-
knowable, the pressure to sell units nevertheless creates a tendency for
labels to reshape their artists in the mold dictated by their perceptions of
the market. This move, however, is claimed to create a "dishonesty" that
strikes at the core of Transformational CCM's legitimating rationales, leaving artists in an uncomfortable position: compromise your art or find yourself without the opportunity to produce it. So, while perhaps
overemphasizing their commitment to artistic purity, Steve Hindalong and
Derri Daugherty describe the tensions that defined their efforts to produce a series of worship albums on their own Glasshouse label:

> We don't have it in our hearts to compromise the creative process at all. I
> mean, the song "Beautiful Scandalous Night" from *At the Foot of the Cross*
> is a Christian radio song if we've ever written one. And it's sincere and
> from the heart; nothing phony about it. And we could have brought it
> home production-wise. But no, we had to put that backwards guitar loop
> in there, and get a good backbeat on the snare. And I had to play African
> percussion and nail it! We could not break ourselves and I don't think we
> ever will.[49]

And if the final result was considered an artistic success, generating not
only critical acclaim but also a significant (and growing) number of imita-
tors, from a business standpoint the decision not to "bring it home pro-
duction-wise" ultimately proved costly. The causal links are difficult to
trace, but it is nonetheless worth noting that the pair's Glasshouse label

subsequently went out of business, and *At the Foot of the Cross, Volume 1: Clouds, Fire, Rain* (Glasshouse, 1992) quickly went out of print while the imitative but far more conventional *Corem Deo* (Sparrow, 1992) won a Dove Award for Best Praise and Worship album.[50]

If Christian record labels have been known to pressure (transformational) artists to produce what is perceived to be more commercially viable music, more frequent and more public have been conflicts between artists and labels over the phrasing and subject matter of the lyrics the artists are writing. Examples of record labels changing album titles, excising songs, and demanding rewrites are rife throughout the history of Christian music: Tonio K.'s previously discussed "What Women Want"—removed from the Word version of *Notes from the Lost Civilization* (What? Records, 1988); Jacob's Trouble's "About Sex"—pulled at the last minute from *Knock, Breathe, Shine* (Alarma, 1990); Julie Miller's "S.O.S." (short for "Sick of Sex")—delayed until Miller's third album and included there only because Miller had, without informing Word, spent much of her promotional budget on a video for the song; The 77's *Pray Naked*—retitled *The Seventy Sevens* (BAI, 1992); The Choir's "Everybody in the Band"—originally penned to include the line "He smokes a lot of Camels" (and occasionally performed as such in concerts), as recorded for *Chase the Kangaroo* (Myrrh, 1988), the line reads, "In tears for man's condition"; The 77's "Dave's Blues"—originally recorded to include the line "this ol' world has kicked my ass," Word had the song remixed and the offending line replaced with that section of the vocal track played in reverse.[51] The list continues.

Tensions, however, don't revolve solely around smoking, sex, and swearing.[52] As the late Mark Heard once said:

> I remember I used to have these discussions with the label people, and they would try to get me to change almost any words that had some kind of negative connotations into positive words—it was silly because they were only afraid that large droves of Christian record buying people would get scared of the music because it didn't fit their expectations of something from a "Christian Singer". . . . I've had record companies tell me, "Oh this song has six negative words in it. We have to get rid of this word, this word, this word. Rewrite the song and get rid of those words."[53]

For the Christian record labels, then, not only are particular topics considered anathema, so too are particular attitudes and approaches to the experience of living considered difficult to market. Artists hoping to explore those areas face considerable pressure from the record labels to alter their music. Indeed, the pressure can at times become overwhelming. After representatives from Rode Dog, a subsidiary label of Reunion Records, sent The Prayer Chain back into the studio to record two new songs after deciding that the product being offered was not "Christian enough," bassist Eric Campuzano vented his frustrations to *Kamikaze* magazine:

> I think it's a joke. I think the "Christian industry" is selling Jesus. I think they're selling mediocrity. I think what they're doing is wrong. I think that they're building a wall around themselves and losing touch with reality. . . . I would like to see the industry re-think its role in the world. I feel really out of place in this industry, and I feel like that's how they want it. People won't take us on tour with them because they don't think we're "Christian" enough and that our music is not the type of music that the youth pastors want to hear.[54]

Yet, to a very real extent, "selling Jesus" is exactly what much of the CCM industry does. "Spirituality" (of the evangelical bent) is used to sell a musical product in the industry much as sex appeal is used to sell products in the wider marketplace. It's an arrangement that many transformational artists find difficult to accept. Allan Aguirre of Scaterd Few laments, "Christians are the only ones who put 'Christian' before anything to justify something or make something passable. . . . It's just the most crass thing I've ever experienced."[55] Perhaps not surprisingly, the casualty rate among the bands that constitute Transformational CCM is particularly high; both The Prayer Chain and Scaterd Few are included among the dead.

So, beyond disbanding, how do transformational artists deal with the commercialization and "evangelicalization" of their art? In the attempt to mediate the pressures of commodification, transformational artists have frequently set up their own record labels in the hopes of finding the freedom to produce the music they want to create. While the 1990s in particular have seen a sudden burst of independent companies making inroads into a CCM art world long dominated by Word, Sparrow, and Benson, independent labels have existed since the earliest days of Christian music. One of the first experiments was Larry Norman's Solid Rock Records, which, in the late 1970s and early 1980s, launched the Christian music careers of Randy Stonehill and Mark Heard and released music from CCM pioneers Daniel Amos, Tom Howard, and Pantano Salisbury. According to Norman, the goal in forming the label was "to help other artists who didn't want to be consumed by the business of making vinyl pancakes but who wanted to say something 'non-commercial' to the world."[56] However, while highly praised by critics and fans alike, the innovative label proved to be short-lived. Randy Stonehill's take on the situation—circumstances that to this day remain shrouded in controversy[57]—has been to conclude that, while artistically Solid Rock was a great experience, artists often make lousy businessmen: "As artistically heady as the days at Solid Rock were . . . and as good as the ideas were on paper, the business end was always very loose-knit. . . . We were young guys with good ideas but not a whole lot of business sense."[58] This, however, is only one explanation. Other explanations include the suggestion made by some of the artists who recorded for Solid Rock that Norman made promises he didn't keep (due, in part, to a head injury that contributed to an inability to complete projects). Norman, however, argues that he never set out to promote anyone's career and ultimately became frustrated with artists who were more interested in selling records than sharing Jesus: "I got really disillusioned when they were talking about Jesus before the album, but then as soon as their career started, they stopped talking and started emphasizing that they'd be at the record table as soon as the concert was over. Wouldn't stay for the afterglow service and they wouldn't pray with people. And I just finally got disillusioned and quit producing people. If they aren't going to advance God's kingdom, I don't care to help them advance their kingdom."[59] Norman felt he had lived up to his obligation to educate Solid Rock artists to help them become self-reliant. Whatever really happened at Solid Rock, the debate illustrates the tensions that exist between the divergent CCM art worlds, as well as those between art and business. Whatever the religious rhetoric, with Norman's role as label executive came a separational perspective that clashed with the transformational approach of the artists he was producing. In many ways, then, Solid Rock can be seen as a microcosm for the industry as a whole.

Solid Rock was not the last such effort. The 1980s brought another highly acclaimed, short-lived venture in artist-run record labels with Exit Records. Begun in 1982 by Mary Neely, Exit Records was the recording arm of the Sacramento-based Warehouse Ministries. Distributed to the Christian market by Word, Exit also had secular distribution for its product, first through A&M and then Island Records. Because of these distribution agreements (as well as a general belief in the quality of the Exit bands), there were great expectations concerning the mainstream potential for the artists on the Exit roster. As Brian Q. Newcomb later noted, "In the Summer of '86 when *Harvest Rock Syndicate* put Charlie Peacock on the cover, it was our prophetic bet that he was about to break, in a big way."[60] At first, Exit appeared to be achieving no small measure of success: videos by The 77's and Vector went into light rotation on MTV, and a few Exit artists found their songs receiving radio airplay; Charlie Peacock toured with bands like The Fixx and General Public; and at least three Exit albums were released to the mainstream marketplace: *Lie Down in the Grass* (Exit, 1984) and a self-titled follow-up from Charlie Peacock, as well as The 77's eponymous third album (which was one of only two Christian rock albums—Leslie Phillips's *The Turning* [Myrrh LA, 1987] was the other—to be reviewed by *Rolling Stone* in the 1980s).[61] In each case, however, the songs went nowhere, the albums went nowhere, and the artists went nowhere. Consequently, in March 1989, Exit went out of business with the departure of every one of its artists.[62]

While there is no doubt much that went into Exit's eventual failure—and much that may never be known[63]—there are a number of factors that clearly hampered the Exit artists in their efforts and that were frequently repeated elsewhere in Christian music. In at least one case, conflict between the goals for a band and an unwillingness to work in pursuit of those goals thwarted the efforts of the label. As Vector member Steve Griffith notes, "Exit . . . did not want us to become a mainstream Christian band. So, we deliberately avoided the Christian concert circuit. They wanted Vector to direct its music to a non-Christian audience, which was fine with us. But at the same time, the people who ran Exit, who incidentally were the same people who pastored our church, were not comfortable with us playing in clubs."[64] Vector, then, was kept out of the Christian marketplace by the desire to avoid being labeled a "Christian band," and yet the consternation caused by the idea of evangelicals entering the secular club scene kept them out of the mainstream marketplace as well. Unable to generate a following, the band's chances for success dissipated. The 77's shared a similar experience. This, too, was a group attempting to avoid the "Christian band" label, and so shunning the Christian press, they hired an independent promoter for the release of their second album *All Fall Down* (Exit, 1984). With a mild hit on the college radio charts ("Ba Ba Ba"), the success of *All Fall Down* in part led to the distribution agreement between Exit and Island Records.[65] The band's Island release, however, had the misfortune of being released just one week prior to U2's *The Joshua Tree* (Island, 1987), and when Island turned its attention toward promoting U2—the band's frontman Mike Roe claims "All of Island Records' staff left the office for about six weeks to go on tour with U2"—The 77's became another casualty in Christian music's crossover campaign.[66]

Beyond the issues of promotions and marketing, there was a third consideration that mitigated against Exit's chances for success in mainstream music. With the release of their first two albums, *Mannequin Virtue* (Exit, 1983) and *Please Stand By* (Exit, 1985), Vector had attracted the interest of A&M and Billy Graham Presents (the rock promoter, not the evangelist) personnel. At the time, however, Exit was committed to the "stubborn insistence that these companies take on all the Exit bands in a package deal," and, while Vector was free to negotiate with A&M on their own, the members "did not want to sever the empathetic and spiritually reinforcing relationships they had with Exit."[67] As guitarist Jim Abegg laments, "We made a purely spiritual decision to go with Exit and blow A&M off . . . [but] we should have evaluated the A&M deal from a purely business viewpoint. We should have taken A&M's three record deal and $60,000 budget for PR"—particularly after Exit later informed them that the label would be focusing on the careers of Peacock and The 77's.[68] The hard lesson learned by the members of Vector and the rest of the artists at Exit was that, despite any religious agenda, creating and marketing popular music—Christian or secular—was, at its core, a financial endeavor. Moreover, the commitment to community found at Exit, while entirely appropriate to running a church, ran directly contrary to the workings of the music industry, which is designed to exploit those artists who are popular while they are popular.

Moving on from Exit, the 1980s featured other significant efforts by established CCM artists to create a niche where they and others could make the type of music they wanted to create with less interference from market pressures. Broken Records claimed to be "a radical restructuring of relationships between music and the church; between artists and audience; between business and labor" that would place "people over product, vision over vinyl."[69] Blonde Vinyl was created by Mike Knott to release his own music but evolved into an innovative alternative label. Terry Taylor and Daniel Amos created their own label, Alarma! Records and Tapes (ART), and their own production company, Rebel Base Productions, with the goal of bringing something of what they had learned to other groups and artists.[70] Fingerprint Records was formed in 1987 by Heard and Dan Russell, first as a vehicle for Mark Heard's music and later as a Boston-based label promoting both regional and national acts. Describing the vision of Fingerprint, Russell repeats the transformational rationales of artistic integrity and honesty: "At Fingerprint Records we're looking for *characters,* we're constantly trying to emphasize the artists finding out who they really are, and getting them to identify the things that are maybe attacking their true self—to get that on the table and encourage them to affirm who they really are."[71]

While these early attempts at creating labels that would put artistic concerns before commercial considerations were generally (though not always) short-lived, the 1990s brought renewed attempts by established transformational artists to make the vision a reality. Gene Eugene of Adam Again and Ojo Taylor of Undercover joined to form Brainstorm Artists International (BAI), which artist Jon Gibson described as "more of an artist type of company. They really are art first, art-oriented."[72] In 1996, Taylor sold his share of the company to Eugene and formed yet another "artist label," Innocent Media, which would promote a wider variety of musical genres than the alternative-music-oriented BAI. Also in 1996, Charlie Peacock formed a multimedia company called Re:think. According to marketing director Nick Barre, Re:think was designed to encourage people to "rethink what it means to be a Christian and what it means to be an artist at the same time, to rethink the place of music in the church."[73] Peacock noted the constraints placed on artists to turn their music into commodities: "Now, artists tend to do one thing, and try to do it well. In our consumer culture, music has become more commodity-oriented. You want to know that Joe PopStar does this one thing and does it well. When you buy the record, you want to know what you're going to get. Very few people have the privilege of changing from record to record. But when I was a kid, that's what we looked forward to."[74] Transformational artists have established a track record of creating their own venues—however small and insignificant they may be relative to the major CCM labels and even more so relative to the mainstream labels—to allow themselves the freedom to create art as they see fit.

Although the independent labels created by the transformational artists have routinely been started in the name of artistic freedom, the labels have generally been less than successful in escaping the tensions between art and commerce. Beyond the simple fact that most of these labels have gone bankrupt as a result of their inability to generate the profits necessary to stay in business, there are a number of significant points to be drawn from the experiences of labels such as Solid Rock and Exit. First, commerce is a necessary evil. As the writers at Comedia (a/k/a Minority Press Group) have charged with regard to alternative newspapers, the success or failure of independent media outlets like the transformational labels can often be attributed to the philosophical biases of those involved. Hence, the repeated failures of the alternative presses during the 1970s and 1980s could be attributed to the inability to conceive of target audiences, adapt marketing strategies, and budget and develop skills in financial planning; in other words, the failures among the alternative press "derive from the 'blind spots' in the libertarian political perspective which has dominated this sector."[75] Similar charges can be made against many of CCM's independent labels. Committed to "art" and artistic freedom, the artist-run labels frequently misunderstand the fundamentals of the economic environments in which they are attempting to work. As Brian Quincy Newcomb notes of his failed effort to successfully publish a Christian music magazine operating from a transformational perspective, "We could've made far better—and I don't mean better in the strict sense of the term, I mean better in the commercial sense of the term—we could've made smarter moves."[76] Unwilling to compromise and thereby largely kept out of the retail distribution channels, Newcomb's magazine—like many of the labels it discussed—ultimately folded.

It should be noted, however, that not all artists-cum-label-executives ignore the demands of the marketplace. Among successful and unsuccessful labels alike there have been numerous examples of transformational artists whose transformational assumptions have given way in the face of commercial realities. John Austin describes his experience recording for Glasshouse Records as similar to those of artists recording for the giants. With his debut album, *The Embarrassing Young* (Glasshouse, 1992)—a collection of ten songs produced by Mark Heard and focused on Austin's singing, songwriting, and acoustic guitar—largely complete, Austin turned the album in to the label and was told to record two additional "radio ready" tracks. The irony here is the fact that Glasshouse was the label created by Derri Daugherty and Steve Hindalong. Hence, despite Daugherty and Hindalong's claim that they can't "break themselves" and "don't have it in [their] hearts to compromise the creative process" when it comes to recording their own music, they apparently have little diffi-culty recognizing the constraints of the marketplace as it applies to others. *The Embarrassing Young* was eventually released with twelve songs—the original ten plus the two overtly religious rock numbers Hindalong and Daugherty co-produced.[77]

The point here is not to hold up Daugherty and Hindalong as hypo-crites. Rather, it is to suggest that the tensions between art and commerce that underlie much of Transformational CCM should not be understood as "the good artist" battling "the evil CEO" (though this is frequently how it is presented). Instead, we are back to Marx's suggestion that, while humans make history, they must do so under circumstances not of their own choosing. In this case, in order to survive in the competitive music industry, transformational artists have struggled with the structural and commercial constraints that industry imposes. As Weinstein has noted, the standards for a successful commodity sharply contrast with those of art. Celebrity and image, not profundity and proficiency, are the key re-quirements for successful audience appeal.[78] In the case of contemporary Christian music, one can add explicit religiosity to Weinstein's list. Celeb-rity, image, or explicit religiosity, the underlying point remains: the choice to pursue artistic purity has often meant commercial obscurity, both in contemporary Christian music and in popular music more generally. But despite the claims of a homogenizing co-optation, in both realms one finds artists willing to risk obscurity—and in some cases perhaps even en-joying it—if it means they will be allowed to enjoy artistic freedom.

Integrational CCM: Watered Down Religion?

For the musicians, critics, and fans of Transformational CCM, the com-mercialization and co-optation of contemporary Christian music are defined by the continual tracing of the line between the authentic artifact on the one hand and the inauthentic, commercial commodity on the other. For Integrational CCM, however, the difficulties associated with the com-mercialization of Christian music aren't perceived to be the result of com-mercialism in general but rather the particular forms of commercialization entailed in the effort to penetrate mainstream markets. In other words, while the critics of Integrational CCM generally see little to be concerned with in the commercial exchanges taking place in the Christian Family Bookstores, they see, potentially at least, a great deal to be concerned with in the parallel activities of Tower Records. The difference can be seen in the following debate between John W. Styll and Keith Green over the purpose of the corporate infrastructure of the Christian music industry. Responding to Green's decision to remove himself from the Christian music industry, Styll argues that "the reason that there *are* such things as [Christian] record companies is primarily to take the burdens of business, distribution, and manufacturing headaches and hassles off of an artist so that the artist can concentrate on what they do best."[79] Green disagrees, arguing that "the central reason that there are record companies is for corporations to make money."[80] Significantly, the issue here is not activity or behavior (making and selling records) but motive; profit is acceptable so long as it's not the primary goal. Thus, the risk run by Integrational CCM regarding commercialized Christian music is not commodification—as implied by Styll's words, business is, after all, perceived to be ministry—but rather the possible perception that the pursuit of profit has taken priority over religious motivations and the concomitant appearance of "watering down the message" as a means of reaching that goal.

Undoubtedly, the risks are real. If Christian music is to be successful within the context of mainstream popular culture, the music must necessarily be commercially viable above and beyond whatever sales it generates in the Christian bookstores. And to be successful in American popular music requires not only touching the hearts and minds of the audience but also moving its members to purchase the music. So, claims Peter Wicke, everything that comes into contact with the music industry is made to serve the economic and ideological interests of capital; and so, claim critics of Integrational CCM, there is a price to be paid for the attention of mainstream audiences.[81] Indeed, "Christian" and "commercially viable" are perceived by many to be antithetical. Adopting this argument, in May 1996 the prominent evangelical magazine *Christianity Today* published a profile on the state of Christian music titled, "Can't Buy Me Ministry."[82] In this essay, separational artist Michael Card accuses—at least by implication—his integrational colleagues of omitting the cross from the gospel: "What happens to the message when we start getting the music to as many people as possible? There is an essential part of the gospel that's not ever going to sell. The gospel is good news, but it is also bad news: 'You are a sinner, and you are hopeless.' How is a multimillion-dollar record company going to take that? That's part of the message, too, and if that's taken out—and it frequently is in Christian music—it ceases to be the gospel."[83] According to Card, then, by virtue of omitting what he sees as an essential part of the gospel message (the fallen nature of humanity) from the music, Integrational CCM no longer qualifies as "Christian" music. Thus, for Card, crossing over can amount only to selling out; no truly Christian music will ever garner mainstream attention or success.

Card is not the only one making such arguments. Steve Taylor, drawing on his experience as a Christian musician, makes a similar case. One of Christian music's central but more enigmatic figures, Taylor spent the 1980s as the industry's self-appointed court jester, recording albums comprising fairly scathing social critique cloaked in New Wave rhythms and pun-filled lyrics. However, when critics saw a tarot card in the cover art to 1987's *I Predict 1990* (Myrrh), Taylor dropped out of CCM. After spending a number of years in pseudo-retirement followed by an attempt at mainstream success with the band Chagall Guevara, Taylor returned to Christian music in 1993 with the album *Squint* (Warner Alliance), this time as an unabashed separational artist. Relating his experiences with mainstream music, Taylor questioned the value of Integrational CCM's positive pop: "I had been looking for freedom in the alternative pop sector, but all I found was a different set of rules, a whole political agenda to follow. Now having returned to the Christian music industry, I realize that what's critically important about Christian music is its distinctiveness. If it loses the Cross, if it loses Christ, if it becomes just 'positive pop,' then I'd rather be cut off from it. I just can't imagine anything more insipid."[84] For Taylor, crossover success seemed to require not only the excision of the gospel but also the adoption of a "politically correct" agenda, at least parts of which (adopting a pro-choice stance) were antithetical to his faith. The bottom line, implied by both Card and Taylor, is that crossover success demands a tempered Christianity, devoid of the gospel.

While separational artists argue that Integrational CCM has little that is Christian about it, there are those who, at least by extension, can be seen to defend the integrational approach. Again, the issue is authenticity. Speaking of black music crossover attempts, Steve Perry notes that the "rhetoric of sellout" is based on very narrow ideas about what counts as authentic musical expressions and what doesn't. Therefore, soulful grunts are considered authentically black, while pop crooning is not.[85] Responding to such critiques, Perry contends that those who criticize crossover attempts generally ignore changes in social relations, technology, and prevailing musical styles in making their judgments about authenticity. Musical genres, he argues, are not static but dynamic, evolving entities. These genres, moreover, evolve in a social context that clearly shapes and steers the music produced, though the music remains to some extent rooted in the assumptions of the subculture from which it rises. Applying Perry's argument to the case of contemporary Christian music, if lyrical content, as opposed to the musical sound, tends to define authenticity in CCM, the underlying thrust of the argument nevertheless remains true. As with black gospel crossovers, the difficulty for Integrational CCM is its deviance from the narrowly defined parameters of authenticity in Christian music. According to the established separational conventions, songs with blatantly gospel messages that explicitly mention Jesus are perceived to be authentically Christian, while pop songs about love and faithfulness, however consistent they may be with Christian "family values," are not. Here too, however, authenticity is largely defined by a particular constellation of cultural forces (the Jesus Movement, sixties protest music, etc.) that integrational artists suggest are no longer in play. What separational critics, working from their cultural assumptions, see as watered-down Christianity and/or inauthentic and commercialized CCM, integrational artists see as a new cultural form.

Comparing the music and careers of Bruce Springsteen and Madonna, Mary Harron takes another approach to this question of authenticity. According to Harron, while Madonna is generally considered a product of commercial manipulation and Bruce Springsteen an authentic rock and roll artist, both are inextricably involved with hype.[86] The difference between them, suggests Harron, lies in the underlying values surrounding the music. If, as in the case of Springsteen, the music is believed to have intrinsic value (the rock belief), then hype is an attempt to distort the audience's perceptions for commercial gain; through the market, the public is manipulated into accepting something trite and flashy in place of the serious and the good. On the other hand, if, as in the case of Madonna, the value of music is determined by what people buy (the pop belief), then value becomes an entirely subjective matter. What sells is good, what doesn't is not; there is no absolute standard of authenticity. Applying these ideas to contemporary Christian music, one can argue that the distinction between the integrational artists and their critics is defined by the distinction between the rock and pop aesthetics; specifically, while integrational artists are more likely to adopt the pop belief, their critics generally adhere to an evangelical take on the rock belief. Illustrating this rock aesthetic, John

Styll argues that "Christian music, by definition, has a fundamentally spiritual purpose" and further suggests that while "there isn't necessarily anything wrong with an album that is not specifically Christian . . . those who market such music should avoid labeling it 'Christian' unless it really is."[87] Integrational artists, on the other hand, suggest that Christian music "really is" whatever the industry and audiences determine it to be. As Amy Grant said of her album *Behind the Eyes* (A&M/Myrrh, 1997), "Being able to label it Christian or non-Christian is not the point for me. The point was to make available the songs I wrote between 1995 and 1997, and to let them find their own audience."[88]

If commercialism brings to Transformational CCM the threat of commodification and the prostitution of art, to Integrational CCM it brings questions of motivation and the tension of competing rock and pop aesthetics. Pursuing or finding success in the mainstream marketplace, integrational artists are accused of giving up religious pursuits for profit and popularity—of giving up the (Christian) rock aesthetic. This, then, is what makes Grant's move to let the songs "find their own audience" such a powerful one within Integrational CCM. If separational critics argue that evidence for authentic Christianity is to be found in explicit (if potentially formulaic) expressions of the gospel and that commercial success is a sign of watered-down religion, integrational artists suggest that authenticity is a question of motivation and impact and that commercial success is in fact a sign of something "real." Commercialism is thus equated with authenticity, with the pop aesthetic translated into terms resonating more closely with the those of the rock aesthetic. The move is perhaps best illustrated by Michael W. Smith's experience. Looking back on his career, Smith suggests that the album he made with crossing over specifically in mind (*The Big Picture* [Reunion, 1986]) was a "mistake." According to Smith, mainstream success was accidental, the result of both his decision "just . . . to make a record" and God's timing.[89] Arguably, this concept of "just making a record" is crucial to Integrational CCM, denying as it does the idea that success is the artist's primary goal. As Amy Grant puts it, "I can look at a fan and say, '. . . this is the record I made for you. Not because I am trying to create a stir, not because I am trying to rock anybody's boat, but because it was what I was able to do.'"[90] Significantly, then, in Integrational CCM's rereading of the pop aesthetic, success emerges only when one isn't explicitly pursuing it, and, more important, is believed to signify authenticity. It does this either by symbolizing a connection between the artist and the audience rooted in common (and thereby authentic) thoughts, feelings, and/or experiences or by indicating some external validation of the music's authenticity (God's timing). Ultimately, integrational artists argue that because the music sells it must speak to the hearts and minds of Christians and non-Christians alike; therefore, it must be authentic. Sales don't threaten authenticity, they guarantee it.

Contemporary Christian music, like popular music more generally, is a realm ruled by the rock aesthetic. Privileging particular forms of expression that are considered to be authentic, it is the belief in the rock aesthetic that, first, allows for the dismissal of expression that finds success in the commercial marketplace, and second, allows for claims like Romanowski's that suggest commercialism signals co-optation. In choosing a commercial path, then, artists face two choices. They can, as Kurt Cobain of Nirvana did in the wake of *Nevermind* (DGC, 1991), attempt to buttress their claim to rock authenticity. Cobain's claim of "It's not our fault we sold two million records. We didn't try very hard," like his appearance on the cover of *Rolling Stone* wearing a T-shirt that read, "Corporate magazines still suck!" clearly worked to reaffirm the band's rock authenticity, which had been threatened by its commercial success, by distancing the members of the group from the commercial mechanisms responsible for *Nevermind*'s astounding sales.[91] The alternative is to challenge the very notion of authenticity as defined by the rock aesthetic. This has been the approach of Integrational CCM. Thus, while the transformational artists, still working from a rock aesthetic, recognize the presence of commercialism and commodification as a threat to their artistry and frequently use their lack of sales as evidence for both their continued commitment to art and the authenticity of their creative output, integrational artists argue that the commercialization of Christian music poses no such threat. Indeed, integrational artists challenge the assumptions that value the noncommercial over the commercial. Whether the claim is that the music has been co-opted by commercialism or that Integrational CCM is neither "Christian" nor of value, integrational artists argue that such claims are nothing more than an elitism that unreasonably privileges one cultural form over another. Emphasizing their desire to say something they feel is important and to find common ground with an audience on the basis of shared personal experiences, the artists of Integrational CCM argue that commercial success is a testament to, not contradictory of, musical authenticity and that, provided the motivation remains pure, co-optation is a nonissue.

Separational CCM: Selling the Gospel?

While critics of Integrational CCM charge that the artists are watering down the gospel message by focusing solely on the positive, critics of Separational CCM make the far more stinging claim that Christian music is essentially a practice in "selling the gospel." With the stated objectives of reaching the non-Christian with the gospel message, encouraging Christians in the daily exercise of their faith, and/or offering praise and worship to God, Separational CCM faces the uncomfortable circumstance of then placing a $15.99 price tag on that message.[92] Given this circumstance, it is not surprising that pointed questions are frequently asked: What happens to the "good news" of the gospel when it gets packaged in a three-and-one-half-minute pop song and sold in the marketplace? Can ministry be maintained under these circumstances or is the music reduced to mere entertainment? Do the harder demands of the Christian lifestyle disappear from the gospel in favor of a more generic moral message that is not distinctively Christian (as is claimed to be the case for Integrational CCM)? Does God's wrath and judgment over sin disappear in favor of sentimental songs of praise? How does one maintain the lyrical distinctiveness of Separational CCM in the face of pressure to make a profit for record companies that are increasingly owned by people whose investments are based on profitability rather than ministry? As Christian music has commercialized, these have been the issues with which Separational CCM has struggled.

The questions surrounding the commercialization of Christian music were brought into sharpest relief by Keith Green. As John Styll argues, Green's "impact on the contemporary Christian music scene is possibly without equal."[93] This arguably has as much to do with Green's stance on the business of Christian music as it does with the songs he recorded. According to Green, record labels—Christian record labels included—exist so that corporations can make money; and, as Green put it, "Anybody who honestly believes that a record company is there as a service, that that's the real reason they exist, or the main reason they are formed, is *grossly* mistaken."[94] Feeling that God was calling him to disassociate himself from a system rooted in the motives and machinations of profit-driven corporations and arguing that it is "wrong to put a price on an item that contains a spiritual message that came free from God," Green withdrew from the Christian music industry's established production and distribution systems.[95] Beginning with *So You Wanna Go Back to Egypt?* (Pretty Good Records, 1980), Green's Last Days Ministries distributed his albums via mail order, priced according to "whatever people can afford, or want, to give."[96] Although ambitious, the system was only partially successful.[97] Whatever the success of Green's mail-order scheme in terms of getting albums to fans, his decision to withdraw from CCM's established distribution channels certainly served to highlight the inherent tensions that Separational CCM faces in juggling ministry with business. As CCM's self-appointed psychoanalyst, Green brought to light what most would have preferred to have stayed repressed. The only member of the Christian music community to offer albums for whatever a fan was willing to pay— at least the only one to do so publicly and on a wide-scale basis—Green, by his actions, forced those involved in Christian music to wrestle, to some degree or another, with the apparent contradictions between the ideals of Christian ministry and the economic realities of the music industry.[98]

Perhaps not surprisingly, the solutions to the dilemma of ministry versus commerce have been rhetorical far more frequently than they have been structural, and even Green, despite his withdrawal from much of the CCM machinery, found it necessary to offer a rhetorical "out" to his fellow artists. At the same time he was vociferously arguing that the "basic system [was] wrong," Green was also suggesting that "the Lord used the gospel music industry," attesting that the majority of the people that he had been dealing with in CCM were "sweet brothers and sisters serving God in the capacity that God called them to."[99] For Green, then, although the commercial system was perceived to be antithetical to the tenets of Christianity, this character neither colored the Christians who were employed by the system nor prevented God from redeeming it. Green was not the only Christian to assert a distinction between the system and the individuals who constitute it. Examining the state of Christian music in 1993, Tim Stafford was able to find plenty of people willing to make statements condemning the Christian music industry as a system—"If you say Jesus a lot . . . you'll definitely sell more albums"; "Pride and greed are . . . tolerated if you sell enough albums"—but none who would claim to know an individual in Christian music who was "insincere in his or her faith."[100] Thus, for many the solution is to separate the system from the participants and focus on the latter. As Sparrow recording artist Margaret Becker puts it, "In the U.S., in order to have a ministry, you must have the business side. If you do a concert for a love offering, chances are you will walk away with nothing. It's just the way we are as a culture; we aren't too quick to hand over the dollars. . . . What I've done is to allow the record company to think of the business. If I am doing bad, they tell me. Otherwise, I don't want to know chart numbers or record sales."[101] Faced with the economic realities of commercialized Christian music, many artists adopt a position of plausible deniability: they acknowledge its existence but argue that part of the music is of an altogether different realm. As Dana Key so plainly puts it in his apologetic for Christian music, "The gospel must always be free; entertainment is not."[102] For artists such as Becker and Key, the commerce that permeates the Christian music industry is that of an entertainment industry, not of a ministry. The two are fundamentally distinct and, like oil and water, can be mixed without corrupting or even influencing one another.

While events such as Keith Green's attempt to circumvent the established commercial distribution system for Christian music have occasionally led to moments of acute crisis, there are also more chronic manifestations of the tensions between ministry and commerce that plague Separational CCM. The most notable of these is the debate over bootlegs (unauthorized recordings) and home taping (unauthorized duplicatation of authorized recordings). The conflict is fairly intuitive. Adopting Separational CCM's primary rationales, those who support these unauthorized recordings do so in the name of ministry and evangelism, arguing that by making duplicates of albums and performances bootleggers are enlarging the audience for the artist's music and expanding the reach of his or her message. Unauthorized taping is thus defended on much the same grounds as the industry itself: as facilitating ministry. The argument is a valid one. If the primary purpose of the music is in fact ministry (communicating a particular message to as many people as possible), then the unauthorized duplication and distribution of albums makes perfect sense. Provided the duplicate albums get into the hands of those who otherwise wouldn't hear the music, the size of the audience—the number of people who hear the message—will be increased. At this point, the artists—the ministers—are faced with an uncomfortable choice: they can allow unauthorized taping in the name of ministry or they can attack it as theft on commercial grounds, acknowledging in the process that ministry does indeed take a backseat to profit. Not surprisingly, most attempt to navigate a third way, by condemning the practice of home taping in explicitly religious terms. Exemplifying this move, Brian Tong of the Frontline Music Group writes on the issue of home taping: "Many artists' families sacrifice personal desires so that they can commit a full-time service to their ministry. If you want to support these 'warriors' for God, you can help by purchasing their music. The hard reality is that everytime you don't, in no uncertain terms, you stand strongly against their efforts."[103]

Although intended as a response to those who would duplicate albums without permission, the statement more significantly illustrates the ultimate reconciliation of business and ministry, for here commerce does not compete with religion and ministry but rather completes it. According to Tong, the act of consumption is an explicitly religious act, and to purchase a Christian record is to cast a blow for right in the spiritual warfare between good and evil. Home taping is defined not as theft, but as a spiritual attack. Business is ministry.

Arguably, however, the difficulties with commerce for Separational CCM do not end with this argument, for while commercialization and co-optation have largely been approached in Separational CCM in terms of "selling the gospel," like the transformational and integrational forms of the music, Separational CCM has also had to deal with the impact of the system on the music itself. Specifically, separational artists, too, have often found themselves at risk of adhering too closely to the musical formulas of Separational CCM (generally a light pop fare coupled with lyrics abounding in Christian catch phrases), thereby trading ministry for sales. Peter Fuhler of Newsboys admits, "We've definitely done our share of cliché-driven songs . . . [and] sometimes we border on spoon-feeding a little too much."[104] In a similar fashion, the members of Audio Adrenaline describe their first two albums, *Audio Adrenaline* (Forefront, 1992) and *Don't Censor Me* (Forefront, 1993), as being filled with "cheerleader songs."[105] Notably, both Newsboys and Audio Adrenaline have been able to move albums based on this cliché-driven cheerleading. A quarter of a million copies of *Don't Censor Me* were sold—impressive numbers for a Christian band. So it may be formulaic, it may be cliché-driven, it may even distort the gospel, but it sells albums; and therein lies the rub: ministry is again brought into tension with business.[106]

Given these conditions, the task separational artists face is that of finding ministry without either resorting to toothless clichés on the one hand or alienating the audiences they hope to minister to on the other. The range is undoubtedly limited. As transformational artists charge, warm sentiments sell in the evangelical subculture; and holy anger, unless specifically directed at non-Christians, generally does not. Consequently, with rare exceptions—Keith Green and Steve Camp both maintained great popularity despite (or possibly because of) their critiques of the Christian music industry and of evangelicals more generally for insufficient demonstrations of piety[107]—separational artists have had to focus on messages that, while potentially producing feelings of guilt, are nevertheless willingly received by evangelicals: calls to greater feelings of devotion, regular "quiet times" of Bible reading and prayer, more fervent witnessing, and so forth. Attempting more zealous messages can leave an artist without an audience, while turning to less explicitly religious topics (homelessness, poverty, etc.) can lead to marginalization as a result of the perception by the vast majority of evangelicals that such issues, abortion excepted, are of secondary importance. Seeking to minister, separational artists face a limited range of appropriate religious subjects to address.

Attempting to move beyond religious issues, separational artists find similar limitations with regard to the contemporary issues they are able to discuss while remaining marketable to Christian audiences. Just as turn-of-the-century fundamentalists had their favorite sins to condemn (smoking, drinking, dancing, card-playing, and theater attendance), Separational CCM has its list of "big sins" as well.[108] At the top of this list is sexual activity outside of marriage and, corresponding to it, abortion. Hence, concerts from groups such as the female quartet Point of Grace are routinely peppered with admonitions to remain "sexually pure" and reminders that "abortion is not an option," while there is no shortage of songs making the same points.[109] The group also released a book, titled *Life, Love & Other Mysteries* (1996), that, beyond the usual artist biographies, seeks to answer the questions regarding sex and abstinence that the band members frequently hear at concerts.[110] Likewise, separational artist Rebecca St. James has become a vocal advocate of sexual abstinence until marriage in her concert performances, as have members of DC Talk.[111] Significantly, these admonitions are largely directed toward the female audience, with even the male members of DC Talk describing abstinence in terms of female behavior.[112] Further manifesting this concern for Christian girls is Lisa Bevill, who, after describing her struggles with depression and suicidal thoughts as a teen in a cover story of *Brio* (Focus on the Family's magazine for young girls), was flooded with letters and organized an annual retreat for girls ages fifteen to eighteen to help them deal with issues such as sex, love, self-esteem, weight control, and how to determine God's will.[113] And if the list of separational sins does not end with premarital sex, relatively speaking, the issues that follow are largely ignored.

By redefining "ministry" to include both praise and worship and exhortation, separational Christian artists were able to escape the paradox of attempting to reach the lost while largely playing to the found; but even as they turned to these alternative definitions, the primacy of proselytism was never far from mind. Rooted in these paradoxical contradictions between the artists' stated goals and the realities of their situation, "ministry" thus became a convoluted notion able to incorporate almost any evangelical behavior. Faced with the challenges of commerce, Separational CCM simply defined consumption as religion. The move was far from persuasive. Record company executives such as Darrell Harris, founder and president of Star Song Communications, could proclaim that they were in the "message" business not the "record" business, but for many there can be little doubt that decisions in these companies are made with the bottom line in mind.[114] As CCM veteran Barry McGuire suggests, when it came to choosing between an artist who sells a lot of records and an artist who truly ministers to people, the minister will lose every time: "Record companies sometimes must choose between people who minister and people who sell records. The person who sells records is gonna win every time because the company has to keep the cash flow going or they are out of business. That is the reality of business. But that has very little to do with ministry; it's business. It's dollars and cents."[115] Recognizing these inherent difficulties, some separational artists have begun to respond. Citing the dangers of "celebrity-ism" in the Christian music industry, wherein the messenger becomes the focus instead of the message, some artists (Michael Card, Steve Green) have established "boards of accountability" that ask the artist hard questions concerning their use of finances, their marriage and family, temptation on the road, and spiritual growth.[116] Such efforts, however, can do little to change the systemic difficulties that plague Christian music. Ultimately accepting business as ministry,

Separational CCM has limited itself to the marketable, producing "romantic Sunday School" art known by its mediocrity rather than its excellence.[117] These warm sentiments and propositional statements about moral right and wrong, combined with the zealous drive toward "ministry" above all else, have embedded Separational CCM in its exclusive subculture.

For Separational CCM, then, like Integrational CCM, the issues of commodification and co-optation are largely resolved through a redefinition of the terms. Drawing on the evangelical tendency to see all of life as a spiritual battle between good and evil, business and commerce are understood as ministry in their own right. Interpreted weakly, this means the industrialization and commercialization of Christian music is understood to have enabled the Christian artists—the music ministers—to go about their work on an otherwise unfathomable scale. More strongly, it is argued that the proper commercial behaviors (buying a Christian album) are constructive and beneficial acts—acts of ministry—within the context of the spiritual warfare that defines modern life. At the same time, ministry within the context of the music itself is limited to a narrow range of topics that are believed to be both significant enough and religious enough to warrant any discussion of them to be labeled "Christian." Whether advocating abstinence, demanding chastity, opposing abortion, or objecting to homosexuality, adopting the appropriate political/theological stance on an appropriate topic is often enough to insure the song's Christian credentials. Provided the artist is willing to remain within the appropriate parameters of "ministry," commercialism remains a nonissue.

In his *Christ and the Media,* British media commentator Malcolm Muggeridge wonders what the result would have been if Christ, during his forty days in the wilderness, had been presented with a fourth temptation, that of network prime-time TV appearances to proclaim and expound His gospel.[118] According to Muggeridge, because the media inherently distort the truth, Christ would have turned down the offer, just as he did the other three. In a similar vein, some have wondered about the potential distortions associated with the gospel presented in a pop-song format. Primarily, the concern is that the Christian music industry—particularly in its associations with mainstream music—will excise Christ and the cross from Christian music. The stories of temptation abound. Dana Key describes an occasion on which one company executive told his band, "We will put you on tour with a group that has never sold anything less than platinum, on any album, ever. You can open for them, and you can do 45 minutes in 100 cities worldwide. All we want you to do is not mention Jesus in concert."[119] In a similar vein, Petra's Bob Hartman describes a time he and his bandmates "were told by a particular distributor of secular and Christian records that they could do a lot more with us if we were less 'gospel' and more 'inspirational,' as they put it. What that translates to is: 'Take the Jesus out.'"[120] The presence of such tensions, however, does not necessarily lead to the conclusion that in CCM evangelicalism has been co-opted. One could note, for example, that, while almost every Christian act seems to have its tale of secular temptations (real or imagined), few have actually given in. More significant, the dilemma is not new to CCM. Don Cusic describes Dwight Moody as a former shoe salesman who used the pulpit to sell Christianity to the masses, and Billy Sunday's singer, Homer Rodeheaver, as gospel music's first "'lady's man' or sex symbol who mixed ministry with entertainment."[121] More generally, Moore argues that once churches start seeking new converts they are engaged in the business of selling. When this happens, compromises are inevitably made in order to continue selling. A part of the gospel may be omitted or something may be added to make it a more attractive product.[122] Despite such considerations, however, Moody's revivals are identified by many as the epitome of evangelicalism. In many ways, commercialism is inherent to the evangelical experience.

In their attempts to be in the world but not of the world, evangelicals and contemporary Christian music face inevitable dilemmas. The desire to change the world, to proselytize, necessitates contact. Contact, then, necessarily presents the possibility of being changed as well as the possibility of changing those whom one is seeking to convert. For CCM to win either converts (the goal of Separational CCM) or merely gain a hearing for the music (that of Integrational and Transformational CCM), the artists must become respectable by the standards of the mainstream music industry. The great evangelical fear is that, in the process of becoming respectable, they may lose any distinctiveness.[123] Ultimately, however, the measure of success or failure in that endeavor can only be determined by one's particular assumptions about the proper relationship between Christians and their culture, not by externally imposed standards of religious behavior. As Amy Grant notes, contemporary Christian music is "a musi-

cal genre that says context validates the song. The context of a relationship with Christ validates even a poorly-written gospel song."[124] As long
as the artist can attest to the reality of his or her relationship with Jesus
Christ according to the standards of evidence of contemporary
evangelicalism more generally, all other sins can be forgiven.

Interlude:
Sunday Services

It is Sunday morning at a Brethren in Christ church in Southern California. A small congregation quietly waits in the recently completed sanctuary for the morning service's "special music" to begin. A male member of the congregation walks to the center of the pulpit. Blonde, in his mid-thirties, and clean-cut in his jeans, athletic shoes, and an Oxford shirt, there is little to distinguish him from the rest of the congregation. After a self-deprecating comment intended as much to soothe his nerves as to introduce his song, he nods to the teenager running sound in the back of the church, and the hiss of an audio tape fills the air. Seconds pass, and the hiss subsides in the wake of the opening strains of Petra's "Somebody's Gonna Praise His Name." The sound of electric guitars, drums, keyboards, and background vocalists flow from the speakers mounted to the ceiling. Indeed, the only thing that distinguishes the tape being played from Petra's original recording is the absence of John Schlitt's lead vocals, with the singer on stage happily standing in. With a stage presence revealing both enthusiasm and restraint—one foot marks time to the music, the other remains firmly planted to the carpet; one hand gestures for emphasis, the other holds the microphone steady—the singer courses flawlessly through the song's lyrics and then patiently waits for the music to fade. Eventually it does, and there is a brief embarrassed silence as the congregation wrestles with its response. Was this a performance or an act of worship? Is applause required or inappropriate? Finally, to a smattering of indecisive clapping and the thanks of the pastor, the singer returns to his seat, and the service moves on.

Elsewhere, at Community Church of Columbus, an interdenominational church of approximately four hundred located in south-central Indiana, "The Levites"—one male and three female vocalists accompanied by a pair of acoustic guitars, an electric bass, flute, and electric keyboard—lead the congregation in singing, "As the deer panteth for the

The Levites, Community Church of Columbus. (Photograph courtesy of Joe Harpring and Community Church of Columbus.)

water/So my soul longs after thee/Thou alone are the true joy giver/And I long to worship thee."[1] Written in 1984, the song has become a standard piece among many evangelical and mainline Protestant churches. Through the combined efforts of The Levites and the congregation, as performed here the song works to create an atmosphere of reverence and the emotions of worship. The ambiance is reaffirmed as one of the singers addresses the congregation over the beginning notes of the next song, "Let's focus our attention on Him and lift our voices in praise." The verses build to the chorus, where the tempo quickly picks up and the congregation sings with enthusiasm, "Lord, I Lift Your Name on High." Experiencing the music as worship, several congregants raise their hands, close their eyes, and sway as they sing.

Conclusion: Contemporary Christian Music and the Contemporary Christian Life

What the gramophone listener actually wants to hear is himself, and the artist merely offers him a substitute for the sounding image of his own person, which he would like to safeguard as a possession. . . . Most of the time records are virtual photographs of their owners, flattering photographs—ideologies.

Theodor W. Adorno

Rodney Dangerfield built a career on the tag line, "I don't get no respect," and the artists and executives of contemporary Christian music have seemingly founded an industry on it. Slings and arrows fly from every direction. The genre has been lampooned on MAD-TV and harpooned in a roundtable discussion on VH-1; magazine articles describe Christian music as "rock 'n' roll (kind of)" and "innocuous ditties in the name of the Lord"; scholars suggest the music to be "counterfeit culture" and "religious propaganda."[1] But the harshest criticism has frequently come, not from those working outside the genre, but from those whose livelihood, or at least ambition, lies within the realm of CCM. The album marking Steve Taylor's 1993 return to Christian music includes a critique of CCM in the song "Easy Listening." With a faux-reggae beat marking time in the background, Taylor satirically adopts the persona of an old man looking back on life today from the year 2044. Criticizing the Christians of the future for their "radical" ideas, Taylor sings:

> Color me old-fashioned, but I still remember when
> The sermons were affirming, 'cause the Lord liked us better then

It's 2044
And I don't want to be my brother's keeper no more . . .

Tickle my ear and I'll pay for your show
Sing about stuff that I already know
Whisper sweet nothings
Pour a nightcap
Gimme that old-time easy listening[2]

Taylor isn't the only critic operating from within the walls, nor is he the only songwriter to employ the easy listening metaphor in describing CCM. Twelve years prior to Taylor's *Squint* (Warner Alliance, 1993), Resurrection Band (a/k/a Rez Band) included a similar critique of the Christian music industry on their album *Mommy Don't Love Daddy Anymore* (Light Records, 1981). With Rez Band's hard rock cacophony underlying his point, singer Glenn Kaiser mocks in a song called "Elevator Muzik" the warm and fuzzy, sentimental tendencies he sees motivating most Christian music: "Who needs rock 'n' roll/Who needs songs about savin' your soul/Plastic muzik, plastic food/Cellophane tunes for that synthetic mood." The song further casts a critical eye at the influence of the capitalist industry, which is implied to be, at least in part, the source of the shallowness: "Controlling your wallet/Coaxing your soul/The corporate big brother/It's an overload." Finishing with the band's prescription for Christian music, Kaiser sings, "What this world needs/Is music that feeds/Not elevator muzik!"[3] Publicly, at least, few in the CCM art world would disagree.

But if those who participate in the creation and consumption of contemporary Christian music can agree that what the world needs is "music that feeds," difficulties nonetheless arise in attempting to determine which songs qualify as members of such a category and which songs do not. Steve Taylor presumably isn't including the seven albums he released for Myrrh and Sparrow during the 1980s in the category of "easy listening"; similarly, Glenn Kaiser and Rez Band are unlikely to characterize their output as "elevator muzik." In the course of their careers, however, both Rez Band and Taylor have faced critics who suggested that their music was less edifying than the artists claimed it to be. As one writer noted of Taylor's *I Predict 1990* (Myrrh, 1987), "A quick look at the album doesn't reveal a lot of 'God words.'"[4] And while dismissed by Taylor as little more than "concern . . . with being commercial in the Christian marketplace," the presence or absence of "God words" is an important issue for the Christian music industry (something Taylor himself recognized when he joked that he "almost made a little count of the 'God words' and put that on the lyric sleeve so that people wouldn't wear themselves out trying to make the connection").[5] Indeed, audiences and industry personnel *do* wear themselves out looking for the connections. What Taylor argued to be a marketing concern is, for many, crucial evidence testifying to spiritually-based and spiritually-edifying music.[6] Ultimately, then, as the ubiquitous debates around albums such as *I Predict 1990* indicate, what one individual finds to be "music that feeds" another will find to be "elevator muzik," and vice versa.

In the preceding chapters we have argued that the roots of this dilemma lie in the diverse assumptions concerning the proper relationship between the Christian and secular cultures that those responsible for contemporary Christian music bring to their craft. As they coalesce into discrete belief sets, these differing assumptions have led to distinct artistic motivations and rationales, distinct generic forms, and distinct responses to the Christian-capitalist paradoxes that emerge from the marriage of religious thought with commercial entertainment. In short, they have led to the creation of distinct CCM art worlds. And so, for the separational artist, music is ministry and the ever-present danger of the commercial system is the risk of becoming too much like the world—in more religious terminology, of the salt losing its saltiness (see Matthew 5:13 NIV). For the integrational artist, music is entertainment and such dangers do not exist. Offering a positive alternative to the hedonism generally found in mainstream pop music—even when the music is only marginally different from standard pop fare—is an acceptable, appropriate role for CCM. Finally, for the transformational artist, music is believed to be a form of artistic expression. Rooted in a vocabulary of "truth," "honesty," and "reality," Transformational CCM demands that the artist and audience enter into what are perceived to be the painful and broken experiences of life, seeking to transform them in the light of Christ's restoration. The commercialization of contemporary Christian music threatens this project by potentially transforming artistry into commodity, with expression giving way to expedience.

Admittedly, like the positions that it describes, this analysis is rooted in a particular set of assumptions concerning the production of popular entertainment. Specifically, it is based on the presumption that "works of art . . . are not the products of individual makers, 'artists' who possess a rare and special gift. They are, rather, the joint products of all the people who cooperate via an art world's characteristic conventions to bring works like that into existence."[7] There are alternative approaches. Those who believe contemporary Christian music to be just another product of the culture industries, characterized by the same meaningless, illusory distinctions and the same underlying ideologies that characterize all of commercial culture, will no doubt find little meaningful difference between Separational, Integrational and Transformational CCM. Those who accept the idea of the musician as auteur—the isolated individual striving to produce unadulterated and uncompromised expression—will likely find our presentation of contemporary Christian music as the product of a three-housed social system unpersuasive. Competing perspectives notwithstanding, it is our contention that there is power in the approach we have adopted.

Tearing Down the Monolith

It is perhaps ironic that one of the principal advantages of approaching contemporary Christian music as an art world is rooted in one of the inherent difficulties associated with such an approach: the problem of assigning boundaries to such worlds. Art worlds, suggests Howard Becker, have no clearly demarcated perimeters; there are no obvious lines marking who (or what) is in, and who (or what) is out. Crucial to Becker's analysis is the assumption that the key to understanding the nature of an art world is the examination of the ways in which its members assign borders between "us" and "them," "art" and "non-art." Becker writes: "One important facet of a sociological analysis of any social world is to see when, where, and how participants draw the lines that distinguish what they want to be taken as characteristic from what is not to be so taken. Art worlds typically devote considerable attention to trying to decide what is and isn't art, and who is and isn't an artist; by observing how an art world makes those distinctions . . . we can understand much of what goes on in that art world."[8] But while the particulars of a given art world are to be found through this observation of the members' efforts at self-determination, Becker further argues that there are key features to the art world as a general model: the integrated professionals who define the central core of a given art world; the mavericks who work at the fringe, continually challenging the boundaries; and the conventions that bind the whole together.

Becker's concepts are reasonably intuitive: the integrated professionals—"canonical artist[s], fully prepared to produce, and fully capable of producing the canonical art work" ("a work done exactly as the conventions current in that world dictate"); the mavericks—"artists who have been part of the conventional art world of their time, place and medium but found it unacceptably constraining" and who therefore "retain some loose connection with it [the art world] but no longer participate in its activities directly"; conventions—the established language, customs, and routinized practices that define the activities of the art world.[9] However, while the concepts are straightforward, their application in the case of CCM is less so. The difficulty lies in what Becker discusses in the context of change.[10] As Becker describes it, art worlds are subject to both drift (the slight but continual innovation and alteration to the works being produced) and change (the continual and/or revolutionary reorganization of an art world's underlying structure). From a sociological perspective, change is the more important of the two, leading not only to distinct art forms but also to distinct institutions, organizations, and social relations. For CCM, things have not been so simple.

To date, CCM has largely been investigated, discussed, and presented as a singular and monolithic phenomenon. Articles in the popular press routinely link the distinct musical styles and, more important, the distinct social and theological rationales found in the likes of Audio Adrenaline, Debby Boone, Steven Curtis Chapman, DC Talk, Kirk Franklin and the Family, Grammatrain, Amy Grant, Larry Norman, Point of Grace, Stryper, and Michael W. Smith into the single concept, "contemporary Christian music."[11] The same has been true for the majority of what little scholarly analysis has been done on the genre.[12] There is justification for this approach. Seen in terms of their common history, common audiences, and reliance on a common infrastructure, the artists constituting CCM undoubtedly share some similarities.[13] At the same time, however, as has been argued here, there are a number of significant social divisions that fragment the genre. These divisions go beyond questions of drift and internal change. In other words, while the artists of the Integrational and Transformational forms of CCM can be approached as maverick responses to Separational CCM, the utility and veracity of such an approach quickly

breaks down in the face of CCM's social, institutional, and industrial relations. So Amy Grant may have begun by challenging the conventions of
the Separational CCM that she had previously internalized, but in the
wake of her doing so a second set of conventions—aural, visual, rhetorical, and economic—crystallized around her. In some cases the new patterns were obvious and readily acknowledged; even Michael W. Smith
recognizes *The Big Picture* (Reunion, 1986) to be blatantly derivative of
Grant's *Unguarded* (A&M/Myrrh, 1985).[14] In other cases, the patterns
are more subtle and less frequently discussed. Consider Margaret Becker's
Simple House (Sparrow, 1991) and Grant's *Heart in Motion* (A&M/Myrrh,
1991). There are parallels in the music: although electric guitars seem
more prominent on Becker's album and keyboards more prominent on
Grant's, *Entertainment Weekly*'s charge that *Heart in Motion* was "top-
level radio pop for flight attendants and office assistants" could as easily be
applied to *Simple House*.[15] There are parallels in the songwriting: Grant
sings, "You like to dance and listen to the music/I like to sing in the
band/You like your hands splashing in the ocean/Well I like my feet in
the sand," while Becker prefers, "You and me/We're not alike/You like
to walk I ride my bike."[16] There are parallels in the imagery: photos included with the albums present Grant in a red T-shirt dress, surrounded
by a halo of brunette curls and light; Becker is in a red formal, with a halo
of blonde curls and light surrounding her. Key personnel are involved
with both albums: Charlie Peacock writes for Grant's album and produces
Becker's; Jerry McPherson, Tommy Sims, Chris Eaton, and Chris
Rodriguez, among others, play for both Becker and Grant. While the list
of similarities goes on, it should be emphasized that this comparison between *Simple House* and *Heart in Motion* is by no means meant to suggest
that Becker's album was conceived as a mere copy of Grant's. What the
similarities (and differences) between the two albums imply is two artists
by this point drawing from the same pool of artistic conventions and at
the same time offering their own interpretations of those conventions. In
other words, if it had been possible in 1985 to view Grant as a CCM
maverick, with artists like Smith following her to the fringe, by 1991 this
conception no longer held; rather Grant, along with Michael W. Smith,
Margaret Becker, Jars of Clay, and others, by then had become integrated
professionals at the center of a distinct CCM art world that they drew
from as much as defined. And in much the same fashion, as artists and
bands like Daniel Amos, The 77's, Vector, Steve Taylor, Charlie Peacock,

and others rejected the constraints of Separational CCM for still another approach, a third art world has emerged. Christian music, then, can be seen to have evolved into three distinct art worlds, each with its own conventions, its own integrated professionals, and its own mavericks. At the same time, these three art worlds remain bound together by their reliance on common resources, not the least of which is the label "Christian."

If art worlds spend a great deal of effort wrestling with their boundaries, that effort can only be extended in the situation found in the Christian music industry, for despite their distinct motivations and distinct rationales, the three approaches to Christian music—Separational CCM, Integrational CCM, Transformational CCM—are still inextricably bound to one another. What defines authentic Christian music? Who makes authentic Christian music? Who has access to the resources of the art world? Problematic even within the confines of any single perspective, these questions become almost impossible to answer as one moves between the three. And while many choose to dismiss such debates, they are more than mere puffery. There is power in the label "art." To produce art—or, in this case, "Christian music"—is to receive the art world's recognition, and that recognition guarantees access to the resources that allow (or at least enable) the artist to continue working. It is not surprising, then, that the people who make up the distinct art worlds of CCM—artists, producers, audience members, and critics—frequently accuse one another of producing (or enjoying) "elevator muzik," for, whatever else they may be, such debates are a competition over resources. They validate some forms of music and dismiss others; place audiences, retail space, and dollars here and take the same from there. At one level, this is of course no different than the debates that characterize popular music more generally. Rock pretensions aside, Kurt Cobain's dismissal of Pearl Jam as "corporate, alternative . . . cock-rock" was at least in part a result of the fact that both Nirvana and Pearl Jam depended on the resources of the Seattle grunge scene.[17] Therefore Pearl Jam is a threat to Nirvana (and thus deserving of comment) in a way that the Spice Girls or Michael Bolton are not because, relative to the Spice Girls and Bolton, Seattle grunge exists in a whole different world. In the case of CCM, however, there are characteristics that render these intra-genre battles unique. First, while Pearl Jam and Nirvana largely work from shared aesthetic sensibilities, the same does not hold for Christian musicians. There is little in the music to suggest that, say, Sandi Patti and Miss Angie should be competing with one another over resources, yet their common association with Word (if not the Christian music industry more generally) places them in just such competition.[18] Second, despite annual record sales nearing $600 million, the resources available to most Christian musicians—unlike those available to Pearl Jam or Nirvana (or the Spice Girls or Michael Bolton)—remain relatively sparse. Audiences are smaller, radio and video outlets are limited, and the production and promotion budgets for all but the biggest Christian stars pale in comparison to those of mainstream acts.[19] Finally, while mainstream bands like Nirvana and Pearl Jam are fairly free to take potshots at one another (and in some cases perhaps are encouraged to do so), the Christian musicians' adherence to a common belief system—a belief system whose founding figure instructed, "You shall love your neighbor as yourself" (Matthew 23:39 NAS), no less—makes such outright conflict more difficult. Those few who name names and point fingers frequently find themselves excoriated by fans. Consequently, the tensions that define CCM are frequently manifested, as they must be, behind a mask of shared community and Christian unity.

Christian unity, however, cannot disguise the fact that conflict and suspicion emerge as members of one CCM camp cast a critical eye toward those located in others. Whether a result of competition over scarce material resources, tension between conflicting aesthetics, concern over the manner in which the gospel message is being communicated, or simple differences in taste, there is little doubt that contemporary Christian music is now the product of an art world as fragmented as it is cohesive. Expressed by both artists and industry personnel as well as audience members and fans, this fragmentation manifests itself in songs, magazine articles, and letters, and in both formal and informal debates. There is no shortage of voices chiming in to the choruses begun by Steve Taylor and Rez Band. So, suggesting that "God Is Not a Secret," the members of Newsboys sing, "Your in-depth research shows/Drop the God emphasize the beat/I've heard that positive pop you dig/I'd rather be buried in wet concrete."[20] Contradicting this position, transformational artist Terry Taylor describes the Separational CCM (e.g., Newsboys) that dominates Christian radio as "syrupy sweet, positive thinking claptrap." This claptrap, claims Taylor, "may provide a spiritual fast food fix and a great sugar high, but the rush doesn't last."[21] Taylor, too, has his critics. Responding to the views that Terry Taylor expresses, one fan writes to *Contemporary Christian Music*, "I am weary of the recurring theme among those who speak for the rock/alternative crowd. The inference that those who enjoy inspirational/pop music are spiritually shallow and musically ignorant not only offends me, but is against the very artistic freedom that many of these musicians support."[22] Elsewhere, another fan expresses concern that the radio single of DC Talk's "Just Between You and Me" may have been edited either by the band or the record company in a conscious effort to remove any overt Christian content from the song.[23] To paint CCM with too broad a brush is to miss—or at least to misunderstand—the significance of such disagreements.

And they are significant. While it is possible to characterize the debates fragmenting the Christian music industry as mere echoes of the long-standing tensions between high culture and mass culture more generally (particularly as those debates come to focus on the costs of popularizing the genre), the religious element arguably adds a new twist to those established patterns.[24] Simply put, arguments that could, in the context of the conflict between high culture and mass culture, be characterized—and thus dismissed—as mere matters of taste are, in the evangelical context of contemporary Christian music, approached as matters of (spiritual) life and death. Lyrics espousing "bumper sticker theology" are not only dismissed as poor art but as morally wrong; writing music for the purpose of entertainment or "casual use" risks not only aesthetic offense but also religious offense through the sin of "self-glory."[25] Fundamentally, the problem is this: from the evangelical perspective, to live and let live is to live and let die. As Mylon LeFevre so succinctly puts it, "There are a hundred million kids that are going to die and go to hell if somebody doesn't do something about it."[26] If one accepts this premise and augments it with the assumption that "authentic" Christian music (however that may be defined) can in fact "do something about it," then the debates between Separational, Integrational, and Transformational CCM emerge as matters of nothing less than life and death.

Desperately Seeking Authenticity

Seeing significant contradictions between the goals and ideals of American consumer culture on the one hand and those of evangelicalism on the other, there is no shortage of critics who dismiss contemporary Christian music as a misplaced effort to merge the two. From religious scholars who suggest that CCM illustrates that "American consumer culture co-opts religious subcultures" to secular music critics who find CCM a watered-down replica of mainstream rock and roll, writers have almost universally focused on contemporary Christian music as a "peculiar hybrid" that unites two disparate and irreconcilable cultures into a compromised cultural form.[27] But without dismissing the tensions that exist between evangelicalism and commercial culture, in dealing with contemporary Christian music one must also recognize the ways in which evangelical culture and pop music culture in fact resonate with one another, rather than contradict. The broad cultural themes that link evangelicals to mainstream American culture more generally have already been discussed, as have the religious roots of popular music. One can also argue, however, that mainstream pop music has long been understood—both consciously (sometimes) and unconsciously—from within a religious framework. So one frequently finds artists, fans, critics, and/or scholars describing pop music in terms of divine inspiration and transcendent states. Furthermore, the adoption of slogans such as "Death before disco" and "There are only two kinds of music: country and western" on the part of pop music audiences suggests a quasi-religious approach to popular music, with the artists and genres becoming focal points in the creation of individual identities as well as in-groups and out-groups in a manner similar to that of religious identification. Elsewhere, the idea that critics of pop music can meaningfully identify rock and roll as "devil music" is suggestive of the fact that there is an underlying religious sensibility to popular music.[28] In this context, then, contemporary Christian music seems less a peculiar hybrid than a reasonable and natural progression. Arguably, the distance between pop music as religion and religious pop music is not as great as some seem to think.

Whatever else the connections between pop music culture and evangelical culture may mean for CCM, their common reliance on a religious sensibility and religious language has important consequences for the ways in which the music, at least as a social phenomenon, should be understood. Specifically, terms that would be assigned clear and distinct meanings in the context either of evangelicalism or of popular music become, in the context of contemporary Christian music, highly ambiguous. Whether the product of deliberate intention or inadvertent chance, one finds in CCM that the language of aesthetics is confounded with the language of religion, and the language of religion with the language of aesthetics. Aesthetic judgments are thus peppered with terms such as "ministry" and "anointing" and religious judgments with terms such as "artful" and "intelligent," while the ambiguity built into words such as "inspired" or "touching" (which have distinct meanings in both contexts) is exploited for all it is worth. Religious value and aesthetic value thus become one. But if the temptation here is to dismiss this double-coding of the CCM vocabulary as little more than a kind of evangelical double-speak, it is a temptation that must be resisted. There is more to this than religion hiding behind aesthetics and/or aesthetics being cloaked in "Christianese." Specifically, while CCM is conventionally understood to be a blending of pop music with evangelicalism, the double-coded vocabulary of CCM suggests that better metaphors exist and that the best of these is perhaps the metaphor of projection. CCM, in other words, does not merge evangelicalism with pop music but rather projects evangelicalism onto pop music and pop music onto evangelicalism. The end result, then, is not a "peculiar hybrid," distinct from and only partially related to each of its parents, but rather a cultural form that absorbs both as completely as possible. The double-coding of terms such as "ministry," then, reveals not artifice on the part of those who use them but rather the essential nature of CCM.

While the frequent employment of a double-coded vocabulary offers the most visible evidence of CCM's essential dualism, more meaningful manifestations of this exist as well. One of the most significant of these involves the concept of authenticity. As with pop music more generally, the demand for authenticity—for "true Christian music," however that may be defined—is, along with its corresponding opposition to music that is perceived to be somehow false or artificial, a driving force in CCM.[29] So, like the mainstream audiences who questioned the consequences of Bob Dylan's electric guitar, those involved with Christian music seem unrepentantly obsessed with determining the parameters of authenticity as this particular art world defines it. There is, of course, little consensus. At the same time, however, while there is no overarching agreement on the standards of authenticity in Christian music, important patterns have developed concerning the issues considered relevant to its determination.

It perhaps goes without saying that any effort to assign authenticity to a particular set of musical characteristics will necessarily presuppose a set of value judgments and criteria for determining worth. Authenticity, in other words, is a matter of perspective, and the assumptions one holds concerning what is to be valued necessarily entail a particular response to the inquiry, a particular set of possibilities and constraints. And one finds among those concerned with the authenticity of Christian music a variety of such assumptions. Throughout this book we have attempted to show how the assumptions held by certain groups of artists and industry personnel, as well as by Christian music audiences, create a "splintered" art world that can be divided into three distinct camps. But even across these three very different social groupings one finds commonalties. Specifically, whether one is speaking of Separational CCM, Integrational CCM, or Transformational CCM, authenticity can be recognized as the product of two distinct determinants, the musical and the religious. To define authenticity in the realm of Christian music, then, demands assumptions both about the nature of the music and about the nature of the faith. Authentic Christian music, in other words, is defined relative not only to evangelical Christianity but also to mainstream pop music.

As a religious issue, the authenticity of Christian music is most prominently a question of utility. Must Christian music ultimately be functional? Must it proselytize, foster worship, admonish, or instruct? From a separational perspective, the standards of authenticity are indeed dependent on the endeavor to make music and art the servants of religion, to create what Paul Weiss labels "sacramental works." As described by Weiss, sacramental works must serve the purposes of religion; the criteria for judging the quality and authenticity of the art is its efficacy in furthering the faith.[30] The category of "great art" thus includes only those works that can be seen to resonate with the Christian's responsibility to the Great Commission, communicating the essential messages of the Christian faith. Accepting these principles by believing that the essence of Christianity is found in its missionary impulse (which, it should be noted, may include educating Christians in the ways of the faith), Separational CCM attempts to subordinate the music it produces to this end. Christian music that fails to accomplish those goals is believed to be a misguided squandering of resources and talent. Authenticity here demands that the songs express in no uncertain terms the basic principles of the Christian faith.

Others challenge the idea that creative expressions must come clearly labeled as "Christian" in order to be legitimate. Clyde Kilby notes that, while "the heavens declare the glory of God" (Psalm 19:1 NIV), God "hangs no moral tags on the stars and pastes none to the clouds."[31] Kilby therefore concludes that, because the morality of the universe is built in, not accessory, Christian art can "be moral rather than state morals."[32] From Kilby's perspective, it would be argued that authentic Christian music does not find its value in its utility for achieving religious goals of evangelism, worship, or instruction. Similarly, Andrew Greeley argues for a less restrictive conception of artistic integrity/authenticity that he suggests better approximates the model of early Christianity: "Let us find what is good, true, and beautiful, the early Christians said, and then define it as 'naturally Christian.'"[33] Authentic Christian music, then, is good, truthful, and beautiful music; utility is irrelevant. According to this approach, one could write lyrics with an overtly Christian message yet still produce music that is not Christian due to its lack of goodness (quality), truthfulness, or beauty. Amy Grant's "Baby, Baby," although devoid of overt gospel messages, might thus be considered more authentically Christian than Petra's "Creed," despite the latter's explicit basis in the doctrine of the Apostles' Creed. In any case, the songs would be evaluated without regard to their respective messages.

In part a continuation of the integrational approach and in part a synthesis of the integrational with the separational, the transformational perspective again redefines authenticity in relation to religion. While still concerned with communicating a Christian message, Terry Taylor argues that, rather than clear, propositional statements of the gospel, ambiguity may be a better hallmark of authentically Christian art: "In the best prose and lyric, more often than not, there is no specific moral, message or sermon attached. The most effective works are often filled with shadow, ambiguity, questions, doubt and longing, mirroring our own lives and the great unfathomable mystery which is God, in such a way that we are at once troubled, touched, and ultimately moved closer to the light."[34] For Transformational CCM, mystery, ambiguity, and struggle are at the heart of authentic Christianity and, therefore, authentic Christian music. According to the transformational perspective, "art resists being completely subordinated to religion," and when it is so subsumed it is necessarily hobbled or distorted.[35] Subordinated to religion, artistic works—contemporary Christian music, for example—are believed to lose their artistic qualities, becoming Sunday School lessons and/or religious propaganda. So, while at one level committed to the same ideals that drive the separational perspective (the communication of a religious message), those adhering to the transformational make a commitment to art a necessary condition for reaching those goals, suggesting that it is through the revelation of the artist's struggles with Christianity that the gospel message achieves its redemptive power. In Taylor's words, "Failures, estrangements, contradictions, betrayals and self-betrayals all conspire to bring us to that dark place where only the Spirit of God can reach down and redeem us. It is argued that many times the vessel for His Spirit is the courageous, transparent artist."[37] And so, by serving the demands of art, contemporary Christian music will serve the demands of religion; authentic Christian music is artistic Christian music.

As noted above, however, religion is only one-half of the equation(s) defining authenticity within the Christian music industry. Linking pop music to American evangelicalism, contemporary Christian music is committed to both. The concept of authenticity, then, draws as much from the demands of mainstream pop music as it does the demands of evangelicalism. Thus, the competing definitions for authenticity put forth by Separational CCM, Integrational CCM, and Transformational CCM rely not only on distinct assumptions concerning the nature and role of religion in informing the artistic work, but also in terms of the assumptions they hold concerning the values of the mainstream music industry—more specifically, those of commercial success and cultural relevance.

There can be little doubt that the rhetoric of the Christian music industry is one rooted in the language and issues of religion. So the efforts to define authenticity in regard to Christian music generally do so in religious terms. Advocating particular religious goals or a particular approach to religious life, the writers move on to articulate the vision for Christian music that most easily fits with those assumptions. Commercial considerations are expressed far more subtly, generally providing an important if unrecognized subtext to the arguments. So it is interesting to note that, while *Contemporary Christian Music* has printed articles and columns that have advocated both an expanded definition for Christian music (the integrational and/or transformational position) as well as a more restrictive approach (the separational position), the position taken seems to be keyed to commercial considerations. Specifically, the editorials that have defended "sanctified entertainment" and "positive pop" as authentic forms of Christian expression and have thus argued that the Christian music industry ought to expand its conception of what Christian music is all about have largely followed on the heels of successful crossover albums such as Amy Grant's *Unguarded* (A&M/Myrrh, 1985). Correspondingly, those periods in which crossover attempts have largely failed and Christian music has seemed most heavily isolated within the evangelical subculture have resulted in the magazine's advocation of far more restrictive definitions of CCM.[37] Hence, for at least one prominent voice in the Christian music industry, it would seem that authenticity is a function of the market; and while there are undoubtedly those who believe that the commercial is necessarily the inauthentic, for many in the Christian music industry "authentic Christian music" is, by definition, Christian music that sells. As with popular music more generally, there is some validation to be found in the ability to find an audience; the pop aesthetic, for the most part, rules. The question is: Who does it serve?

The answer to this question can be found each week in the back pages of *Contemporary Christian Music* and other magazines where radio airplay and commercial sales become performance charts. The picture is fairly clear. Looking at the twenty-five best selling albums of 1996, for example, one finds twenty-two albums that can be best categorized as Separational CCM, two albums of Integrational CCM, and one with a separational tone overall but also including two tracks produced by Adrian Belew (King Crimson) and having been heavily promoted to mainstream radio stations, falling somewhere between the two.[38] Transformational CCM is nowhere to be found. While it is foolish to extrapolate too much from this one data point, the chart is nevertheless suggestive of the overall trends within CCM. At this point, there can be little doubt that, while the occasional integrational artist will rise to superstardom, it is Separational CCM that controls the evangelical marketplace. And while the artists of Transformational CCM may fancy themselves aesthetically superior, their music generally does not sell. Furthermore, as one considers the state of the Christian music industry more generally, the significance of both the transformational artists' inability to find an audience and Separational CCM's control of the charts arguably increases. Simply put, the stakes are getting higher. Drawing on data provided by the Recording Industry Association of America, *Contemporary Christian Music* estimates that sales of recorded Christian music grew by $298 million in the years between 1985 and 1995. In 1996, sales climbed 30 percent over the previous year to some $538 million;[39] and if concert ticket sales and other ancillary products are included, the total rises to somewhere between $750 million and $1 billion.[40] Consequently, although finding an audience in the mainstream market remains a goal for many, it is no longer necessary for financial success or for the validation that success provides. If few outside Christian music knew of DC Talk prior to the release of *Jesus Freak* (Forefront,

1995), that didn't prevent the album from selling more than eighty-five thousand copies during its first week in release.[41] The evangelical marketplace is now big enough to produce its own superstars.

Commercial success is not the only mainstream value adopted by the Christian music industry. While there is validation to be found in record sales and airplay, there are other considerations that mitigate against those forces. Chief among these is the question of whom the music can be claimed to reach. In terms of artistic validation and authenticity, audiences are not created equal, and some are invested with more cultural capital than others.[42] Within the realm of CCM, the distinctions take place on many levels and draw on numerous stereotypes, but the most essential of these is the distinction between mainstream audiences on the one hand and evangelical audiences on the other. Simply put, throughout the Christian music industry, it appears that the ability to attract mainstream audiences offers a greater sense of validation than does the ability to attract evangelicals. And from Larry Norman to Jars of Clay, the history of Christian music is replete with artists whose music has been validated largely in terms of its success in the mainstream market. The first-week performance of *Jesus Freak* is considered impressive, but many find the mainstream airplay of "Between You and Me" and the band's new relationship with Virgin Records more impressive yet. Whether justified in evangelical terms and presented as an opportunity for evangelism or in capitalistic terms and presented as an external, nonreligious validation for the quality of an artist's music, the ability to reach mainstream audiences—to prove oneself relevant to those outside the evangelical subculture—remains a significant validation of the music.

At this point, then, authenticity in Christian music is explicitly tied to the currents and trends of the mainstream marketplace. But while there have been crossover successes and while the growth of Christian music can only be described as impressive, the fact remains that CCM's frequently projected genre-wide breakthrough into mainstream success has yet to be seen. The problem should by now be obvious: on the one hand the Christian music industry seems to want mainstream commercial success and what that success entails, but at the same time it does not want to compromise its religious ideals. As numerous CCM and quasi-CCM bands have experienced, this ambivalence creates problems for those who attempt to bridge the gap between CCM and mainstream music. Recently, while the jury remains out on the possibilities available to groups such as DC Talk and Jars of Clay (the current players in the crossover lottery), artists such as The Aunt Bettys (Aunt Betty's Ford prior to complaints from the Ford Motor Company's legal department), Vigilantes of Love, Newsboys, and Kim Hill have each fallen victim to the difficult relationships that connect the mainstream and evangelical markets. Their experiences are illuminating.

Perhaps the most intriguing cases are those of The Aunt Bettys and Vigilantes of Love, two bands operating on the fringes of CCM. The problem for The Aunt Bettys was one of history. Although signed to the Elektra label and making no claim to being a "Christian band," the fact that band leader Mike Knott had a substantial history with CCM, first as a member of the groundbreaking Lifesavers Underground and then as the driving force behind Blonde Vinyl Records, was enough to cause Christian music fans and some industry personnel to position The Aunt Bettys as a Christian crossover. This led to feelings of betrayal when the band's first album, *The Aunt Bettys* (EastWest/Elektra, 1996), was released. With profanity-laden lyrics and a cover that presented Jesus as a bartender, the album was considered by many to be a clear revocation of Christian standards of behavior, if not of Christian belief.[43] In a never-before-taken position, True Tunes, a Christian music retail house and mail-order service known for its extremely broad conception of "Christian music," chose not to stock or distribute the album. Following a lukewarm review of the album in the store's magazine (*True Tunes News*), the editor wrote:

> Due to the extremely controversial nature of this recording, including, but not limited to, profanity and explicit subject matter, True Tunes will not carry this record. As long-time supporters of Mike Knott and his various bands, we believe we owe our readers a solid review, but please do not take it as a recommendation. If you are an LSU/Knott fan, consider carefully the purchase of this record. This is the first time [True Tunes] has decided not to carry the work of a known Christian, but due to the nature of this release we feel this is the best position to take. Meanwhile, we're trying to get an interview with Knott to address the many questions with which our readers have been deluging us.[44]

Here, then, CCM's traditional crossover move, that of promise to defeat, was traded for the move from promise to betrayal—despite the fact that The Aunt Bettys had made it clear that the evangelical expectations were misplaced. Unfortunately for The Aunt Bettys, in its search for the validation provided by the mainstream market the Christian music industry expands at will; unfortunately for the industry, in doing so it sometimes gets more than it has bargained for.

If the experience of The Aunt Bettys was one of a band trying to distance itself from CCM, Vigilantes of Love illustrates the problems faced by a band trying to walk the line between CCM and the mainstream markets. Rooted in the Athens music scene, Vigilantes of Love was, in the early 1990s, a marginally successful folk-rock outfit that, while fronted by an evangelical Christian, had little or no connection to the Christian music industry. This changed with the album *Killing Floor* (Fingerprint/Sky, 1992). Produced by Mark Heard and released through Heard's Fingerprint label, *Killing Floor* brought Vigilantes of Love first to the attention of the Christian music press and then to a growing body of evangelical fans. But with the exception of performing at the Cornerstone music festival, the band made little effort to exploit its evangelical fan base or to tap in to the CCM infrastructure. However, after an association with Capricorn Records ultimately proved unable to generate greater exposure for the band, the decision was made to reach out to Christian music listeners by signing a one-album contract with Warner Resound. The album was to be a collection of previously released material designed to acquaint Christian bookstore shoppers with the music of Vigilantes of Love. Unfortunately, difficulties with the label over the song selection for *V.O.L.* (Warner Resound, 1996), followed by conflict with the largest of the Christian retail chains over the inclusion of "Love Cocoon" (an unabashed ode to marital sex) on *Slow Dark Train* (Capricorn, 1997) rendered the band's efforts to tap the evangelical market less than successful. Moreover, these events, along with an increasing number of performances in churches and other Christian venues, led to a growing perception that Vigilantes of Love had become "a Christian band"—a perception that further hindered the band's efforts to expand its mainstream audience. Christian fans now felt free to criticize the band for not writing music in line with their expectations for Christian music while in at least one case a scheduled club appearance was canceled due to the club manager's discomfort with bringing in a Christian act. Attempting to negotiate a path that would include elements of both the evangelical and the mainstream industries, Vigilantes of Love wound up alienating key elements of both. By the end of 1997 the band was left contemplating a name change as a way to distance itself from this history and looking to release future albums without the help of a record company, mainstream or Christian.[45]

Attempting to parlay their popularity among evangelicals into mainstream success, Newsboys found themselves face to face with a bikini-clad model and a dilemma faced by many Christian artists: how to respond to the sex and self-promotion they see permeating the mainstream music industry. (Photograph courtesy of EMI Christian Music Group, used by permission of Star Song Records.)

While bands such as The Aunt Bettys and Vigilantes of Love amply illustrate the problems faced by groups that operate on the fringes of the Christian music industry, equally problematic has been life at the center. Kim Hill, for example, made the transition from CCM to country music in 1994. With "Janie's Gone Fishin'" in the video rotations on Country Music Television and VH-1, Hill achieved a moderate degree of success with her first country album, *So Far So Good* (BNA, 1994). Hill's foray into country music was cut short, however, when BNA dropped the artists who had no platinum albums from its roster. Once again a part of the Christian music industry, Hill confessed her discomfort with the "dog and pony show to sell myself" she had experienced in mainstream music.[46] Hill isn't the only artist to express such qualms. Taping a video they hoped would have crossover appeal, the Christian pop band Newsboys chose to work with a producer and director, neither one a Christian, from the mainstream music industry. Coming to the set, the band was surprised to find that a model in a bikini was to be included in the video. Peter Fuhler described the band members' reaction: "We met with the producer who said, 'If you want us to take you into a new market, you're going to have to do new things.' We didn't freak out and throw scriptures at them . . . [but] I said, 'If that's what we need to sell ourselves, then we're not sellable. This is a good three minute pop song, and if it can't carry itself, then it doesn't need to be going anywhere.' I thank God that happened now and not three years ago because we were so moldable."[47] Wes King captured the dilemma for both Hill and Newsboys, suggesting that self-promotion and the use of sex to sell music, which is believed inevitable in mainstream music, are both inherently problematic for Christians.[48] Undoubtedly, such hesitations will continue to make crossover success difficult for the majority of CCM artists (which is not to say that many won't still pursue it).

While the success of acts such as Jars of Clay (who sold seven hundred thousand copies of their debut album and saw "Flood" rise to the Top 20), DC Talk (who saw *Jesus Freak* climb to number sixteen on *Billboard*'s Top 200 album chart), and Bob Carlisle (whose "Butterfly Kisses" became a number one Adult Contemporary single, carrying *Shades of Grace* [Diadem, 1996] to number one on the *Billboard* album chart) seems to bode well for the potential of contemporary Christian music as a whole, the music industry downsizing that occurred in 1996 does not.[49] Mainstream corporations have again grown impatient with the lack of return on their CCM investments and have begun to extract themselves from the perils of the religious marketplace.[50] In such an environment, suggests one music industry executive, record labels tend to seek out the "sure thing"; and according to Liquid Disc president Steve Griffith, for contemporary Christian music this means increasing pressure to produce "music for youth pastors": songs containing obvious religious messages and a "safe sound" three to five years behind the musical times.[51] But while such music will sell briskly within the confines of the Family Christian Bookstores, at Tower Records things will be quite different. As Terry Hemmings of Reunion Records points out, groups such as 4Him and Point of Grace, while immensely popular within the separatist Christian subculture, are, in terms of musical style alone, alien to mainstream record buyers.[52] Add to this the religious message—the "essential part of the gospel that's not ever going to sell"— and the gap grows wider yet.[53] Recognizing that CCM is isolated both stylistically and by virtue of its message, Stan Moser, the Word executive who originally signed Amy Grant and went on to serve as CEO of Star Song, concludes that contemporary Christian music will never be a breakthrough genre.[54]

Seeking validation for the music it produces, the Christian music industry has produced an intricate tapestry of rationales to justify the concept of religious pop music. Incorporating threads drawn from both evangelical Christianity and the culture of mainstream pop music, authenticity in Christian music has become a function of religious motivations, aesthetic judgments, sales figures, airplay, and audience demographics. However, there is no one equation explaining how these elements come together to produce "authentic Christian music." Although fearful of the concessions believed to be necessary for mainstream success, Separational CCM nevertheless draws validation from sales figures in the evangelical market. Threatened by the lack of similar sales, Transformational CCM takes refuge in the demographics of an audience it finds superior to the "blue-haired ladies" who shop at the Christian bookstores. The equations are fluid, changing in response to the environments in which they appear, but one thing remains clear: Rooted in both American evangelicalism and commercial pop music, the Christian music industry remains committed to the values of both. The manifestation of those values may differ between Separational CCM, Integrational CCM, and Transformational CCM, and within those camps the particular values held may change across time, but the commitment to the Christian faith, the commitment to at least some degree of commercial success, and the commitment to reaching an audience remain.

Historical Roots to Contemporary Music

Manifested in definitional debates over the permissible forms that contemporary Christian music can take, and played out in competition over shared resources and high-stakes arguments over doctrinal purity, the fragmentation of the Christian music art world has implications—and causes—that extend well beyond the boundaries of Christian music. At this point, the task becomes one of seeking causes and identifying consequences. Where did this tangle of competing definitions and discourses come from? Why do they matter?

"No art world can protect itself fully or for long against all the impulses for change," suggests Howard Becker, "whether they arise from external sources or internal tensions."[55] Drift and change, whether evolutionary or revolutionary, are inherent to the art world. To some degree we have already seen this of CCM in the argument made earlier that Integrational CCM and Transformational CCM both evolved out of the separational approach. And indeed, the fragmentation of CCM can at least in part be seen as the final result of the unavoidable process of evolution. As the individual artists who make Christian music have aged and matured, changes in their lives—death, marriage, divorce, parenthood, poverty, wealth, popularity, etc.—have frequently been translated into changes in the music. As one artist puts it, "Some fans of our band would be like us to just kind of do the same thing all the time. . . . But, you know, I'm different now. I'm 31 years old and I'm going through different things."[56] Individuals evolve, and the social worlds they participate in absorb the changes. At the same time, however, individuals not only change in and of themselves, but also as members of a collective; and examining contemporary Christian music across time reveals not only changes among the artists as individuals but also as a collective body. So, while early Christian artists were hassled by church elders for their rock music, long hair, and shabby clothes, years later many of those same artists are criticizing the subsequent generations of Christian artists for their own music and clothes. The focus may have changed—long hair on men versus earrings on men, denim versus spandex, etc.—but the essential arguments remain the same: external markers adopted by one generation are denounced by another as signifiers of questionable beliefs. Like popular music more generally, there is an age-specific quality to contemporary Christian music.

While contemporary Christian music—and contemporary Christian musicians—have undoubtedly evolved, it would be a mistake to attribute CCM's fragmented state to the forces of evolution alone. Because of the extreme hostility that Christian lyrics set to rock and roll music evoked from the evangelical church as a whole, Christian musicians and their support personnel have, from the very beginning, been forced to articulate clear rationales to justify the existence of the music. "You can't stop rock!"

shouts the Alan Freed character in a movie about the early days of rock and roll, but in the case of Christian rock, the fact of the matter is that the church could, and often did, stop the music.[57] The ability to articulate clear rationales for their efforts thus became a matter of self-defense and self-preservation for Christian artists. So driven, it can be of little surprise that Christian musicians came up with a variety of potential responses to their critics. In fact, one peculiar consequence of the need to justify the music has been the emergence of an ironic contrast between CCM and the larger evangelical subculture. If, as Michael Horton argues, American evangelicalism has become too proud for self-examination, the long-term result of the struggle to articulate rationales for CCM has been the creation of an art world that is, quite simply, obsessed with it.[58] And although this self-examination often fails to produce much in the way of a critical understanding of Christian music—undoubtedly evocative, the suggestion that CCM has become the "fat Elvis in Vegas . . . ready to die" perhaps offers less analytical insight than one might desire—there is nevertheless no lack of questioning, claims, and counterclaims concerning the state of CCM.[59] From the very first issue of *Contemporary Christian Music* magazine in which Don Cusic asked, "Should We Take the Jesus Out of Christian Music?" to the May 1997 issue, which wondered, "What Does God Think of the CCM Industry?" contemporary Christian music has been an art world obsessed with introspection and self-definition.[60] As a result, minor differences that would otherwise have little impact on the social whole have become for the Christian music industry the lines of scrimmage in unending battles.

More fundamentally, however, in searching for the sources of CCM's competing discourse, it is necessary to adopt an historical perspective that looks well beyond the Jesus Movement to the ambivalence toward secular culture felt by evangelicals throughout the last century. George Marsden points out that, while America's evangelical Protestants were considered respectable in the 1870s, by 1920 they had become a laughingstock. In the course of a single generation, evangelicals both transformed themselves and were transformed from cultural insiders responsible for defending America's dominant cultural traditions to relics of a religious past irrelevant to the modern world.[61] Not surprisingly, this cultural shift left evangelical and fundamentalist Christians with what was at best an ambivalent relationship toward their surrounding culture. Hence, while some

Christians attempted to reconcile their faith with the condition of modernity, convinced "that the broader American culture had turned hostile to their interests," others "busied themselves devising various institutions to insulate themselves and their children from the depredation of the world."[62] In other words, while many Christians expanded outward into modernity and the secular world, still more retreated inward. This ambivalence would be manifested in a number of distinct cultural realms and would eventually be absorbed into, and fragment, CCM.

Although it is beyond the scope of this project to describe completely the relationship between evangelicals and secular culture over the last century, it is nevertheless important to identify key elements of this relationship, identifying the ways in which the current state of CCM can be traced to larger historical trends. In particular, under the broader umbrella of the Christ and culture dilemma, one must look more specifically at the evangelical attitudes toward both intellectualism and the concept of a social gospel, for in these one finds the underlying conflicts that have led to CCM's fragmented state.

As they reacted to the adaptation of Christianity to a modern culture that, at the expense of traditional religious cosmologies, embraced Darwin, evolution, and the humanist epistemologies they were perceived to entail, fundamentalist Christians and their evangelical descendants were left alternating between trust and distrust of the intellect. More often than not, distrust carried the day. At core, it is a problem of method. As Andrew Greeley notes: "The slow, methodical poking around of the scholar, his dispassionate suspension of judgment, his proclivity for nuance and qualification, and his refusal to provide the kind of answers that are wanted when they are wanted are intolerable if the enemy is at the gates. Indeed it is not at all clear that the scholar might not be on the side of the enemy."[63] Fundamentally, the ways of evangelicalism and the ways of academia are not the same; they pursue different goals. On the part of evangelicals, "a hunger for safe and simple solutions has caused evangelicals to become increasingly nervous about serious academics and academic life."[64] Searching for confirmation of their fundamental beliefs, evangelicals find much of scholarly life, from Darwinism to deconstruction, to be threatening. Not surprisingly, then, evangelicals spent much of the twentieth century founding colleges and universities in an effort to create an evangelical academy—an effort most critics dismiss as having more to do with isolating evangelicals than educating them. As evangelical scholar Mark Noll so scathingly puts it, "The scandal of the evangelical mind is that there is not much of an evangelical mind."[65]

While intellectual life sits at the center of one major debate for evangelicals, social life is the focus of another. Much as the twentieth century saw evangelicals grow increasingly suspicious of scholars and intellectuals, so too have they grown suspicious of those Christians who argue that social agendas are as important as spiritual ones. Watching once doctrinally conservative denominations embrace more liberal theologies as they increasingly emphasized "love" rather than doctrine as the mark of the true Christian, fundamentalist Christians have responded by attempting to reaffirm and preserve what they perceive to be essential doctrinal positions. Hence, social issues have been largely deleted from the fundamentalist version of Christianity.[66] Social actions such as feeding the hungry, housing the homeless, and caring for widows and orphans are no longer held to be marks of the true Christian; rather, one's identity as a Christian is dependent upon one's agreement with particular doctrinal positions (the virgin birth, the substitutionary atonement of Christ) as well as participation in selected "spiritual" activities (prayer, Bible reading, church attendance) and nonparticipation in others (smoking, consuming alcohol). Deviation from these standards on virtually any issue, either by degree or by kind, would be enough to evoke apprehension.[67] And while important in and of itself, this move to minimize social action and emphasize individual belief has had significant repercussions for evangelicals. In focusing on individual belief, evangelicals have necessarily focused on individuals, frequently discounting the influence of what might be labeled "structural sins." Poverty, hunger, abortion, drug abuse, and other such issues are thus approached as personal failings rather than social problems. Systemic elements simply aren't included in the equation.

Under the condition of modernity, the Christian experience eventually came to represent a wide range of beliefs and actions—political, social, and theological. And although largely isolated to one end of the spectrum, within evangelicalism alone would be manifested distinct strains of thought; modernity, to use Erling Jorstad's terms, subjected evangelicalism to an ongoing process of "fragmentation or tribalization."[68] Rooted in the evangelical culture, it is not surprising that contemporary Christian music came to reflect the larger social system in which it exists. Manifested in CCM are evangelicalism's larger debates over its ties to secular culture, the role of intellectualism in the evangelical life, and the appropriate emphasis to place on social concerns and systemic sins. In the splintered art world of CCM, one finds the larger categories—and larger issues—that divide evangelicalism more generally.

Without suggesting that the whole of CCM's social fragmentation can be attributed to evangelical qualms over intellectualism and social action, it is clear that the two nevertheless color much of the debate in CCM. So, much as the hunger for safe and simple solutions has left many evangelicals suspicious of the academic life, separational artists have criticized those who use their music for anything beyond simple statements of the most basic Christian doctrine.[69] Clarity, not mystery or ambiguity, is presented in their music. At the same time, however, integrational artists find that this propositional approach omits too much of life from the scope of the gospel's influence. Sociologist, novelist, and Catholic priest Andrew Greeley contends that the purpose of religious discourse, at least in its most elementary forms, is not to communicate doctrinal propositions but to "stir up in the other person resonances of experiences similar to those which the religious storyteller himself or herself has had."[70] Religion, Greeley concludes, is transmitted from imagination to imagination and only then, if at all, from intellect to intellect.[71] Working from similar assumptions, the integrational artist wants to find God in all of life, not merely in prayer, Bible reading, evangelism, and statements of faith. These evangelicals want to examine their marriages, their parenting, their careers, and their entertainment in light of a Christian worldview, and they see a strict separation between the sacred and the profane as a distortion of Christianity (as well as a contradiction of reality).

But while integrational Christians accuse their separational counterparts of creating an artificial dichotomy between the sacred and secular aspects of life, those operating with transformational assumptions take the point further. Dissatisfied with the emphasis on either clear propositional statements of doctrine or on the overwhelming focus on the positive aspects of the Christian life, the transformational perspective criticizes both the separational and integrational approaches for presenting an image of Christianity that is, at best, incomplete, and, at worst, a lie. It is argued that both separationalists and integrationalists, to borrow from Thomas Moore, have a tendency "to idealize and romanticize a story, winnowing out the darker elements of doubt, hopelessness, and emptiness."[72] The intellect seeks summary meaning, Moore argues, but "the soul craves depth of reflection, many layers of meaning, nuances without end, references and allusions and prefigurations" that "enrich the texture of an image or story" and give the soul "food for rumination."[73] One finds in both evangelicalism more generally and in CCM that, while separational artists/evangelicals are seemingly quite satisfied with summary meaning and propositional statements (hence the popularity of bands that attempt to provide "musical Bible studies"), transformational artists/evangelicals seek out Moore's rumination and mystery. In a similar vein, the integrational stress on positive feelings and messages of hope are also seen as deceptive according to the transformational viewpoint. Reflecting this, George Buttrick writes: "Pollyanna, who looked for the 'silver lining' until she convinced herself that we can have the lining without the black cloud, is a nasty little girl. She is a liar, and she peddles a mirage. Imagine her in a bombed city or the city morgue. There is no dodging the 'problem of pain.' And there is no easy answer."[74] To deny the struggle, failure, sin, and pain is, according to the transformational resolution to the Christ and culture dilemma, no resolution at all.

These debates over the "problem of pain" get carried forward into the question of social action. At this point, contemporary evangelicals can be found locating themselves at numerous points along a continuum defined by an emphatically individualistic faith at one end and a strongly social version at the other. A similar range defines CCM. Displaying one extreme are bands such as Undercover and Carman who, at least at particular moments in their careers, have rejected the use of Christian music for social commentary or in the service of social agendas. "I just don't want to spend my time on social commentary," says Carman, "because there's too much of it going on and it doesn't deliver anyone from sin."[75] "You can feed the world, you can disarm the world and still go to hell," suggest the members of Undercover. "Issues are great, but there's no transforming or cleansing power in them."[76] In the separational approach advocated by these artists, there is a nearly total rejection of any social component of the Christian message. This approach came under fire as early as 1947 when Carl F. Henry published his manifesto, *The Uneasy Conscience of Modern Fundamentalism*. Lambasting the nearly exclusive emphasis of fundamentalists on individual sin rather than social evil, Henry charged that in the hands of the fundamentalists "a world changing message narrowed its scope to the changing of isolated individuals."[77] According to Henry, "The redemptive message has implications for all of life; a truncated life results from a truncated message."[78] Perhaps not coin-

cidentally, Henry saw the popular religious music of his day as contributing to the problem, as great church music came to be replaced by a barn-
dance variety of semireligious choruses that often made churches seem a
sort of spiritualized juke box.[79]

While likely rejecting Henry's "high culture" biases, many contemporary Christian artists—and contemporary evangelicals—have echoed his
critique and have begun to incorporate, whether in part or in full, social
agendas into their faith and music. One of the best examples of this is
perhaps Jesus People, USA (JPUSA). While still primarily focused on evangelism, believing that "pollution won't clear up, politics will not become
honest, racial issues will not be solved, the broken family will not be mended,
useless wars will not cease—until men's hearts change," the people of
JPUSA have nonetheless spent the last twenty years in Chicago's South
Side offering shelter for the homeless, sanctuary for battered women, food
for the hungry, medical supplies for the sick, and numerous other services
to those in need.[80] And as the home to Resurrection Band, JPUSA has seen
its message incorporated into, and communicated through, the machinery
of the Christian music industry. In a similar fashion, Evangelicals for Social
Action (ESA) have adopted numerous social causes in their desire "that
every Christian be a faithful disciple—marked by service to the poor and
powerless, reverence for life, care for creation, and passionate witness to
Jesus Christ."[81] This effort, too, has been connected to CCM, most recently in the form of *Demonstrations of Love* (Prism Magazine, 1997), a
compilation album designed to garner subscriptions for *Prism Magazine*,
ESA's publishing voice.[82] The precise manner in which the concern for
social conditions comes to be manifested may differ, but groups such as
JPUSA and ESA have added a clear social element to their conceptions of
evangelicalism. This commitment to a social agenda, if occasionally manifesting itself in Separational and Integrational CCM (e.g. C.A.U.S.E.),
has become an essential characteristic of Transformational CCM.[83]

According to cultural critic Kenneth Myers, evangelicals cannot be
defined by their beliefs. Orthodoxy does not unite evangelicals as a community. Indeed, disagreements over the nature and extent of salvation,
the sacraments, revelation, church authority, and eschatology all serve to
fragment the evangelical church, not unite it.[84] And firmly wedded to the
ways of the church, contemporary Christian music has inevitably fallen
victim to the same social divisions, the same fragmentation. Still, however,
there is a sense of unity, both among the divisive factions of the evangelical

church and among the various camps that define CCM. And what defines that unity? Suggests Myers, the fundamental unifying force for evangelicals is their common association with the sentimental trappings of the faith: feelings of acceptance, of familiarity, and, often, of superiority relative to non-Christians.[85] For better or worse, it is in the service of this master that contemporary Christian music has most frequently been employed.

Contemporary Christian Music and the Contemporary Christian Life

In the 1980s, the so-called televangelists became both cause célèbres and whipping boys for the evangelical church. At once wildly successful and yet the objects of derision, these flamboyant preachers were united in their almost universal adherence to prosperity doctrine—a "health and wealth" theology rooted in a strain of pietistic Calvinism that suggests worldly success to be the sign of God's favor. The Christian life was presented as the good life (in all its commercial connotations), for Christians were believed to be God's elect. While the televangelists have largely lost control of the evangelical ship at sea, much of their theology has been institutionalized into the evangelical church. Randall Balmer describes a sermon delivered by the president of an unnamed Christian college in which the speaker "used the New Testament . . . to 'baptize' American consumerism and extol the virtues of prosperity theology, the notion that God is itching to fulfill the material desires of every Christian. The president, preaching on a text from the third chapter of Paul's epistle to the Philippians, implied that his recently acquired sports car was God's reward for his work and faithfulness." The college president's argument that "God never intended us to be poor or deprived" underlies much of contemporary evangelicalism.[86] Within this context, it is not surprising that, while transformational artists work to address the dark side of life, contemporary Christian music as a whole has instituted an informal ban on anything that implies negativity. As transformational artists have discovered, their efforts at depicting a broken world, a fallen humanity, and, more significant, broken and fallen Christians have been met with serious censoring from an industry that is dominated by the separational perspective. Horror stories abound. Mark Heard describes a record company executive's suggestion that he avoid any "ethnic" instrumentation and any "negative words" in producing an unnamed artist's album. In response, Heard tells of his "play it stupider" sessions: Heard and the artist collaborated to embellish a "stupid and inane" chorus with "bell-piano-shimmery-ish" keyboards, bell trees, sleigh bells, claves, little bongos, and shakers, along with a buried drum track. The end result was a "really sappy" song that the company loved and "went to number two on Nationwide Christian radio and stayed on the chart a good while"—something none of Heard's own transformational music accomplished.[87] Musician Bob Bennett echoes Heard's charge, claiming that "the 'Keep-it-simple-stupid' dictum is a very pervasive thing" in Christian music.[88] Violating it, as Bennett did when he "was foolish enough to make a record about [his] divorce" (*Songs from Bright Avenue* [Urgent, 1991]), can lead to serious commercial consequences.[89]

In a very real sense, any admissions of failure that are not overwhelmed with hope-filled and neatly wrapped conclusions are viewed with suspicion in a Christian music industry controlled by the separational perspective that defines the subculture more generally. Thus, while God's presence in times of struggle is a major theme, "happy endings" are also required. In the end, God must solve all difficulties, reveal the meaning of suffering, and/or point to some greater good. Confession, if potentially good for the soul, is only appropriate after all problems have been solved and one has been restored to the requisite Christian joy. Confessions of being sinful to the core or confessions of a perpetual struggle between the old sinful nature and the new Christian nature are strongly discouraged in Separational CCM. The separational approach to Christ and culture suggests that CCM is to be always positive, always hopeful, and, apart from some tidy resolution, to never address one's own continuing failures and brokenness; such a topic might suggest that evangelical Christianity is ineffectual. Most Christians have learned the lesson well. Jimmy Carter's "cultural malaise" does not inspire and sell; Ronald Reagan's perpetual optimism does. But if depictions of failure and sin are not allowed in Separational CCM, can the genre fulfill its self-proclaimed mission to "save the lost"? If one cannot admit to failure, sin, doubt, and struggle, can one speak to those who do fail, sin, doubt, and struggle? Kilby suggests not: "Can the Christian ever be true witness to his neighbor, until with some vividness he imagines his neighbor different from what he is now? And is it not this very process of creative imagination which enables brotherly love to move forth dynamically in relation to another human being? In fact, apart from such imaginative participation, will not one's neighbor become mere spiritual merchandise, mere object-to-be-saved, to whom a

Professional and predictable, the straightforward statements of romanticized Christian life coming from artists like Steven Curtis Chapman sell extremely well among evangelicals. (Photograph courtesy of EMI Christian Music Group, used by permission of Sparrow Records.)

formula of regeneration is indiscriminately spoken robot-fashion and apart from genuine sympathy and love?"[90] Whether or not this critique of Separational CCM is valid, the music is clearly popular. So, while a concert review in *Contemporary Christian Music* called a Steven Curtis Chapman concert "a thoroughly top-notch, though thoroughly predictable, performance," Chapman's *Signs of Life* (Sparrow, 1996) became his fourth gold record, and *Heaven in the Real World* (Sparrow, 1994) was eventually certified platinum—something no transformational artist can claim.[91] Audiences are unapologetically buying these straightforward statements of a romanticized Christian life.

Additionally, like the larger evangelical subculture of which it is a part, the Christian music art world tends to ignore the notion that evil can be structural. By reducing all concerns to the state of individuals' hearts, one overlooks such questions as those once raised by Keith Green about the appropriateness of "selling the gospel" and his subsequent decisions to not charge for concerts (though collecting a voluntary offering) and to offer his albums for whatever a person could afford to pay. It also ignores Bill Mallonee's concerns with selling that which is most precious through a commercial medium. According to Mallonee, "No matter what you do, you can make the most precious thing in the world and it's still kind of coming through this vending machine format that is pop culture, so some of it gets a little lost around the edges for us."[92] Yet for separational artists such as Point of Grace's Shelly Phillips, selling the gospel presents no dilemma: "To me, it's the same thing as when you go in and buy a Bible, you're selling the Word of God. That whole selling Jesus thing is totally weightless, to us anyway, because I don't feel like we're involved in that at all."[93] Such stubborn refusals to consider the question of the commercialism inherent in selling music and the impact on the nature of CCM and the version of Christianity it presents may often make the introspection found in the genre ineffectual, but the fact of the matter is that the version of Christianity being presented sells—and sells well.

One reason for the lack of success in critiquing the CCM art world, and the concomitant level of sales, is the aforementioned individualistic approach to both Christianity and industry that predominates in evangelicalism and CCM.[94] In the May 1997 issue of *Contemporary Christian Music*, Lindy Warren ponders the opinion God might have of the Christian music industry. The conclusions drawn are framed in individualistic terms that ignore completely the social structures of the industry.[95] The attitude is pervasive in Christian music. Jim Chafee, general manager of Myrrh Records, quickly reduces the question to the state of the souls of the individuals who work in the industry: "I don't think God gives a flying flip about our industry in terms of companies and systems. I do think He cares what happens to us as individuals."[96] Neal Joseph, president of Warner Alliance, echoes this perspective, claiming that God's "concern is the condition of the hearts of the men and women who have been called to use music as a part of the work of His kingdom."[97] And Bruce Koblish, recently appointed president of Reunion Records and former president of the Gospel Music Association, also ignores the social structures of the industry in his assertion, "I don't think God cares hardly at all about the Christian music industry. . . . I know that He cares an awful lot about the lives of the people who are in the industry."[98] In the same issue, *Contemporary Christian Music* publisher and original editor John W. Styll wonders whether God is pleased with the industry. He then proceeds to sidestep the question by reducing the industry to its constituent individuals, concluding that individuals' attitudes are more important than their activities and that "our hearts mean more to God than our habits."[99] It is difficult to critique an industry and the structures it has developed if only the attitudes of individuals' hearts—something further argued to be beyond the measure of humankind—are deemed important. The approach ignores the possibility that "anti-Christian" practices have been embedded into the structures of the industry. Thus hard questions often go unasked, as well as unanswered.[100]

If the popularity of CCM can be credited, first, to its unceasing optimism, and second, to its willingness to turn a blind eye to social ills structurally defined, there is finally a more basic explanation for the sales of Christian music, of whatever quality. Christians buy music not only for its artistic value or religious utility but also because it serves as an identity marker. Colleen McDannell argues that identifying oneself as a Christian through the purchasing of so-called "Jesus junk" or "holy hardware" (for example, "Jesus ♥ You" coffee mugs) is granted much more importance among conservative American Christians than thinking critically about their religion.[101] Christians purchase these "christianized" products not because they are great works of art but because they serve as signifiers to both the buyer and others of the owner's Christian identity.[102] Thus, a collection of shield decals carrying the legend "PROTECTED BY SHED-BLOOD SECURITY UNLTD." are promoted with the claim that "SHED-BLOOD SECURITY UNLTD. offers the consumer the advantage of both discouraging would-be prowlers and an opportunity to witness to neighbors about their security in Christ."[103] SHED-BLOOD decals, "Testamints,"

"Witness Panty Hose" (hose that feature "a fish design woven into the nylon and a Bible verse around the ankles"[104]), ichthus and dove stickers, T-shirts ("This blood's for you"), Christian aerobics tapes, Christian romance and horror novels, and, perhaps most significant and most extensive, contemporary Christian music, all provide a material basis on which to establish, first, a Christian identity, and second, a Christian subculture.[105] Consumption becomes religion as these objects proclaim the buyer's Christian identity. As McDannell summarizes: "The stress that is placed on critically *thinking* about religion in liberal traditions holds less importance in conservative Christianity than doing religious activities and *identifying* oneself as Christian. Making, selling, marketing, and purchasing link Christians together."[106]

Assuming the preceding arguments to be valid, the question that follows is: So what? What does it matter what evangelicals are buying? Sociologist Andrew Greeley has argued that popular culture is a "locus theologicus," a place where one may encounter God; it is in the realm of popular culture, he argues, that people tell stories of their own encounters with the divine.[107] Whether such stories actually lead to God is a question that obviously cannot be answered here. What is clear, however, is that it is in popular culture that many Christians are currently finding the foundation for their faith. So, while some have argued contemporary Christian music to be, as is popular music more generally, an accessory—like "witness wear" or a fish on the car, an icon that identifies one as a member of the group—there is reason to believe the impact of Christian music to be far greater. Beginning in 1517, when Martin Luther nailed his ninety-five theses to the church door at the castle in Wittenberg and thereby inaugurated the Protestant Reformation, Christianity arguably began a slow turn from authority rooted in the church to an authority rooted in the individual. Today the trend is coming into full bloom. Within the modern evangelical church, articulating the principles and assumptions of the faith has largely become an activity for armchair theologians. The authority of ministers and church councils, resting on the foundations of scholarly training in theology, biblical exegesis, history, and the like is giving way to the authority of the individual, rooted in experience. From mass organizations such as Promise Keepers (a movement begun by the University of Colorado's football coach focused on rearticulating gender roles within an evangelical context) to the listservs, newsgroups, and chatrooms of the Internet, the basis for much contemporary Christian theology has moved outside the church; it has moved beyond church authority, beyond privately interpreted scripture, and come to rest in private experience. Theology is now less a matter of logical argument founded on biblical exegesis than an impressionist collage emerging from the raw materials of what's available in the surrounding culture. For millions of evangelicals, contemporary Christian music is a crucial source; it is grist for the mills of their personal theologies. As Bob Hartman relates, "Kids will come up to us and say, 'I was reading the Bible and I saw this verse, and I thought "That's in a Petra song."' Which may be a sad commentary on practices in Bible study, but it helps them to connect."[108] But the question is: Connect with what? And while Hartman, like the youth ministers who use his music, sees Christian music leading listeners to scripture, what such arguments miss is the fact that the lyrics have at the same time come to complement scripture, if not replace it outright, as the locus of "Truth." In important ways, then, CCM no longer accessorizes contemporary Christianity; it essentializes it. Separational CCM, Integrational CCM, Transformational CCM—these are not merely musical subgenres, but the foundations to distinct bodies of religious thought.

If it is true, as Ray Browne and Michael Marsden argue, "that through our entertainment forms we reveal ourselves," then what does CCM reveal? "Popular entertainments," claim Browne and Marsden, "can be used as windows into the attitudes and values of the many who participate in and enjoy them. They function as mirrors or lenses, reflecting/refracting the immediate society, and, in some instances, affecting it."[109] In the case of contemporary Christian music, this argument can be taken much further. Whether the praise and worship choruses of Sandi Patti, the radio pop of Amy Grant, the folk rock of Mark Heard, the "heavenly metal" of Bride, the alterno-rock of Third Day, or whatever, contemporary Christian music has become essential listening for a great many contemporary evangelicals, inextricably intertwined with their religious experiences. There are significant consequences of this. Most important, as the separational artists have long argued, the fact of the matter is that the musicians who constitute CCM have become de facto ministers. Many deny the role (and many more would deny it for them), but as CCM comes to be incorporated both into the daily life of evangelical Christians and into the liturgies of the evangelical church, the equation of the lyric with the holy writ, the musician with the minister, becomes all but unavoidable. Whatever else this may mean in terms of the theologies it enables, this elevation of Christian music to the level of scripture ultimately renders doctrine a matter of musical taste.[110] Numerous examples have been discussed: the critic who finds listening to Amy Grant's *Age to Age* a "knee-bending experience," the letter writer whose distaste for Grant's *Heart in Motion* is disguised as a demand for an intellectual faith, the writer who finds sincerity and honesty in darkness, the artists who locate truth in sloganeering. Personal doctrine may not be solely the product of musical taste, but, in their willingness to ascribe such purely religious motivation or result to the music, examples like these leave little doubt that, in the realm of CCM, taste and doctrine merge.

Discography

Alba, Ric. *Holes in the Floor of Heaven*. Glasshouse, 1991.

All Star United. *All Star United*. Reunion, 1997.

The Allies. *The Allies*. Light, 1985.

———. *Shoulder to Shoulder*. Dayspring, 1987.

Arkangel. *Warrior*. Star Song, 1980.

Audio Adrenaline. *Audio Adrenaline*. Forefront, 1992.

———. *Don't Censor Me*. Forefront, 1993.

———. *Bloom*. Forefront, 1996.

The Aunt Bettys. *The Aunt Bettys*. EastWest/Elektra, 1996.

Austin, John. *The Embarrassing Young*. Glasshouse, 1992.

Becker, Margaret. *Simple House*. Sparrow, 1991.

Bennett, Bob. *Songs from Bright Avenue*. Urgent, 1991.

Boltz, Ray. *The Concert of a Lifetime*. Word, 1995.

Boone, Debbie. *You Light Up My Life*. Curb/Warner, 1977.

Bride. *Show No Mercy*. Pure Metal, 1986.

Camp, Steve. *For Every Man*. Myrrh, 1981.

———. *Shake Me to Wake Me*. Sparrow, 1985.

Carlisle, Bob. *Shades of Grace*. Diadem, 1996.

Carman. *Addicted to Jesus*. Sparrow, 1993.

———. *R.I.O.T*. Sparrow, 1995.

Chapman, Steven Curtis. *Heaven in the Real World*. Sparrow, 1994.

———. *Signs of Life*. Sparrow, 1996.

The Choir. *Chase the Kangaroo*. Myrrh, 1988.

———. *Circle Slide*. Myrrh, 1990.

———. *Kissers and Killers*. ICCD, 1993.

———. *Speckled Bird*. REX, 1994.

Cockburn, Bruce. *Christmas*. Columbia/Myrrh, 1993.

DA [Daniel Amos]. *Darn Floor—Big Bite*. Frontline, 1987.

Dakoda Motor Company. *Into the Son*. Myrrh, 1993.

————. *Welcome Race Fans*. Myrrh, 1994.

Daniel Amos. *Shotgun Angel*. Maranatha!, 1977.

————. *Horrendous Disc*. Solid Rock, 1981.

————. *Alarma!* Newpax, 1981.

————. *Doppelgänger*. Alarma, 1982.

————. *Vox Humana*. Refuge, 1984.

————. *Motorcycle*. Brainstorm Artists Int'l, 1993.

Dave Perkins. *The Innocence*. What? Records, 1987.

DC Talk. *Free at Last*. Forefront, 1992.

————. *Jesus Freak*. Forefront, 1995.

Dead Artists Syndrome. *Prints of Darkness*. Blonde Vinyl, 1991.

DeGarmo & Key. *Commander Sozo & the Charge of the Light Brigade*. Powerdiscs, 1985.

————. *Street Light*. Powerdiscs, 1986.

————. *D&K*. Powerdiscs, 1987.

————. *The Pledge*. Powerdiscs, 1989.

————. *Heat It Up*. Benson, 1994.

Eugene, Gene, Michael Knott, and Terry Taylor. *Alternative Worship: Prayers, Petitions, and Praise*. Alarma, 1994.

4Him. *The Message*. Benson, 1996.

4•4•1. *Sacrifice*. Broken, 1988.

Franklin, Kirk and the Family. *Kirk Franklin and the Family*. GospoCentric, 1993.

————. *Whatcha Lookin' 4*. GospoCentric, 1996.

Giantkiller. *Valley of Decision*. Star Song, 1981.

Gideon's Army. *Warriors of Love*. A&R, 1987.

Grant, Amy. *Age to Age*. Myrrh, 1982.

————. *Straight Ahead*. Myrrh, 1984.

————. *Unguarded*. Myrrh/A&M, 1985.

————. *Lead Me On*. Myrrh/A&M, 1988.

————. *Heart in Motion*. Myrrh/A&M, 1991.

————. *House of Love*. Myrrh/A&M, 1994.

————. *Behind the Eyes*. Myrrh/A&M, 1997.

Green, Keith. *No Compromise*. Sparrow, 1978.

————. *So You Wanna Go Back to Egypt?* Pretty Good Records, 1980.

————. *Songs for the Shepherd*. Pretty Good Records, 1982.

Griffith, Andy. *I Love to Tell the Story*. Sparrow, 1996.

Heard, Mark. *Eye of the Storm*. Home Sweet Home/Myrrh, 1983.

————. *Dry Bones Dance*. Fingerprint, 1990.

————. *Satellite Sky*. Fingerprint, 1992.

———. *High Noon*. Fingerprint/Myrrh, 1993.

Hester, Benny. *Perfect*. Frontline, 1989.

Hill, Kim. *So Far So Good*. BNA, 1994.

iDEoLA. *Tribal Opera*. What? Records, 1987.

The Imperials. *No Shortage*. Impact, 1975.

———. *Sail On*. Impact, 1977.

———. *Heed the Call*. Dayspring, 1979.

———. *Priority*. Dayspring, 1981.

Jacob's Trouble. *Door Into Summer*. Alarma, 1989.

———. *Knock, Breathe, Shine*. Alarma, 1990.

Jars of Clay. *Jars of Clay*. Essential/Silvertone, 1995.

K., Tonio. *Romeo Unchained*. What? Records, 1986.

———. *Notes from the Lost Civilization*. What? Records, 1988.

Keaggy, Phil. *Ph'lip Side*. Sparrow, 1980.

———. *Phil Keaggy and Sunday's Child*. Myrrh, 1988.

Kemper Crabb. *The Vigil*. Star Song, 1980.

LeFevre, Mylon and Broken Heart. *Crack the Sky*. Myrrh, 1987.

Lost Dogs. *Scenic Routes*. Brainstorm Artists Int'l, 1992.

LSU. *Shaded Pain*. Frontline, 1987.

Lust Control. *We Are Not Ashamed*. Enclave, 1993.

Marks, Kenny. *Attitude*. Dayspring, 1986.

———. *Make It Right*. Dayspring, 1987.

Matthews, Randy. *All I Am Is What You See*. Myrrh, 1972.

Miller, Julie. *Meet Julie Miller*. Myrrh, 1990.

Newsboys. *Take Me To Your Leader*. Star Song, 1996.

Nirvana. *Nevermind*. DGC, 1991.

Norman, Larry. *Upon This Rock*. Capitol, 1969.

———. *Only Visiting This Planet*. MGM, 1972.

———. *In Another Land*. Solid Rock, 1976.

Paris, Twila. *Where I Stand*. Sparrow, 1996.

Peacock, Charlie. *Lie Down in the Grass*. Exit, 1984.

———. *West Coast Diaries: Volumes 1, 2, 3*. Sparrow, 1990.

———. *Love Life*. Sparrow, 1991.

———. *Everything That's On My Mind*. Sparrow, 1994.

———. *strangelanguage*. Re:think, 1996.

Peek, Dan. *Doer of the Word*. Home Sweet Home, 1984.

People. *I Love You*. Capitol, 1968.

Petra. *Never Say Die*. Star Song, 1981.

———. *More Power To Ya*. Star Song, 1982.

———. *Beat the System*. Star Song, 1984.

———. *This Means War!* Star Song, 1987.

———. *Beyond Belief*. Dayspring, 1990.

PFR. *Great Lengths*. Sparrow, 1994.

Philadelphia. *Search and Destroy*. Patmos, 1985.

Phillips, Leslie. *Black and White in a Grey World*. Myrrh, 1985.

———. *The Turning*. Myrrh LA, 1987.

Point of Grace. *The Whole Truth*. Word, 1995.

———. *Life, Love, and Other Mysteries*. Word, 1996.

Resurrection Band. *Mommy Don't Love Daddy Anymore*. Light Records, 1981.

Rob Cassells Band. *Kamikaze Christian*. Morada, 1984.

Rogers, Kenny. *The Gift*. Magnatone, 1996.

Saint. *Warriors of the Son*. Quicksilver Records, 1984.

The 77's. *All Fall Down*. Exit, 1984.

———. *The 77's*. Exit/Island, 1987.

———. *The Seventy Sevens*. Brainstorm Artists Int'l, 1992.

———. *Drowning with Land in Sight*. Myrrh, 1994.

Smith, Michael W. *The Big Picture*. Reunion, 1986.

———. *Go West Young Man*. Reunion, 1990.

———. *Change Your World*. Reunion, 1992.

———. *I'll Lead You Home*. Reunion, 1995.

St. James, Rebecca. *Rebecca St. James*. Forefront, 1994.

———. *God*. Forefront, 1996.

Stonehill, Randy. *Love Beyond Reason*. Myrrh, 1985.

———. *Can't Buy a Miracle*. Myrrh, 1988.

———. *Return to Paradise*. Myrrh, 1989.

Stryper. *Yellow and Black Attack*. Enigma, 1984.

———. *Soldiers Under Command*. Enigma, 1985.

———. *To Hell With the Devil*. Enigma, 1986.

Sunday Drive. *Sunday Drive*. Brentwood, 1997.

Sweet Comfort Band. *Hearts of Fire!* Light, 1981.

———. *Cutting Edge*. Light, 1982.

T-Bone. *Tha Hoodlum's Testimony*. Metro One, 1997.

Talbot, John Michael. *The Lord's Supper*. Sparrow, 1979.

Taylor, Steve. *I Predict 1990*. Myrrh, 1987.

———. *Squint*. Warner Alliance, 1993.

Taylor, Terry Scott. *A Briefing for the Ascent*. Frontline, 1987.

Third Day. *Third Day*. Reunion/Arista, 1995.

Thum, Pam. *Feel the Healing*. Benson, 1996.

U2. *The Joshua Tree*. Island, 1987.

Various Artists. *At the Foot of the Cross, Volume 1: Clouds, Fire, Rain*. Glasshouse, 1992.

———. *Corem Deo*. Sparrow, 1992.

———. *Demonstrations of Love*. Prism Magazine, 1997.

———. *My Utmost for His Highest*. Myrrh, 1995.

———. *My Utmost for His Highest: The Covenant*. Myrrh, 1996.

———. *Orphans of God*. Fingerprint, 1996.

———. *Strong Hand of Love*. Fingerprint, 1994.

———. *WOW 1996*. Sparrow, 1996.

———. *WOW 1997*. Sparrow, 1997.

Vector. *Mannequin Virtue*. Exit, 1983.

———. *Please Stand By*. Exit, 1985.

Velasquez, Jaci. *Heavenly Place*. Myrrh, 1996.

Vigilantes of Love. *Killing Floor*. Fingerprint/Sky, 1992.

———. *V.O.L.* Warner Resound, 1996.

———. *Slow Dark Train*. Capricorn, 1996.

White Heart. *Emergency Broadcast*. Sparrow, 1987.

Winans, CeCe. *Alone in His Presence*. Sparrow, 1995.

Youth Choir [The Choir]. *Shades of Gray*. Shadow Records, 1986.

Lyrics were quoted from the following songs:

"Armed and Dangerous," from the Petra album *Beyond Belief* (Dayspring, 1990), words and music by Bob Hartman © 1990 Petsong Publishing (SESAC).

"As the Deer," words and music by Marin Nystrom © 1984 Maranatha! Music.

"Asleep in the Light," from the Keith Green album *No Compromise* (Sparrow, 1978), words and music by Keith Green © 1978 Birdwing Music/BMG Songs/Cherry Lane Music Publishing Co./Ears to Hear Music.

"Black and White in a Grey World," from the Leslie Phillips album *Black and White in a Grey World*/Leslie Phillips/Word Music (100%)/ASCAP. © 1985 Word Music, Inc. All Rights Reserved. Used By Permission.

"Bush League," from the Lost Dogs album *Scenic Routes* (BAI, 1992), words by Gene Eugene and Terry Taylor, music by Gene Eugene © 1992 Brainstorm Artists Int'l (ASCAP).

"Church of Do What You Want To," from the Jacob's Trouble album *Door Into Summer* (Alarma, 1989), words and music by Steve Atwell, Mark Blackburn, and Jerry Davison © 1989 Broken Songs.

"Closer Than a Brother," from The Allies album *Shoulder to Shoulder* (Dayspring,

1987), words and music by Randy Thomas and Bob Carlisle © 1987 Carlisle & Thomasongs (ASCAP).

"Dave's Blues," from The 77's album *Drowning with Land in Sight* (Word, 1994), words and music by The 77's © 1994 Fools of the World Ltd. (ASCAP).

"Don't Break Down," from the Randy Stonehill album *Can't Buy a Miracle* (Myrrh, 1988), words and music by Randy Stonehill © 1988 Stonehillian Music/Word Music (ASCAP).

"Dry Bones Dance," from the Mark Heard album *Dry Bones Dance* (Fingerprint, 1990), words and music by Mark Heard © 1990 Ideola Music (ASCAP).

"Easy Listening," from the Steve Taylor album *Squint* (Warner Alliance, 1993), words and music by Steve Taylor © 1993 Warner Alliance Music/Soylent Tunes (ASCAP).

"Elevator Muzik," from the Resurrection Band album *Mommy Don't Love Daddy Anymore* (Light Records, 1981), words and music by Glenn Kaiser © 1981 Luminar Music.

"Everybody in the Band," from The Choir album *Chase the Kangaroo* (Myrrh, 1988), words and music by Steve Hindalong © 1988 Word Music (ASCAP).

"Fashion Fades," from the White Heart album *Emergency Broadcast* (Sparrow, 1987), words and music by Gordon Kennedy, Billy Smiley, and Mark Gersmehl © 1987 Hall-Clement Pub./Yellow Jacket Music, Inc./Birdwing Music/Kid And The Squid Music/Word Music (ASCAP).

"Find A Way," from the Amy Grant album *Unguarded* (Myrrh/A&M, 1985)/ Amy Grant/Word Music (50%)/ASCAP ©1985 Word Music, Inc. and Meadowgreen Music. All Rights Reserved. Used By Permission.

"Ghost of the Heart," from the Daniel Amos album *Alarma!* (Newpax, 1981), words and music by Terry Taylor © 1981 Paragon Music Corp. (ASCAP).

"God Good, Devil Bad," from the DeGarmo & Key album *Heat It Up* (Benson, 1994), words and music by Eddie DeGarmo and Dana Key © 1993 DKB Music.

"God Is Not a Secret," from the Newsboys album *Take Me To Your Leader* (Star Song, 1996), words by Steve Taylor, music by Peter Furler © 1996 Dawn Treader Music/Warner Alliance Music/Soylent Tunes (ASCAP).

"Good for Me," from the Amy Grant album *Heart in Motion* (Myrrh/A&M, 1991), words and music by Tom Snow, Jay Grushka, Amy Grant and Wayne Kirkpatrick © 1991 Tom Snow Music (BMI)/J-88 Music (ASCAP)/Age to Age Music, Inc. (ASCAP)/Emily Boothe, Inc. (BMI).

"He's the Rock That Doesn't Roll," from the Larry Norman album *In Another Land* (Solid Rock, 1976), words and music by Larry Norman © 1973 Beechwood Music Corporation/J.C. Love Publishing Co.

"Hymn," from the Randy Stonehill album *Love Beyond Reason* (Myrrh, 1985), words and music by Randy Stonehill © 1985 Stonehillian Music/Word Music (ASCAP).

"I Could Laugh," from The 77's album *The 77's* (Exit/Island, 1987), words and music by Mike Roe © 1987 Fools of the World, Ltd. (ASCAP).

"I Have Decided," from the Amy Grant album *Age to Age* (Myrrh, 1982), words and music by Michael Card © 1981 Whole Armor Publishing Co./ Singspiration.

"I Use the J-Word," from the DeGarmo & Key album *Heat It Up* (Benson, 1994), words and music by Eddie DeGarmo and Dana Key © 1993 DKB Music.

"I Wish We'd All Been Ready," from the Larry Norman album *Only Visiting This Planet* (MGM, 1972), words and music by Larry Norman. © 1969 Beechwood Music.

"If God Is For Us (Who Can Be Against Us)," from the DeGarmo & Key album *The Pledge* (Powerdiscs, 1989), words and music by Eddie DeGarmo and Dana Key © 1989 DKB Music (ASCAP).

"If You Die Before You Die," from the Benny Hester album *Perfect* (Frontline, 1989), words and music by Benny Hester and Niles Borop © 1989 Benny Hester Music/Broken Songs/Word Music (ASCAP).

"Never Been a Stranger," from the Kenny Marks album *Make It Right* (Dayspring, 1987), words and music by Kenny Marks, Pamela Marks and George Cocchini © 1987 Comatone Music (ASCAP)/Dayspring Music (BMI).

"Reader's Digest," from the Larry Norman album *Only Visiting This Planet* (MGM, 1972), words and music by Larry Norman. © 1972 Strawbed Music.

"See You In Person," from the Ric Alba album *Holes in the Floor of Heaven* (Glasshouse, 1991), words and music by Ric Alba © Never Say Never Songs/Word Music (ASCAP).

"Shot Down," from the Larry Norman album *In Another Land* (Solid Rock, 1976), words and music by Larry Norman. © 1976 Beechwood Music.

"Side by Side," from the Rebecca St. James album *Rebecca St. James* (Forefront, 1994), words and music by Bob Farrell and Eddie DeGarmo © 1994 DKB Music (ASCAP).

"Sing Your Praise to the Lord," from the Amy Grant album *Age to Age* (Myrrh, 1981), words and music by Rich Mullins © 1981 Meadowgreen Music, Inc.

"Six Sixty Six," from the Larry Norman Album *In Another Land* (Solid Rock, 1976), words and music by Larry Norman. © 1973 Glenwood Music.

"Stand Like Steel," from the Randy Stonehill album *Return to Paradise* (Myrrh, 1989), words and music by Randy Stonehill © 1989 Stonehillian Music/ Word Music (ASCAP).

"Talk About Love," from the Margaret Becker album *Simple House* (Sparrow, 1991), words and music by Margaret Becker and Charlie Peacock © 1991 His Eyes Music (SESAC)/Sparrow Song/Andi Beat Goes On Music (BMI).

"The New Physics," from the Lost Dogs album *Scenic Routes* (BAI, 1992), words and music by Mike Roe and Gene Mascoli © 1992 Brainstorm Artists Int'l (ASCAP).

"U.F.O." from the Larry Norman Album *In Another Land* (Solid Rock, 1976), words and music by Larry Norman. © 1973 Glenwood Music.

"Walk in Two Worlds," from the Phil Keaggy album *Phil Keaggy and Sunday's Child* (Myrrh, 1988), words and music by Randy Stonehill and Phil Keaggy © 1988 Sebastian Music/Stonehillian Music/Word Music.

"What Women Want," from the Tonio K. album *Notes from the Lost Civilization* (What? Records, 1988), words and music by Tonio K. © 1986 Bibo Music Publishers/N.Y.M. (ASCAP).

"Window," from the Gene Eugene, Michael Knott, and Terry Taylor album *Alternative Worship: Prayers, Petitions, and Praise* (Alarma, 1994), words and music by Michael Knott © 1994 Ttonk Publishing (ASCAP).

Notes

Introduction: What, Pray Tell, Is Contemporary Christian Music?

Epigraph from Fishwick, "Pop Theology," 268.

1. Bloom, *Closing of the American Mind*, 68.
2. Eisenberg, *Recording Angel*, 65.
3. Ross, *Microphone Friends*, 1–13.
4. Quoted in Boehlert, "Holy Rock & Rollers," 24.
5. Kruse, "Subcultural Identity," 33–41.
6. Pirsig, *Zen and the Art of Motorcycle Maintenance*, xiii; Hebdige, *Subculture*, 17.
7. Gaines, *Teenage Wasteland*.
8. Jorstad, *Popular Religion in America*.
9. Rivers, *Shake*.
10. The included artists were: Philip Bailey; Kim Boyce; Derri Daugherty and Steve Hindalong (The Choir); Ron Hemby, Jimmy Lee, Armand Morales and David Will (The Imperials); Benny Hester; Phil Keaggy; Chris Kearney, Jamie Kearney, Keith Lancaster and Mark Townsend (Bash-n-the-Code); Mylon LeFevre; David Meece; Randy Stonehill; Russ Taff; Steve Taylor; Greg X. Volz; and Sheila Walsh. Noticeable by her absence was Amy Grant, who at the time was both the cornerstone of the Myrrh stable but also negotiating her way to mainstream pop stardom.
11. Rivers, *Shake*.
12. Artists quoted in ibid.
13. The statement read: "At Myrrh Records we challenge ourselves daily as to who we are and why we are here. Ultimately, after we shake off the dust of the daily business we are here to speak about Jesus Christ. . . . Through in-depth conversation we have captured a glimpse of the hearts and desires of our artists on tape. The result is a two hour insight into the lives of the people who are this label. . . . This interview package was created for you to understand the intent of our artists. Music is the universal language and the redemption of Jesus Christ is

the universal message. We feel honored to be a part of a medium which involves both."

14. Weinstein, *Heavy Metal,* 6.

15. At least there are no sonic codes for contemporary Christian music as a genre. While numerous artists and critics have argued CCM to possess certain production conventions that might make it distinguishable from mainstream music (e.g., "the Nashville fade"), these conventions work only within the parameters of larger musical genres. While Christian heavy metal, for example, might be distinguishable from heavy metal more generally on the basis of certain sonic qualities, those characteristics will likely not be shared with other forms of contemporary Christian music.

16. Pat Boone, "Prelude," vii.

17. Cusic, *Sound of Light,* 219.

18. Fischer, "Watering Down God," 76. It perhaps goes without saying that among evangelicals God is still most commonly gendered male.

19. Steve Camp quoted in Granger, "Steve Camp," 19.

20. See *Syndicate,* 6–8; Faris, "DeGarmo & Key," 14–15.

21. See Styll, "Jesus Junkie?" 54.

22. Hale, "State of Christian Music," 34.

23. Fischer, "Field of Themes," 86

24. Seay, "Backbeat," 72–73, 81.

25. It should be noted that this has not been a one-way process. For example, long-time Columbia Records artist Bruce Cockburn's 1993 Christmas album (appropriately titled, *Christmas)* was released both on the Columbia and Myrrh labels, the latter in an effort to tap into the evangelical market.

26. See Styll, "Enlarging the Vision," 49.

27. A *Prime-Time Live* segment on Amy Grant and Sandi Patty argued that contemporary Christian music includes "over two hundred artists signed to dozens of labels" (see ABC News, "A Song and a Prayer").

28. See Howard and Streck, "Splintered Art World," 37–53.

29. Becker, *Art Worlds.*

30. Altman, "Ten Theses," 1.

31. Ibid., 3.

32. Becker, *Art Worlds,* 36.

33. Niebuhr, *Christ and Culture.*

34. Key argues the telephone, automobile, and gun to be similarly "neutral" (*Don't Stop the Music,* 68).

35. Payton, "Prelude or Quaalude?" 14.

36. Ibid.

37. Ibid.

38. The most obvious example of this can be found when "secular" songs are covered by Christian artists. For example, when The Lost Dogs cover The Beatles' "I'm a Loser," The 77's Led Zeppelin's "Nobody's Fault but Mine" (borrowed from Blind Willie Johnson), or Petra a reworked version of Argent's "God Gave Rock and Roll to You" (popularized by KISS), they enter into explicit negotiation with the meanings surrounding the original bands and the songs as originally performed.

39. Shepherd, "Music, Culture, and Interdisciplinarity," 127–41.

40. Frith, "Aesthetic of Popular Music," 133–50.

41. Flake, *Redemptorama*, 11, 22, 184, 184.

42. Ibid., 184.

43. Cohen, "Ethnography and Popular Music Studies," 123–38.

44. Quebedeaux, *Worldly Evangelicals*; Balmer, *Mine Eyes*, xii.

45. Towns, *Today's Most Innovative Churches*, 15; Miller, *Contemporary Christian Music Debate*, 1.

46. Romanowski, *Rock 'n' Religion*, 286; Miller, *Contemporary Christian Music*, 1.

47. "Yet Another Door Interview," 24; Joey Taylor quoted in Newcomb, "Joey Taylor," 20.

48. See Boehlert, "Holy Rock & Rollers"; St. James and Green, *St. James Place*.

Interlude: Larry Norman

1. "U.F.O.," words and music by Larry Norman.

2. "I Wish We'd All Been Ready" and "Six Sixty Six," words and music by Larry Norman.

3. "Reader's Digest" and "Shot Down," words and music by Larry Norman.

1. Origins and Oppositions

Epigraph quoted in Friedenthal, *Luther*, 462.

1. Ennis, *Seventh Stream*, 1.

2. Ibid.

3. Ibid., 2.

4. Anderson, "Roots of Rock," 13; Ennis, *Seventh Stream*, 17; Santino, "Spirit," 23.

5. Gaines, *Contested Culture*, 77.

6. Ennis, *Seventh Stream*, 233; Curtis, *Rock Eras*, 30.

7. Cusic, *Sound of Light*, 76.

8. Hilburn and Willman, "Rock of Ages," 50.

9. Baker, *Why Should?* 45.

10. Santino, "Spirit," 25.

11. Anderson, "Roots," 13. See also Curtis, *Rock Eras;* Gillett, *Sound of the City;* Frith, *Sound Effects.*

12. Curtis, *Rock Eras,* 60.

13. Anderson, "Roots," 14; Stanislaw, "Should We Rock the Boat?" 25.

14. Hilburn and Willman, "Rock of Ages," 50.

15. See ibid.; Hill, "Enemy Within," 39–71; Martin and Segrave, *Anti-Rock.*

16. Hill, "Enemy Within," 48.

17. Larson, *Rock and the Church,* 59.

18. Ibid.

19. Hilburn and Willman, "Rock of Ages," 50.

20. Moore, *Selling God,* 168–69.

21. Cusic, *Sound of Light,* 70–71.

22. Quoted in ibid., 174.

23. While Swaggart's condemnation of contemporary Christian music must be seen, at least at some level, as logically inconsistent with the celebration of his honky-tonk gospel playing, Swaggart nonetheless draws a clear separation between his music and CCM based on motivations, volume, and context. Specifically, Swaggart sees his music as "preparing people's hearts to hear the Word of God" but argues the motivation of CCM to be nothing more than making money (see Swaggart, *Religious Rock'n'Roll,* 151; Trott, "Like a Wolf among Chickens?" 38–40, 44). After airing a series of TV programs explicitly condemning a number of CCM bands, Swaggart was approached in a telephone interview by members of Jesus People USA, whose Rez Band had been among those criticized. In the interview, Swaggert's position was defended by his son Donny, who argued that "My father's music is not modern, it isn't rock'n'roll. . . . it's sacred" (Trott, 40). He further stated, "We disagree totally with what you're doing. We're appalled at the fact that you're appearing in bars, that you look the way you do, and that your music sounds the way it does" (Trott, 44). The similarities in sound between Swaggart's gospel and contemporary rock music are apparently anything but obvious to the Swaggarts.

24. The confusion over the appropriate label for the genre—known variously as "contemporary Christian music," "Contemporary Christian Music," "CCM," "C.C.M.," "contemporary gospel," and "Jesus rock," among a host of other terms—is complicated by the fact that the Christian music industry's premier trade publication is also known both as *Contemporary Christian Music* and *CCM.* (During a brief period in the 1980s the magazine became *Contemporary Christian Maga-*

zine in a failed effort to expand its subject matter and audience.) For the purposes of clarity, the magazine will henceforth be referred to exclusively as *Contemporary Christian Music* (or, where appropriate, *Contemporary Christian Magazine*), and the music as "contemporary Christian music" or "CCM."

25. Hilburn and Willman, "Rock of Ages," 50.

26. Huffman, *Jesus Christ Superstar,* 266.

27. See Baker, *Why Should?* 62–63. It should perhaps be noted that while the story of Larry Norman, "I Love You," and People is frequently repeated in historical treatments of contemporary Christian music, the cited source, as it is here, is almost always Paul Baker.

28. McClary, "Same As It Ever Was," 29–40.

29. "Waltz Is of Hell," 9. See also Sheinfeld, "Ratings," 12; Wolmuth, "Parents vs. Rock," 46–51.

30. Kamin, "Parallels," 415. Of course controversy over rock and roll music in mainstream American culture did not die away completely. There have been flare ups from time to time, the most recent example of this perhaps being the debates over album ratings begun by the PMRC.

31. Noebel, *Marxist Minstrels,* iii.

32. Ibid., iv.

33. Larson, *Hippies,* 60.

34. Larson, *Day the Music Died,* 69, 134.

35. See, for example, Godwin, *Dancing With Demons;* Aranza, *Backward Masking Unmasked;* Haynes, *God of Rock;* Peters and Peters, *Why Knock Rock?* and *Rock's Hidden Persuader,* among numerous others.

36. Spurred by the success of the PMRC and the climate of the times that allowed the group to flourish, the most recent religious crusades against rock music—at least the most recent to garner media attention—took place in the mid-1980s. The anti-rock seminars held by Dan and Steve Peters, for example, received substantial music industry attention. In addition, the expansion of the Internet and the World Wide Web has created a new venue for the anti-rock crusades (see, for example, among numerous others, Brown, "'Christian' Rock"; Llewellyn, "Christian Rock?"; Watkins, "Rock Music"; Watkins, "It's Only Rock and Roll"; Watkins, "Christian Rock"; Godwin, "Aging Hippies"; Noebel, "Christian Rock"; Marrs, "Dragon's Hot Breath").

37. See, for example, Payton, "Prelude or Quaalude?" 10–16.

38. Dawidoff, "No Sex," 40.

39. Ross, *Microphone Friends,* 1–13; Gaines, *Teenage Wasteland.*

40. Wilkerson, *Set the Trumpet,* 85.

41. Quoted in Styll, "Jimmy Swaggart," 135.

42. Godwin, *Dancing*, 17.

43. Miller, *Christian Music Debate*, 29.

44. Menconi, *Today's Music*, 40.

45. Quoted in Flake, *Redemptorama*, 181.

46. See Baker, *Why Should?* 181–84; Peters and Peters, *Hidden Persuader*, 187.

47. Larson, *Day the Music Died*, 88; "Door Interview," 17.

48. Larson, *Day the Music Died*, 88.

49. Larson, *Rock and Roll*, 66.

50. Godwin, *What's Wrong?* 76.

51. Larson, *Day the Music Died*.

52. Noebel, *Christian Rock*, 27.

53. Larson, *Rock and Roll*, 17; Godwin, *What's Wrong?* 29.

54. Larson, *Rock and the Church*, 57.

55. See Miller, *Christian Music Debate*, for a more exhaustive list of these complaints.

56. Noebel, *Christian Rock*, 29.

57. Routley, *Words*, 118.

58. Ibid., 120.

59. Ibid., 118.

60. Larson, *Rock and the Church*, 39.

61. Payton, "Prelude or Quaalude?" 14.

62. Ibid.

63. Ibid.

64. Quoted in Ferraiuolo, "Church Leaders Troubled," 65.

65. Godwin, *Dancing*, 252.

66. Larson, *Rock and the Church*, 42, italics original.

67. Ibid., 44.

68. Schaeffer, *Art and the Bible*, 9.

69. Fischer, "Consider This: The Meaning of Words," 86.

70. Enroth, Ericson, and Peters, *Jesus People*, 157.

71. Quoted in Willman, "Call," 16.

72. Dawidoff, "No Sex," 68; quoted in Hefner and Smeby, "Christian Music Finds," 14.

73. See Dawidoff, "No Sex"; Stafford, "Has Christian Rock," 14–19.

74. See, for example, Key, *Don't Stop the Music*. In addition, seminars defending and defining CCM are frequently held at Cornerstone.

75. "An Open Letter," 5.

76. Ibid. 5–6.

77. Ibid.

78. Ibid.

79. Niebuhr, *Christ and Culture*, 29.

80. Howard and Streck, "Splintered Art World," 37–53.

81. Recording Industry Association of America, "Recording Industry Releases 1996."

82. See Styll, "Cross Purposes?" 45–46, 48; "Survey Reports"; Farley, "Reborn to Be Wild," 62; Dawidoff, "No Sex," 40.

83. Christian Booksellers Association, "1997 CBA Customer Profile," 63.

84. There have, of course, been the occasional exceptions to this, the most recent being the scandal that erupted when Michael English publicly confessed (the week after winning six Dove awards) to an extramarital affair with singer Marabeth Jordan, also married, of First Call. Following the announcement, radio stations banned English's songs, retailers removed his records from the shelves, and Warner Alliance dropped him from the label (see O'Donnell, "God and the Music Biz," 62–63).

Interlude: Rebecca St. James

1. Demarco, "In Concert," 120.

2. St. James, *40 Days with God* (1996). The success of the book led to the similarly formatted follow-up, *You're the Voice* (1997).

3. Phillips, "Rebecca St. James Concert Review."

2. Separational CCM: "It's Ministry"

Epigraph from Nee, *Love Not the World*, © 1985, 37–38.

1. "Black and White in a Grey World," words and music by Leslie Phillips, © Word Music, Inc.

2. "Walk in Two Worlds," words and music by Randy Stonehill and Phil Keaggy.

3. See, for example, Granger, "Taking Stryper Seriously," 131.

4. A reference to Matthew 28:19–20a, "The Great Commission": "Therefore go and make disciples of all nations, baptizing them in the name of the Father and of the Son and of the Holy Spirit, and teaching them to obey everything I have commanded you" (NIV).

5. Newcomb, "Larry Norman," 23.

6. "Yet Another Door Interview," 24.

7. See Key, *Don't Stop the Music*, 36–44.

8. Hebdige, *Subculture*, 3

9. "Yet Another Door Interview," 25, emphasis original.

10. Boone, "Prelude," vii.

11. Marvin, "Album Reviews," 5.

12. Phillips, *Fresh Air* interview.

13. "God Good, Devil Bad," words and music by DeGarmo & Key. "He's the Rock That Doesn't Roll," words and music by Larry Norman. The songs identified in the text appear on the following albums: "You Light Up My Life," Debbie Boone, *You Light Up My Life* (Curb/Warner, 1977); "Life is Hard (God is Good)," Pam Thum, *Feel the Healing* (Benson, 1996); "You Are the Answer," Point of Grace, *Life, Love, and Other Mysteries,* (Word, 1996); "Boycott Hell," DeGarmo & Key, *The Pledge* (Powerdiscs, 1989); "This Means War!" Petra, *This Means War!* (Star Song, 1987); "Run to the Battle," Steve Camp, *For Every Man* (Myrrh, 1981).

14. See, for example, Giantkiller, *Valley of Decision* (Star Song, 1981); DeGarmo & Key, *Commander Sozo & the Charge of the Light Brigade* (Powerdiscs, 1985); The Allies, *The Allies* (Light, 1985); and Petra, *This Means War!* (Star Song, 1987).

15. Quoted in Hendrickson, "And the Beat Goes On," 24.

16. See Cusic, *Sound of Light.*

17. Hunter, *American Evangelicalism,* 7.

18. Ibid., emphasis added.

19. Ibid., 67.

20. Drane, *New American Reformation,* 112.

21. Interview with Jay Howard.

22. Ellwood, *One Way,* 20.

23. Ibid., 63–64.

24. Shaw, "Jesus Rocks," 63.

25. Enroth, Ericson, and Peters, *Jesus People,* 164.

26. Green and Hazard, *No Compromise,* 162.

27. Baker, *Why Should?* 65.

28. Lindsey, *Late Great Planet Earth.*

29. Baker, *Why Should?* 65.

30. Styll, "Why Are We?" 4.

31. See Enroth, Ericson, and Peters, *Jesus People.*

32. Styll, "Why Are We?" 4.

33. "Eve of Destruction" (words and music by P.F. Sloan) reached Number 1 on *Billboard's* Pop Chart on Aug. 28, 1965.

34. Donaldson, "Celebrating Ten Years," 35.

35. Styll, "Celebrating Ten Years," 40. Gaither's mention of John 3:16 manifests the tendency of evangelicals to reduce the Christian experience—as well as the message of Christ—to that one passage. Explaining his song "Bannerman,"

which appeared on the 1993 album *Squint* (Warner Alliance) and celebrated the individual(s) who appear at sporting events with signs reading "John 3:16," artist Steve Taylor rejected interpretations of the song that suggested he was disparaging such efforts, arguing that there was something admirable in presenting this simple, straightforward message (see Newcomb, "Steve Taylor," 38–41; "Steve Taylor," 18–20).

36. Smith-Newcomb, "Interview with Greg Volz," 4.

37. See Romanowski, "Contemporary Christian Music," 143–69; Romanowski, "Roll Over Beethoven," 79–88.

38. Styll, "Carman," 25–27.

39. "Undercover," 24.

40. Granger, "Taking Stryper Seriously," 131.

41. Even today bands that are perceived as Christian can have a difficult time. The Vigilantes of Love, for example, found their performance at a Knoxville, Tenn., club canceled when the manager learned that they were "a Christian band" (see VoL-list archive). It should be noted, however, that while many interpret such actions as clear evidence of an anti-Christian bias, there are alternative explanations. Most notably, given that Christian audiences tend not to drink, there is little incentive for bar owners dependent on drink sales for revenues to book Christian acts.

42. Baker, *Why Should?* 107.

43. Among the most notable of the regular music festivals are Cornerstone (Ill.), Creation (Penn.), Fishnet (Va.), Icthus (Ky.), Greenbelt (Great Britain), and Flevo (Norway).

44. Steve Taylor quoted in Tapia, "Evangelicals," 10.

45. Tapia, "Evangelicals," 10.

46. Price, "Point of Grace," 30.

47. On Jan. 8, 1996, Point of Grace's "God Is With Us" reached Number 1 on *Contemporary Christian Music's* Adult Contemporary chart. The group's accomplishment of ten Number 1 singles in a row is unsurpassed by any artist in the eighteen years *Contemporary Christian Music* has been publishing its charts ("Point of Grace Makes History").

48. As Garry Wills suggests, this may have had less to do with the decreasing numbers of evangelical believers than it did the fact that the media were no longer paying attention to them (Wills, *Under God*).

49. Mike Roe quoted in Knight, "The 77's Michael Roe," 48.

50. Camp, "Kiss the Son," 47.

51. Holm, *My Story,* 128–29.

52. Burns, "What's New," 30.

53. While Grant would continue releasing records through CCM's Myrrh label, from 1985's *Unguarded* (Myrrh/A&M) on, her albums would also be released to the mainstream market by A&M.

54. McCormick, "A&M/Word Impact," G-33.

55. For a complete analysis of Amy Grant's career through 1993's *Heart in Motion* from a cultural/critical perspective, see Romanowski, "Move Over Madonna," 47–68.

56. O'Neill, *Troubadour,* 75.

57. As described by O'Neill, "The Third Order is made up of vowed and non-vowed brothers and sisters, as well as married couples, who seek to follow the example of the saint from Assisi, either in community or private homes." The First Order consists of celibate, vowed men, while the Second Order is comprised of cloistered nuns sometimes called "Poor Clares" in honor of the first Franciscan sister (ibid., 102).

58. Green and Hazard, *No Compromise,* 247.

59. See LaRue, "Contemporizing," 72.

60. It is important to note that despite the increasing popularity of contemporary worship music, some religious authorities find the pop styled choruses of "Praise and Worship" music to be insufficient when used without some more traditional music in the mix. Barry Liesch, for example, labels traditional hymns the "enduring stars" but praise choruses only "momentary fireworks." The difference is that of the transcendent, substantive, intellectually complex and vocally demanding song which appeals to the mature Christian on the one hand, versus the simple, repetitive, intimate and emotional chorus which appeal to most anybody on the other. Such choruses, Liesch claims, while excellent for communicating the freshness of one's faith by expressing an intimate, personal relationship with God, lack intellectual rigor and fail to offer a mature exposition of biblical doctrines. Still, despite the complaints of critics such as Liesch, there's little doubt that choruses are carrying the day both in terms of the number of churches which use them in worship and in the size and growth of those churches versus churches relying primarily or exclusively on traditional hymns (see Liesch, *New Worship*).

61. Trouten, "Paris in June," 34.

62. "Open Letter," 6.

63. Miller, *Contemporary Christian Music,* 176.

64. Ibid., 189. In 1986 the number was pegged at 52,000 (see Styll, "Mylon LeFevre," 82).

65. To varying degrees many of the artists themselves recognize the shortcomings involved in merely counting decision cards as a means of evaluating success. Petra's Louie Weaver, for example, claims that "if I share Christ with you, I

want to make sure you have a Bible, I want you to know there's a church down the street that would love to have you come and grow there. . . . There's more than just accepting Christ. Most of it is growing, and I don't think a whole lot of the new groups want to accept that responsibility" (quoted in Hendrickson, "And the Beat Goes On," 24). The issue, however, is infrastructure. While groups as large as Petra, especially when they tour with the likes of Billy Graham or Josh McDowell, are able to provide at least minimal support to those who convert to Christianity at their concerts, most artists simply aren't in a position to do so. More fundamentally, given the nature of a system in which bands come in for one or two nights and then move on to the next location, providing long-term support is something that the Christian music industry is simply not set up to accomplish.

66. It is perhaps a truism to suggest that when it comes to proselytism, no one is so zealous as the recent convert. Whether the belief system in question is one of computer platform, political ideology, religion proper, or something else altogether, those who have recently been convinced of a particular body of thought are often the most eager to convince others of its merits. Thus, the fact that early Christian music was so frequently the product of new believers suggests that the turn from evangelism to exhortation could be at least in part the result of those artists' maturation and their increasing awareness of the issues involved in living a Christian life.

67. While the Biblical arguments of Dallas Holm, Steve Miller and the like claimed that God was indeed listening, asking, "Would Jesus listen to CCM?" has become a frequent pastime for critics and audiences alike. See, for example, Warren, "What Does God Think?" 16; Styll, "What Makes Music Christian?" 35–36; Hafer, "Music in Ministry," 28, 33; Austin, "158 Questions"; among numerous others.

68. Donaldson, "Randy Stonehill," 126.

69. Stonehill's evocation of the seed planter is a clear reference to the parable found in Matthew 13, Mark 4 and Luke 8. Here, the Christian is likened to a sower whose seed (words) falls first on the road side where it is eaten by crows, then on rocky ground, thorny ground and finally good soil. Perhaps most significant here is the focus not on the actions of the sower but rather the character of the ground. Unlike the evangelist who works to elicit a declaration of conversion from an audience, the "seed planter" merely states his or her piece and moves on.

70. "Hymn," "Don't Break Down," "Stand Like Steel," words and music by Randy Stonehill.

71. Smith-Newcomb, "Interview," 4; Miller, *Contemporary Christian Music*, 174.

72. Newcomb, "Petra's Battle," 99.

73. Ibid.

74. Rabey, "Rock Steady," 40.

75. Ozard, "Music Notes," 33. The songs from Carman identified in the text appear on the albums *Addicted to Jesus* (Sparrow, 1993) and *R.I.O.T.* (Sparrow, 1995).

76. Rabey, *Rock the Planet.*

77. Hartman, *More Power to Ya.*

78. "If You Die Before You Die," words and music by Benny Hester and Niles Borop. The songs identified in the text appear on the following albums: "Soul Reviver," Kenny Marks, *Attitude* (Dayspring, 1986); "Doer of the Word," Dan Peek, *Doer of the Word* (Home Sweet Home, 1984); "Love God, Hate Sin," Mylon LeFevre and Broken Heart, *Crack the Sky* (Myrrh, 1987); "El Shaddai," Amy Grant, *Age to Age* (Myrrh, 1982).

79. "Effective death" because while some CCM bands continued to make efforts to gain access to mainstream markets and some fans continued to search for the next Amy Grant, the expectations that CCM would become a force within secular culture were largely abandoned, at least temporarily, after a period of some hope in the mid to late 1980s.

80. Romanowski, "Move Over Madonna," 56.

81. Newcomb, "Petra," 21.

82. "Armed and Dangerous," words and music by Bob Hartman.

83. "Asleep in the Light," words and music by Keith Green.

84. The fact that Green died prematurely in a light plane crash in July 1982 has also served to color perceptions of him. As in mainstream pop culture, the premature death of the Christian artist can lead to a reverence for the memory that often comes in reverse proportion to the apathy and disdain the individual received in life. Thus, Green is often cited by both fans and industry personnel as a hero to emulate, a musician passionate about his calling to the ministry (see, for example, Pagano's comments about Green in Mineo, "Jonathan Finds New Freedom," 28). Similar responses followed the deaths of Mark Heard and Rich Mullins.

85. Hinchman, "Christian Artists," 19.

86. Ibid.

87. See Granger, "Steve Camp," 18–21; Camp, "Call for Reformation."

88. Fischer, "Relevancy Isn't Everything," 62; Fischer, "View from a Window," 38; Fischer, "It's Over," 70.

89. Farley estimates the number of radio stations playing CCM to have grown from less than 200 in the mid-1980s to more than 500 by 1996 (see Farley, "Reborn to Be Wild," 62–64). It should be noted, however, that the numbers

may be somewhat misleading. As the National Christian Music Research Project learned, Christian music radio, despite its gains, still faces substantial obstacles; most notably, the mixing of too many diverse musical styles, the broadcasting of too much talk and preaching, and the low visibility of most stations because of low power transmitting and a lack of promotion (see Seward and Dodds, "Christian Music Radio," 70–77). A poll taken by *Christianity Today* in 1988 revealed that "Christian radio remained fourth—behind friends' recommendations, magazine ads, and music reviews—as a means of exposure for new Christian music" (Romanowski, *Rock 'n' Religion,* 187).

Interlude: DC Talk

1. See Parker, "DC Talk," 14–15.

3. Integrational CCM: "It's Entertainment"

Epigraph from Capon, *The Supper of the Lamb,* 86

1. *Unguarded* was released with four distinct covers, although each adhered to the same format: large block letters in hot pink reading "Amy Grant" across the top of the cover, "unguarded" in small italics three-quarters of the way down on the right hand side, and Grant in her leopard skin jacket (which, for a time, would become her trademark) filling the whole of the frame. Together, then, the four covers suggested an image of Grant in motion, caught in the act by an unnoticed camera. This was particularly true of the *Billboard* advertisement, where all four covers appeared together (though without the lettering).

2. A&M Records advertisement, *Billboard,* Apr. 20, 1985, 5.

3. Romanowski, "Move Over Madonna," 50.

4. See Romanowski, "Move Over Madonna"; Bhatia, "Amy Grant FAQ."

5. At least one critic argued that the success of *Heart in Motion* had "more to do with A&M's desperate situation (i.e., losing Janet Jackson, Sting's record stiffed and no other real hit-makers are currently on the label), and their need for her to be a money-making success, than any thing special or new in the music over against *Unguarded* which got no real airplay" (Newcomb, "Letters to the Editor," 3). Another common argument was that Amy Grant was drawing on the same "church-going" audiences with *Heart in Motion* that she had been relying on all along, the albums were simply being stocked in more stores (see Porter, "Steve Hindalong," 19–23).

6. "Sing Your Praise to the Lord," words and music by Rich Mullins; "I Have Decided," words and music by Michael Card

7. "Find a Way," words and music by Amy Grant and Michael W. Smith. © 1985 Word Music, Inc. and Meadowgreen Music.

8. In the case of "Baby, Baby" the readings were further confused by the fact that while Grant claimed to have written the song for her newborn daughter, the video, three minutes and fifty-seven seconds of Grant flirting with a male model/actor, presented the song as a clear expression of heterosexual *eros.*

9. Gill, "Music of Amy Grant," 19.

10. Willman, "Faithful in her Fashion," F3.

11. Styll, "Intro," 4; Millard, *Amy Grant,* 162. The Usenet newsgroups rec.music.christian and rec.music.artists.amy-grant are also useful for illustrating the continual debates between fans and non-fans concerning Grant.

12. See Quinn, "Michael Blanton," 34–37. In the article, Blanton states that Grant "typified the type of artist who needed development. There was nobody doing that. . . . [and] nobody to help motivate or take it [Grant's music] to the next level" until he and Harrell stepped in (34, 36). Harrell further notes that with regard to the business side of her career, Grant "just really entrusts us to take care of the major decisions" (37).

13. The fact that all the people identified here are male should not be read to suggest that Grant, as a woman, would not have been successful without male assistance. Rather it is an artifact of the Christian music industry, which, like its mainstream counterpart, is constructed around a definite gender hierarchy.

14. Romanowski, for example, quotes one Word executive's claim that while some 50 percent of Americans call themselves (or could be called) evangelical, less than 10 percent of those people shop at the Christian bookstores where CCM is sold (see Romanowski, "Roll Over Beethoven," 3).

15. See Seay, "Daniel Amos," 6–7; Platt, "Whatever Happened?" 32–33, 35.

16. Well, "Record Reviews," 14.

17. For a fuller discussion of Hill and The 77's, see chapter 5.

18. Quoted in Ciani, "All Aboard!" 37–38. It should be noted that the original lead singer left the band after recording the second album.

19. Quoted in Seay, "Daniel Amos," 7.

20. Wicke, *Rock Music,* 117.

21. For more on Darrell Mansfield, see Bullock, "Darrel Mansfield," 22, 29.

22. Quoted in Platt, "B.J. Thomas' View," 11, emphasis original.

23. Ironically enough, it is conventional wisdom that audiences for Christian music concerts can be some of the worst an artist can face. Shows are frequently held in venues such as church auditoriums and theme parks where general seating can lead, first, to stampedes, and second, to a crowd mentality that erases many standards of civility. In addition (and to many an artist's annoyance), Christian audiences are not shy about shouting out song requests during shows or, in cases such as Thomas's, vocalizing their displeasure with a performance. The most no-

torious example of this was a 1987 performance by Leslie Phillips at Knott's Berry Farm that culminated in the audience booing her from the stage and Phillips's subsequent departure from Christian music.

24. See "82 Issues," 44; Platt, "B.J. Thomas's View," 10–13; Styll, "Cool Crowds," 37–38.

25. Styll, "Editor's Comment," 4.

26. Niebuhr, *Christ and Culture*.

27. "Church of Do What You Want To," words and music by Steve Atwell, Mark Blackburn, and Jerry Davison. For a more substantive treatment of this subject, see Guiness, *Fit Bodies;* Horton, *Made in America;* Horton, *Where in the World?*

28. Niebuhr, *Christ and Culture*, 108.

29. Indeed, in terms of its institutional practices, CCM has largely been isolated from the workings of black gospel music. Thus, while there have been black gospel artists who have recorded for CCM labels (Al Green, Phillip Bailey, Denise Williams, the Mighty Clouds of Joy, and Shirley Caesar among others), efforts to blur the lines between black gospel and CCM that went beyond these individual contacts have met with strong resistance. The most obvious case of this occurred when the publishers of CCM attempted to start a new publication, *American Gospel*, for the purposes of exploring and promoting black gospel. Seen as an effort by white culture to dominate black expression, the attempt met with significant opposition when the black gospel art world leveled charges of racism at the Christian music infrastructure (see Styll, "Intro," 4).

30. Curtis, *Rock Eras*, 59. See also Cusic, *Sound of Light*, 121–25.

31. See "25 Years," 23–32; Widner and Carter, *Oak Ridge Boys*, 196–97.

32. Widner and Carter, *Oak Ridge Boys*, 1.

33. See ibid., 193, 197–98, for a complete list of the band's achievements.

34. Ibid., 40.

35. Similar arguments have been made about Leslie Phillips, who left Christian music after 1987's *The Turning* (Myrrh LA) to record for Virgin Records as Sam Phillips. Like The Oak Ridge Boys and unlike most Christian acts seeking to crossover, Phillips attempted to "disassociate herself from her pre-*Turning* albums and the Christian music industry as much as possible." As a result, she was frequently accused of "losing her faith or deserting Christianity, or of having been brainwashed into theological liberalism by her producer and frequent companion [later, husband], T Bone Burnett" (Willman, "Sam Phillips," 8).

36. Further attesting to the separation of white and black gospel is the fact that The Imperials were also the first southern gospel group to feature a black singer, Sherman Andrus, the addition of whom resulted in canceled concert dates

and exile from venues where the group had once been welcomed. See Cusic, *Sound of Light*, 191–94, for a more detailed account of the controversy surrounding The Oak Ridge Boys and The Imperials.

37. When the argument is pushed to its most extreme formulations it is claimed that the split between the secular and the Christian ("sacred") is an artifact of the Enlightenment, that in reality "all of creation is God's handiwork. . . . [and] if it's not sin, God calls it 'good,'" and thus that it makes no sense to talk of "Christian music" and "secular music" (Styll, "Enlarging the Vision," 49).

38. It should be noted that there is some confusion concerning the precise year Word, Inc., was founded. Romanowski and Cusic cite 1950, Ferré claims 1951, and Baker prefers 1953 (see Cusic, *Sound of Light*, 134; Romanowski, "Contemporary Christian Music," 153; Ferré, "Searching," 103; Baker, *Why Should?* 111).

39. Again, there is some confusion concerning the date of the sale. Cusic argues it was 1976, while Romanowski and Baker claim 1974 (see Cusic, *Sound of Light*, 137; Romanowski, *Rock 'n' Religion*, 163; Baker, *Contemporary Christian Music*, 152).

40. Romanowski, *Rock 'n' Religion*, 164.

41. Ibid. See also Cusic, *Sound of Light*, 137–38.

42. See Seay, "Backbeat," 72–73, 81; Gubernick and LaFranco, "Rocking with God," 40–41.

43. Long, "Can't Buy Me Ministry," 25.

44. Quoted in Styll, "*Billboard* Conference," 38.

45. Jim Fogelson (MCA Records president, Nashville Division) quoted in "MCA Gears Down," 58.

46. Romanowski, "Contemporary Christian Music," 159.

47. Styll, "CBA Attendance Down," 44.

48. Styll, "*Billboard* Conference," 38.

49. See Styll and Baker, "Pursuit of a Dream," 12–26.

50. Despite the repetitive formula of such reporting, few ever bothered to consider the increasing pattern of CCM's failure with the mainstream audience. Manifesting more than their fair share of Christian optimism, the implied sentiment in almost every report on a mainstream distribution deal was that this time things would be different.

51. "I Use the J-Word," words and music by DeGarmo & Key.

52. See Young, "Contemporary Christian Music," 156–57; Romanowski, "2 Hot 2 Handle?" 14–18.

53. Romanowski, "2 Hot 2 Handle?"

54. Stillion and Estey, "Tonio K. Interview," 7.

55. Willman, "What's New?" 10, 12.

56. Quoted in Willman, "What's New?" 10.

57. The What? Records name and logo have since been resurrected for use in the UK.

58. While most of the attention received by albums released through What? Records came from the Christian music press, there were a few mainstream writers paying attention as well. Steve Simels of *Stereo Review,* for example, wrote of *Romeo Unchained:* "Altogether . . . a thrilling piece of vinyl, and as Robert Schumann is reputed to have observed upon first hearing Chopin, 'Hats off, gentlemen.' Let me add, at the risk of repeating myself, 'This is the greatest album ever recorded'" (Simels, "Best of the Month," 100).

59. "What Women Want," words and music by Tonio K.

60. Godwin, *What's Wrong?* 5.

61. Ibid., 47–48, emphasis original.

62. Quoted in Long, "Can't Buy Me Ministry," 27.

63. Ibid.

64. Denisoff, *Sing a Song.*

65. Friedlander, *Rock and Roll.*

66. Quoted in Granger, "Steve Camp," 17.

67. Payton, "Prelude or Quaalude?" 14.

68. Quoted in Granger, "Steve Camp," 18.

69. See Styll, "Editor's Comment"; Styll, "Wanted," 4; Styll, "Enlarging the Vision," 49.

70. Emerson, "Self-Reliance," 183.

71. Styll, "Wanted," 4.

72. Bultman, "Editorial/Christian Muzak," 32.

73. Mellers, *Darker Shade of Pale,* 209.

74. Faris, "Critique," 12.

75. Liner notes can also be used to help determine the object of a song's indeterminate pronouns: a capitalized "You" referred to God, a lowercase "you" to a person. Frequently, however, the clever artist who wants to thwart efforts at an obvious reading will have the liner notes, or at least the lyrics, printed either without capitalization or in all capital letters.

76. Margaret Becker quoted in Stafford, "Has Christian Rock?" 18.

77. Van Matre, "Move Over, Fanny Crosby," 18.

78. See Smith, "Guest Editorial," 12, emphasis original.

79. Quoted in Romanowski, "Move Over Madonna," 57.

80. Balmer, *Mine Eyes,* 93.

81. See Baker, *Contemporary Christian Music,* 214.

82. Brown, "Records," 40.

83. Marion, "Critique," 17.

84. Ciani, "What's New," 52.

85. Thunder, "What's New," 52; Urbanski, "What's New," 53.

86. Boehlert, "Holy Rock & Rollers," 24.

87. See Baker, *Contemporary Christian Music*, 242–57.

88. Romanowski, *Rock 'n' Religion*, 53, note 31.

89. See "Music Recommendation Chart," World Wide Web document available at http://www.biblenet.net/media/musicrec.html.

90. It should perhaps be noted that the debate concerning sanctified entertainment extends well beyond the "official" voices of CCM to include fans of the genre. In response to the magazine's review of *Unguarded*, for example, *Contemporary Christian Music* was subjected to a continuous stream of letters on the topic of Grant and her new approach to Christian music. Letters, both pro and con, appeared in every issue from Aug. 1985 to Jan. 1986.

91. See Rookmaaker, *Creative Gift*; Schaeffer, *Addicted to Mediocrity*; Schaeffer, *Sham Pearls*.

92. These are: "(1) God loves you and offers a wonderful plan for your life; (2) Man is sinful and separated from God. Therefore, he cannot know and experience God's love and plan for his life; (3) Jesus Christ is God's only provision for man's sin. Through Him you can know and experience God's love and plan for your life; and, (4) We must individually receive Jesus Christ as Savior and Lord; then we can know and experience God's love and plan for our lives" (Bill Bright, *Four Spiritual Laws*).

93. Fischer, "Spirit of CCM," 55.

94. Styll, "Enlarging the Vision," 49.

95. Ibid., 52.

96. Ibid.

97. Adair, "Feedback," 6.

98. Ibid.

99. Ibid.

100. Quoted in Heyn, "Looking Below," 17.

101. Quoted in Donaldson, "Amy Grant," 60.

102. Quoted in Newcomb, "Margaret Becker," 10.

103. Rookmaaker, *Creative Gift*.

104. Steve Hindalong quoted in Kauffman, "Choir," 10; Well, "Michael W. Smith," 13.

105. Quoted in Well, "Michael W. Smith," 13.

106. See Weber, *On the Other Side*.

107. Well, "Michael W. Smith," 13.

108. If a continual theme of Smith's music, his teen focus arguably culminated with the (nearly) simultaneous release of *The Big Picture* (with songs such as "You're Alright," "Old Enough to Know," and "Pursuit of the Dream") and Smith's book, *Old Enough to Know*, a how-to manual "written as a way of helping junior high and high school kids find better ways to cope with life's demands than 'sex and drugs and rock & roll'" (Well, "Michael W. Smith," 21).

109. Hefner, "Mike and the Mechanics," 37.

110. Well, "Michael W. Smith," 21.

111. Ibid.

112. Andre Crouch quoted in Tatum, "Celebrating Ten Years," 43.

113. Schaeffer, *Addicted to Mediocrity*, 47.

114. Thompson, "Grand Architecture," 14."

4. Transformational CCM: "It's Art"

Epigraph from Kipling, "The Conundrum of the Workshops," 100.

1. Becker, *Art Worlds*, 133.

2. Ibid., 131.

3. See Vanderpoel, "Strong Hand of Love," 10–11, 16–19.

4. Quoted in ibid., 17.

5. Fischer, "Consider This: Heard Again," 78.

6. Michael Been quoted in Vanderpoel, "Strong Hand of Love," 10.

7. Leppert and Lipsitz, "'Everybody's Lonesome for Somebody,'" 259, 261.

8. The effort to position Heard's music as explicitly authentic went so far as to focus on the instruments he played in recording his songs. Much was made in the Christian music press of the 1939 National Steel mandolin Heard played on his final albums, as well of the version of "What Kind of Friend," played on a "broken upright piano," which appeared on *High Noon*.

9. Leppert and Lipsitz, "'Everybody's Lonesome,'" 272.

10. As David Miner projected, a lot of people "start[ed] talking about how incredible . . . [Heard was] that wouldn't give him the time of day when he was alive" (quoted in Vanderpoel, "Strong Hand of Love," 16).

11. Newcomb, "Staying Up Late," 15.

12. Ashley Cleveland quoted in Vanderpoel, "Strong Hand of Love," 11.

13. See Bultman, "Editorial/Christian Muzak," 32.

14. Niebuhr, *Christ and Culture*.

15. Lefieste, "Re: copying/recording."

16. Ozard, "Interview," 26.

17. This theme was explored on the DA (Daniel Amos) album *Darn Floor—Big Bite,* the title of which was taken from the words used by Koko, the gorilla taught to use sign language, to describe an earthquake.

18. See Matthew 5:48.

19. In the words of the Apostle Paul, "Creation groans in suffering awaiting its restoration to God's original intent" (Romans 8:22 [NIV]).

20. Ozard, "At the Foot of the Cross," 26.

21. Ibid.

22. See Vanderpoel, "Strong Hand of Love," 16.

23. Newcomb, "Q Thoughts," 4.

24. MacIntosh, "Mark Heard," 11.

25. It should be noted that at least in some cases members of the Christian music industry working from the transformational perspective define themselves as something other than evangelical (see, for example, "Syndicate," 6–8).

26. Hunter, *American Evangelicalism.*

27. See, among numerous others, Anders, *God;* Packer, *Knowing God;* Stafford, *Knowing the Face of God;* Swindoll, *Intimacy with the Almighty.*

28. Hybels, *God You're Looking For,* xxvi.

29. Otto, *Idea of the Holy,* 12–13, emphasis original.

30. Hunter, *American Evangelicalism,* 124–25.

31. "Never Been a Stranger," words and music by Kenny Marks, Pamela Marks and George Cocchini.

32. "Side by Side," words and music by Bob Farrell and Eddie DeGarmo.

33. "If God Is For Us (Who Can Be Against Us)," words and music by DeGarmo & Key.

34. "Closer Than a Brother," words and music by Randy Thomas and Bob Carlisle.

35. Lovelace, *Dynamics of Spiritual Life,* 349.

36. See ibid., 344.

37. Fischer, "Spirit of CCM," 49–50ff.

38. Nouwen, *Wounded Healer,* 25.

39. Gene Eugene quoted in Heyn, "Looking Below the Surface," 17.

40. Quoted in *Syndicate,* 7, emphasis original.

41. Michael Been quoted in Urbanski, "Tracing the Call," 9.

42. "I Could Laugh," words and music by Mike Roe; "Fashion Fades," words and music by Gordon Kennedy, Billy Smiley, and Mark Gersmehl.

43. The songs identified in the text appear on the following albums: Point of Grace, *The Whole Truth* (Word, 1995); DeGarmo & Key, *Street Light* (Powerdiscs, 1986); Phil Keaggy, *Ph'lip Side* (Sparrow, 1980); Julie Miller, *Meet Julie Miller*

(Myrrh, 1990); All Star United, *All Star United* (Reunion, 1997); PFR, *Great Lengths* (Sparrow, 1994).

44. Well, "Critique," 23.

45. Grossberg, "Is Anybody Listening?" 51.

46. Lipsitz, "We Know What Time It Is," 17–28.

47. McClary, "Same As It Ever Was," 29–40.

48. Hirschberg, "ENDD Notes." The concert was significant for, as Hirschberg describes it, "Singer Robert Smith came on-stage in his trademark white-face makeup and his cherry red lipstick and his black smock, stared out at the sea of white-faced faces and black smocks before him, and said, 'God, you all look more like Robert Smith than I do.'"

49. Simpson, "Shadows of Anxiety," 55–73.

50. Mootown Records advertisement, *Visions of Gray,* Apr. 1994, 16.

51. Styll, "'Jesus Junk' Revisited," 4. At the same time, however, the number of Christian acts (Audio Adrenaline, The Newsboys, One Bad Pig) whose stated purposes include showing that "Christianity can be fun" further testifies to a conception of the faith that is largely connected to issues of (adolescent) popularity and fashion (see Ferraiuolo, "Interview," 51–52, 54; Ridley, "Christianity Is Serious Fun," 20–23).

52. Harbinson, "Arts," 3.

53. See, among others, Havelock, *Muse Learns to Write;* Innis, *Bias of Communication;* McLuhan, *Gutenberg Galaxy;* Ong, *Orality & Literacy.*

54. Christians, "Redemptive Media," 331–56.

55. Schultze, "Keeping the Faith," 33 .

56. Ibid., 34.

57. Christians, "Redemptive Media," 332.

58. Schultze, "Keeping the Faith," 41.

59. Christians, "Redemptive Media," 354.

60. Ibid., 343.

61. Cone, *Spirituals and the Blues.*

62. Christians, "Redemptive Media," 351.

63. Fischer, "Spirit of CCM," 55.

64. Christians, "Redemptive Media," 353.

65. Sayers, *Christian Letters.*

66. See Genesis 1:27.

67. Schaeffer, *Art of Life.*

68. Sayers, *Christian Letters,* 28–29.

69. See, for example, Rookmaaker, *Modern Art;* Rookmaaker, *Creative Gift;* Schaeffer, *Hidden Art;* Schaeffer, *Art of Life;* Schaeffer, *Art and the Bible.*

70. Rookmaaker, *Modern Art,* 228.

71. Ibid.

72. Myra and Merrill, *Rock, Bach and Superschlock,* 120.

73. Peck, "Englishman Comments," 41.

74. *"Syndicate,"* 6.

75. Rookmaaker, *Creative Gift,* 230.

76. Ibid., 113.

77. Schaeffer, *Art and the Bible,* 25.

78. Rookmaaker, *Creative Gift,* 154–55.

79. Sayers, *Christian Letters,* 80.

80. Fischer, "The Spirit of CCM," 50.

81. Ibid., 53.

82. Ibid.

83. Myra and Merrill, *Rock, Bach and Superschlock.*

84. See I Corinthians 13:12; Isaiah 55:8.

85. Fischer, "Consider This: Handle with Care," 86.

86. *"Syndicate,"* 6.

87. Peacock, "Few Words."

88. Quoted in Faris, "Charlie Peacock."

89. Ibid., 7.

90. *"Syndicate,"* 6.

91. Newcomb, "Q Thoughts," 4.

92. Quoted in Bajkiewicz, "Interview," 43.

93. Quoted in Rocker, "Adam Again," 6.

94. Newcomb, "Q Thoughts," 4.

95. Ibid.

96. See Farley, "Reborn to Be Wild," 62–64.

97. See Rake, "Kevin Smith," 16–17; Rake, "Jimmy A.," 17–18; Smith, *At the Foot of Heaven.*

98. Rake, "Kevin Smith," 16.

99. Rumburg, "Unguarded," 24–32.

100. Scott, "Scratching the Surface," 22, emphasis original.

101. Ibid.

102. Peacock, "Few Words."

103. The juxtaposition of black and white versus shades of gray is undoubt-edly one of Christian music's more widely used metaphors, finding application in album titles (Leslie Phillips, *Black and White in a Grey World* [Myrrh, 1985]; Youth Choir, *Shades of Gray* [Shadow Records, 1986]), band names (Black and White World, Out of the Grey), and trade magazine titles (*Visions of Gray*).

104. Nouwen, *Wounded Healer,* 38.

105. Quoted in MacIntosh, "Michael Roe," 29.

106. Ibid.

107. "The New Physics," words and music by Mike Roe and Gene Mascoli; The 77's, *Drowning with Land in Sight* (Myrrh, 1994).

108. Quoted in Newcomb, "The 77's," 19.

109. See Parks, "Human Migration," 888–96; Simmel, "Stranger," 402–8.

110. The songs identified in the text appear on the following albums: Mark Heard, *Eye of the Storm* (Home Sweet Home/Myrrh, 1983); Daniel Amos, *Motorcycle* (BAI, 1993); The Choir, *Speckled Bird* (REX, 1994).

111. "Window," words and music by Michael Knott.

112. See "Orphans of God," words and music by Mark Heard; "Hollow Man," words and music by Daniel Amos; "See You In Person," words and music by Ric Alba.

113. Steve Taylor, however, is also one of the better examples of the problems associated with making hard-and-fast distinctions between Separational, Integrational and Transformational CCM (see pages 19-21). Perhaps more than any other artist, Taylor has moved fairly freely between the categories. Thus, clearly transformational with his early work, Taylor's participation in Chagall Guevara moved him toward a more integrational approach; and following the failure of Chagall Guevara, Taylor returned to CCM, this time taking an explicitly separational approach (see "Steve Taylor," *Campus Life Christian Music Annual,* M24; Ervin, "Chagall Guevara," 6–7; "Steve Taylor," *CounterCulture,* 18–20).

114. Pritchard, "From the Editor," 2, emphasis original.

115. "Steve Taylor," *CounterCulture,* 19.

116. Pritchard, "From the Editor," 2.

117. Nouwen, *Wounded Healer,* 63.

118. See Faris, "The Choir," 13.

119. "Ghost of the Heart," words and music by Terry Taylor.

120. "Dry Bones Dance," words and music by Mark Heard.

121. The band comprises Terry Taylor (Daniel Amos), Gene Eugene (Adam Again), Derri Daugherty (The Choir), and Mike Roe (The 77's).

122. "Bush League," words and music by Gene Eugene and Terry Taylor.

123. Gene Eugene quoted in Caviness, "Lost Dogs," 14.

124. Bill Mallonee quoted in Knight, "Choosing to Believe," 16.

5. The Materialist Critique: "It's Business"

Epigraph from Marx, "Eighteenth Brumaire," 595.

1. Harbinson, "Arts," 3.

2. Vanderpoel, "Cover Story." The article was also posted to the Usenet newsgroup rec.music.christian on Feb. 25, 1995.

3. Mike Roe quoted in Vanderpoel, "Cover Story."

4. See Carey, *Communication as Culture,* for a fuller discussion of the distinctions between transmission-based and ritual-based models of communication.

5. Phillips, "Busting the Media Trusts," 23, emphasis original.

6. See Farley, "Reborn to Be Wild," 62–64.

7. See "An Open Letter," *Contemporary Christian Magazine,* 5; "An Open Letter: Editor's Response," *Contemporary Christian Magazine,* 5–6.

8. Hirsch, "U.S. Cultural Production," 111.

9. Compaine, "Expanding Base," 90.

10. See, for example, Bagdikian, *Media Monopoly;* Compaine, *Who Owns the Media?;* Gomery, "Media Economics," 43–60; Picard, *Media Economics.*

11. See, for example, Romanowski, "Roll Over Beethoven," 79–88; Flake, *Redemptorama;* Warren, "What Does God Think?" 16; Hefner, "Alternative Views," 63–64; Long, "Can't Buy Me Ministry," 20–28.

12. See Baker, *Contemporary Christian Music,* 85.

13. Quoted in Molina, "Randy Matthew's [*sic*]Son of Dust," 11.

14. For a more complete discussion of Myrrh's history, see Romanowski, *Rock 'n' Religion,* 133–37.

15. Compaine, *Who Owns the Media?* 275. See also, Frith, "Industrialization of Pop Music," 49–74; Frith, "Art versus Technology," 263–80.

16. Owen, *Economics and the Freedom of Expression,* 14; Compaine, *Who Owns the Media?* 275.

17. See Baker, *Contemporary Christian Music,* 83.

18. Baker, *Why Should?* 137; Romanowski, *Rock 'n' Religion,* 136.

19. Romanowski, "Contemporary Christian Music," 158. Note, however, that this figure would drop over the next decade, bottoming out in 1993 at 15 percent (see Christian Booksellers Association, "1997 CBA Customer Profile," 63).

20. Flake, *Redemptorama;* Balmer, *Mine Eyes;* Weber, *Protestant Ethic.*

21. Lull, "Popular Music and Communication," 21–22.

22. Dawidoff, "No Sex," 40.

23. See Romanowski, "Move Over Madonna," 59–60.

24. Romanowski, *Rock 'n' Religion,* 15.

25. Frith, "Art versus Technology," 265.

26. Ibid., 267.

27. See Denisoff, "Folk-Rock," 214–30; Kruse, "Subcultural Identity," 33–41; Lont, "Redwood Records," 233–49; Lont, "Women's Music," 241–53.

28. There are myriad examples of such studies. See, for example, Gitlin, "Prime Time Ideology," 507–32; Grossberg, "Is Anybody Listening?" 41–58; Hall, "Culture," 315–48; Weinstein, "Rock," 3–23. The approach as a whole can be traced largely to the work of the Frankfurt School and, more specifically, Horkheimer and Adorno, "Culture Industry," 120–67.

29. See Lont, "Persistence," 1–12.

30. For one of the better attempts at this, see Grossberg, "Another Boring Day," 225–58.

31. Flake, *Redemptorama*, 1, 17.

32. Ibid., 21.

33. For a discussion of the commercial/institutional nature of the contemporary church, see Windes, "Cost of Living," 6.

34. Lont, "Persistence," 5–6.

35. Grossberg, "Politics of Youth," 105.

36. Grossberg, "Another Boring Day," 252.

37. Ibid., 255.

38. Ibid., 254; Weber, *Protestant Ethic*; Schultze, "Keeping the Faith," 23–45.

39. Cf. Barry Manilow, *Sweet Life*; Radano, *New Musical Figurations*.

40. Mike Roe quoted in Ozard, "Interviews: Mike Roe," 20; Bob Hartman quoted in Newcomb, "Petra," 21; Tai Anderson quoted in DeMarco, "Conspiracy Theories," 40; Scott Hunter quoted in Smiles, "Spotlight," 8; John James quoted in Ferrairuolo, "Interview: Newsboys," 52.

41. While there are no doubt exceptions and executives who do make decisions based on personal belief, publicly at least the controversial decisions made by the Christian music industry are by and large justified in terms of the market. So, for example, The 77's album title *Pray Naked* was rejected by Word because executives for the label "did not feel the title was appropriate for this retail market" (quoted in Gascón, "The 77's Expose Their Faith," 28–29). Similarly, Family Christian Bookstores refused to carry the Vigilantes of Love's *Slow Dark Train* because the song "Love Cocoon" was considered potentially offensive to customers (see Selby, "On the Beat," 10–11).

42. Dixon, "Curious Fools," 24.

43. Ibid., 24; Nouwen, *In the Name of Jesus*.

44. See Hirsch, *Structure*; DiMaggio and Hirsch, "Production Organizations," 735–52; Hirsch, "Processing Fads," 639–59; Rothenbuhler and Streck, "Structure and Performance."

45. So, for example, while the aforementioned Daniel Amos album *Darn Floor—Big Bite* is considered by some critics (as well as the band members) to be

one of the best albums the group ever recorded, less than 10,000 copies of the album were sold (see Newcomb, "Terry S. Taylor," 12, 18).

46. See Well, "Hoi Polloi," 8–11.

47. Brown, "Julie Miller," 33. Conventional wisdom holds that the label was hoping Miller would become a replacement for Leslie Phillips.

48. See Newcomb, "Mercy Mercy," 13–14; Ozard, "Interviews: Mike Roe"; Newcomb, "Jacob's Trouble," 10–12; Willman, "Sam Phillips," 8, 11; Akins, "Pretty in Pink," 64–65; Hefner, "Is Image Everything?" 90–99; Rumburg, "Cindy Morgan," 60–62; Price, "Kim Hill," 50–51; Smeby, "Keeping Promises," 56–57; Long, "Bryan Duncan," 96–98.

49. Palmer, "The Choir," 24.

50. See Hefner, "Charlie Peacock's Cry," 42–43.

51. "Everybody in the Band," words and music by Steve Hindalong; "Dave's Blues," words and music by The 77's. For obvious reasons, documented sources describing such conflicts are often difficult to find (but see Stillion and Estey, "Tonio K. Interview," 3–9; Well, "Critique," 25; Ozard, "Interview: Mike Roe"; Gascón, "The 77's Expose Their Faith"). Live performances, however, often find artists either describing their conflicts with the labels and/or performing their songs as originally written.

52. While the issue seems quite trivial to the uninitiated, the difficulty is that behaviors like smoking and cussing—or rather, not smoking and not cussing—are frequently employed as identity markers by evangelicals to distinguish themselves from non-Christians. Illustrating this point, evangelist and author Tony Campolo has been known to provoke his evangelical audiences by claiming (to paraphrase), "Forty thousand children will die of starvation today and, frankly, you don't give a damn. And now, most of you are more concerned that I just said 'damn' than you are about the forty thousand children who are dying."

53. Quoted in MacIntosh, "Mark Heard," 11.

54. Knight, "Prayer Before Dying," 12.

55. Knight, "Dancing on Silver Lakes," 19.

56. Platt, "Original Christian Street Rocker," 8.

57. See, for example, Platt, "Whatever Happened to *Horrendous Disc?*" 32–33, 35; Newcomb, "Larry Norman," 22–25; Styll, "Feedback: Larry Norman," 4; Newcomb, "Taylor, Part I," 9–10; Newcomb, "Taylor, Part II," 14, 16; Newcomb, "Taylor, Part III"; Cash and Mason, "Is Larry Norman Through?" 8–9.

58. Vanderpoel, "Inner-View: Randy Stonehill," 9.

59. Cash and Mason, "Is Larry Norman Through?," 8–9.

60. Newcomb, "Charlie Peacock," 9.

61. Capone, "See What Sacramento Hath Spawned," 20–22; Newcomb,

"Charlie Peacock"; Guterman, "Records: *The Turning*," 84–85; Mifflin, "Records: *77's*," 104.

62. Roe and Hershey, "The 77's, Part 1," 7; Roe and Hershey, "The 77's, Part 2," 6.

63. Asked to comment on his failure to achieve the predicted stardom, for example, Charlie Peacock's response was, "somethings [*sic*] are better left unsaid" (quoted in Newcomb, "Charlie Peacock").

64. Quoted in Marion, "Vector," 20.

65. Delaney, "What 7 & 7 Is," 14; Roe and Hershey, "The 77's, Part 2," 6.

66. Roe and Hershey, "The 77's, Part 2," 6. If there is a recurring theme in the joint distribution deals between Christian labels and the mainstream record industry, it's promotion—or the lack thereof. All too often the Christian music industry seems to assume that if their products are on the record store shelves they are going to sell; that, however, is simply not the case. As has been repeatedly shown, unless the record industry is willing to put its marketing forces behind an album, that album is unlikely to sell.

67. Marion, "Vector," 20.

68. Quoted in Marion, "Vector," 20. While Exit ultimately obtained its group distribution deal with Island, as shown by the performance of both The 77's and Charlie Peacock, there was little commitment from A&M to the label and "the contract was a joke" (Roe and Hershey, "The 77's, Part 2," 6).

69. Broken Records advertisement, *Cornerstone* 13, 73 (1985): 2–3. While this initial advertisement suggested the label to be an artist-run label controlled by Ojo Taylor (Undercover), Derri Daugherty (The Choir), Mike Stand (Altar Boys), and Stephen Crumbacher (Crumbächer), Broken Records was at that point the rock-oriented arm of Maranatha! Music. With the sale of Maranatha! Music, however, Broken Records became, in the hands of Taylor and Adam Again's Gene Eugene, what it had to that point only pretended to be: an artist-owned and-operated company (see Hershey, "New Life," 9; Pritchard, "Behind the Scenes," 10).

70. Bajkiewicz, "Interview: Daniel Amos," 43.

71. Quoted in Adams, "Interview With Dan Russell," emphasis original.

72. MacIntosh, "Everybody Loves Jon Gibson," 6. BAI was essentially a continuation of Taylor and Eugene's efforts at Broken Records. The name change was prompted when Maranatha! Music reasserted its interest in the name "Broken Records" (see note 69).

73. Rumburg, "In the News: Charlie Peacock," 22.

74. Long, "Charlie Peacock," 30.

75. Comedia, "Alternative Press," 95.

76. Quoted in *"Syndicate,"* 7.

77. Orteza, "John Austin," 14.

78. Weinstein, "Rock," 3–23.

79. Styll, "Keith Green," 70, emphasis original.

80. Quoted in ibid.

81. Wicke, *Rock Music*, 117.

82. Long, "Can't Buy Me Ministry," 20–28.

83. Quoted in Long, "Who's the Leader," 23.

84. Ibid.

85. Perry, "Ain't No Mountain," 51–87.

86. Harron, "McRock," 219.

87. Styll, "Wanted," 4.

88. Quoted in Rumburg, "Unguarded," 32.

89. Well, "Michael W. Smith," 12–13, 21.

90. Quoted in Rumburg, "Unguarded," 32.

91. *Rolling Stone,* Apr. 16, 1992. In the case of the *Rolling Stone* cover, moreover, Cobain's proclamation arguably worked to legitimize *Rolling Stone*'s own authenticity, which has come to be questioned in recent years.

92. With the exception of the occassional coupon offered by some of the larger chains and the now abandoned "1 Free with 4" incentive program of the Christian record distributors—a long standing practice of affixing to every Christian release stickers that could collectively be redeemed for free albums, participation in the "1 Free with 4" program dwindled through the 1990s, ending completely on Aug. 1, 1997 when Chordant Distribution, the sole remaining participant, pulled out—Christian retailers rarely discount tapes and CDs they sell.

93. Styll, "Keith Green," 65.

94. Ibid., 70, emphasis his.

95. Ibid., 68.

96. Ibid.

97. See Romanowski, *Rock 'n' Religion,* 199–206.

98. While giving away his albums made Green a singular character in the Christian music industry, it was a common practice during the late '70s and early '80s to recoup the costs for live performances by taking a voluntary "love offering" at some point during the performance rather than charging a fixed price for tickets.

99. Styll, "Keith Green," 69–70.

100. Margaret Becker and John W. Styll quoted in Stafford, "Has Christian Rock?" 18.

101. Margaret Becker quoted in Metzler, "Margaret Becker," 8.

102. Key, *Don't Stop the Music*, 146. It should be noted, however, that along with partner Eddie DeGarmo, Key made a significant concession to Green's argument with the release of the 1987 album *D&K* (Powerdiscs). Although sold for the standard industry price, initial shipments of the cassette version of the album were packaged in twos with the admonition to the consumer to give one copy away to a non-Christian friend.

103. Brian Tong quoted in Styll, "Intro," 4.

104. Granger, "No More Funny Business," 35.

105. Selby, "Flower Power," 31.

106. The moves made by Audio Adrenaline and Newsboys (i.e., the dismissal of one's previous albums as cliché-driven cheerleading) have become formulaic in their own right. In order to position themselves for either mainstream success or rock authenticity, separational bands must generally distance themselves from their earlier, explicitly Christian and/or overtly commercial (vis-à-vis the evagelical market) efforts.

107. See, for example, Green's *So You Wanna Go Back to Egypt* (Pretty Good Records, 1980) and Camp's *Shake Me to Wake Me* (Sparrow, 1985) for examples of these musicians' critical perspectives.

108. Marsden, *Reforming Fundamentalism*, 204.

109. Quoted in Dawidoff, "No Sex," 40.

110. Hefner, "Point of Grace," 35, 47–51; Point of Grace and David Seay, *Life, Love & Other Mysteries*.

111. Within this context it is perhaps not surprising that while confessions of drug use by Christian artists (e.g., Michael W. Smith, Gary Chapman) receive relatively little comment, the sexual affairs of artists such as Sandi Patti, Michael English and Marybeth Jordan are particularly problematic for, and soundly condemned by, the Christian music industry (see chapter 1, note 84).

112. See, for example, "That Kinda Girl" from the album *Free at Last*.

113. Randolph, "Bevill-May-Care," 70; Hefner, "On the Beat," 13–14.

114. Long, "Conversations: Darrell A. Harris," 28.

115. Donaldson, "Celebrating Ten Years: Barry McGuire," 35. Contributing to this state of affairs is the fact that many Christian record companies are now owned by large mainstream media corporations whose interest in CCM is limited to its ability to generate revenue. Ministry is fine, provided it doesn't interfere with profits.

116. See Long, "Can't Buy Me Ministry."

117. Schaeffer, *Art and the Bible*, 9.

118. Muggeridge, *Christ and the Media*. Muggeridge was no doubt in part responding to *Jesus Christ Superstar,* which, in the grand finale, poses that very question.

119. Long, "Dana Key," 31.

120. Long, "Petra's Bob Hartman," 39.

121. Cusic, *Sound of Light,* 58, 70–71.

122. Moore, *Selling God,* 264.

123. See, for example, Quebedeaux, *Worldly Evangelicals.*

124. Quoted in Rumburg, "Unguarded," 30.

Interlude: Sunday Services

1. "As the Deer," words and music by Marin Nystrom.

Conclusion: Contemporary Christian Music and the Contemporary Christian Life

Epigraph from Adorno, "Curves of the Needle," 54.

1. Dawidoff, "No Sex," 40; Boehlert, "Holy Rock & Rollers," 23; Flake, *Redemptorama,* 22; Romanowski, "Roll Over Beethoven," 81.

2. "Easy Listening," words and music by Steve Taylor.

3. "Elevator Muzik," words and music by Glenn Kaiser.

4. Metzler, "Steve Taylor," 11.

5. Quoted in ibid.

6. See, for example, Matthews, "Letters" 3–4; Long, "Who's the Leader? 22–25.

7. Becker, *Art Worlds,* 35.

8. Ibid., 36.

9. Ibid., 229, 228, 233.

10. See ibid, chap. 10.

11. See, for example, Clarke, "New Lyrics"; Dawidoff, "No Sex"; Farley, "Reborn to be Wild," 62–64.

12. See, for example, Romanowski, "Roll Over Beethoven"; Young, "Contemporary Christian Music," 141–58.

13. Important in this regard are, first, the view the industry has of itself, and, second, the views of the audience. Hence, while there are exceptions, those involved in contemporary Christian music generally take a monolithic approach to the industry, attempting to apply their reasoning and rationales to all of Christian music. Similarly, in listening to Christian audiences speak about themselves (as on the Usenet newsgroup rec.music.christian, for example), one finds, first, that more often than not the audience members will identify themselves as "Chris-

tian music fans," and second, that audience tastes generally vary across a wider range of musical styles than do those of mainstream audiences. It's not uncommon to find individuals lauding at once the praise and worship of Michael Card or Rich Mullins, the arena rock of White Heart or Petra, and the alterno-rock of The 77's or The Prayer Chain. Consequently, while a few integrational artists may have fans who are unaware of the larger body of Christian music available, most Christian acts borrow their audiences—audiences who hear it all as "Christian music"—from one another.

14. See Well, "Michael W. Smith," 21.

15. Eddy, "Amy Grant," 64.

16. "Good for Me," words and music by Tom Snow et. al.; "Talk About Love," words and music by Margaret Becker and Charlie Peacock.

17. Quoted in Colapinto, "Who Are You Eddie Vedder?" 146.

18. It can of course be argued that artists like Miss Angie are in fact dependent upon artists like Sandi Patti, the high sales of the latter's albums compensating for the low sales of the former's. At the same time, it has also been argued that access to the production and promotion budgets afforded artists like Patti could elevate lesser known artists to those earning levels.

19. Comparing production budgets is a somewhat problematic task as it's not always clear just what an album costs to make. As Tom Moon notes, "ask a producer how much it costs to make a record and you're likely to get standup comedy" (Moon, "What it Costs," 90). Still, Moon suggests that for mainstream rock music low end production budgets (nevermind your Michael Jackson or Rolling Stones) can range from a few thousand dollars for an indie effort to $200,000 for "your average mid-profile rock act"; while in comparison, that same average mid-profile rock act in CCM would, according to some insiders, be given a budget of roughly $15,000 (see Newcomb, "Adam Again Digs Deep," 10; Blinn, "The Choir").

20. "God Is Not a Secret," words and music by Steve Taylor and Peter Furler.

21. Terry Scott Taylor, "Further Up and Further In."

22. Harris, "Feedback: Rock/Alt Elitists?" 6.

23. "Ask CCM: Cut!," 11.

24. For more on the tensions between high culture and mass culture see, among others: Rosenberg and White, *Mass Culture*; Gans, *Popular Culture and High Culture*.

25. See *"Syndicate,"* 6–8; Camp, "Call for Reformation."

26. Quoted in Rivers, *Shake.*

27. Romanowski, "Move Over Madonna," 63; Flake, Redemptorama, 22.

28. See, for example, Goldman, "That Old Devil Music," 28–31, 59.

29. For more on authenticy in popular music, see, among others, Frith, "Art versus Technology," 263–80; Grossberg, "Another Boring Day," 225–58; Denisoff, "Folk-Rock," 214–30; Kruse, "Subcultural Identity,"33–41; Lont, "Redwood Records," 233–49.

30. Weiss, *Religion and Art.*

31. Kilby, *Christianity and Aesthetics,* 30.

32. Ibid., emphasis original.

33. Greeley, *God in Popular Culture,* 14.

34. Taylor, "Further Up and Further In."

35. Weiss, *Religion and Art,* 5.

36. Taylor, "Further Up and Further In."

37. See, for example, Styll, "Editor's Comment: Amy Grant's Sanctified Entertainment," 4; Styll, "Wanted: Explicit Lyrics," 4; Styll, "Enlarging the Vision," 49–52.

38. "On the Beat: 1996's Top-Selling Albums," 14. In order, the albums listed were: Jars of Clay, *Jars of Clay* (Essential/Silvertone, 1995); DC Talk, *Jesus Freak* (Forefront, 1995); Kirk Franklin and the Family, *Whatcha Lookin' 4* (GospoCentric, 1996); Any Griffith, *I Love to Tell the Story* (Sparrow, 1996); Newsboys, *Take Me to Your Leader* (Star Song, 1996); Steven Curtis Chapman, *Signs of Life* (Sparrow, 1996); Michael W. Smith, *I'll Lead You Home* (Reunion, 1995); Point of Grace, *Life, Love, and Other Mysteries* (Word, 1996); Audio Adrenaline, *Bloom* (Forefront, 1996); Various Artists, *W.O.W 1996* (Sparrow, 1996); CeCe Winans, *Alone in His Presence* (Sparrow, 1995); Carman, *R.I.O.T.* (Sparrow, 1996); Twila Paris, *Where I Stand* (Sparrow, 1996); Kirk Franklin and the Family, *Kirk Franklin and the Family* (GospoCentric, 1993); Various Artists, *My Utmost for His Highest* (Myrrh, 1995); Point of Grace, *The Whole Truth* (Word, 1994); Various Artists, *WOW 1997* (Sparrow, 1997); 4Him, *The Message* (Benson, 1996); Ray Boltz, *The Concert of a Lifetime* (Word, 1995); Third Day, *Third Day* (Reunion/Arista, 1995); Jaci Velasquez, *Heavenly Place* (Myrrh, 1996); Kenny Rogers, *The Gift* (Magnatone, 1996); Amy Grant, *House of Love* (Myrrh/A&M, 1994); Various Artists, *My Utmost for His Highest: The Covenant* (Myrrh, 1996); Rebecca St. James, *God* (Forefront, 1996).

39. Styll, "Cross Purposes?" 45–46, 48; "Survey Reports."

40. See Farley, "Reborn to be Wild," 62; Dawidoff, "No Sex," 40; Boehlert, "Holy Rock & Rollers," 24.

41. Akins, "DC Talk's 'Freak.'"

42. For a discussion of the concept of "cultural capital," see Bourdieu, *Outline of a Theory of Practice.*

43. See Peepo, "Aunt Betty's Mike Knott," 11, 13–14.

44. Pratt, "*Aunt Bettys,* Aunt Bettys," 9.

45. For more information on Vigilantes of Love, see the VoL-list archive.

46. Quoted in Selby, "Take the Long Way Home," 33.

47. Quoted in Hefner, "Is Image Everything?" 97.

48. See ibid.

49. Boehlert, "Holy Rock & Rollers," 24; Akins, "DC Talk's 'Freak'"; Warren, "Bob Carlisle Album."

50. Styll, "Facing the Music: Christian Labels Downsize," 20, 22.

51. Hendrickson, "In the News: Indie City," 21–22.

52. "Industry Growth Tempered."

53. Long, "Who's the Leader?" 23.

54. Michael Card quoted in Long, "We Have Created a Monster," 26–27.

55. Becker, *Art Worlds,* 300.

56. Gene Eugene quoted in Heyn, "Looking Below the Surface," 17.

57. Randy Matthews, for example, describes a time when, at a Pennsylvania music festival, his band was unplugged because "the people [in charge] thought we were satanic" (see Molina, "Randy Matthew's Son of Dust, 11). Similar tales are told by most of the artists active during the early days of CCM.

58. Horton, *Made in America.*

59. Mike Roe quoted in Ozard, "Interviews: Mike Roe," 31.

60. Cusic, "Should We Take the Jesus Out?" 6; Warren, "What Does God Think?" 16. In 1981 *Contemporary Christian Music* published *The Best of Contemporary Christian Music,* 1978–1980, a volume drawing on their two-and-a-half year publication history, which illustrates both the Christian music industry's disproportionate sense of self-importance and its continual introspection and efforts at self-definition. Articles such as Cusic's (43), John Fischer's "Biblical Foundations for a Music Ministry" (7, 17–20, 50–51) and B.J. Thomas's "The Power of Positive Pop" (43, 60), along with letters to the editor (6) which claimed Christian music to be more than "a platform for preaching," expressed concern over "gospel hype" in Christian music, and condemned "the commercialization of CCM" all worked to resolve the Christian music identity crisis—unsuccessfully, one might add. And while a comprehensive list of similar efforts would run for pages, the following offers a rough sampling of the viewpoints generally expressed: Menconi, "What's Wrong with Christian Music?" 19–20; Hafer, "Music in Ministry: A Christian Looks at the Arts," 45, 49; Hafer, "Music in Ministry: The Purpose of Music," 28, 33; Long, "Can't Buy Me Ministry," 20–28; Peck, "An Englishman Comments," 40–41, 43; Pritchard, "From the Editors," 2; Schaeffer, "Edith Schaeffer: Backstage Pass," 35, 37; Styll, "What Makes Music Christian?" 35–36.

61. Marsden, *Fundamentalism.*

62. Balmer, *Mine Eyes,* 95.

63. Quoted in Hatch, "Our Shackled Scholars," 13. While Greeley writes specifically of Catholic suspicions of the intellectual, as Hatch argues, his analysis is equally applicable to evangelicals.

64. Hatch, "Our Shackled Scholars," 12.

65. Noll, *The Scandal of the Evangelical Mind,* 3.

66. The single exception to this has been the issue of abortion, opposition to which at this point has arguably become an essential tenet to fundamentalist Christianity.

67. See Marsden, *Reforming Fundamentalism,* especially 148 and following.

68. Jorstad, *Popular Religion,* 156.

69. Interestingly enough, the argument could be made that such statements can be so simplistic as to become empty of what would generally be understood to be doctrine. So, in a study of twenty-seven songs which appeared in the Top Ten of Contemporary Christian Music's 1986 charts, Gary Richard Drum, while hypothesizing that Christian music would "reflect an evangelical-Pentecostal-charismatic doctrinal perspective," in fact found CCM "to be almost devoid of doctrinal content in any direction" (Drum, *The Message in the Music*).

70. Greeley, *God in Popular Culture,* 67.

71. Ibid., 67.

72. Moore, *The Care of The Soul,* 235.

73. Ibid., 236.

74. Buttrick, *God, Pain, and Evil,* 16.

75. Styll, "Carman," 27.

76. "Yet Another Door Interview: Undercover," 26.

77. Henry, *Uneasy Conscience,* 22.

78. Ibid., 68

79. Ibid., 19. A more current critique of evangelical church music can be found in Leonard Payton, "Prelude or a Quaalude?" 10–16.

80. "In the Beginning," 8

81. "ESA—Our Vision."

82. The cost of the album included a one year subscription to the magazine.

83. C.A.U.S.E. (Christian Artists United to Save the Earth) was contemporary Christian music's 1985 answer to Band Aid's "Do They Know It's Christmas?" and USA for Africa's "We Are the World." Embarrased by the fact that Christian musicians hadn't taken the lead in responding to world hunger, Steve Camp brought together ninety-seven CCM artists to perform on a song titled, "Do Something Now" (written by Camp, Phil Maderia, and Rob and Carol

Frazier). Released on Sparrow Records, proceeds from the record were directed to Compassion International, a Christian child development organization (see Ted Ojarovsky, "Ya Gotta Do Something!" 20–26ff).

84. Myers, *All God's Children,* 186.

85. Ibid.

86. Balmer, *Mine Eyes,* 212.

87. Heard, "Musician's Diary," 15.

88. Quoted in Harris, "What About Bob?" 56.

89. Ibid.

90. Kilby, *Christianity and Aesthetics,* 36.

91. Randolph, "In Concert: Steven Curtis Chapman," 58; Hefner, "On the Beat: Everything Changes," 12; "Growing Sales," 3.

92. Knight, "Choosing to Believe," 16.

93. Hefner, "Point of Grace," 50.

94. For a discussion of the origins and influence of individualism in evangelicalism, see Marsden, *Fundamentalism.*

95. Warren, "What Does God Think?" 16.

96. Quoted in ibid.

97. Ibid., emphasis original.

98. Ibid.

99. Styll, "Cross Purposes?" 48.

100. There have been occasional exceptions—such as DC Talk's Toby McKeehan, who on multiple occasions has suggested that CCM has a racial bias which leads it to overlook urban hip-hop music—but generally, critical questions such as, "How does the medium of rock music affect the nature of the Christian message presented?" and "How does the CCM industry's participation in a capitalist economic system impact the types of music produced?" go unasked (see Nappa, "Destination Known," 34–36; Morrison, "Nitty Gritty," 80–81). Moreover, McKeehan is speaking from the perspective of a frustrated record label owner, not as an artist. Unfortunately, questions of racism within the CCM industry are most likely to be raised when a record company finds itself saddled with an artist who is getting less attention and fewer sales than what might be deserved because of a perceived racial bias. In a similar incident, Linda Klosterman, vice president of marketing for Word Distribution, noted that the relegation of God's Property featuring Kirk Franklin's Nu Nation to the Gospel Chart rather than the Top Contemporary Christian Chart hurt the album's sales in Christian bookstores (see "Christian Music Claims Spots").

101. McDannell, *Material Christianity.*

102. Ibid.

103. Quoted in Balmer, *Mine Eyes,* 166–67.
104. Ibid., 166
105. McDannell, *Material Christianity,* 267.
106. Ibid., 223, emphasis original.
107. Greeley, *God in Popular Culture,* 9.
108. Quoted in Newcomb, "Petra," 21.
109. Browne and Marsden, "Introduction," 1.
110. For a discussion of the potential heresies to be found in CCM, see Payton, "Prelude or a Quaalude?" 11, 14.

Bibliography

"25 Years of Gospel Music from The Imperials." *Contemporary Christian Music* 11, 9 (Mar. 1989): 23–32.

"82 Issues." *Contemporary Christian Music* 5, 7 (Jan. 1983): 44.

A&M Records advertisement. *Billboard,* Apr. 20, 1985, 5.

ABC News, "A Song and a Prayer: Christian Music Stars Amy Grant and Sandi Patti," *Prime-Time Live,* aired Dec. 3, 1997. Transcripts available at http://www.abcnews.com/onair/ptl/html_files/transcripts/ptl1203c.html.

Adair, Mark. "Feedback: Fat Babies in Shallow Water" [letter to the editor]. *Contemporary Christian Music* 14, 10 (Apr. 1992): 6.

Adams, Chris. "Interview with Dan Russell." World Wide Web document available at http://www.xensei.com/users/bobhouse/about.htm.

Adorno, Theodor W. "The Curves of the Needle" [trans. T. Y. Levin]. *October* 55 (Winter 1990): 49–55.

Akins, Debra. "DC Talk's 'Freak' Sets First Week Sales Record." *CCM Update* [electronic], Dec. 4, 1995. World Wide Web document available at http://www.ccmcom.com/ccmupdate/95_12_04/120495freak_story.html.

———. "Pretty in Pink." *Contemporary Christian Music* 18, 11 (May 1996): 64–65.

Altman, Rick. *Ten Theses About Genre* [unpublished manuscript]. University of Iowa, 1995.

"An Open Letter." *Contemporary Christian Magazine* 8, 8 (Feb. 1986): 5.

"An Open Letter: Editor's Response." *Contemporary Christian Magazine* 8, 8 (Feb. 1986): 5–6.

Anders, Max. *God: Knowing Our Creator.* Nashville: Thomas Nelson Publishers, 1995.

Anderson, Tim. "The Roots of Rock: Did Gospel Music Give Birth to the Devil's Rock 'n' Roll?" *Contemporary Christian Magazine* 6, 8 (Feb. 1984): 12–14, 42.

Aranza, Jacob. *Backward Masking Unmasked: Backward Satanic Messages of Rock and Roll Exposed*. Shreveport, La.: Huntington, 1983.

"Ask *CCM:* Cut!" *Contemporary Christian Music* 19, 11 (May 1997): 11.

Austin, John. "158 Questions (and a Quote from Jesus) for Those Who Buy and Sell Contemporary Christian Music." World Wide Web document available at http://www.geocities.com/SunsetStrip/Stage/9900/ja.html.

Bagdikian, Ben. *The Media Monopoly*. Boston: Beacon Press, 1983.

Bajkiewicz, Chris. "Interview: Daniel Amos." *Cornerstone* 12, 68 (1983): 43.

Baker, Paul. *Contemporary Christian Music: Where It Came From, What It Is, Where It's Going*. Westchester, Ill.: Crossway, 1985.

———. *Why Should the Devil Have All the Good Music?* Waco, Tex.: Word Books, 1979.

Balmer, Randall. *Mine Eyes Have Seen the Glory: A Journey into the Evangelical Subculture of America*. Oxford: Oxford Univ. Press, 1989.

Bate, Barbara, and Anita Taylor, eds. *Women Communicating: Studies of Women's Talk*. Norwood, N.J.: Ablex, 1988.

Becker, Howard. *Art Worlds*. Berkeley: Univ. of California Press, 1982.

Bhatia, Pradeep. "Amy Grant FAQ" [unofficial web page]. World Wide Web document available at http://www.cs.ruu.nl/wais/html/na-dir/music/amy-grant-faq/part2.html.

Blinn, Beth. "The Choir." *The Lighthouse* [electronic]. World Wide Web document available at http://tlem.netcentral.net/old/choir_9407.html.

Bloom, Allan. *The Closing of the American Mind*. New York: Simon & Schuster, 1987.

Boehlert, Eric. "Holy Rock & Rollers." *Rolling Stone,* Oct. 3, 1996, 23–24.

Boone, Pat. "Prelude." In *Why Should the Devil Have All the Good Music?* Paul Baker. Waco, Tex.: Word Books, 1979.

Bourdieu, Pierre. *Outline of a Theory of Practice* [trans. R. Nice]. Cambridge: Cambridge Univ. Press, 1986.

Bright, Bill. *The Four Spiritual Laws*. N.p.: Campus Crusade for Christ, 1965/1995.

Broken Records advertisement. *Cornerstone* 13, 73 (1985): 2–3.

Brown, Bruce A. "Dakoda Motor Company: Same Model, New Name." *True Tunes News* 5, 8 (1993): 26–27, 35.

———. "Julie Miller: Helping Heal the World's Scars." *Contemporary Christian Music* 17, 5 (Nov. 1994): 32–33.

———. "On the Beat: Rock/Alternative." *Contemporary Christian Music* 19, 5 (Nov. 1996): 19–20.

———. "Records: *Vox Humana,* Daniel Amos." *Contemporary Christian Magazine* 7, 6 (Dec. 1984): 38, 40.

Brown, David L. "'Christian' Rock Is The Devil's Music." World Wide Web document available at http://www.execpc.com/~dlbrown/logos/rock.html.

Browne, Ray B., and Michael T. Marsden, eds. *Ten Cultures of Celebrations.* Bowling Green, Ohio: Popular Press, 1994.

Browne, Ray B., and Michael T. Marsden. "Introduction." In *Ten Cultures of Celebrations,* ed. Ray B. Browne and Michael T. Marsden. Bowling Green, Ohio: Popular Press, 1994.

Bubel, Kathy. "Dakoda Motor Co. Revs It Up!" *Syndicate* 9, 1 (May 1994): 24–27.

Bullock, Kathy. "Darrel Mansfield: Rock Is His Pulpit." *Contemporary Christian Music* 3, 3 (Sept. 1980): 22, 29.

Bultman, Bud. "Editorial/Christian Muzak." *HIS* 42, 5 (Feb. 1982): 32.

Burns, C.A. "What's New: A Stunning Collection." *Contemporary Christian Music* 4, 12 (June 1982): 30.

Buttrick, George A. *God, Pain, and Evil.* Nashville: Abingdon, 1966.

Camp, Steve. "Kiss the Son." *Contemporary Christian Music* 19, 9 (Mar. 1995): 46–48.

Camp, Steven John. "A Call for Reformation in the Contemporary Christian Music Industry." World Wide Web document available at http://pages.prodigy.net/berrykl/theses/thesopen.html.

Capon, Robert Farrar. *The Supper of the Lamb.* Garden City, N.Y.: Doubleday, 1969.

Capone, Dean. "See What Sacramento Hath Spawned." *Contemporary Christian Magazine* 8, 11 (May 1986): 20–22.

Carey, James. *Communication as Culture.* New York: Routledge, 1989.

Cash, Michael and Steve Mason. "Is Larry Norman Through?" *Visions of Gray* 4, 8 (Apr. 1994): 8–9.

Caviness, Brad. "Lost Dogs: Pound Puppies Pitching in for a Perfect Partnership." *Syndicate* 9, 1 (1994): 13–14.

Christian Booksellers Association (CBA). "1997 CBA Customer Profile Satisfaction Survey." N.p.: CBA, 1997.

"Christian Music Claims Spots in Nation's Top 5." *CCM Update* [electronic], June 9, 1997. World Wide Web document available at http://www.ccmcom.com/ccmupdate/97_06_09/news.html#story1.

Christians, Clifford G. "Redemptive Media as the Evangelical's Cultural Task." In *American Evangelicals and the Mass Media,* ed. Quentin J. Schultze. Grand Rapids, Mich.: Zondervan, 1990.

Ciani, Michael. "All Aboard!" *Contemporary Christian Music* 19, 1 (July 1996): 34–39.

———. "What's New: *Sunday Drive*—Sunday Drive." *Contemporary Christian Music* 20, 2 (Aug. 1997): 52.

Clarke, Gerald. "New Lyrics for the Devil's Music." *Time*, Mar. 11, 1985.

Cohen, Sara. "Ethnography and Popular Music Studies." *Popular Music* 12, 2 (1993): 123–38.

Colapinto, John, with Eric Boehlert and Matt Hendrickson. "Who Are You Eddie Vedder?" *Rolling Stone*, Nov. 28, 1996, 50–59ff.

Comedia. "The Alternative Press: The Development of Underdevelopment." *Media, Culture and Society* 6, 2 (1984): 95–102.

Compaine, Benjamin M., et al. *Who Owns the Media? Concentration of Ownership in the Mass Communication Industry.* White Plains, N.Y.: Knowledge Industry, 1982.

Compaine, Benjamin M. "The Expanding Base of Media Competition." *Journal of Communication* 35, 3 (summer 1985): 81–96.

Cone, James H. *The Spirituals and the Blues: An Interpretation.* New York: Seabury, 1972.

Curtis, Jim. *Rock Eras: Interpretations of Music and Society, 1954–84.* Bowling Green: Popular Press, 1987.

Cusic, Don. *Music in the Market.* Bowling Green, Ohio: Popular Press, 1996.

———. "Should We Take the Jesus Out of Christian Music?" *Contemporary Christian Music* 1, 1 (July 1978): 6.

———. *The Sound of Light: A History of Gospel Music.* Bowling Green, Ohio: Popular Press, 1990.

Dawidoff, Nicholas. "No Sex. No Drugs. But Rock 'n' Roll (Kind of)." *New York Times Magazine*, Feb. 5, 1995, 40–44ff.

DeCurtis, Anthony, ed. *Present Tense: Rock & Roll and Culture.* Durham: Duke Univ. Press, 1992.

Delaney, Michael. "What 7 & 7 Is: Michael Roe." *Harvest Rock Syndicate* 5, 1 (1990): 14.

DeMarco, John M. "Conspiracy Theories." *Contemporary Christian Music* 20, 3 (Sept. 1997): 38–40.

———. "In Concert: Rebecca St. James." *Contemporary Christian Music* 19, 11 (May 1997): 120.

Denisoff, R. Serge. "Folk-Rock: Folk Music, Protest, or Commercialism." *Journal of Popular Culture* 3, 2 (1969): 214–30.

———. *Sing a Song of Social Significance.* Bowling Green, Ohio: Popular Press, 1972.

DiMaggio, Paul and Paul M. Hirsch. "Production Organizations in the Arts." *American Behavioral Scientist* 19 (1976): 735–52.

Dixon, Amy E. "Curious Fools: Admire the Cat." *Contemporary Christian Music* 17, 8 (Feb. 1995): 24.

Donaldson, Devlin. "Amy Grant: Leading the Way." In *The Heart of the Matter: The Best of CCM Interviews, Volume 1,* ed. John W. Styll. Nashville: Star Song, 1991. (Originally published in *Contemporary Christian Music,* Sept. 1988.)

———. "Celebrating Ten Years: Barry McGuire." *Contemporary Christian Music* 10, 12 (June 1988): 35, 73–74.

———. "Randy Stonehill: Between the Glory and the Flame." In *The Heart of the Matter: The Best of CCM Interviews, Volume 1,* ed. John W. Styll. Nashville: Star Song, 1991. (Originally published in *Contemporary Christian Music,* Oct. 1981.)

"Door Interview: Bob Larson." *Wittenburg Door,* Apr.-May 1979, 7–12, 14–17.

Drane, James. *A New American Reformation: A Study of Youth Culture and Religion.* Totowa, N.J.: Littlefield, 1974.

Drum, Gary Richard. *The Message in the Music: A Content Analysis of Contemporary Christian and Southern Gospel Song Lyrics.* Ph.D. diss., University of Tennessee, 1987.

Eddy, Chuck. "Amy Grant: *Heart in Motion.*" *Entertainment Weekly,* Apr. 5, 1991, 64.

Eisenberg, Evan. *The Recording Angel: Explorations in Phonography.* New York: McGraw-Hill, 1987.

Ellwood, Robert S., Jr. *One Way: The Jesus Movement and Its Meaning.* Englewood Cliffs, N.J.: Prentice-Hall, 1973.

Emerson, Ralph Waldo. "Self-Reliance." In *Ralph Waldo Emerson: Selected Essays,* ed. Larzar Ziff. New York: Penguin Books, 1982.

Ennis, Philip H. *The Seventh Stream: The Emergence of Rock'n'roll in American Popular Music.* Hanover and London: Wesleyan Univ. Press, 1992.

Enroth, Ronald M., Edward E. Ericson, Jr., and C. Breckinridge Peters. *The Jesus People: Old-Time Religion in the Age of Aquarius.* Grand Rapids, Mich.: Eerdmans, 1972.

Epstein, Jonathan S., ed. *Adolescents and Their Music: If It's Too Loud, You're Too Old.* New York: Garland, 1994.

Ervin, Kathleen A. "Chagall Guevara, How'd You Get So Good?" *Harvest Rock Syndicate* 6, 2 (1991): 6–7.

"ESA—Our Vision." World Wide Web document available at http://www.libertynet.org:80/~esa/vision.html.

Faris, T.L. "Charlie Peacock: The Fine Craft of Living Artfully." *Syndicate* 7, 2 (1992): 6–7.

———. "Critique: *Circle Slide,* The Choir." *Harvest Rock Syndicate* 5, 4 (1990): 12.

———. "DeGarmo & Key: On the Road Again." *Syndicate* 8, 5 (1993): 14–15.

———. "The Choir: Serious Music." *Harvest Rock Syndicate* 6, 1 (1991): 13.

Farley, Christopher John. "Reborn to Be Wild." *Time*, Jan. 22, 1996, 62–64.

Ferrairuolo, Perucci. "Church Leaders Troubled by Christian Music." *Contemporary Christian Music* 17, 11 (May 1995): 65.

———. "Interview: Newsboys." *Cornerstone* 21, 100 (1993): 51–52, 54.

Ferré, John P. "Searching for the Great Commission: Evangelical Book Publishing Since the 1970s." In *American Evangelicals and the Mass Media,* ed. Quentin J. Schultze. Grand Rapids, Mich.: Zondervan, 1990.

Fischer, John. "Consider This: Handle With Care." *Contemporary Christian Music* 18, 10 (Apr. 1996): 86.

———. "Consider This: Heard Again." *Contemporary Christian Music* 20, 3 (Sept. 1997): 78.

———. "Consider This: The Meaning of Words." *Contemporary Christian Music* 18, 1 (July 1995): 86.

———. "Field of Themes." *Contemporary Christian Music* 17, 10 (Apr. 1995): 86

———. "It's Over . . . Go Home." *Contemporary Christian Music* 12, 10 (Apr. 1990): 70.

———. "Relevancy Isn't Everything." *Contemporary Christian Music* 14, 12 (June 1992): 62.

———. "The Spirit of CCM Alive and Well." *Contemporary Christian Music* 10, 12 (June 1988): 49–50ff.

———. "View From a Window." *Contemporary Christian Music* 12, 3 (Sept. 1989): 38.

———. "Watering Down God." *Contemporary Christian Music* 17, 7 (Jan. 1995): 76.

Fishwick, Marshall. *Great Awakenings: Popular Religion and Popular Culture.* New York: Haworth, 1995.

———. "Pop Theology." *Journal of Popular Culture* 3, 2 (fall 1969): 268–73.

Fishwick, Marshall, and Ray B. Browne, eds. *The God Pumpers: Religion in the Electronic Age.* Bowling Green, Ohio: Popular Press, 1987.

Flake, Carol. *Redemptorama: Culture, Politics, and the New Evangelicalism.* New York: Penguin, 1984.

Foster, Arnold W., and Judith R. Blau, eds. *Art and Society: Readings in the Sociology of the Arts.* Albany, N.Y.: SUNY Press, 1989.

Friedenthal, Richard. *Luther: His Life and Times.* New York: Harcourt, 1967.

Friedlander, Paul. *Rock and Roll: A Social History.* Boulder, Col.: Westview, 1996.

Frith, Simon, ed. *Facing the Music: Essays on Pop, Rock, and Culture.* London: Mandarin, 1990.

Frith, Simon. "Art versus Technology: The Strange Case of Popular Music." *Media, Culture and Society* 8, 3 (1986): 263–80.

———. *Sound Effects: Youth, Leisure, and the Politics of Rock*. London: Constable and Company Ltd., 1983.

———. "The Industrialization of Pop Music." In *Popular Music and Communication* [2nd ed.], ed. James Lull. Newbury Park, Calif.: Sage, 1992.

———. "Towards an Aesthetic of Popular Music." In *Music and Society: The Politics of Compositions, Performance, and Reception*, ed. Richard D. Leppert and Susan McClary. Cambridge: Cambridge Univ. Press, 1987.

Gaines, Donna. *Teenage Wasteland: Suburbia's Deadend Kids*. New York: Pantheon, 1991.

Gaines, Jane M. *Contested Culture: The Image, the Voice, and the Law*. Chapel Hill: Univ. of North Carolina Press, 1991.

Gans, Herbert J. *Popular Culture and High Culture*. New York: Basic, 1974.

Garofalo, Reebee, ed. *Rockin' the Boat: Mass Music & Mass Movements*. Boston: South End, 1992.

Gascón, Ana. "The 77's Expose Their Faith." *Inside Music* 6, 4 (Nov.-Dec. 1992): 28–29.

Gill, Mary. "The Music of Amy Grant: A New Wrapping for a Timeless Message." *Journal of Communication and Religion* 13, 1 (Mar. 1990): 12–24.

Gillett, Charlie. *The Sound of the City: The Rise of Rock and Roll*. New York: Pantheon, 1983.

Gitlin, Todd. "Prime Time Ideology: The Hegemonic Process in Television Entertainment." In *Television: The Critical View*, ed. Horace Newcomb. New York: Oxford Univ. Press, 1987.

Godwin, Jeff. "Aging Hippies and a Deadend Dream." World Wide Web document available at http://www.av1611.org/crock/godwin1.html.

———. *Dancing With Demons*. Chino, Calif.: Chick, 1988.

———. *What's Wrong With Christian Rock?* Chino, Calif.: Chick, 1990.

Goldman, Stuart. "That Old Devil Music." *National Review*, Feb. 24, 1989, 28–31, 59.

Gomery, Douglas. "Media Economics: Terms of Analysis." *Critical Studies in Mass Communication* 6, 1 (Mar. 1989): 43–60.

Granger, Thom. "No More Funny Business." *Contemporary Christian Music* 18, 8 (Feb. 1996): 32–38.

———. "Steve Camp: The Grace That Covers Him." *Contemporary Christian Music* 9, 5 (Nov. 1986): 18–21.

———. "Steve Camp: The Grace That Covers Him." In *The Heart of the Matter: The Best of CCM Interviews, Volume 1*, ed. John W. Styll. Nashville: Star Song

Communications, 1991. (Originally published in *Contemporary Christian Music,* Nov. 1986.)

―――. "Taking Stryper Seriously." In *The Heart of the Matter: The Best of CCM Interviews, Volume 1,* ed. John W. Styll. Nashville: Star Song, 1991. (Originally published in *Contemporary Christian Music,* Aug. 1988.)

Greeley, Andrew. *God in Popular Culture.* Chicago: Thomas More, 1989.

Green, Melody and David Hazard. *No Compromise: The Life Story of Keith Green.* Chatsworth, Calif.: Sparrow, 1989.

Grossberg, Lawrence. "Another Boring Day in Paradise: Rock and Roll and the Empowerment of Everyday Life." In *Popular Music 4: Performers and Audiences,* ed. Richard Middleton and David Horn. Cambridge: Cambridge Univ. Press, 1984.

―――. "Is Anybody Listening? Does Anybody Care?: On the 'State of Rock.'" In *Microphone Friends: Youth Music and Youth Culture,* ed. Andrew Ross and Tricia Rose. New York: Routledge, 1994.

―――. "The Politics of Youth: Some Observations on Rock and Roll in American Culture." *Social Text* 8 (1983–84): 104–26.

"Growing Sales." *Sound and Spirit Magazine* 1, 16 (1997): 3.

Gubernick, Lisa and Robert LaFranco. "Rocking with God." *Forbes,* Jan. 2, 1995, 40–41.

Guiness, Os. *Fit Bodies, Fat Minds: Why Evangelicals Don't Think and What to Do About It.* Grand Rapids: Baker, 1994.

Gurevitch, Michael and Janet Woollacott, eds. *Mass Communication and Society.* London: Open Univ. Press, 1987.

Guterman, Jimmy. "Records: *The Turning.*" *Rolling Stone,* June 18, 1987, 84–85.

Hafer, Jack. "Music in Ministry: A Christian Looks at the Arts." *Contemporary Christian Music* 2, 1 (July 1980): 45, 49.

―――. "Music in Ministry: The Purpose of Music." *Contemporary Christian Music* 3, 2 (Aug. 1980): 28, 33.

Hale, Johnny. "The State of Christian Music: A Conversation with Michael Card and Scotty Smith." *Contemporary Christian Music* 17, 11 (May 1995): 36–40.

Hall, Stuart. "Culture, the Media and the 'Ideological Effect.'" In *Mass Communication and Society,* ed. Michael Gurevitch and Janet Woollacott. London: Open Univ. Press, 1987.

Harbinson, Colin. "The Arts: A Biblical Framework." In *Art Rageous,* by Colin Harbison, et al.. Chicago: Cornerstone Press, 1992.

Harbison, Colin, et al. *Art Rageous.* Chicago: Cornerstone Press, 1992.

Harris, Beth. "Feedback: Rock/Alt Elitists?" *Contemporary Christian Music* 19, 9 (Mar. 1997): 6.

Harris, Laura. "What About Bob?" *Contemporary Christian Music* 19, 5 (Nov. 1996): 55–56, 58.

Harron, Mary. "McRock: Pop as a Commodity." In *Facing the Music: Essays on Pop, Rock, and Culture,* ed. Simon Frith. London: Mandarin, 1990.

Hartman, Bob. *More Power To Ya.* Ohio: Standard Publishing, 1997.

Hatch, Nathan O. "Our Shackled Scholars." *Christianity Today,* Nov. 22, 1993, 12–13.

Havelock, Erik. *The Muse Learns to Write: Reflections on Orality and Literacy from Antiquity to the Present.* New Haven: Yale Univ. Press, 1986.

Haynes, Michael K. *The God Of Rock: A Christian Perspective of Rock Music.* Lindale, Tex.: Priority, 1982.

Heard, Mark. "A Musician's Diary." *CounterCulture* 2, 4 (July-Aug. 1994): 14–15.

Hebdige, Dick. *Subculture: The Meaning of Style.* London: Routledge, 1979.

Hefner, April and Mark A. Smeby. "Christian Music Finds Widespread Attention: Recent Coverage Proclaims Music 'Mediocre' with 'Hidden Agenda.'" *Contemporary Christian Music* 17, 11 (May 1995): 14–20.

Hefner, April. "Alternative Views." *Contemporary Christian Music* 19, 11 (May 1997): 63–64.

———. "Charlie Peacock's Cry of Coram Deo." *Contemporary Christian Music* 16, 8 (Feb. 1994): 42–43.

———. "Is Image Everything?" *Contemporary Christian Music* 18, 11 (May 1996): 90–99.

———. "Mike and the Mechanics." *Contemporary Christian Music* 18, 3 (Sept. 1995): 32–37.

———. "On the Beat: Everything Changes." *Contemporary Christian Music* 19, 9 (Mar. 1997): 12.

———. "On the Beat: Pop/Insp/Country." *Contemporary Christian Music* 18, 1 (July 1995): 13–14.

———. "Point of Grace: Road Life." *Contemporary Christian Music* 19, 3 (Sept. 1996): 35, 47–51.

Hendrickson, Lucas W. "And the Beat Goes On." *Contemporary Christian Music* 19, 10 (Apr. 1997): 20–22ff.

———. "In the News: Indie City." *Contemporary Christian Music* 19, 2 (Aug. 1996): 21–22.

Henry, Carl F. *The Uneasy Conscience of Modern Fundamentalism.* Grand Rapids, Mich.: Eerdmans, 1947.

Hershey, Brent. "New Life for Broken Records," *Notebored* 4, 1 (Jan.-Feb. 1988): 9.

Heyn, Chris. "Looking Below the Surface (An Interview with Gene Eugene)." *Notebored* 6, 1 (July-Aug. 1991): 16–17.

Hilburn, Robert and Chris Willman. "Rock of Ages: There's a New Spirituality in Pop Music." *Los Angeles Times,* Calendar, June 7, 1987, 50.

Hill, Trent. "The Enemy Within: Censorship in Rock Music in the 1950s." In *Present Tense: Rock & Roll and Culture,* ed. Anthony DeCurtis. Durham: Duke Univ. Press, 1992.

Hinchman, Gary J. "Christian Artists: Today's Prophets?" *Contemporary Christian Music* 10, 2 (Aug. 1987): 19.

Hirsch, Paul M. "Processing Fads and Fashions: An Organization-Set Analysis of Cultural Industry Systems." *American Journal of Sociology* 77 (1972): 639–59.

———. *The Structure of the Popular Music Industry.* Ann Arbor, Mich.: Institute for Social Research, 1969.

———. "U.S. Cultural Production: The Impact of Ownership." *Journal of Communication* 35, 3 (summer 1985): 110–21.

Hirschberg, Glen. "ENDD Notes—A Diary." *Seattle Weekly,* Jan. 8, 1992, 43–44.

Holm, Dallas, with Robert Paul Lamb. *This Is My Story.* Nashville: Impact, 1980.

Horkheimer, Max, and Theodor Adorno. "The Culture Industry: Enlightenment as Mass Deception." In *Dialectic of Enlightenment,* Max Horkheimer and Theodor Adorno. New York: Continuum, 1994. (Originally published in German as *Dialektik der Aufklärung* in 1944.)

Horton, Michael S. *Made in America: The Shaping of Modern American Evangelicalism.* Grand Rapids, Mich.: Baker, 1991.

———. *Where in the World is the Church?* Chicago: Moody, 1995.

Howard, Jay R., and John M. Streck. "The Splintered Art World of Contemporary Christian Music." *Popular Music* 15, 1 (1996): 37–53.

Huffman, James R. "*Jesus Christ Superstar*—Popular Art and Unpopular Criticism." *Journal of Popular Culture* 6, 2 (fall 1972): 259–69.

Hunter, James Davison. *American Evangelicalism: Conservative Religion and the Quandary of Modernity.* New Brunswick, N.J.: Rutgers Univ. Press, 1983.

Hybels, Bill. *The God You're Looking For.* Nashville: Thomas Nelson Publishers, 1997.

"In the Beginning . . ." *Cornerstone* 21, 99 (1992): 8.

"In the News: Artists, Pastors and Industry Leaders Discuss Issue of 'Fame and Ministry.'" *Contemporary Christian Music* 19, 1 (July 1996): 22, 24.

"Industry Growth Tempered by Heavy Returns, Slimmer Margins." *CCM Update* [electronic], Apr. 1, 1996. World Wide Web document available at http://www.ccmcom.com/ccmupdate/96_04_01/news.html#story1.

Innis, Harold. *The Bias of Communication.* Toronto: Univ. of Toronto Press, 1951.

Jorstad, Erling. *Popular Religion in America: The Evangelical Voice.* Westport, CN: Greenwood, 1993.

Joseph, Mark, Patrick Cavanaugh and Kerry Livgren. "Can 'Christian' Music Exist?" *Contemporary Christian Music* 18, 2 (July 1995): 55–57.

Kamin, Jonathan. "Parallels in the Social Reactions to Jazz and Rock." In *Art and Society: Readings in the Sociology of the Arts,* ed. Arnold W. Foster and Judith R. Blau. Albany, N.Y.: SUNY Press, 1989.

Kauffman, Michael J. "The Choir: A Step Beyond." *Harvest Rock Syndicate* 4, 3 (1989): 10.

Key, Dana, with Steve Rabey. *Don't Stop the Music.* Grand Rapids, Mich.: Zondervan, 1989.

Kilby, Clyde S. *Christianity and Aesthetics.* Chicago: InterVarsity, 1961.

Kipling, Rudyard. "The Conundrum of the Workshops." In *Departmental Ditties and Ballads and Barrack Room Ballads,* Rudyard Kipling. Garden City, N.Y.: Doubleday, Page & Company, 1926.

Knight, Stephen Andrew. "A Prayer Before Dying: The Making and Breaking of Prayer Chain." *Kamikaze* 4, 34 (1995): 12–13.

———. "Dancing on Silver Lakes: A Pseudo-conversation with the Scaterd Few." *Kamikaze* 3, 31 (1994): 18–20.

———. "Choosing to Believe the Unbelievable Truth: A Real Conversation with Bill Malonnee from the Vigilantes of Love." *Kamikaze* 3, 31 (1994), 14–16.

———. "The 77's Michael Roe: Just For Us, It's Safe as Milk." *Kamikaze* 4, 32 (1994): 49–47, 22 (pages numbered backward).

———. "The Changing Face of CCM Through the Eyes of John Fischer." *Kamikaze* 4, 33 (1995): 12–13.

Kruse, Holly. "Subcultural Identity in Alternative Music Culture." *Popular Music* 12, 1 (Jan. 1993): 33–41.

Larson, Bob. *Hippies, Hindus and Rock & Roll.* McCook, Neb.: Larson, 1969.

———. *Rock and Roll: The Devil's Diversion.* McCook, Neb.: Larson, 1967.

———. *Rock and the Church.* Carol Stream, Ill.: Creation House, 1971.

———. *The Day the Music Died.* Carol Stream, Ill.: Creation House, 1972.

LaRue, John C. Jr., "The Contemporizing of Worship Music." *Your Church* 43, 3 (1997): 72.

Lefieste, Terry. "Re: copying/recording" [posting to rec.music.christian]. Oct. 22, 1996.

Leppert, Richard, and George Lipsitz. "'Everybody's Lonesome for Somebody': Age, the Body and Experience in the Music of Hank Williams." *Popular Music* 9, 3 (1990): 259–74.

Leppert, Richard D., and Susan McClary, eds. *Music and Society: The Politics of Compositions, Performance, and Reception.* Cambridge: Cambridge Univ. Press, 1987.

Liesch, Barry. *The New Worship: Straight Talk on Music and the Church.* Grand Rapids, Mich.: Baker, 1996.

Lindsey, Hal. *The Late Great Planet Earth.* New York: Bantam, 1973.

Lipsitz, George. "We Know What Time It Is: Race, Class and Youth Culture in the Nineties." In *Microphone Friends: Youth Music and Youth Culture,* ed. Andrew Ross and Tricia Rose. New York: Routledge, 1994.

Llewellyn, Ric. "Christian Rock?" World Wide Web document available at http://www.av1611.org/crock/crock1.html.

Long, James. "Bryan Duncan: Slowly Revived." *Contemporary Christian Music* 17, 11 (May 1995): 96–98.

———. "Can't Buy Me Ministry." *Christianity Today,* May 20, 1996, 20–28.

———. "Charlie Peacock: Everything That's On His Mind." *Contemporary Christian Music* 18, 9 (Mar. 1996): 30–31.

———. "Conversations: Darrell A. Harris: Taking Care of Business." *Contemporary Christian Music* 18, 12 (June 1996): 28–29.

———. "Dana Key: 'Elvis Has Left the Building.'" *Contemporary Christian Music* 18, 8 (Feb. 1996): 30–31.

———. "Petra's Bob Hartman: No Doubt About It." *Contemporary Christian Music* 18, 11 (May 1996): 38–39.

———. "We Have Created a Monster." *Christianity Today,* May 20, 1996, 26–27.

———. "Who's the Leader of This Band?: Michael Card and Steve Taylor Wonder What the Industry Won't Do For Money." *Christianity Today,* May 20, 1996, 22–25.

Lont, Cynthia. "Persistence of Subcultural Organizations: An Analysis Surrounding the Process of Subcultural Change." *Communication Quarterly* 38, 1 (Winter 1990): 1–12.

———. "Redwood Records: Principles and Profit in Women's Music." In *Women Communicating: Studies of Women's Talk,* ed. Barbara Bate and Anita Taylor. Norwood, N.J.: Ablex, 1988.

———. "Women's Music: No Longer a Small Private Party." In *Rockin' the Boat: Mass Music & Mass Movements,* ed. Reebee Garofalo. Boston: South End, 1992.

Lovelace, Richard F. *Dynamics of Spiritual Life: An Evangelical Theology of Renewal.* Downers Grove, Ill.: InterVarsity, 1979.

Lull, James, ed. *Popular Music and Communication.* Newbury Park, Calif.: Sage, 1987.

―――. *Popular Music and Communication* [2nd ed.]. Newbury Park, Calif.: Sage, 1992.

Lull, James. "Popular Music and Communication: An Introduction." In *Popular Music and Communication,* ed. James Lull. Newbury Park, Calif.: Sage, 1987.

Lyon, Robert. Interview with author (Howard). July 15, 1993.

MacIntosh, Dan. "Everybody Loves Jon Gibson." *Syndicate* 44 (1995): 6.

―――. "Mark Heard: Music to Make Dry Bones Dance." *Harvest Rock Syndicate* 5, 3 (1990): 11.

―――. "Michael Roe: Roe Knows." *Syndicate* 43 (1995): 20, 25, 29.

Manilow, Barry. *Sweet Life: Adventures on the Way to Paradise.* New York: McGraw-Hill, 1987.

Marion, Sheree. "Critique: *Sacrifice*—4•4•1." *Harvest Rock Syndicate* 3, 3 (1988): 17.

―――. "Vector: Challenging Success In All It's [*sic*] Hollow Ways." *Harvest Rock Syndicate* 5, 1 (1990): 20.

Marrs, Texe. "The Dragon's Hot Breath: Unmasking the Awful Truth About 'Christian' Rock Music." World Wide Web document available at http://www.av1611.org/crock/crocmars.html.

Marsden, George M. *Fundamentalism and American Culture: The Shaping of Twentieth-Century Fundamentalism: 1870–1925.* Oxford: Oxford Univ. Press, 1980.

―――. *Reforming Fundamentalism.* Grand Rapids, Mich.: Eerdmans, 1987.

―――. *Understanding Fundamentalism and Evangelicalism.* Grand Rapids, Mich.: Eerdmans, 1991.

Martin, Linda and Kerry Segrave. *Anti-Rock: The Opposition to Rock 'n' Roll.* Hamden, Connecticut: Archon Books, 1988.

Marvin, Sam. "Album Reviews: *Horrendous Disc*—Daniel Amos." *Encore,* June 1981, 5.

Marx, Karl. "The Eighteenth Brumaire of Louis Bonaparte." In *The Marx-Engels Reader* [2nd. ed.], ed. Robert C. Tucker. New York: W.W. Norton & Company, 1978.

Matthews, Stephen. "Letters" [letter to the editor]. *Syndicate* 8, 4 (1993): 3–4.

"MCA Gears Down Songbird Division." *Contemporary Christian Music* 5, 5 (Nov. 1982): 58.

McClary, Susan. "Same As It Ever Was: Youth Culture and Music." In *Micro-*

phone Friends: Youth Music and Youth Culture, ed. Andrew Ross and Tricia Rose. New York: Routledge, 1994.

McCormick, Moira. "The A&M/Word Impact: Next Six Months Are 'Critical' for Gospel's Mainstream Voyage." Billboard, Oct. 19, 1985, G-33.

McDannell, Colleen. *Material Christianity.* New Haven, CN: Yale Univ. Press, 1995.

McLuhan, Marshall. *The Gutenberg Galaxy: The Making of Typographic Man.* Toronto: Univ. of Toronto Press, 1962.

Mellers, Wilfred. *A Darker Shade of Pale: A Backdrop to Bob Dylan.* New York: Oxford Univ. Press, 1985.

Menconi, Al with Dave Hart. *Today's Music: A Window to Your Child's Soul.* Elgin, Ill.: Cook, 1990.

Menconi, Al. "What's Wrong with Christian Music?" *Contemporary Christian Music* 9, 12 (June 1987): 19–20.

Metzler, George. "Margaret Becker: Praising Her Own Way." *Notebored* 2, 5 (Mar.-Apr. 1989): 8–9.

———. "Steve Taylor: Ever Unpredictable." *Notebored* 1, 4 (Jan.-Feb. 1987): 10–11.

Middleton, Richard and David Horn, eds. *Popular Music 4: Performers and Audience.* Cambridge: Cambridge Univ. Press, 1984.

Mifflin, Margot. "Records: *77's.*" *Rolling Stone,* May 21, 1987, 104.

Millard, Bob. *Amy Grant: A Biography.* New York: Doubleday, 1986.

Miller, Steve. *The Contemporary Christian Music Debate: Worldly Compromise or Agent of Change.* Wheaton, Ill.: Tyndale House Publishers, Inc., 1993.

Mineo, Robert. "Jonathan Finds New Freedom." *Contemporary Christian Music* 17, 9 (Mar. 1995): 28.

Molina, Jay. "Randy Matthew's *[sic]* Son of Dust . . . Still in the Father's Hands." *Harvest Rock Syndicate* 6, 3 (1991): 11.

Moon, Tom. "What it Costs to Make an Album." *Musician,* Dec. 1990, 90–94.

Moore, R. Lawrence. *Selling God: American Religion in the Marketplace of Culture.* New York: Oxford Univ. Press, 1994.

Moore, Thomas. *The Care of The Soul.* New York: HarperCollins, 1992.

Mootown Records advertisement. *Visions of Gray,* Apr. 1994, 16.

Morrison, Shawn. "Down to the Nitty Gritty." *Contemporary Christian Music* 19, 11 (May 1997): 80–81

Muggeridge, Malcom. *Christ and the Media.* Grand Rapids, Mich.: Eerdmans, 1977.

"Music Recommendation Chart." World Wide Web document available at http://www.biblenet.net/media/musicrec.html.

Myers, Kenneth A. *All God's Children and Blue Suede Shoes: Christians and Popular Culture*. Wheaton, Ill.: Crossway, 1989.

Myra, Harold and Dean Merrill. *Rock, Bach and Superschlock*. New York: Holman, 1972.

Nappa, Mike. "Destination Known." *Contemporary Christian Music* 19, 8 (Feb. 1997): 34–36.

Nee, Watchman [Nee To-sheng]. *Love Not the World*. Wheaton, Ill.: Tyndale House, 1968.

Newcomb, Brian Quincy. "Adam Again Digs Deep." *Syndicate* 7, 4 (1992): 10.

————. "Amy Grant: The Secret of Life." *Harvest Rock Syndicate* 6, 4 (1991): 12–13, 16.

————. "Charlie Peacock: One Hep Cat." *Harvest Rock Syndicate* 5, 1 (1990): 9.

————. "Jacob's Trouble: Let the Truth Run Wilder." *Syndicate* 8, 4 (1993): 10–12.

————. "Joey Taylor: No Longer Undercover." *Contemporary Christian Music* 10, 2 (Aug. 1987): 20.

————. "Larry Norman: The Long Journey Home." *Contemporary Christian Music* 11, 12 (June 1989): 22–25.

————. "Letters to the Editor" [editor's response]. *Harvest Rock Syndicate* 6, 4 (1991): 3.

————. "Margaret Becker: A Woman with Chalk Dust on her Hands." *Harvest Rock Syndicate* 6, 2 (1991): 10–11.

————. "Mercy Mercy." *Harvest Rock Syndicate* 3, 3 (1988): 13–14.

————. "Petra's Battle." In *The Heart of the Matter: The Best of CCM Interviews*, Volume 1, ed. John W. Styll. Nashville: Star Song, 1991. (Originally published in *Contemporary Christian Music*, Oct. 1987.)

————. "Petra: Back to the Rock." *Contemporary Christian Music* 9, 4 (Oct. 1986): 16–19, 37.

————. "Petra: Walking the Dinosaur." *Syndicate* 9, 1 (1994): 20–21.

————. "Q Thoughts." *Syndicate* 8, 1 (1993): 4.

————. "Q Thoughts." *Syndicate* 8, 2 (1992): 4.

————. "Staying Up Late." *Syndicate* 8, 2 (1993): 15.

————. "Steve Taylor: Living Life in the Open." *Contemporary Christian Music* 16, 8 (Feb. 1994): 38–41.

————. "Terry S. Taylor: The *HRS* Interview, Part I." *Harvest Rock Syndicate* 5, 4 (1990): 9–10.

————. "Terry S. Taylor: The *HRS* Interview, Part II." *Harvest Rock Syndicate* 6, 1 (1991): 14, 16.

————. "Terry S. Taylor: The *HRS* Interview, Part III." *Harvest Rock Syndicate* 6, 3 (1991): 12, 18.

————. "The 77's: The Trying Life and Times of Mike Roe," *Syndicate* 7, 5 (1992): 9.

Newcomb, Horace, ed. *Television: The Critical View.* New York: Oxford Univ. Press, 1987.

Niebuhr, H. Richard. *Christ and Culture.* New York: Harper Torchbooks, 1951.

Noebel, David A. "Christian Rock: Paganism in the Church." World Wide Web document available at http://www.av1611.org/crock/crocknob.html.

————. *The Marxist Minstrels: A Handbook on Communist Subversion of Music.* Tulsa, OK: American Christian College Press, 1974.

Noll, Mark A. *The Scandal of the Evangelical Mind.* Grand Rapids, Mich.: William B. Eerdmans Publishing Co., 1994.

Nouwen, Henri J. M. *In the Name of Jesus: Reflections on Christian Leadership.* New York: Crossroad, 1989.

————. *The Wounded Healer: Ministry in Contemporary Society.* New York: Doubleday, 1990.

O'Donnell, Paul with Amy Eskind. "God and the Music Biz." *Newsweek,* 30 May, 1994, 62–63.

Ojarovsky, Ted. "Ya Gotta Do Something!" *Contemporary Christian Magazine* 7, 12 (June 1985): 20–26ff.

O'Neill, Dan. *Troubadour for the Lord: The Story of John Michael Talbot.* New York: Crossroad, 1983.

"On the Beat: 1996's Top-Selling Albums." *Contemporary Christian Music* 19, 8 (Feb. 1997): 14.

Ong, Walter. *Orality & Literacy.* London: Routledge, 1982.

Orteza, Arsenio. "John Austin: Young, Yes—Embarrassing, No." *Syndicate* 7, 5 (1992): 14.

Otto, Rudolf. *The Idea of the Holy* [trans. J. W. Harvey]. London: Oxford Univ. Press, 1923.

Owen, Bruce. *Economics and the Freedom of Expression: Media Structures and the First Amendment.* Cambridge: Ballinger Publishing Company, 1975.

Ozard, Dwight. "Interview: At the Foot of the Cross: Contemporary Worship with a Sense of History." *Prism* 2, 4 (Mar.-Apr. 1995): 24–27.

————. "Interviews: Mike Roe of The Seventy Sevens." *True Tunes News* 6, 10 (Spring 1994): 18–21,31.

————. "Music Notes." *Prism* 4, 3 (Mar.-Apr. 1997): 33.

Packer, J.I. *Knowing God.* Downers Grove, Ill.: InterVarsity Press, 1973.

Palmer, Dave. "The Choir." *Syndicate* 9, 3 (1994): 22–24.

Parker, Mike. "DC Talk." Release, Dec. 1997–Jan. 1998, 14–15.

Parks, Robert. "Human Migration and the Marginal Man." *American Journal of Sociology* 33 (1928): 888–896.

Payton, Leonard. "Is It a Prelude or a Quaalude?" *Modern Reformation,* Jan.-Feb. 1993, 10–16.

Peacock, Charlie. "A Few Words About the Art House." In *West Coast Diaries: Volumes 1, 2, 3* [liner notes]. Sparrow, 1990.

Peck, John. "An Englishman Comments on the Revolution: British Thinker on Rock in the Church." *Cornerstone* 14, 77 (1985): 40–41, 43.

Peepo, Meepo. "Aunt Betty's Mike Knott—LSU." *Raw Tuna* 9 (summer 1996): 11, 13–14.

Perry, Steve. "Ain't No Mountain High Enough: The Politics of Crossover." In *Facing the Music: Essays on Pop, Rock, and Culture,* ed. Simon Frith. London: Mandarin, 1990.

Peters, Dan and Steve Peters with Cher Merrill. *Rock's Hidden Persuader: The Truth About Backmasking.* Minneapolis: Bethany, 1985.

———. *Why Knock Rock?* Minneapolis: Bethany, 1984.

Phillips, James. "Rebecca St. James Concert Review." World Wide Web document available at http://rsjames.com/concert_hall/10962rev.html.

Phillips, Kevin. "Busting the Media Trusts." *Harper's Magazine,* July 1977, 23–34.

Phillips, Sam. *Fresh Air* interview. Broadcast Mar. 16, 1994.

Picard, Robert. *Media Economics.* Beverly Hills, Calif.: Sage, 1990.

Pirsig, Robert M. *Zen and the Art of Motorcycle Maintenance: An Inquiry into Values.* New York: Bantam Books, 1974.

Platt, Karen Marie. "B.J. Thomas' View from the Stage." *Contemporary Christian Music* 4, 10 (Mar. 1982): 10–13.

———. "The Original Christian Street Rocker: Larry Norman." *Contemporary Christian Music* 3, 9 (Mar. 1981): 8–11, 25.

———. "Whatever Happened to *Horrendous Disc?*" *Contemporary Christian Music* 3, 9 (Mar. 1981): 32–33, 35.

Point of Grace and David Seay. *Life, Love & Other Mysteries.* New York: Pocket Books, 1996.

"Point of Grace Makes History: 10 Number Ones In a Row." *CCM Update* [electronic], Jan. 29, 1996. World Wide Web document available at http://www.ccmcom.com/ccmupdate/96_01_29/012996pog.html.

Porter, Tim. "Steve Hindalong: Paint on Canvas." *Art Clippings* 2, 2 (Aug. 1993): 19–23.

Pratt, Dirk. "Aunt Bettys, *Aunt Bettys*" [staff note]. *True Tunes News* 8, 2 (1996): 9.

Price, Deborah Evans. "Kim Hill: Walking a Country Road." *Contemporary Christian Music* 18, 1 (July 1995): 50–51.

———. "Point of Grace: Tired and True." *Contemporary Christian Music* 17, 9 (Mar. 1995): 30–35.

Pritchard, Kathy. "Behind the Scenes: Broken Records." *CounterCulture*, May-June 1994, 10.

———. "From the Editors." *CounterCulture* 2, 4 (July-Aug. 1994): 2.

Quebedeaux, Richard. *The Worldly Evangelicals.* San Francisco: Harper & Row, 1978.

Quinn, Walt. "Michael Blanton and Dan Harrell: Managing Amy Grant." *Contemporary Christian Music* 11, 3 (Sept. 1988): 34–37.

Rabey, Steve, ed. *Rock the Planet.* Grand Rapids, Mich.: Zondervan, 1989.

Rabey, Steve. "Rock Steady: Petra Embraces the Future While Honoring Its Past." *Contemporary Christian Music* 18, 3 (Sept. 1995): 40–42.

Radano, Ronald M. *New Musical Figurations: Anthony Braxton's Cultural Critique.* Chicago: The Univ. of Chicago Press, 1993.

Rake, Jamie Lee. "Jimmy A." *Syndicate* 9, 5 (1994): 17–18.

———. "Kevin Smith." *Syndicate* 9, 5 (1994): 16–17.

Randolph, Karly. "Bevill-May-Care." *Contemporary Christian Music* 18, 10 (Apr. 1996): 70.

———. "In Concert: Steven Curtis Chapman/Audio Adrenaline/Carolyn Arends." *Contemporary Christian Music.* 19, 8 (Feb. 1997): 58.

Recording Industry Association of America (RIAA). "Recording Industry Releases 1996 Consumer Profile." World Wide Web document available at http://www.riaa.com/market/releases/demosu96.htm.

Ridley, Jim. "Christianity Is Serious Fun." *Inside Music* 4, 6 (Nov.-Dec. 1992): 20–23.

Rivers, Jon [producer]. *Shake: Christian Artists Face the Music.* Syndicated radio program aired Feb. 6, 1988.

Rocker, Randy. "Adam Again." *Syndicate* 47 (1995): 6.

Roe, Mike and Brent Hershey. "The 77's—An Authorized Time Line, Part 1." *Notebored* 4, 1 (July-Aug. 1990): 7.

———. "The 77's—An Authorized Time Line, Part 2." *Notebored* 4, 2 (Sept.-Oct. 1990): 6.

Romanowski, William D. "2 Hot 2 Handle?" *Contemporary Christian Music* 8,1 (July 1985): 14–18.

———. "*Contemporary Christian Music*: The Business of Music Ministry." In *American Evangelicals and the Mass Media,* ed. Quentin J. Schultze. Grand Rapids: Zondervan Publishing House, 1990.

———. "Move Over Madonna: The Crossover Career of Gospel Artist Amy Grant." *Popular Music and Society* 17, 2 (summer 1993): 47–68.

———. *Rock 'n' Religion: A Socio-Cultural Analysis of the Contemporary Christian Music Industry,* Ph.D. dissertation, Bowling Green State University, 1990.

———. "Roll Over Beethoven, Tell Martin Luther the News: American Evangelicals and Rock Music." *Journal of American Culture* 15, 3 (1992): 79–88.

Rookmaaker, Hans. *Modern Art and the Death of a Culture.* London: Inter-Varsity, 1970.

———. *The Creative Gift: Essays on Art and the Christian Life.* Westchester, Ill.: Cornerstone, 1981.

Rosenberg, Bernard and David Manning White, eds. *Mass Culture: The Popular Arts in America.* New York: The Free Press, 1957.

Ross, Andrew and Tricia Rose, eds. *Microphone Friends: Youth Music and Youth Culture.* New York: Routledge, 1994.

Ross, Andrew. "Introduction." In *Microphone Friends: Youth Music and Youth Culture,* ed. Andrew Ross and Tricia Rose. New York: Routledge, 1994.

Rothenbuhler, Eric W. and John M. Streck. "The Structure and Performance of the Recorded Music Industry." In *Media Economics: Theory and Practice* [2nd. Ed], ed. Alison Alexander, James Owers and Rod Carveth. Hillsdale, N.J.: Lawrence Erlbaum Associates, Publishers, 1998.

Routley, Erik. *Words, Music, and the Church.* Nashville: Abingdon, 1968.

Rumburg, Gregory. "Cindy Morgan: Real Life Revisited." *Contemporary Christian Music* 17, 11 (May 1995): 60–62.

———. "In the News: Charlie Peacock Starts Multimedia Company." *Contemporary Christian Music* 18, 9 (Mar. 1996): 22.

———. "Unguarded: Is Amy Grant the Apple of Christian Music's Eye or the Outcast on Her Knees?" *Contemporary Christian Music* 20, 3 (Sept. 1997): 24–32.

Santino, Jack. "The Spirit of American Music: 'Nobody Ever Told Me it Was the Blues.'" *Journal of American Culture* 5, 4 (1982): 20–26.

Sayers, Dorothy. *Christian Letters to a Post-Christian World: A Selection of Essays.* Grand Rapids, Mich.: Eerdmanns, 1969.

Schaeffer, Edith. "Edith Schaeffer: Backstage Pass." *Cornerstone* 14, 75 (1985): 35, 37.

———. *Hidden Art.* Wheaton, Ill.: Tyndale, 1971.

———. *The Art of Life.* Westchester, Ill.: Crossway, 1987.

Schaeffer, Francis A. *Art and the Bible: Two Essays.* Downers Grove, Ill.: InterVarsity, 1973.

Schaeffer, Franky. *Addicted to Mediocrity.* Wheaton, Ill.: Crossway, 1985.

———. *Sham Pearls for Real Swine.* Brentwood, TN: Wolgemuth & Hyatt, Publishers, Inc., 1990.

Schultze, Quentin J., ed. *American Evangelicals and the Mass Media.* Grand Rapids, Mich.: Zondervan, 1990.

Schultze, Quentin J. "Keeping the Faith: American Evangelicals and the Media." In *American Evangelicals and the Mass Media,* ed. Quentin J. Schultze. Grand Rapids, Mich.: Zondervan, 1990.

Scott, Steve. "Scratching the Surface." In *Art Rageous,* Colin Harbinson, et al. Chicago: Cornerstone Press, 1992.

Seay, David. "Backbeat: Christian Music: The Record Industry's Saving Grace?" *High Fidelity* 32, 2 (Feb. 1982): 72–73, 81.

Seay, Davin and Mary Neely. *Stairway to Heaven: The Spiritual Roots of Rock 'n' Roll.* New York: Ballantine Books, 1986.

Seay, Davin. "Daniel Amos: Christian Music's Angry Young Men?" *Contemporary Christian Music* 2, 7 (Jan. 1980): 6–7.

Selby, Marykay. "Flower Power: Audio Adrenaline Opens Up (and Grows Up) on the New *Bloom.*" *Contemporary Christian Music* 18, 10 (Apr. 1996): 30–35.

———. "On the Beat: Too Sexy for Your Church?" *Contemporary Christian Music* 20, 2 (Aug. 1997): 10–11.

———. "Take the Long Way Home." *Contemporary Christian Music.* 19, 9 (Mar. 1997): 30–33.

Seward, Matt and Duncan Dodds. "Christian Music Radio: Out of the Closet and Into the Spotlight." *Religious Broadcasting* 25, 2 (Feburary 1993): 70–77

Shaw, William. "Jesus Rocks." *Details,* Oct. 1996, 62–78ff.

Sheinfeld, Lois P. "Ratings: The Big Chill." *Film Comment* 22 (June 1986): 9–14.

Shepherd, John. "Music, Culture, and Interdisciplinarity: Reflections on Relationships." *Popular Music* 13, 2 (1994): 127–141.

Simels, Steve. "Best of the Month: Grit and Glitz in New Songs by Tonio K." *Stereo Review,* Sept. 1986, 100.

Simmel, Georg. "The Stranger." In *The Sociology of Georg Simmel,* ed. Kurt Wolff. New York: The Free Press, 1950.

Simpson, Charles. "Shadows of Anxiety: Popular Culture in Modern Society." In *Art and Society: Readings in the Sociology of the Arts,* ed. Arnold W. Foster and Judith R. Blau. Albany, N.Y.: SUNY Press, 1989.

Smeby, Mark A. "Keeping Promises." *Contemporary Christian Music* 18, 1 (July 1995): 56–57.

Smiles, Dutch. "Spotlight: Poor Old Lu." *Syndicate* 9, 2 (July 1994): 8.

Smith, Kevin. *At the Foot of Heaven*. Nashville: Star Song, 1994.

Smith, Michael W. and Fritz Ridenour. *Old Enough to Know*. Waco, Tex.: Word, 1987.

Smith, Steve. "Guest Editorial: What's Wrong With Christian Music? Part 2." *Encore*, Aug. 1981, 12.

Smith-Newcomb, Quincy. "An Interview with Greg Volz and Bob Hartman of Petra." *Progressive Pacer*, Nov. 1982, 4–7.

St. James, Rebecca and Sam Green. "St. James Place" [official web page]. World Wide Web document available at http://www.rsjames.com.

St. James, Rebecca. *40 Days with God: A Devotional Journey*. Ohio: Standard Publishing, 1996.

———. *You're the Voice: Forty More Days with God—A Contemporary Devotional*. Nashville: Thomas Nelson Publishers, 1997.

Stafford, Tim. "Has Christian Rock Lost Its Soul?" *Christianity Today*, Nov. 22, 1993, 14–19.

———. *Knowing the Face of God*. Colorado Springs: NavPress, 1996.

Stanislaw, Richard. "Should We Rock the Boat Over Rock Music?" *Eternity*, Mar. 1977, 25.

"Steve Taylor." *Campus Life Christian Music Annual*, 1985, M-24.

"Steve Taylor." *CounterCulture*, Mar.-Apr. 1994, 18–20.

Stillion, Martin and Chris Estey. "Tonio K. Interview." *CounterCulture*, Jan.-Feb. 1993, 3–9.

Styll, John W. and Paul Baker. "Pursuit of a Dream: A History of Contemporary Christian Music." *Contemporary Christian Music* 10, 12 (June 1988): 12–26.

Styll, John W., ed. *The Heart of the Matter: The Best of CCM Interviews, Volume 1*. Nashville: Star Song, 1991.

Styll, John W. "Billboard Conference Reveals Gap Between Gospel and Secular." *Contemporary Christian Music* 4, 8 (Jan. 1982): 38.

———. "Carman: The *CCM* Interview." In *The Heart of the Matter: The Best of CCM Interviews, Volume 1*, ed. John W. Styll. Nashville: Star Song, 1991. (Originally published in *Contemporary Christian Music*, Mar. 1988.)

———. "CBA Attendance Down Slightly as Industry Tightens Belt." *Contemporary Christian Music* 5, 3 (Sept. 1982): 44.

———. "Celebrating Ten Years: Bill Gaither." *Contemporary Christian Music* 10, 12 (June 1988): 38, 40.

———. "Cool Crowds Fuel Hot Tempers." *Contemporary Christian Music* 5, 4 (Oct. 1982): 37–38.

———. "Cross Purposes?" *Contemporary Christian Music* 19, 11 (May 1997): 45–46, 48.

———. "Editor's Comment: Amy Grant's Sanctified Entertainment." *Contemporary Christian Music* 9, 1&2 (July-Aug. 1986): 4.

———. "Enlarging the Vision of Contemporary Christian Music." *Contemporary Christian Music* 14, 10 (Apr. 1992): 49–52.

———. "Facing the Music: Christian Labels Downsize." *Contemporary Christian Music* 19, 6 (Dec. 1996): 20, 22.

———. "Feedback: Larry Norman." *Contemporary Christian Music* 12, 2 (Aug. 1989): 4.

———. "Intro." *Contemporary Christian Music* 13, 12 (June 1991): 4.

———. "Intro." *Contemporary Christian Music* 14, 3 (Sept. 1991): 4.

———. "Intro: To Tape or Not to Tape." *Contemporary Christian Music* 10, 9 (Mar. 1988): 4.

———. "'Jesus Junk' Revisited." *Contemporary Christian Music* 11, 2 (Aug. 1988): 4.

———. "Jesus Junkie?" *Contemporary Christian Music* 14, 5 (Nov. 1991): 54.

———. "Jimmy Swaggart: Christian Rock Wars." In *The Heart of the Matter: The Best of CCM Interviews, Volume 1,* ed. John W. Styll. Nashville: Star Song, 1991. (Originally published in *Contemporary Christian Music,* June 1985.)

———. "Keith Green: A Non-Profit Prophet?" In *The Heart of the Matter: The Best of CCM Interviews, Volume 1,* ed. John W. Styll. Nashville: Star Song, 1991. (Originally published in *Contemporary Christian Music,* Mar. 1980.)

———. "Mylon LeFevre: The Solid Rocker." In *The Heart of the Matter: The Best of CCM Interviews, Volume 1,* ed. John W. Styll. Nashville: Star Song, 1991. (Originally published in *Contemporary Christian Music,* Mar. 1986.)

———. "Wanted: Explicit Lyrics." *Contemporary Christian Music* 10, 3 (Sept. 1987): 4.

———. "What Makes Music Christian?" *Contemporary Christian Music* 9, 10 (Apr. 1987): 35–36.

———. "Why Are We Doing This, Anyway? That's Contemporary Christian Show Business!" *Wittenburg Door,* Oct.-Nov. 1984, 2, 4.

"Survey Reports Gospel as Fastest Growing Genre." *CCM Update* [electronic], Mar. 25, 1996. World Wide Web document available at http://www.ccmcom.com/ccmupdate/96_03_25/032596survey.html.

Swaggart, Jimmy. *Religious Rock'n'Roll: A Wolf in Sheep's Clothing.* Baton Rouge, La.: Swaggart, 1987.

Swindoll, Charles R. *Intimacy with the Almighty.* Dallas: Word, 1996.

"*Syndicate:* Death of a Magazine," *CounterCulture* 2, 1 (Jan.-Feb. 1994): 6–8.

Tapia, Andreas. "Evangelicals Stage Their Own Lollapaloozas to Save Teen Souls." *Icon* (Iowa City, Iowa), July 25, 1996, 10.

Tatum, Renee. "Celebrating Ten Years: André Crouch." *Contemporary Christian Music* 10, 12 (June 1988): 43, 71–73.

Taylor, Terry Scott. "Further Up and Further In." World Wide Web document available at http://members.aol.com/StuntRec/Further.html (also published in *Release*, 1993).

Thomas, B.J. "The Power of Positive Pop." *The Best of CCM, 1978–80* (1981): 43, 60.

Thompson, John J. "Grand Architecture and the World of Positive Pop." *True Tunes News* 6, 14 (1994): 12–15.

Thunder, Scott. "What's New: *Supertones Strike Back*—The Supertones." *Contemporary Christian Music* 20, 3 (Sept. 1997): 52.

Towns, Elmer. *Ten of Today's Most Innovative Churches.* Ventura, Calif.: Regal Books, 1990.

Trott, Jon. "Like a Wolf among Chickens?" *Cornerstone* 15, 82 (1987): 38–40, 44.

Trouten, Doug. "Paris in June." *Contemporary Christian Music* 18, 12 (June 1996): 30–34.

Tucker, Robert C, ed. *The Marx-Engels Reader* [2nd. ed.]. New York: W.W. Norton & Company, 1978.

Urbanski, Dave. "Tracing The Call." *Contemporary Christian Music* 20, 3 (Sept. 1997): 8–9.

———. "What's New: *Plumb*—Plumb." *Contemporary Christian Music* 19, 12 (June 1997): 53.

Van Matre, Lynn. "Move Over, Fanny Crosby . . . Here Comes Donna Summer." *HIS* 42, 5 (Feb. 1982): 16–18.

Vanderpoel, David. "Cover Story: Michael Roe." *VOG* [*Visions of Gray*], Mar. 1995, np. (The article was also posted to the Usenet newsgroup rec.music.christian on Feb. 25, 1995).

———. "Inner-View: Randy Stonehill." *Visions of Gray* 4, 2 (Oct. 1994): 8–9, 12.

———. "Strong Hand of Love: Prophet, Artist, Friend: Musicians Remember John Mark Heard III." *Visions of Gray,* Apr. 1994, 10–11, 16–19.

Vigilantes of Love listserv archive. World Wide Web document(s) available at http://www.coaster.com/VOL/vol-list/Digests.

"Waltz Is of Hell." *The Morning Oregonian,* May 13, 1907, 9.

Warren, Lindy. "Bob Carlisle Album Soars to No. 2 in Nation." *CCM Update* [electronic], May 26, 1997. World Wide Web document available at http://www.ccmcom.com/ccmupdate/97_05_26/news.html#story1.

———. "What Does God Think of the CCM Industry?" *Contemporary Christian Music* 19, 11 (May 1977): 16.

Watkins, Terry. "Christian Rock: Blessing or Blasphemy?" World Wide Web document available at http://www.av1611.org/crock.html.

———. "It's Only Rock and Roll, But It Kills!" World Wide Web document available at http://www.av1611.org/rockm.html.

———. "Rock Music: The Devil's Advocate." World Wide Web document available at http://www.av1611.org/rock.html.

Weber, Alexa N. "On the Other Side—Michael W. Smith" [unofficial web page]. World Wide Web document available at http://www.nauticom.net/www/catspaw/mwshome2.htm.

Weber, Max. *The Protestant Ethic and the Spirit of Capitalism*. New York: Scribner, 1958.

Weinstein, Deena. *Heavy Metal: A Cultural Sociology*. New York: Lexington Books, 1991.

———. "Rock: Youth and Its Music." In *Adolescents and Their Music: If It's Too Loud, You're Too Old*, ed. Jonathan S. Epstein. New York: Garland, 1994.

Weiss, Paul. *Religion and Art*. Milwaukee: Marquette Univ. Press, 1963.

Well, Chris. "Critique: *Diggin' Up Bones*, Jacob's Trouble." *Syndicate* 41 (1994): 25.

———. "Critique: *We Are Not Ashamed*, Lust Control." *Syndicate* 8, 1 (1993): 23.

———. "Hoi Polloi: It's a Long Way from New Zealand." *7–Ball* 1 (1995): 8–11.

———. "Michael W. Smith: Picture Perfect, In Progress." *Syndicate* 7, 4 (1992): 12–13, 21.

———. "Record Reviews: *This Means War!*—Petra." *Harvest Rock Syndicate* 2, 3 (1987): 14.

Wicke, Peter. *Rock Music: Culture, Aesthetics and Sociology*. Cambridge: Cambridge Univ. Press, 1990.

Widner, Ellis and Walter Carter. *The Oak Ridge Boys*. Chicago: Contemporary, 1987.

Wilkerson, David. *Set the Trumpet to Thy Mouth*. Springdale, PA: Whitaker, 1985.

Willman, Chris. "Faithful in her Fashion." *Los Angeles Times*, Apr. 16, 1991, F-3.

———. "Sam Phillips: Has She Turned Away?" *Contemporary Christian Music* 11, 5 (Nov. 1988): 8, 11.

———. "The Call: Singing the Struggle." *Contemporary Christian Music* 13, 5 (Nov. 1990): 16ff.

———. "What?'s New." *Contemporary Christian Music* 8, 12 (June 1986): 10, 12.

Wills, Garry. *Under God: Religion and American Politics.* New York: Simon and
    Schuster, 1990.
Windes, Deborah. "The Cost of Living in Suburban Paradise." *Books & Culture:
    A Christian Review,* Jan.-Feb. 1998, 6.
Wolmuth, Roger. "Parents vs. Rock." *People Weekly,* Sept. 16, 1985, 46–51.
"Yet Another Door Interview: Undercover." *Wittenburg Door,* Oct.-Nov. 1984,
    22–26.
Young, Bill. "Contemporary Christian Music: Rock the Flock." In *The God Pump-
    ers: Religion in the Electronic Age,* ed. Marshall Fishwick and Ray B. Browne.
    Bowling Green, Ohio: Popular Press, 1987.
Ziff, Larzar, ed. *Ralph Waldo Emerson: Selected Essays.* New York: Penguin Books,
    1982.

Index